FALLACIES

Edited by
Hans V. Hansen and Robert C. Pinto

FALLACIES

Classical and
Contemporary Readings

The Pennsylvania State University Press
University Park, Pennsylvania

Library of Congress Cataloging-in-Publication Data

Fallacies : classical and contemporary readings / edited by
Hans V. Hansen, Robert C. Pinto.

     p.   cm.
   Includes bibliographical references and index.
   ISBN 0-271-01416-4 (cloth : alk. paper)
   ISBN 0-271-01417-2 (paper : alk. paper)
  1. Fallacies (Logic) I. Hansen, Hans V.   II. Pinto, Robert C.
   BC175.F35   1995
  165—dc   94-20973
                                             CIP

Published by The Pennsylvania State University Press,
University Park, PA 16802-1003

It is the policy of The Pennsylvania State University Press to use acid-free paper for the
first printing of all clothbound books. Publications on uncoated stock satisfy the minimum
requirements of American National Standard for Information Sciences—Permanence of
Paper for Printed Library Materials, ANSI Z39.48–1992.

Contents

Part II Contemporary Theory and Criticism

Part III Analyses of Specific Fallacies

Part IV Fallacies and Teaching

Preface

In 1970 Charles Hamblin published a book simply titled *Fallacies*, which since then has exercised an extraordinary influence on scholars in several fields. Perhaps the most significant theme in the book is its trenchant criticism of the state of fallacy theory in the twentieth century—a criticism that many have taken as a challenge to begin work anew on the nature of fallacies and associated problems in the theory of argumentation.

If Hamblin intended to issue a call for renewed research on fallacies, then his call has been answered to an extent greater than he could have hoped. Stimulated by *Fallacies*, a considerable literature has developed—part of it devoted to the theory of fallacies and part of it concerned with giving improved analyses of individual fallacies. Contributions have appeared in journals including, but not limited to, *Informal Logic, Argumentation,* and *Philosophy and Rhetoric*; more recently a trickle of monographs has begun to appear. However, most of the fallacy literature is still not readily accessible to either the researcher, teacher, or student of the field; furthermore, the existence of the newer literature is not generally recognized among educators, philosophers, and logicians, or by those who teach speech and communication skills and forensic science. As a result, the best work on fallacies is not finding its way into the classroom, nor is it informing the educational and intellectual experiences available to most college and university students.

A major purpose of this anthology is to make the post-Hamblin work on fallacies available to a wider audience in a single, convenient volume; another purpose is to present a selection of the most important historical texts on fallacies. It is our hope that this collection will stimulate a new generation of more careful, more informed introductory level texts, and make it easier for educators to relay the fruits of the best recent work on fallacies available to their students.

Each of the book's four parts brings together what we believe to be crucial conceptualizations or essential information on a different aspect of fallacy theory.

I. *Historical Selections.* Chapters 1–6 offer representative texts from important contributors to fallacy theory from Aristotle to John Stuart Mill.

II. *Contemporary Theory and Criticism.* (i) In the period after Hamblin, there have been a number of attempts to provide a solid theoretical framework for a theory of fallacies. Chapters 7–10 illustrate four such attempts. (ii) There has been a debate, occasioned by Gerald Massey, about whether a theory of fallacy is even possible. Chapters 11–13 present three contributions to that debate.

III. *Analyses of Specific Fallacies.* In the post-Hamblin period, sophisticated attempts to illuminate the nature of the traditional fallacies have become common. Part III samples the work that is being done by presenting analyses of eight of the traditional informal fallacies. The analyses are from a variety of theoretical perspectives: indeed, there is a pair of analyses of *ad hominem*, illustrating two very different views of the nature of that fallacy.

IV. *Fallacies and Teaching.* Two papers present opposing views of the value of teaching the fallacies in undergraduate courses in critical thinking and informal logic.

All but a few of the papers in sections II–IV constitute new work.

In addition to being the first anthology explicitly devoted to fallacies and fallacy theory, the four parts of the anthology, taken together with the Select Bibliography, constitute a volume that will serve a number of purposes in both teaching and research. First, it is suitable as a text for upper-level undergraduate courses as well as graduate courses in philosophy, informal logic, argumentation theory, critical thinking, education theory, speech communication, and forensics. Second, it will serve as a source and reference book for researchers and students in these fields.

This book was made possible by the generous help of our friends and colleagues on both sides of the Atlantic. We gladly acknowledge their help and express our appreciation to them. Indeed, the book would have been impossible if not for the efforts of those who have contributed papers, advice, encouragement, and criticisms. For its shortcomings, we take full responsibility.

From the very beginning of the project, crucial advice and assistance were given by J. Anthony Blair, James B. Freeman, Joseph W. Wenzel, and John Woods. David Hitchcock generously allowed us to tap his knowledge of Greek and settle some important details in the historical selections. Phyllis Wright and Douglas Walton helped us locate and obtain important material. Sandy Thatcher of Penn State Press provided encouragement, support, and guidance without which this book would not have been possible. Cherene Holland and Betty Waterhouse's expert copyediting improved the book in a great many ways as well as saved us a number of embarrassments. Unfortunately, projects like this do not get completed unless others agree to put their own projects and plans on hold. For graciously postponing their own plans on many occasions, and for their constant encouragement and support, as well as for practical assistance in many ways, we affectionately thank our families—Brone, Rob, and Laura Pinto, and Jane McLeod.

Hans V. Hansen, Thorold
Robert C. Pinto, Windsor

PART I

Historical Selections

Introduction

Charles Hamblin's book, *Fallacies*, first published in 1970, not only presents a criticism of twentieth-century work on fallacies and a constructive contribution to fallacy theory, it also contains several important chapters that trace the history of the development of fallacy theory. In this introduction it is not our purpose to attempt another history of the subject, but rather to provide an introduction to the historical sources selected below. Those who seek a broad historical overview of the history of the fallacies can do no better than to turn to the first five chapters of Hamblin's excellent book.

For this volume we have excerpted those passages from historical works that we think will be most useful to those who have an interest in informal logic, argumentation theory, and critical thinking. It would have been ideal to reprint entire chapters and treatises; but given that we want to present selections from a number of authors, this has not been possible. We have, however, included a large part of Aristotle's *Sophistical Refutations* and followed that with excerpts that signal subsequent major developments; for example, the expansion of the traditional list of sophisms in the *Port-Royal Logic*, the development of the category of '*ad*' arguments in Locke and Watts, and the new classifications introduced by Whately and Mill.

Aristotle (384–322 B.C.)

The history of the study of fallacies begins with Aristotle's *On Sophistical Refutations*. It is among his earlier writings, following the *Topics* and Book I of the *Posterior Analytics*, and predating the *Prior Analytics* and Book II of the *Posterior Analytics*. There is reason to think that Aristotle thought of the *Sophistical Refutations* as being the last book of the *Topics*, his treatise on dialectics. It seems likely, then, that he found the study of fallacies to be a natural extension of the study of dialectical arguments.

Aristotle begins his examination of sophistical refutations as part of the study of what he calls sophistical, or contentious, arguments. Such arguments he defines as either proceeding from premises that only appear to be generally accepted, or as only appearing to be reasonings. Arguments like these were used in the Greek academies in dialogues that were intellectual contests, and that formed part of the education of the students. However, Aristotle's interest in fallacious arguments goes beyond his study of contentious and eristic dialogues. About halfway through the *Sophistical Refutations* he explains why the study of such arguments is important.

> The use of . . . [contentious arguments] . . . , then, is, for philosophy, two-fold. For in the first place, since for the most part they depend upon the expression, they put us in a better condition for seeing in how many senses any term is used, and what kind of resemblances and what kind of differences occur between things and between their names. In the second place they are useful for one's own personal researches; for the man who is easily committed to a fallacy by someone else, and does not perceive it, is likely to incur this fate of himself also on many occasions. Thirdly and lastly, they further contribute to one's reputation, viz. the reputation of being well trained in everything, and not inexperienced in anything: for that a party to arguments should find fault with them, if he cannot definitely point out their weakness, creates a suspicion, making it seem as though it were not the truth of the matter but merely inexperience that put him out of temper. (*Soph. Ref.* 16 175a5–17)[1]

The importance of studying fallacies and contentious arguments, then, has a deeper significance than mere training for argumentative contests. Such studies alert us to problems with language, improve our own reasoning, and help us establish reputations as sound argument analysts.

The contrast between apparent reasoning and refutation, on the one hand, and their genuine counterparts, on the other, is of the utmost importance to the history of fallacies. It is to Aristotle that we owe what might be called the standard definition of "fallacy" as an invalid argument, or invalid reasoning, that seems to be valid although it is really invalid (Hamblin 1970, 12). But there are important differences between a merely deductively valid argument and what Aristotle took to be good reasoning. Not all arguments that we would accept as valid will count as genuine reasonings for Aristotle. The word translated as "reasoning" is the Greek *syllogismos*, which Aristotle defines in the second paragraph of the *Sophistical Refutations*. Three condi-

---

1. In this introduction all quotations from the *Sophistical Refutations* are taken from the W. A. Pickard-Cambridge translation published in *The Works of Aristotle Translated into English, Volume I* (Oxford: Oxford University Press, 1928), edited by W. D. Ross.

tions are necessary: the conclusion must follow necessarily, it must be different from any of the premises, and it must be due to the premises (*Soph. Ref.* 1 165a1–2).[2] Apparent or pseudoreasoning, then, is "reasoning" that *seems* to satisfy all of the three conditions mentioned but that in fact fails to do so. The definition of "refutation," in turn, depends on the definition of "reasoning"; for a refutation is just a syllogism (a reasoning) that takes as premises the answers to questions given by someone else and concludes with a contradictory of that someone else's thesis. An apparent or sophistical refutation is thus either an apparent syllogism that appears to be a syllogism, or a syllogism that fails to reach the required contradictory, but seems to do so. Such apparent refutations will contain a fallacy.

Aristotle classifies refutations into those that depend on language and those that do not. In the first group there are six kinds of sophistical refutations: equivocation, amphiboly, combination of words, division of words, accent, and form of expression. Of these the first two have survived pretty much as Aristotle thought of them. Equivocation results from the exploitation of a term's ambiguity, and amphiboly comes about through indefinite grammatical structure. However, the way that Aristotle thought of the combination and division fallacies in the *Sophistical Refutations* differs significantly from modern treatments of composition and division. In Aristotle's view these fallacies are combinations and divisions of *words* that alter meanings: e.g., "walk while sitting" vs. "walk-while-sitting," (i.e., to have the *ability* to walk while seated vs. being able to walk and sit at the same time). However, contemporary accounts of these fallacies treat them not as fallacies dependent on language but rather as deceptive inferences involving parts and wholes of extralinguistic objects. Also in the category of refutations dependent on language is the fallacy of accent, which involves altering the meaning through the use of accents in written Greek; still another fallacy closely tied to the classical Greek language is form of expression, which can also result in a change of meaning.

There are seven kinds of sophistical refutations that can occur in the

---

2. Recent editions translate *syllogismos* as "deduction" rather than "reasoning"; for example, Pickard-Cambridge's revised translation in *The Collected Works of Aristotle*, edited by J. Barnes (Princeton: Princeton University Press, 1984), and Robin Smith (trans.) *Prior Analytics* (Indianapolis: Hackett, 1989). Definitions of *syllogismos* nearly identical to the one just given occur both earlier and later in Aristotle: see *Topics* I,1, 100a25–27 and *Prior Analytics* A I,1 24b18–20. The use of "syllogism" in the *Topics* and *Sophistical Refutations* predates the formal theory of the syllogism in the *Prior Analytics*. Thus we may talk of informal and formal syllogisms. Aristotle's eventual claim that all informal syllogisms could be rendered into formal syllogisms turns out to be false.

category of refutations not dependent on language: accident, *secundum quid*, consequent, non-cause, begging the question, *ignoratio elenchi*, and many questions.

Aristotle's fallacy of accident is perhaps the most difficult of all his fallacies to understand. The intuitive idea is that what can be predicated of a subject cannot necessarily be predicated of the properties of that subject. In Aristotle's own example where (1) Coriscus is different from Socrates, and (2) Socrates is a man, it is a mistake to conclude that (3) Coriscus is different from a man. Here the subject of predication is Socrates, and "man" is a property predicated of him. A further property or attribute, "Coriscus is different from . . ." may be predicated of Socrates but may not be predicated of the property of Socrates, "man." Part of the difficulty in understanding Aristotle's account is that he treats "man" as an accidental property of Socrates whereas we are inclined to think it is a necessary property of him. But Aristotle is here using "accidental" property to indicate any nonsynonymous property.[3]

The fallacy that has become known as *secundum quid et simpliciter*[4] involves a confusion about whether an expression is used in a qualified respect or absolutely. Concluding that a robin is red (absolutely, without qualification), for example, because it is red in respect to its breast, is an example of this fallacy. Aristotle gives more challenging examples, namely, that because something exists *in thought* does not mean that it also exists without that qualification, i.e., in extra-mental reality.

Ignoratio elenchi (literally, "ignorance of refutation") results from failing to meet any of the necessary conditions of a successful refutation (*Soph. Ref.* 5 167a21–26). Thus all the other sophistical refutations are cases of *ignoratio elenchi*, including those that are classified as dependant on language. That *ignoratio elenchi* is given such broad scope again emphasizes Aristotle's position that sophistical refutations are mistakes in deduction, since a refutation (*elenchus*) is a "proof," and it is "altogether absurd to discuss Refutation without first discussing Proof" (*Soph. Ref.* 10 171a1–2). *Ignoratio elenchi* also includes another mistake of refutation, namely, proving the wrong contradictory, even if it is proved by a genuine syllogism.

The fallacy of the consequent is clearly an early version of what we now

---

3. See *Topics* I, 5, 101b37–102b26 for Aristotle's discussion of the predicables: definition, property, genus and accident. In our explanation of the fallacy of accident we have followed Bueno (1988).
4. A name acquired during the Middle Ages.

know as the fallacy of affirming the consequent. Aristotle means it to apply both to conversion of universal affirmative propositions and to conditional propositions. Begging the question—asking to have granted what one is supposed to prove—gets remarkably short discussion in the *Sophistical Refutations*; perhaps this is because it has been discussed earlier (*Topics*, VIII, 13 162b34–163a28), or perhaps because Aristotle's definition of "reasoning" (*syllogismos*) explicitly declares it to be invalid. The same definition guards against non-cause ("treating as a cause what is not a cause") which, in *reductio per impossibile* refutations occurs when a concession that was not used in the deduction of a contradiction appears to have been refuted.[5]

The last of Aristotle's thirteen fallacies is many questions. It occurs when we fail to realize that more than one question is being asked and thus that the starting point of the refutation is not a genuine proposition, in Aristotle's sense.[6] Most modern analyses of this fallacy turn it into a case of unrecognized assumptions, but it is doubtful that this is the mistake Aristotle had in mind.

It should be noted that Aristotle recognizes several senses of "fallacy" in addition to the thirteen that are at the center of discussion in the *Sophistical Refutations*. In the *Topics* he tells us that there are four kinds of false reasoning (*Topics* VIII, 12 162b3–15): (1) reasoning that appears to be syllogistic but really is not, (2) syllogistic reasoning that reaches the wrong conclusion, (3) syllogistic reasoning that derives its conclusion from inappropriate subject matter, and (4) reasoning that, although syllogistic, starts from false premises. It is the first two kinds that receive the most attention in *Sophistical Refutations*, but the third kind, Aristotle reminds us, is also important: "By a sophistical refutation and syllogism I mean not only a syllogism or refutation which appears to be valid but is not so, but also one which, though it is valid,

5. Hamblin takes Aristotle's non-cause fallacy to depend on a problem that may arise with indirect arguments, namely, that when a contradiction is deduced from two or more premises it is uncertain which of the premises has been shown false (Hamblin 1970, 78). Thus Hamblin thinks the logical mistake contained in non-cause should be expressed as:

(a) $\{[(S \ \& \ T) \supset U] \ \& \ \text{-}U\} \supset \text{\textasciitilde}S$

But this analysis of the mistake does not show that S is logically a non-cause of U, since U may be a consequence of the conjunction, $S \ \& \ T$, and not of either of the conjuncts by themselves. The syllogistic error in Aristotle's fallacy of non-cause can be correctly depicted, however, by the following schema:

(b) $\{W \ \& \ [(S \ \& \ T) \supset U] \ \& \ \text{\textasciitilde}U\} \supset \text{\textasciitilde}W$

6. A proposition, says Aristotle, "is a single statement about a single thing" (*Soph. Ref.* 6 169a7). This rules out multiple subjects and predicates.

only appears to be appropriate to the thing in question" (*Soph. Ref.* 8, 169b21–23). Aristotle's examples of this kind of sophistical refutation are that of a nonmedical argument appearing to be a medical argument, and that of a nongeometrical argument appearing to be a geometrical argument. We may wonder why Aristotle thinks such arguments to be fallacious. The answer is that he takes a scientific demonstration to be not only a deduction *that* a proposition is true but also a demonstration of *why* it is true. Thus, in a proper demonstration the premises must also be able to play the role of explanans. Given Aristotle's strict compartmentalization of the sciences, the premises and conclusion of an argument must all belong to the same science. Thus a nongeometrical premise cannot be used in a geometrical argument, nor can a nonmedical premise be used in a medical argument. A genuine demonstration of a proposition proceeds from the principles of the science to which that proposition belongs; hence, when premises inappropriate to a subject matter are inserted into an argument it becomes a false reasoning. If the inappropriateness goes undetected, the argument will be a fallacy. The thirteen fallacies that Aristotle first named and identified, however, are nearly all instances of the first kind: invalid syllogisms that appear valid. The exception is *ignoratio elenchi*, which may sometimes be of the second kind identified, i.e., a syllogism, but to the wrong conclusion.

To gain a better sense of Aristotle's different concepts of dialogue and the roles of questioners and answerers it is useful to read the *Topics* in conjunction with the *Sophistical Refutations*, especially Books I and VIII. We also remind the reader that we have only reprinted part of the *Sophistical Refutations*. Aristotle gave directions for how to solve (that is, defend against) each of the thirteen fallacies in chapters 19–30 of the same work. These chapters shed additional light on how Aristotle meant his fallacies to be understood.

Although the *Sophistical Refutations* is Aristotle's main work on the fallacies, there are also, in addition to what we find in the *Topics*, important passages in the *Prior Analytics* and the *Rhetoric*. The discussion in the *Rhetoric* seems to be somewhat looser and less focused than it is in *Sophistical Refutations*, and only seven or so from the original list are reviewed. Still, the account of the fallacies in the *Rhetoric* is historically important since it contains an early version of *post hoc ergo propter hoc*; it also gives an account of combination and division that is like the modern nonlinguistic accounts. In the *Prior Analytics* only begging the question and non-cause are discussed at length, and Aristotle considers them especially with regard to the problems of demonstration. The following summary indicates where in Aristotle's works the individual fallacies are discussed.

Equivocation: *Soph. Ref.* 4 (165b31–166a7); 6 (168a24); 7 (169a22–25); 17 (175a36–b8); 19; 23 (179a15–19); *Rhet.* II, 24 (1401a13–23).

Amphiboly: *Soph. Ref.* 4 (166a7–23); 7 (169a22–25); 17 (175a36–b8); 19; 23 (179a19).

Combination of words: *Soph. Ref.* 4 (166a23–32); 6 (168a27); 7 (169a25–27); 20; 23 (179a12–13); *Rhet.* II, 24 (1401a24–b3).

Division of words: *Soph. Ref.* 4 (166a33–39)); 6 (166a27); 7 (169a25–27); 20; 23 (179a12–13); *Rhet.* II, 24 (1401a24–b3).

Accent: *Soph. Ref.* 4 (166b1–9); 6 (168a27); 7 (169a27–29); 21; 23 (179a13–14).

Form of expression: *Soph. Ref.* 4 (166b10–19); 6 (168a25); 7 (169a30–169b3); 22; 23 (179a20–25).

Accident: *Soph. Ref.* 5 (166b28–37); 6 (168a34–b10, 168b26–169a5); 7 (169b3–6); 24; *Rhet.* II, 24 (1401b15–19).

Secundum Quid: *Soph. Ref.* 5 (166b38–167a20); 6 (168b11–16); 7 (169b9–13); 25; *Rhet.* II, 24 (1401b35–1402a28).

Ignorance of refutation: *Soph. Ref.* 5 (167a21–36); 6 (168b17–21); 7 (169b9–13); 26.

Begging the question: *Soph. Ref.* 5 (167a37–40); 6 (168b22–27); 7 (169b13–17); 17 (176a27–32); 27; *Topics* VIII, 11 (161b11–18); VIII, 13 (162b34–163a28); *Pr. Anal.* I, 24 (41b9); II, 16.

Consequent: *Soph. Ref.* 5 (167b1–20); 6 (168b26–169a5); 7 (169b6); 28; *Pr. Anal.* II, 16 (64b33); *Rhet.* II, 24 (1401b10–14, 20–29).

Non-cause: *Soph. Ref.* 5 (167b21–37); 6 (168b22–26); 7 (169b13–17); 29; *Pr. Anal.* II, 17; *Rhet.* II, 24 (1401b30–34).

Many questions: *Soph. Ref.* 5 (167b38–168a17); 6 (169a6–18); 7 (169b13–17); 17 (175b39–176a19); 30.

Hamblin was so discouraged with the current state of fallacy studies that he advises us to return to Aristotle to get a better understanding of the subject. The second chapter of Hamblin's book, in fact, is a useful introduction to the *Sophistical Refutations* and a defense of the dialectical nature of Aristotelian fallacies. Hamblin thinks that a dialectical framework is indispensable for an understanding of Aristotle's fallacies and that part of the poverty of contemporary accounts of fallacies is due to a failure to understand their dialectical genesis. This dialectical approach to the fallacies is continued in the present century by some European argumentation theorists, most notably by van Eemeren and Grootendorst[7] who combine dialectics and pragmatics, and by Hintikka, who analyzes the Aristotelian fallacies as interrogative mistakes, i.e., mistakes of question-dialogues. According to Hintikka, it is an outright mistake to think of Aristotle's fallacies primarily as mistaken inferences, either deductive or inductive.[8] However, other interpretations are possible, especially if we keep in mind Aristotle's repeated reminders that failed refutations are failed proofs. The challenge for those who resist dialectical interpretations is to give a satisfactory nondialectical analysis of each of Aristotle's fallacies.

The Port-Royal Logic

Antoine Arnauld (1611–94) and Pierre Nicole (1625–95) were the authors of *Logic, or the Art of Thinking* (1662), commonly known as the *Port-Royal Logic*.[9] This work is important to the history of fallacy theory for at least two reasons. First, insofar as it continues the Aristotelian list of fallacies it treats them mainly as sophisms of scientific method; second, it seeks to extend the class of sophisms to include fallacies found in popular discourse.

The *Port-Royal Logic* consists of four parts: "Conception," "Judgment," "Reasoning," and "Ordering." The last two chapters of part 3 are given over to a discussion of sophisms, which are described as "the chief sources of bad reasoning." The authors think the study of sophisms is auxiliary to the study of logic and they include the chapters on sophisms because "what is to be avoided is often more striking than what is to be imitated."

The *Port-Royal Logic* does not continue Aristotle's distinction between fallacies that are dependent on language and those that are not; however, the extension of the discussion over two chapters brings with it a different division of sophisms into those associated with scientific subjects and those that may

---

7. See van Eemeren and Grootendorst 1984, 1992a, and their essays in Parts II and III below.

8 Hintikka (1987). See also James Bachman's "Appeal to Authority," Chapter 20.

9. Ian Hacking, in *The Emergence of Probability* (Cambridge: Cambridge University Press, 1975) 73–79, suggests that the last three chapters of the *Port-Royal Logic*, having to do with probability, were written by Blaise Pascal (1623–62).

arise in public discourse. This turns out not to be an exclusive classification since some members from either category would fit as well in the other, and some of them, like hasty generalization, are discussed in both sections. The sophisms of public discourse again subdivide into those that are due mainly to an internal factor (e.g., various forms of bias) and those that result mainly from external factors—supposedly a capacity that objects have to deceive us.

Arnauld and Nicole's treatment of Aristotle's fallacies is interesting in several respects. One reason is that only eight of the original thirteen are included. Another reason is that they are not treated as primarily arising from dialogue, although some of them continue to bear that stamp. *Ignoratio elenchi*, for example, is still recognized as an error of discussion but it is given a new twist, namely, the mistake of intentionally distorting an adversary's position such that it becomes more easily refutable. In hindsight we may see this as the emergence of what is now known as the straw man fallacy. Begging the question is included and so is non-cause. The latter is discussed in several guises, one of which is the mistake of thinking that because "one event occurs after another then the latter event must be the cause of the former"; this sophism Arnauld and Nicole call *post hoc ergo propter hoc* and it has more in common with the non-cause fallacy Aristotle mentions in the *Rhetoric* than the non-cause fallacy we find in the *Sophistical Refutations*. The other Aristotelian fallacies included are accident, combination and division, *secundum quid*, and ambiguity. Two new sophisms are included: the error of overlooking an alternative, and a version of hasty generalization. Although the discussion of the last fallacy is brief, it marks an early entrance of inductive fallacies among the fallacies associated with scientific method.

The last chapter in part 3 of the *Port-Royal Logic* bears the title, "Of the bad reasonings which are common in civil life and in ordinary discourse." It may be seen as the first attempt since Aristotle's *Rhetoric* to study what many contemporary informal logicians think most important, namely, the patterns of arguments used in the public arena. Two successful contemporary texts, Kahane's *Logic and Contemporary Rhetoric* (1992) and Johnson and Blair's *Logical Self-Defense* (1993), might well trace their purpose of improving critical skills through examining actual arguments for fallacies back to the *Port-Royal Logic*.[10] Especially important in this section are what Arnauld and Nicole call the sophisms of authority and manner. Together these form an important discussion of arguments from authority which, unlike Locke's

---

10. Benson Mates in his *Elementary Logic* (Oxford: Oxford University Press, 1965) notices that the *Port-Royal Logic* "is an outstanding early example of the 'how to think straight' *genre*" (214).

discussion of the *ad verecundiam*, seeks to distinguish legitimate from illegitimate uses of authority. Interspersed in Arnauld and Nicole's discussion in this section are allusions to appeals to force and popularity. Although these are not here recognized as distinct sophisms, and although the *ad* label is not used, it is arguable that it is the *Port-Royal Logic* that is the *locus classicus* of the *ad*-fallacies genre, not Locke's *Essay*.

Locke (1632–1704)

It is to Locke that we owe the names of the argument types, *ad verecundiam*, *ad ignorantiam*, *ad hominem*, and *ad judicium*. The discussion of these, almost as an afterthought, is found in *An Essay Concerning Human Understanding* (1690), in a chapter called "Of Reason," in which Locke devotes considerable energy to criticizing syllogistic logic. Reasoning by syllogisms, thought Locke, was neither necessary nor useful for knowledge. Although he never used the term "fallacy" in his discussion of the four *ad* arguments, it does occur earlier in the same chapter in connection with his criticism of syllogistic reasoning.

> [A]nother reason that makes me doubt whether syllogism be the only proper instrument of reason, in the discovery of truth, is, that of whatever use *mode* and *figure* is pretended to be in the laying open of fallacy, . . . *those scholastic forms of discourse are not less liable to fallacies than the plainer ways of argumentation*; and for this I appeal to common observation, which has always found these artificial methods of reasoning more adapted to catch and entangle the mind, than to instruct and inform the understanding. [11]

Thus, there is not only a familiar use of the term "fallacy" to mark breaches of the syllogistic rules, but the term is also applied to "plainer ways of argumentation." It is significant, then, that when we come to the discussion of the *ad* arguments, Locke does not use the term "fallacy" at all, although he clearly thinks that the arguments *ad verecundiam*, *ad ignorantiam*, and *ad hominem* are inferior kinds of arguments in comparison to the *ad judicium*.

11. John Locke, *An Essay Concerning Human Understanding*, edited by A. C. Fraser (New York: Dover, 1959), Book IV, chap. xvii, sec. 4 (399).

His opening remarks are worth quoting: "[I]t may be worth our while a little to reflect on *four sorts of arguments*, that men, in their reasoning with others, do ordinarily make use of to prevail on their assent; or at least so to awe them as to silence their opposition." In noticing their intended effects on others, Locke is here commenting on the dialectical use of these arguments. And since they are "ordinarily" made, we may infer that they occur with noticeable frequency. (This is an interesting remark, for frequency of occurrence is considered by many to be a necessary condition for a kind of mistake to be a fallacy.) Furthermore, the arguments are used against opponents in discussion either to win agreement or stop opposition. But the way that the first three kinds of *ad* arguments achieve this is to be contrasted with *ad judicium* arguments, which alone lead to truth and knowledge. In fact, Locke's complaint against the *argumenta ad verecundiam, ad ignorantium,* and *ad hominem* may be summarized by saying that they fail to meet the standard of arguments *ad judicium*.[12]

Watts (1674–1748)

Isaac Watts in his *Logick; or, The Right Use of Reason* (1725), helped to establish the *ad* argument tradition by repeating the four kinds of arguments introduced by Locke and by adding two additional ones: *argumentum ad fidem* (appeal to faith) and *argumentum ad passiones* (appeal to passion). Like Locke, Watts does not consider the *ad* arguments as fallacies and he does not discuss them in the chapter devoted to sophisms. The *ad* arguments are rather presented as a type, or *rank*, of argument to be distinguished from other kinds such as direct or indirect arguments, certain or probable arguments, etc. It is not until we come to Whately that some uses of *ad* arguments are said to be fallacies.

According to Watts a sophism, or fallacy, is any false argument that "carries the face of truth with it, and yet leads us into mistake." Such mistakes are due either to a false premise or a fault in the deduction or inference. The rationale for including a discussion of fallacies is that "we may with more ease and readiness detect and solve them."

12. The origin of the *ad* arguments has not been decisively settled. Hamblin (1970, 161–62) suggests that it found its way into Locke's work through Latin translations of the *Sophistical Refutations*, especially a passage at 177b33. But see also Finocchiaro (1974) and Nuchelmans (1993).

Although Watts's discussions are brief, the *Logick* is interesting because it shows at once the beginning of the entrenchment of a tradition as well as a transition in the development of some of the fallacies. It is largely Arnauld and Nicole's list of scientific sophisms, adopted from Aristotle, that begins to form the heart of the tradition. Yet minor innovations are made; for example, in the discussion of *ignoratio elenchi* there is a mention of the "Images of Straw" indicating another stage in the evolution of the straw man fallacy, and in his list of *ad* arguments he calls *ad passiones* arguments *ad populum* arguments, if the appeal is made publicly. Finally, we have the introduction of "false cause" as an alternative name for *non causa pro causa* which here, as in the *Port-Royal Logic*, is understood as a fallacy associated with empirical causation. According to Watts it occurs whenever anyone assigns "the reasons of natural appearances, without sufficient experiments to prove them." The other sophisms identified are composition and division, accident and *secundum quid*, and ambiguity. A final sophism, imperfect enumeration or false induction, the mistake of generalizing on insufficient evidence, is mentioned but not discussed in the chapter on sophisms.

Whately (1787–1863)

Richard Whately devotes one of the four books of his *Elements of Logic* (1826) to giving what he thought would be an improved account of the fallacies. He sees himself as approaching the subject from a logical point of view.

> It is on logical principles . . . that I propose to discuss the subject of Fallacies; . . . the generality of logical writers have usually followed so opposite a plan. Whenever they have to treat of anything that is beyond the mere elements of Logic, they totally lay aside all reference to the principles they have been occupied in establishing and explaining, and have recourse to a loose, vague, and popular kind of language; . . . [which] . . . seems strangely incongruous in a professional logical treatise. [13]

13. Richard Whately, *Elements of Logic* (New York: Harper and Row, 1853), 176 (originally published 1826).

Whately's complaint was echoed by Hamblin who, in his indictment of the Standard Treatment of fallacies, says that it is untheoretical and "lacking in logic" (Hamblin 1970, 12). In hindsight we may see Whately as the first to inveigh against the Standard Treatment.

In the spirit of this logical approach, Whately is led to revise the traditional classification of fallacies inherited from Aristotle. "In every fallacy," he says, "the Conclusion either *does*, or *does not follow from the premisses*." There are, then, fallacies, in which the conclusion *is* a logical consequence of the premises. This marks a clear break with what had become the established conception of "fallacy" as an invalid argument that appears to be valid. Accordingly, Whately offers a wider conception of "fallacy" as "any argument, or apparent argument, which professes to be decisive of the matter at hand, while in reality it is not."[14] Thus there are two broad classes of fallacy: the logical fallacies are invalid arguments and contain a mistake in deductive reasoning, the nonlogical (or material) fallacies are fallacies despite the fact that they are deductively valid.[15]

The logical fallacies divide into the purely logical and the semilogical fallacies. The former consist in a violation of one or another of the rules of the syllogism, including the rule that warns against four or more terms. The semilogical fallacies, when properly analyzed, also violate the rule that a syllogism must have exactly three terms, but the existence of the fourth term has to be revealed by identifying an ambiguity in one of the three terms. Under this heading Whately places ambiguity, composition and division, and accident, as well as false analogy. To be exposed, the semilogical fallacies, unlike the purely logical fallacies, require extralogical knowledge; that is, knowledge of the meanings of the terms.

There is more at work in Whately's new classification than the desire to be scientific. It is his view that all real reasoning can be put in the form of a syllogism.[16] Fallacious reasoning, then, that cannot be depicted as a breaking of a syllogistic rule, must be seen to be a violation of good deductive reasoning nevertheless. Since the fault cannot be found in the connection between the premises and the conclusion, it must be either in the premises or in the

14. Whately, *Elements of Logic*, appendix.

15. This is not really a break with Aristotle so much as it is a break with what had become the Aristotelian tradition. Recall that Aristotle thinks that "fallacy" is used in four senses, three of which might well fit Whately's category of material fallacies.

16. Whately, *Elements of Logic* (IV,i,1): "[A]*ll* reasoning, on whatever subject, is one and the same process, which may be clearly exhibited in the form of syllogisms." See also the same work, Book I, sec. i.

conclusion. Hence nonlogical fallacies divide into those that involve a premise mistakenly or unduly assumed (begging the question and false cause) and those that reach an irrelevant conclusion. The *ad* fallacies are placed under the last division and they are claimed to be fallacies only when they are used unfairly. Whately seems to give two distinct accounts, possibly related, of what an unfair use of an *ad* argument amounts to. The main analysis is that such arguments are used unfairly when an absolute rather than a relative proposition is claimed as the conclusion; that is, to take the *ad hominem* as an example, when the conclusion is *p* rather than, say, "you are committed to *p*." In such cases there may well be a valid argument but since the conclusion proved is the wrong one, the argument is an *ignoratio elenchi*. A second analysis, merely suggested in an accompanying note to the *ad hominem* discussion, is that *ad* arguments are fallacious when they are used unjustly to shift a burden of proof. This suggestion has been welcomed by some modern argumentation theorists but unfortunately Whately does nothing in the *Elements of Logic* to distinguish legitimate from illegitimate shiftings of the burden of proof.[17] Whately does not give a separate discussion of any of the other *ad* fallacies but he indicates that what he has said about the *ad hominem* is to apply by extension to the *ad verecundiam* and *ad populum* as well.

Mill (1803–1874)

John Stuart Mill devotes one of the six books of his comprehensive work, *A System of Logic, Ratiocinative and Inductive* (1843), to a detailed study of fallacies. Although Mill's work appeared less than twenty years after Whately's book, and although Mill praises Whately's work on the fallacies, one finds in Mill a much keener interest in the methodology of the inductive sciences and a completely opposite conception to Whately's of what real reasoning is. Whereas Whately held that real reasoning conforms to the syllogism, Mill thinks that only inductive, ampliative inferences count as *reasoning*. Accordingly, there is for the first time the creation of a *category* of inductive fallacies, and the classificatory scheme is revised again to accord with Mill's attempt to treat the fallacies of induction on a par with those of deduction.

Although Mill warns us that "the only complete safeguard against reason-

17. But see Hamblin (1970, 170–75) for a fair discussion of what Whately says about presumption and burden of proof in his *Elements of Rhetoric*.

ing ill is the habit of reasoning well," there are still three discernible reasons for the inclusion of the study of the fallacies in his *Logic*. First is that a complete study of reasoning should include bad reasoning as well as good reasoning, not just for the sake of completeness but also, thinks Mill, because we can know something of good reasoning by studying its opposite. Second, even those who take the most pains to avoid fallacies still commit them. Finally, and obviously, Mill sees himself as being the first to give a systematic account of the fallacies from an inductivist point of view.

Mill's concept of "fallacy" is decidedly undialectical. Basically—with one important exception—he sees fallacies as inferences that simply overestimate the strength of the evidence; hence, in the main, a fallacy involves the mistaking of a bad inference for a good one. He adds the qualifications that casual mistakes, due, say, to inattention, are not fallacies, and that "moral" failings (e.g., being biased or indifferent to truth), although they may predispose us to error, are not themselves fallacies.[18] "A catalogue of the varieties of evidence which are not real evidence," says Mill, "is an enumeration of fallacies." The main division is between fallacies of inference and what he calls fallacies of inspection (or *a priori* fallacies). Although the latter need not involve an inference, they are fallacies nevertheless, roughly analogous to what we might call the fallacies of unwarranted premise.[19] Such fallacies result from neglecting to subject propositions to the appropriate proof procedure. However, these fallacies of inspection, which Mill chose to discuss first, detract attention from what we should see as the core of his classificatory scheme.

For Mill, logic is about proof[20] and proof includes observation, deduction, and generalization.[21] Accordingly, the basic division of fallacies that follows naturally from this conception of logic is three kinds of fallacy of inference: (1) fallacies of observation (overlooking facts that should have been considered); (2) of generalization (e.g., *post hoc ergo propter hoc*, false analogy); and (3) of ratiocination (e.g., *secundum quid*, violations of syllogistic rules, mistakes of hypothetical conversion). A final category, fallacies of confusion,

---

18. In insisting that moral shortcomings are not fallacies, Mill may be distancing himself from the *Port-Royal Logic*, which identified a class of fallacies due mainly to a weakness of the will. See the *Port-Royal Logic*, part 3, chap. xx. He is also rejecting the *ad*-category of fallacies.

19. See also Mill's *Autobiography* (chap. vii., para. 4) where he criticizes the view that empirical truths can be known by intuition.

20. J. S. Mill, A *System of Logic* (London: George Routledge and Sons, 1892), Book II, chap. i, sec. 1.

21. Ibid., Book V, chap. iv, sec. 1.

Mill describes, in contrast to the other fallacies of inference, as resulting from an indistinct conception of the evidence. Some of the traditional fallacies (ambiguity, composition, and division, *petitio principii, ignoratio elenchi*) are placed under this heading.

Mill's work on the fallacies has been much neglected by modern scholars. One reason for this may be that few find his account of inference to be convincing. Another reason may be that Mill's account of the fallacies is tied more closely to scientific methodology than to the problems of public discourse and everyday argumentation, the arena of most interest to contemporary theorists. It is quite clear, however, that Mill cannot be accused of giving a shallow and unoriginal account of the fallacies. His classification flows from a novel conception of logic; his examples are taken from science, politics, economics, religion, and philosophy; and his discussions are for the most part probing and insightful.

As Hamblin's book showed, historically there exists a great deal of interesting and important work on the fallacies. Regrettably, most of it is largely unknown to contemporary logicians and argumentation theorists. We hope that the selections we have excerpted will whet the reader's appetite for further research in the field and that a better understanding of the fallacy tradition will enrich contemporary research. [22]

22. We are grateful to John Woods for extensive discussions on the history of the fallacies, and to the publisher's referee for very helpful suggestions.

1

On Sophistical Refutations

Aristotle

[The following excerpt is from Aristotle, chaps. 1–11 of *De Sophisticis Elenchis*, translated by W. A. Pickard-Cambridge, in vol. 1 of *The Works of Aristotle Translated into English*, edited by W. D. Ross (London: Oxford University Press, 1928).]

[164ᵃ] Let us now discuss sophistic refutations, i.e. what appear to be refutations but are really fallacies instead. We will begin in the natural order with the first. 1

That some reasonings are genuine, while others seem to be so but are not, is evident. This happens with arguments, as also elsewhere, through a certain likeness between the genuine and the sham. For physically some people are in a vigorous condition, while others merely seem to be so by blowing and rigging themselves out as the tribesmen do their victims for sacrifice; and [164ᵇ] some people are beautiful thanks to their beauty, while others seem to be so, by dint of embellishing themselves. So it is, too, with inanimate things; for of these, too, some are really silver and others gold, while others are not and merely seem to be such to our sense; e.g. things made of litharge and tin seem to be of silver, while those made of yellow metal look golden. In the same way both reasoning and refutation are sometimes genuine, sometimes not, though inexperience may make them appear so: for inexperienced people obtain only, as it were, a distant view of these things. [165ᵃ] For reasoning rests on certain statements such that they involve necessarily the assertion of something other than what has been stated, through what has been stated: refutation is reasoning involving the contradictory of the given

conclusion. Now some of them do not really achieve this, though they seem to do so for a number of reasons; and of these the most prolific and usual domain is the argument that turns upon names only. It is impossible in a discussion to bring in the actual things discussed: we use their names as symbols instead of them; and therefore we suppose that what follows in the names, follows in the things as well, just as people who calculate suppose in regard to their counters. But the two cases (names and things) are not alike. For names are finite and so is the sum-total of formulae, while things are infinite in number. Inevitably, then, the same formulae, and a single name, have a number of meanings. Accordingly just as, in counting, those who are not clever in manipulating their counters are taken in by the experts, in the same way in arguments too those who are not well acquainted with the force of names misreason both in their own discussions and when they listen to others. For this reason, then, and for others to be mentioned later, there exists both reasoning and refutation that is apparent but not real. Now for some people it is better worth while to seem to be wise, than to be wise without seeming to be (for the art of the sophist is the semblance of wisdom without the reality, and the sophist is one who makes money from an apparent but unreal wisdom); for them, then, it is clearly essential also to seem to accomplish the task of a wise man rather than to accomplish it without seeming to do so. To reduce it to a single point of contrast it is the business of one who knows a thing, himself to avoid fallacies in the subjects which he knows and to be able to show up the man who makes them; and of these accomplishments the one depends on the faculty to render an answer, and the other upon the securing of one. Those, then, who would be sophists are bound to study the class of arguments aforesaid: for it is worth their while: for a faculty of this kind will make a man seem to be wise, and this is the purpose they happen to have in view.

Clearly, then, there exists a class of arguments of this kind, and it is at this kind of ability that those aim whom we call sophists. Let us now go on to discuss how many kinds there are of sophistical arguments, and how many in number are the elements of which this faculty is composed, and how many branches there happen to be of this inquiry, and the other factors that contribute to this art.

Of arguments in dialogue form there are four classes: 2

Didactic, Dialectical, Examination-arguments, and Contentious arguments. [165^b] Didactic arguments are those that reason from the principles appropriate to each subject and not from the opinions held by the answerer (for the learner should take things on trust): dialectical arguments are those that reason from premises generally accepted, to the contradictory of a given thesis: examination-arguments are those that reason from premises which are accepted by the answerer and which any one who pretends to possess knowledge of the subject is bound to know—in what manner, has been defined in another treatise:[1] contentious arguments are those that reason or appear to reason to a conclusion from premises that appear to be generally accepted but are not so. The subject, then, of demonstrative arguments has been discussed in the *Analytics*, while that of dialectic arguments and examination-arguments has been discussed elsewhere:[2] let us now proceed to speak of the arguments used in competitions and contests.

First we must grasp the number of aims entertained by those who argue as   3 competitors and rivals to the death. These are five in number, refutation, fallacy, paradox, solecism, and fifthly to reduce the opponent in the discussion to babbling—i.e. to constrain him to repeat himself a number of times: or it is to produce the appearance of each of these things without the reality. For they choose if possible plainly to refute the other party, or as the second best to show that he is committing some fallacy, or as a third best to lead him into paradox, or fourthly to reduce him to solecism, i.e. to make the answerer, in consequence of the argument, to use an ungrammatical expression; or, as a last resort, to make him repeat himself.

There are two styles of refutation: for some depend on the language used,   4 while some are independent of language. Those ways of producing the false appearance of an argument which depend on language are six in number: they are ambiguity, amphiboly, combination, division of words, accent, form of expression. Of this we may assure ourselves both by induction, and by syllogistic proof based on this—and it may be on other assumptions as well— that this is the number of ways in which we might fail to mean the same thing by the same names or expressions. Arguments such as the following depend upon ambiguity. 'Those learn who know: for it is those who know their letters who learn the letters dictated to them.' For 'to learn' is ambiguous; it signifies both 'to understand' by the use of knowledge, and also 'to acquire knowledge'. Again, 'Evils are good: for what needs to be is good, and evils must needs be.' For 'what needs to be' has a double meaning: it means what is

1. *Topics* VIII, 5.
2. *Topics* I–VIII.

inevitable, as often is the case with evils, too (for evil of some kind is inevitable), while on the other hand we say of good things as well that they 'need to be'. Moreover, 'The same man is both seated and standing and he is both sick and in health: for it is he who stood up who is standing, and he who [166ª] is recovering who is in health: but it is the seated man who stood up, and the sick man who was recovering.' For 'The sick man does so and so', or 'has so and so done to him' is not single in meaning: sometimes it means 'the man who is sick or is seated now', sometimes 'the man who was sick formerly'. Of course, the man who was recovering was the sick man, who really was sick at the time: but the man who is in health is not sick at the same time: he is 'the sick man' in the sense not that he is sick now, but that he was sick formerly. Examples such as the following depend upon amphiboly: 'I wish that you the enemy may capture.' Also the thesis, 'There must be knowledge of what one knows': for it is possible by this phrase to mean that knowledge belongs to both the knower and the known. Also, 'There must be sight of what one sees: one sees the pillar: *ergo* the pillar has sight'. Also, 'What you profess to-be, that you profess-to-be: you profess a stone to-be: *ergo* you profess-to-be a stone.' Also, 'Speaking of the silent is possible': for 'speaking of the silent' also has a double meaning: it may mean that the speaker is silent or that the things of which he speaks are so.[3] There are three varieties of these ambiguities and amphibolies: (1) When either the expression or the name has strictly more than one meaning, e.g. *aetos* and *kuon;*[4] (2) when by custom we use them so; (3) when words that have a simple sense taken alone have more than one meaning in combination; e.g. 'knowing letters'. For each word, both 'knowing' and 'letters', possibly has a single meaning: but both together have more than one—either that the letters themselves have knowledge or that someone else has it of them.

Amphiboly and ambiguity, then, depend on these modes of speech. Upon the combination of words there depend instances such as the following: 'A man can walk while sitting, and can write while not writing'. For the meaning is not the same if one divides the words and if one combines them in saying that 'it is possible to walk-while-sitting'. The same applies to the latter phrase, too, if one combines the words 'to write-while-not-writing': for then it means that he has the power to write and not to write at once; whereas if one does not combine them, it means that when he is not writing he has the

---

3. Plato, *Euthydemus* 300 B–C.

4. The term *aetos* can mean 'eagle' or 'pediment'; *kuon* can mean 'dog', 'dogstar', or 'Cynic philosopher'. See E. S. Forster (trans.) *On Sophistical Refutations* (Cambridge: Harvard University Press, 1953), 20. [Eds.]

power to write. Also, 'He knows now if he has learnt his letters.'[5] Moreover, there is the saying that 'One single thing if you can carry a crowd you can carry too'.

Upon division depend the propositions that 5 is 2 and 3, and even and odd, and that the greater is equal: for it is that amount and more besides. For the same phrase would not be thought always to have the same meaning when divided and when combined, e.g., 'I made thee a slave once a free man', and 'God-like Achilles left fifty a hundred men'.

[166ᵇ] An argument depending upon accent it is not easy to construct in unwritten discussion; in written discussions and in poetry it is easier. Thus (e.g.) some people emend Homer against those who criticize as unnatural his expression *to men hou kataputhetai ombroi*.[6] For they solve the difficulty by a change of accent, pronouncing the *ou* with an acuter accent. Also, in the passage about Agamemnon's dream, they say that Zeus did not himself say 'We grant him the fulfilment of his prayer', but that he bade the dream grant it. Instances such as these, then, turn upon the accentuation.

Others come about owing to the form of expression used, when what is really different is expressed in the same form, e.g. a masculine thing by a feminine termination, or a feminine thing by a masculine, or a neuter by either a masculine or a feminine; or, again, when a quality is expressed by a termination proper to quantity or vice versa, or what is active by a passive word, or a state by an active word, and so forth with the other divisions previously[7] laid down. For it is possible to use an expression to denote what does not belong to the class of actions at all as though it did so belong. Thus (e.g.) 'flourishing' is a word which in the form of its expression is like 'cutting' or 'building': yet the one denotes a certain quality—i.e. a certain condition—while the other denotes a certain action. In the same manner also in the other instances.

Refutations, then, that depend upon language are drawn from these common-place rules. Of fallacies, on the other hand, that are independent of language there are seven kinds:

(1) that which depend upon Accident:
(2) the use of an expression absolutely or not absolutely but with some qualification of respect, or place, or time, or relation:

---

5. A note in the Forster translation (*On Sophistical Refutations*, 22) indicates that the same words, when differently combined, can mean, "He understands now what he knows because he has understood letters." [Eds.]

6. *Iliad* xxiii, 328. In Aristotle's day there were no marks in written Greek to indicate accent or breathing. [Eds.]

7. *Topics* I, 9.

(3) that which depends upon ignorance of what 'refutation' is:
(4) that which depends upon the consequent:
(5) that which depends upon assuming the original conclusion:
(6) stating as cause what is not the cause:
(7) the making of more than one question into one.

Fallacies, then, that depend on Accident occur whenever any attribute is   5
claimed to belong in a like manner to a thing and to its accident. For since
the same thing has many accidents there is no necessity that all the same
attributes should belong to all of a thing's predicates and to their subject as
well. Thus (e.g.), 'If Coriscus be different from "man", he is different from
himself: for he is a man': or 'If he be different from Socrates, and Socrates be
a man, then', they say, 'he has admitted that Coriscus is different from a
man, because it so happens (*accidit*) that the person from whom he said that
he (Coriscus) is different is a man'.

Those that depend on whether an expression is used absolutely or in a
certain respect and not strictly, occur whenever an expression used in a
particular sense is taken as though it were used absolutely, [167a] e.g. in the
argument 'If what is not is the object of an opinion, then what is not is': for it
is not the same thing 'to be x' and 'to be' absolutely. Or again, 'What is, is
not, if it is not a particular kind of being, e.g. if it is not a man.' For it is not
the same thing 'not to be x' and 'not to be' at all: it looks as if it were, because
of the closeness of the expression, i.e. because 'to be x' is but little different
from 'to be', and 'not to be x' from 'not to be'. Likewise also with any
argument that turns upon the point whether an expression is used in a certain
respect or used absolutely. Thus e.g. 'Suppose an Indian to be black all over,
but white in respect of his teeth; then he is both white and not white.' Or if
both characters belong in a particular respect, then, they say, 'contrary attributes belong at the same time'. This kind of thing is in some cases easily seen
by any one, e.g. suppose a man were to secure the statement that the Ethio-
pian is black, and were then to ask whether he is white in respect of his teeth;
and then, if he be white in that respect, were to suppose at the conclusion of
his questions that therefore he had proved dialectically that he was both white
and not white. But in some cases it often passes undetected, viz. in all cases
where, whenever a statement is made of something in a certain respect, it
would be generally thought that the absolute statement follows as well; and
also in all cases where it is not easy to see which of the attributes ought to be
rendered strictly. A situation of this kind arises, where both the opposite
attributes belong alike: for then there is general support for the view that one

must agree absolutely to the assertion of both, or of neither: e.g. if a thing is half white and half black, is it white or black?

Other fallacies occur because the terms 'proof' or 'refutation' have not been defined, and because something is left out in their definition. For to refute is to contradict one and the same attribute—not merely the name, but the reality— and a name that is not merely synonymous but the same name—and to confute it from the propositions granted, necessarily, without including in the reckoning the original point to be proved, in the same respect and relation and manner and time in which it was asserted. A 'false assertion' about anything has to be defined in the same way. Some people, however, omit some one of the said conditions and give a merely apparent refutation, showing (e.g.) that the same thing is both double and not double: for two is double of one, but not double of three. Or, it may be, they show that it is both double and not double of the same thing, but not that it is so in the same respect: for it is double in length but not double in breadth. Or, it may be, they show it to be both double and not double of the same thing and in the same respect and manner, but not that it is so at the same time: and therefore their refutation is merely apparent. One might, with some violence, bring this fallacy into the group of fallacies dependent on language as well.

Those that depend on the assumption of the original point to be proved, occur in the same way, and in as many ways, as it is possible to beg the original point; they appear to refute because men lack the power to keep their eyes at once upon what is the same and what is different.

[167ᵇ] The refutation which depends upon the consequent arises because people suppose that the relation of consequence is convertible. For when-ever, suppose A is, B necessarily is, they then suppose also that if B is, A necessarily is. This is also the source of the deceptions that attend opinions based on sense-perception. For people often suppose bile to be honey because honey is attended by a yellow colour: also, since after rain the ground is wet in consequence, we suppose that if the ground is wet, it has been raining; whereas that does not necessarily follow. In rhetoric proofs from signs are based on consequences. For when rhetoricians wish to show that a man is an adulterer, they take hold of some consequence of an adulterous life, viz. that the man is smartly dressed, or that he is observed to wander about at night. There are, however, many people of whom these things are true, while the charge in question is untrue. It happens like this also in real reasoning; e.g. Melissus' argument, that the universe is eternal, assumes that the universe has not come to be (for from what is not nothing could possibly come to be) and that what has come to be has done so from a first beginning. If, therefore, the universe has not come to be, it has no first beginning, and is therefore eternal. But this does not necessarily follow: for even if what has come to be always has a first beginning, it does not also follow that what has a first beginning has come to be; any more than it follows that if a man in a fever be hot, a man who is hot must be in a fever.

The refutation which depends upon treating as cause what is not a cause, occurs whenever what is not a cause is inserted in the argument, as though the refutation depended upon it. This kind of thing happens in arguments that reason *ad impossibile*: for in these we are bound to demolish one of the premisses. If, then, the false cause be reckoned in among the questions that are necessary to establish the resulting impossibility, it will often be thought that the refutation depends upon it, e.g. in the proof that the 'soul' and 'life' are not the same: for if coming-to-be be contrary to perishing, then a particular form of perishing will have a particular form of coming-to-be as its contrary: now death is a particular form of perishing and is contrary to life: life, therefore, is a coming-to-be, and to live is to come-to-be. But this is impossible: accordingly, the 'soul' and 'life' are not the same. Now this is not proved: for the impossibility results all the same, even if one does not say that life is the same as the soul, but merely says that life is contrary to death, which is a form of perishing, and that perishing has 'coming-to-be' as its contrary. Arguments of that kind, then, though not inconclusive absolutely, are inconclusive in relation to the proposed conclusion. Also even the questioners themselves often fail quite as much to see a point of that kind.

Such, then, are the arguments that depend upon the consequent and upon false cause. Those that depend upon the making of two questions into one occur whenever the plurality is undetected and a single answer is returned as if to a single question. [168ᵃ] Now, in some cases, it is easy to see that there is more than one, and that an answer is not to be given, e.g. 'Does the earth consist of sea, or the sky?' But in some cases it is less easy, and then people treat the question as one, and either confess their defeat by failing to answer the question, or are exposed to an apparent refutation. Thus 'Is A and is B a man?' 'Yes,' 'Then if any one hits A and B, he will strike a man' (singular), 'not men' (plural). Or again, where part is good and part bad, 'is the whole good or bad?' For whichever he says, it is possible that he might be thought to expose himself to an apparent refutation or to make an apparently false statement: for to say that something is good which is not good, or not good which is good, is to make a false statement. Sometimes, however, additional premisses may actually give rise to a genuine refutation; e.g. suppose a man were to grant that the descriptions 'white' and 'naked' and 'blind' apply to one thing and to a number of things in a like sense. For if 'blind' describes a thing that cannot see though nature designed it to see, it will also describe things that cannot see though nature designed them to do so. Whenever, then, one thing can see while another cannot, they will either both be able to see or else both be blind; which is impossible.

The right way, then, is either to divide apparent proofs and refutations as 6 above, or else to refer them all to ignorance of what 'refutation' is, and make that our starting point: for it is possible to analyse all the aforesaid modes of fallacy into breaches of the definition of a refutation. In the first place, we may see if they are inconclusive: for the conclusion ought to result from the premises laid down, so as to compel us necessarily to state it and not merely to seem to compel us. Next we should also take the definition bit by bit, and try the fallacy thereby. For of the fallacies that consist in language, some depend upon a double meaning, e.g. ambiguity of words and of phrases, and the fallacy of like verbal forms (for we habitually speak of everything as though it were a particular substance)—while fallacies of combination and division and accent arise because the phrase in question or the term as altered is not the same as was intended. Even this, however, should be the same, just as the thing signified should be as well, if a refutation or proof is to be effected; e.g. if the point concerns a doublet, then you should draw the conclusion of a 'doublet', not of a 'cloak'. For the former conclusion also would be true, but it has not been proved; we need to further question to show that 'doublet' means the same thing, in order to satisfy any one who asks why you think your point proved.

Fallacies that depend on Accident are clear cases of *ignoratio elenchi* when once 'proof' has been defined. For the same definition ought to hold good of 'refutation' too, except that a mention of 'the contradictory' is here added: for a refutation is a proof of the contradictory. If, then, there is no proof as regards an accident of anything, there is no refutation. For supposing, when A and B are, C must necessarily be, and C is white, there is no necessity for it to be white on account of the syllogism. So, if the triangle [168^b] has its angles equal to two right-angles, and it happens to be a figure, or the simplest element or starting point, it is not because it is a figure or a starting point or simplest element that it has this character. For the demonstration proves the point about it not *qua* figure or *qua* simplest element, but *qua* triangle. Likewise also in other cases. If, then, refutation is a proof, an argument which argued *per accidens* could not be a refutation. It is, however, just in this that the experts and men of science generally suffer refutation at the hand

of the unscientific: for the latter meet the scientists with reasonings consti-
tuted *per accidens*; and the scientists for lack of the power to draw distinctions
either say 'Yes' to their questions, or else people suppose them to have said
'Yes', although they have not.

Those that depend upon whether something is said in a certain respect
only or said absolutely, are clear cases of *ignoratio elenchi* because the affirmation and the denial are not concerned with the same point. For of 'white in a
certain respect' the negation is 'not white in a certain respect', while of 'white
absolutely' it is 'not white, absolutely'. If, then, a man treats the admission
that a thing is 'white in a certain respect' as though it were said to be white
absolutely, he does not effect a refutation, but merely appears to do so owing
to ignorance of what refutation is.

The clearest cases of all, however, are those that were previously described[8]
as depending upon the definition of a 'refutation': and this is also why they
were called by that name. For the appearance of a refutation is produced
because of the omission in the definition, and if we divide fallacies in the
above manner, we ought to set 'Defective definition' as a common mark
upon them all.

Those that depend upon the assumption of the original point and upon
stating as the cause what is not the cause, are clearly shown to be cases of
ignoratio elenchi through the definition thereof. For the conclusion ought to
come about 'because these things are so',[9] and this does not happen where
the premisses are not causes of it: and again it should come about without
taking into account the original point, and this is not the case with those
arguments which depend upon begging the original point.

Those that depend upon the consequent are a branch of Accident: for the
consequent is an accident, only it differs from the accident in this, that you
may secure an admission of the accident in the case of one thing only (e.g.
the identity of a yellow thing and honey and of a white thing and swan),
whereas the consequent always involves more than one thing: for we claim
that things that are the same as one and the same thing are also the same as
one another, and this is the ground of a refutation dependent on the consequent. It is, however, not always true, e.g. suppose that A and B are 'the
same' as C *per accidens*; for both 'snow' and the 'swan' are the same as
something 'white'. Or again, as in Melissus' argument,[10] a man assumes that

8. 167a21–35.
9. Aristotle, *Prior Analytics*, A. i. 24b18.
10. 167b13.

to 'have been generated' and to 'have a beginning' are the same thing, or to 'become equal' and to 'assume the same magnitude'. For because what has been generated has a beginning, he claims also that what has a beginning has been generated, and argues as though both what has been generated and what is finite were the same because each has a beginning. Likewise also in the case of things that are made equal [169ᵃ] he assumes that if things that assume one and the same magnitude become equal, then also things that become equal assume one magnitude: i.e. he assumes the consequent. Inasmuch, then, as a refutation depending on accident consists in ignorance of what a refutation is, clearly so also does a refutation depending on the consequent. We shall have further to examine this in another way as well.[11]

Those fallacies that depend upon the making of several questions into one consist in our failure to dissect the definition of 'proposition'. For a proposition is a single statement about a single thing. For the same definition applies to 'one single thing only' and to the 'thing', simply, e.g. to 'man' and to 'one single man only'; and likewise also in other cases. If, then, a 'single proposition' be one which claims a single thing of a single thing, a 'proposition', simply, will also be the putting of a question of that kind. Now since a proof starts from propositions and refutation is a proof, refutation, too, will start from propositions. If, then, a proposition is a single statement about a single thing, it is obvious that this fallacy too consists in ignorance of what a refutation is: for in it what is not a proposition appears to be one. If, then, the answerer has returned an answer as though to a single question, there will be a refutation; while if he has returned one not really but apparently, there will be an apparent refutation of his thesis. All the types of fallacy, then, fall under ignorance of what a refutation is, some of them because the contradiction, which is the distinctive mark of a refutation, is merely apparent, and the rest failing to conform to the definition of a proof.[12]

The deception comes about in the case of arguments that depend on ambiguity of words and of phrases because we are unable to divide the ambiguous term (for some terms it is not easy to divide, e.g. 'unity', 'being', and 'sameness'), while in those that depend on combination and division, it is because

7

---

11. Chapters 24 and 28 of On Sophistical Refutations. (Not reprinted here. [Eds.])

12. The revised edition (The Complete Works of Aristotle, Jonathan Barnes, ed., Princeton: Princeton University Press, 1984) is closer to the original Greek. Compare: "All the types of fallacy, then, fall under ignorance of what a refutation is, those dependent on language because the contradiction, which is the proper mark of a refutation, is merely apparent, and the rest because of the definition of deduction." [Eds.]

we suppose that it makes no difference whether the phrase be combined or divided, as is indeed the case with most phrases. Likewise also with those that depend on accent: for the lowering or raising of the voice upon a phrase is thought not to alter its meaning—with any phrase, or not with many. With those that depend on the form of expression it is because of the likeness of expression. For it is hard to distinguish what kind of things are signified by the same and what by different kinds of expression: for a man who can do this is practically next door to the understanding of the truth.[13] A special reason why a man is liable to be hurried into assent to the fallacy is that we suppose every predicate of anything to be an individual thing, and we understand it as being one with the thing: and we therefore treat it as a substance: for it is to that which is one with a thing or substance, as also to substance itself, that 'individuality' and 'being' are deemed to belong in the fullest sense. For this reason, too, this type of fallacy is to be ranked among those that depend on language; in the first place, because the deception is effected the more readily when we are inquiring into a problem in company with others than when we do so by ourselves (for an inquiry with another person is carried on by means of speech, whereas an inquiry by oneself is carried on quite as much by means of the object itself); secondly a man is liable to be deceived, even when inquiring by himself, [169ᵇ] when he takes speech as the basis of his inquiry: moreover the deception arises out of the likeness (of two different things), and the likeness arises out of the language. With those fallacies that depend upon Accident, deception comes about because we cannot distinguish the sameness and otherness of terms, i.e. their unity and multiplicity, or what kinds of predicate have all the same accidents as their subject. Likewise also with those that depend on the Consequent: for the consequent is a branch of Accident. Moreover, in many cases appearances point to this— and the claim is made—that if A is inseparable from B, so also is B from A. With those that depend upon an imperfection in the definition of a refutation, and with those that depend upon the difference between a qualified and an absolute statement, the deception consists in the smallness of the difference involved; for we treat the limitation to the particular thing or respect or manner or time as adding nothing to the meaning, and so grant the statement universally. Likewise also in the case of those that assume the original point, and those of false cause, and all that treat a number of questions as one: for in

---

13. *The Complete Works of Aristotle*, Barnes, ed., is truer to the original in that it adds "and knows best how to assent" immediately after "is practically next door to the understanding of the truth." [Eds.]

all of them the deception lies in the smallness of the difference: for our failure to be quite exact in our definition of 'premiss' and of 'proof' is due to the aforesaid reason.

Since we know on how many points apparent syllogisms depend, we know   8 also on how many sophistical syllogisms and refutations may depend. By a sophistical refutation and syllogism I mean not only a syllogism or refutation which appears to be valid but is not, but also one which, though it is valid, only appears to be appropriate to the thing in question. These are those which fail to refute and prove people to be ignorant according to the nature of the thing in question, which was the function of the art of examination. Now the art of examining is a branch of dialectic: and this may prove a false conclusion because of the ignorance of the answerer. Sophistic refutations on the other hand, even though they prove the contradictory of his thesis, do not make clear whether he is ignorant: for sophists entangle the scientist as well with these arguments.

That we know them by the same line of inquiry is clear: for the same considerations which make it appear to an audience that the points required for the proof were asked in the questions and that the conclusion was proved, would make the answerer think so as well, so that false proof will occur through all or some of these means: for what a man has not been asked but thinks he has granted, he would also grant if he were asked. Of course, in some cases the moment we add the missing question, we also show up its falsity, e.g. in fallacies that depend on language and on solecism. If then, fallacious proofs of the contradictory of a thesis depend on their appearing to refute, it is clear that the considerations on which both proofs of false conclusions and an apparent refutation depend must be the same in number. Now an apparent refutation depends upon the elements involved in a genuine one: [170ª] for the failure of one or other of these must make the refutation merely apparent, e.g. that which depends on the failure of the conclusion to follow from the argument (the argument *ad impossibile*) and that which treats two questions as one and so depends upon a flaw in the premiss, and that which depends on the substitution of an accident for an essential attribute, and—a branch of the last—that which depends upon the consequent: moreover, the conclusion may follow not in fact but only verbally: then, instead of proving the contradictory universally and in the same respect and relation and manner, the fallacy may be dependent on some limit of extent or on one or other of these qualifications: moreover, there is the assumption of the original point to be proved, in violation of the clause 'without reckoning in the original point'. Thus we should have the number of considerations on which the fallacious proofs depend: for they could not depend on more, but all will depend on the points aforesaid.

A sophistical refutation is a refutation not absolutely but relatively to some one: and so is a proof, in the same way. For unless that which depends upon ambiguity assumes that the ambiguous term has a single meaning, and that which depends on like verbal forms assumes that substance is the only category, and the rest in the same way, there will be neither refutations nor proofs, either absolutely or relatively to the answerer: whereas if they do assume these things, they will stand, relatively to the answerer; but absolutely they will not stand: for they have not secured a statement that does have a single meaning, but only one that appears to have, and that only from this particular man.

The number of considerations on which depend the refutations of those who   9
are refuted, we ought not to try to grasp without a knowledge of everything that is. This, however, is not the province of any special study: for possibly the sciences are infinite in number, so that obviously demonstrations may be infinite too. Now refutations may be true as well as false: for whenever it is possible to demonstrate something, it is also possible to refute the man who maintains the contradictory of the truth; e.g. if a man has stated that the diagonal is commensurate with the side of the square, one might refute him by demonstrating that it is incommensurate. Accordingly, to exhaust all possible refutations we shall have to have scientific knowledge of everything: for some refutations depend upon the principles that rule in geometry and the conclusions that follow from these, others upon those that rule in medicine, and others upon those of the other sciences. For the matter of that, the false refutations likewise belong the number of the infinite: for according to every art there is false proof, e.g. according to geometry there is false geometrical proof, and according to medicine there is false medical proof. By 'according to the art', I mean 'according to the principles of it'. Clearly, then, it is not of all refutations, but only of those that depend upon dialectic that we need to grasp the common-place rules: for these stand in a common relation to every art and faculty. And as regards the refutation that is according to one or other of the particular sciences it is the task of that particular scientist to examine whether it is merely apparent without being real, and, if it be real, what is the reason for it: whereas it is the business of dialecticians so to examine the refutation that proceeds from the common first principles that fall under no particular special study. For if we grasp the starting points of the accepted proofs on any subject

whatever we grasp [170ᵇ] those of the refutations current on that subject. For a refutation is the proof of the contradictory of a given thesis, so that either one or two proofs of the contradictory constitute a refutation. We grasp, then, the number of considerations on which all such depend: if, however, we grasp this, we also grasp their solutions as well; for the objections to these are the solutions of them. We also grasp the number of considerations on which those refutations depend, that are merely apparent—apparent, I mean, not to everybody, but to people of a certain stamp; for it is an indefinite task if one is to inquire how many are the considerations that make them apparent to the man in the street. Accordingly it is clear that the dialectician's business is to be able to grasp on how many considerations depends the formation, through the common first principles, of a refutation that is either real or apparent, i.e. either dialectical or apparently dialectical, or suitable for an examination.

It is no true distinction between arguments which some people draw when   10 they say that some arguments are directed against the expression, and others against the thought expressed: for it is absurd to suppose that some arguments are directed against the expression and others against the thought, and that they are not the same. For what is failure to direct an argument against the thought except what occurs whenever a man does not in using the expression think it to be used in his question in the same sense in which the person questioned granted it? And this is the same thing as to direct the argument against the expression. On the other hand, it is directed against the thought whenever a man uses the expression in the same sense which the answerer had in mind when he granted it. If now any one (i.e. both the questioner and the person questioned), in dealing with an expression with more than one meaning, were to suppose it to have one meaning—as e.g. it may be that 'Being' and 'One' have many meanings, and yet both the answerer answers and the questioner puts his question supposing it to be one, and the argument is to the effect that 'All things are one'—will this discussion be directed any more against the expression than against the thought of the person questioned? If, on the other hand, one of them[14] supposes the expression to have many meanings, it is clear that such a discussion will not be directed against the thought. Such being the meanings of the phrases in question, they clearly cannot describe two separate classes of argument. For, in the first place, it is possible for any such argument as bears more than one meaning to be directed against the expres-

14. "Someone" is closer to the original Greek. [Eds.]

sion and against the thought, and next it is possible for any argument whatsoever; for the fact of being directed against the thought consists not in the nature of the argument, but in the special attitude of the answerer towards the points he concedes. Next, all of them may be directed to the expression. For 'to be directed against the expression' means in this doctrine 'not to be directed against the thought'. For if not all are directed against either expression or thought, there will be certain other arguments directed neither against the expression nor against the thought, whereas they say that all must be one or the other, and divide them all as directed either against the expression or against the thought, while others (they say) there are none. But in point of fact those that depend on mere expression are only a branch of those syllogisms that depend on a multiplicity of meanings. For the absurd statement has actually been made that the description 'dependent on mere expression' describes all the arguments that depend on language: whereas some of these are fallacies not because the answerer adopts a particular attitude towards them, but because the argument itself involves the asking of a question such as bears more than one meaning.

[171ª] It is, too, altogether absurd to discuss Refutation without first discussing Proof: for a refutation is a proof, so that one ought to discuss proof as well before describing false refutation: for a refutation of that kind is a merely apparent proof of the contradictory of a thesis. Accordingly, the reason of the falsity will be either in the proof or in the contradiction (for mention of the 'contradiction' must be added), while sometimes it is in both, if the refutation be merely apparent. In the argument that speaking of the silent is possible it lies in the contradiction, not in the proof; in the argument that one can give what one does not possess, it lies in both; in the proof that Homer's poem is a figure through its being a cycle it lies in the proof. An argument that does not fail in either respect is a true proof.

But, to return to the point whence our argument digressed,[15] are mathematical reasonings directed against the thought, or not? And if any one thinks 'triangle' to be a word with many meanings, and granted it in some different sense from the figure which was proved to contain two right angles, has the questioner here directed his argument against the thought of the former or not?

Moreover, if the expression bears many senses, while the answerer does not understand or suppose it to have them, surely the questioner here has directed his argument against his thought! Or how else ought he to put his question except by suggesting a distinction—suppose one's question to be 'Is

15. 170b40.

speaking of the silent possible or not?'—as follows, 'Is the answer "No" in one sense, but "Yes" in another?' If, then, any one were to answer that it was not possible in any sense and the other were to argue that it was, has not his argument been directed against the thought of the answerer? Yet his argument is supposed to be one of those that depend on the expression. There is not, then, any definite kind of arguments that is directed against the thought. Some arguments are, indeed, directed against the expression: but these are not all even apparent refutations, let alone all refutations. For there are also apparent refutations which do not depend upon language, e.g. those that depend upon accident, and others.

If, however, any one claims that one should actually draw the distinction, and say, 'By "speaking of the silent" I mean, in one sense this and in the other sense that', surely to claim *this* is in the first place absurd (for sometimes the questioner does not see the ambiguity of his question, and he cannot possibly draw a distinction which he does not think to be there): in the second place, what else but this will *didactic* argument be? For it will make manifest the state of the case to one who has never considered, and does not know or suppose that there is any other meaning but one. For what is there to prevent the same thing also happening to us in cases where there is no double meaning? 'Are the units in four equal to the twos? Observe that the twos are contained in four in one sense in this way, in another sense in that.' Also, 'Is the knowledge of contraries one or not? Observe that some contraries are known, while others are unknown.' Thus the man who makes this claim seems to be unaware of the difference [171ᵇ] between didactic and dialectical argument, and of the fact that while he who argues didactically should not ask questions but make things clear himself, the other should merely ask questions.

Moreover, to claim a 'Yes' or 'No' answer is the business not of a man who is   11 showing something, but of one who is holding an examination. For the art of examining is a branch of dialectic and has in view not the man who has knowledge, but the ignorant pretender. *He*, then, is a dialectician who regards the common principles with their application to the particular matter in hand, while he who only appears to do this is a sophist. Now for contentious and sophistical reasoning: (1) one such is a merely apparent reasoning, on subjects on which dialectical reasoning is the proper method of examination, even though its conclusion be true: for it misleads us in regard to the cause: also (2) there are those misreasonings which do not conform to the line of inquiry proper to the particular subject, but are generally thought to conform to the art in question. For false diagrams of geometrical figures are not contentious (for the resulting fallacies conform to the subject of the art)—any more than is any false diagram that may be offered in proof of a truth—e.g. Hippocrates' figure or the squaring of the circle by means of the lunules. But Bryson's method of squaring the circle,[16] even if the circle is thereby squared, is still sophistical because it does not conform to the subject in hand.[17] So, then, any merely apparent reasoning about these things is a contentious argument, and any reasoning that merely appears to conform to the subject in hand, even though it be genuine reasoning, is a contentious argument: for it is merely apparent in its conformity to the subject-matter, so that it is deceptive and plays foul. For just as a foul in a race is a definite type of fault, and is a kind of foul fighting, so the art of contentious reasoning is foul fighting in disputation: for in the former case those who are resolved to win at all costs snatch at everything, and so in the latter case do contentious reasoners. Those, then, who do this in order to win the mere victory are generally considered to be contentious and quarrelsome persons, while those who do it to win a reputation with a view to making money are sophistical. For the art of sophistry is, as we said,[18] a kind of art of money-making from a merely apparent wisdom, and this is why they aim at a merely apparent demonstration: and quarrelsome persons and sophists both employ the same arguments, but not with the same motives: and the same argument will be sophistical and contentious, but not in the same respect; rather, it will be contentious in so far as its aim is an apparent victory, while in so far as its aim is an apparent wisdom, it will be sophistical: for the art of sophistry is a certain appearance of wisdom without the reality. The contentious argument stands in somewhat the same relation to the dialectical as the drawer of false diagrams to the geometrician; for it beguiles by misreasoning from the same principles as dialectic uses, just as the drawer of a false diagram beguiles the geometrician. But whereas the latter is not a contentious reasoner, because he bases his false diagram on the principles and conclu- [172a] -sions that fall under the art of geometry, the argument which is subordinate to the principles of dialectic will yet clearly be contentious as regards other subjects. Thus, e.g., though the squaring of the circle by means of the lunules is not contentious, Bryson's

16. On the various methods of attempting to square the circle, here and below (172a2–7), see Poste, *Soph. El.*, Appendix F. (The reference is to Edward Poste, *Aristotle on Fallacies or the Sophistici Elenchi, With a Translation and Notes* (London: Macmillan and Co., 1866. Reprinted in New York and London: Garland, 1987.) [Eds.])

17. Cf. 172a2–7 below.

18. 165a22.

solution is contentious: and the former argument cannot be adapted to any subject except geometry, because it proceeds from principles that are peculiar to geometry, whereas the latter can be adapted as an argument against all the number of people who do not know what is or is not possible in each particular context: for it will apply to them all. Or there is the method whereby Antiphon squared the circle. Or again, an argument which denied that it was better to take a walk after dinner, because of Zeno's argument, would not be a proper argument for a doctor, because Zeno's argument is of general application. If, then, the relation of the contentious argument to the dialectical were exactly like that of the drawer of false diagrams to the geometrician, a contentious argument upon the aforesaid subjects could not have existed. But, as it is, the dialectical argument is not concerned with any definite kind of being, nor does it show anything, nor is it even an argument such as we find in the general philosophy of being. For all beings are not contained in any one kind, nor, if they were, could they possibly fall under the same principles. Accordingly, no art that is a method of showing the nature of anything proceeds by asking questions: for it does not permit a man to grant whichever he likes of the two alternatives in the question: for they will not both of them yield a proof. Dialectic, on the other hand, does proceed by questioning, whereas if it were concerned to show things, it would have refrained from putting questions, even if not about everything, at least about the first principles and the special principles that apply to the particular subject in hand. For suppose the answerer not to grant these, it would then no longer have had any grounds from which to argue any longer against the objection. Dialectic is at the same time a mode of examination as well. For neither is the art of examination an accomplishment of the same kind as geometry, but one which a man may possess, even though he has not knowledge. For it is possible even for one without knowledge to hold an examination of one who is without knowledge, if also the latter grants him points taken not from things that he knows or from the special principles of the subject under discussion but from all that range of consequences attaching to the subject which a man may indeed know without knowing the theory of the subject, but which if he do not know, he is bound to be ignorant of the theory. So then clearly the art of examining does not consist in knowledge of any definite subject. For this reason, too, it deals with everything: for every 'theory' of anything employs also certain common principles. Hence everybody, including even amateurs, makes use in a way of dialectic and the practice of examining: for all undertake to some extent a rough trial of those who profess to know things. What serves them here is the general principles:

for they know these of themselves just as well as the scientist, even if in what they say they seem to the latter to go wildly astray from them. All, then, are engaged in refutation; for they take a hand as amateurs in the same task with which dialectic is concerned professionally; and he is a dialectician who examines by the help of a theory of reasoning. Now there are many identical principles which are true of everything, though they are not such as to constitute a particular nature, i.e. a particular kind of being, but are like negative terms, while other principles are not of this kind but are special to particular subjects; accordingly it is possible from these general principles to hold an examination on everything, and that there should be [172ᵇ] a definite art of so doing, and, moreover, an art which is not of the same kind as those which demonstrate. This is why the contentious reasoner does not stand in the same condition in all respects as the drawer of a false diagram: for the contentious reasoner will not be given to misreasoning from any definite class of principles, but will deal with every class.

These, then, are the types of sophistical refutations: and that it belongs to the dialectician to study these, and to be able to effect them, is not difficult to see: for the investigation of premisses comprises the whole of this study.

2

Concerning Sophisms and Bad Reasonings Which Are Common in Ordinary Discourse

Antoine Arnauld and Pierre Nicole

[The following excerpt is from Antoine Arnauld and Pierre Nicole, *La Logique ou L'Art de Penser*, translated as The *Port-Royal Logic* by Thomas Spencer Baynes, 6th ed. (Edinburgh: Oliver and Boyd, Tweeddale Court, 1865), Part III, chaps. 19 and 20.]

Chapter 19.   Of the Different Ways of Reasoning Ill, Which Are Called Sophisms

Although, if we know the rules of good reasoning, it may not be difficult to recognise those which are bad, nevertheless, as examples to be avoided often strike us more than examples to be imitated, it will not be without its use to set forth the principal classes of bad reasoning, which are called sophisms or paralogisms, since this will enable us yet more readily to avoid them. We have reduced all these to seven or eight, some being so gross that they are not worthy of being noticed.

I. Proving Something Other Than That Which is in Dispute

This sophism is called by Aristotle *ignoratio elenchi*, that is to say, the ignorance of that which ought to be proved against an adversary. It is a very common vice in the controversies of men. We dispute with warmth, and often without understanding one another. Passion, or bad faith, leads us to attribute to our adversary that which is very far from his meaning, in order to carry on the contest with greater advantage; or to impute to him consequences which we imagine may be derived from his doctrine, although he disavows and denies them. All this may be reduced to this first kind of sophism, which an honest and good man ought to avoid above all things. . . .

II. Assuming as True the Thing in Dispute

This is what Aristotle calls *a begging of the question* [*petitio principii*], which is clearly altogether opposed to true reasoning, since, in all reasoning, that which is employed as proof ought to be clearer and better known than that which we seek to prove.

Galileo, however, has accused him, and with justice, of having himself fallen into this error, when he tried to prove that the earth was at the centre of the world, by this argument:—

> *The nature of heavy things is to tend to the centre of the universe, and of light things to go off from it;*
> *Now, experience proves that heavy things tend towards the centre of the earth, and that light things go off from it;*
> *Therefore, the centre of the earth is the same as the centre of the universe.*

It is clear that there is in the major of this argument a manifest begging of the question; for we see well enough that heavy things tend towards the centre of the earth; but where did Aristotle learn that they tend towards the centre of the universe, unless he assumed that the centre of the earth is the same as the centre of the universe?—which is the very conclusion that he wishes to prove by that argument. . . .

We may reduce, also, to this kind of sophism, the proof which is derived from a principle different from that which is in dispute, but which we know is equally contested by him with whom we dispute. There are, for example, two dogmas equally established amongst Catholics; the one, that all the points of faith cannot be proved by Scripture alone; the other, that it is a point of faith that infants are capable of baptism. It would, therefore, be bad reasoning in an Anabaptist to prove against the Catholics that they are wrong in believing that infants are capable of baptism, since nothing is said of it in the Scripture;

because this proof would assume that we ought to believe only what is in the Scripture, which is denied by the Catholics.

Finally, we may bring under this sophism all reasonings in which we prove a thing unknown, by another equally or more unknown; or an uncertain thing, by another which is equally or more uncertain.

III. Taking for a Cause That Which is Not a Cause

This sophism is called *non causa pro causa*. It is very common amongst men, and we fall into it in many ways. One is, through simple ignorance of the true causes of things. It is in this way that philosophers have attributed a thousand effects to the abhorrence of a vacuum, which, in our time, have been proved to demonstration—and by very ingenious experiments—to be caused by the weight of the air alone, as we may see in the excellent treatise of M. Pascal. The same philosophers commonly teach that vessels full of water break when they freeze, because the water contracts, and thus leaves a vacuum which nature cannot endure. It has, however, been discovered, that they break, on the contrary, because water, when frozen, occupies more room than it did before which also occasions ice to float in water. . . .

We may bring under this kind of sophism, too, that common fallacy of the human mind, *post hoc, ergo propter hoc,* —this happens after such a thing, therefore it must be caused by that thing. In this way it has been concluded that the star which is called the dog-star, is the cause of the extraordinary heat we feel during those days which are termed the dog-days, which led Virgil to say, when speaking of that star, which is called in Latin Sirius—

Aut Sirius ardor:
Ille sitim morbosque ferens mortalibus aegris
Nascitur, et laevo contristat lumine coelum.[1]

Although, as Gassendi has very well remarked, there is nothing more unreasonable than this imagination, for that star being on the other side of the line, its influence ought to be much more powerful in those parts, to which it is more perpendicular; notwithstanding which, the days which we call dog-days

---

1. [Eds.] James Dickoff and Patricia James in their translation of the *Port-Royal Logic* (Indianapolis: Bobbs-Merrill, 1964) render this passage as follows:
. . . Even as fiery Sirius:
Bearer of draught and plague to feeble man
Rises and saddens the sky with baleful light.
(*Aeneid* X.273–75)

here are the winter season there; so that, in that country, the inhabitants have much more ground for believing that the dog-star brings them cold, than we have for believing that it is the cause of our heat.

IV. Incomplete Enumeration

There is scarcely any vice of reasoning into which able men fall more easily than that of making imperfect enumerations, and of not sufficiently considering all the ways in which a thing may exist, or take place; which leads them to conclude rashly, either that it does not exist, because it does not exist in a certain way, though it may exist in another, or that it exists in such and such a way, although it may still be in another way, which they have not considered. . . .

V. Judging of a Thing by That Which Only Belongs to it Accidentally

This sophism is called in the schools *fallacia accidentis*, which is, when we draw a simple, unrestricted, and absolute conclusion, from what is true only by accident. This is done by the number of people who decry antimony, because, being misapplied, it produces bad effects; and by others, who attribute to eloquence all the bad effects which it produces when abused, or to medicine the faults of certain ignorant doctors. . . .

VI. Passing from a Divided Sense to a Connected Sense, or from a Connected Sense to a Divided Sense

The former of these sophisms is called *fallacia compositionis*; the latter, *fallacia divisionis*. They will be understood better by examples.

Jesus Christ says, in the Gospel, in speaking of his miracles, *The blind see, the lame walk, the deaf hear.* This cannot be true if we take these things separately, and not together, that is to say, in a divided, and not in a connected sense. For the blind could not see, remaining blind; and the deaf could not hear, remaining deaf;—but those who had been blind before were so no longer, but now saw; and so of the deaf.

It is in the same sense, also, that God is said, in the Scripture, to justify the ungodly. For this does not mean, that he considers as just those who are still ungodly, but that he renders just, by his grace, those who before were ungodly.

There are, on the contrary, propositions which are true only in an opposite sense of the divided sense: as when St. Paul says, that liars, fornicators, and covetous men, shall not enter into the kingdom of heaven. For this does not mean that none of those who have had these vices shall be saved, but only that those who have continued addicted to them, and have never left them by turning to God, shall have no place in the kingdom of heaven.

It is easy to see that we cannot, without a sophism, pass from one of these senses to the other; and that those, for example, would reason ill, who should promise themselves heaven while remaining in their sins, because Jesus came to save sinners, and because it is said in the gospel that women of evil life shall enter into the kingdom of God before the Pharisees; or who, on the other hand, having forsaken evil, should despair of their salvation, as having nothing to expect but the punishment of their sins, because it is said that the anger of God is reserved against all those who live ungodly lives, and that none who are vicious shall have any part in the inheritance of Jesus Christ. The first would pass from the divided sense to the compounded, in promising themselves, though still continuing sinners, that which is only promised to those who cease to be so by true conversion; and the last would pass from the compounded sense to the divided, in applying to those who have been sinners, but who cease to be so by turning to God, that which refers only to sinners remaining in their sins and wicked life.

VII. Passing from What is True in Some Respect, to What is True Absolutely

This is what is called in the schools *a dicto secundum quid ad dictum simpliciter.* The following are examples: The Epicureans proved, again, that the gods must have the human form because it is the most beautiful, and everything which is beautiful must be in God. This was bad reasoning; for the human form is not beautiful absolutely, but only in relation to bodies. And thus, the perfection being only in some respect, and not absolutely, it did not follow that it must be in God because all perfections are in God, it being only those which are perfections absolutely, that is to say, which contain no imperfection, which were necessary in God. . . .

VIII. Abusing the Ambiguity of Words, Which May be Done in Different Ways

We may reduce to this kind of sophism *all those syllogisms which are vicious through having four terms*, whether this be because the middle is taken twice particularly, or because it is taken in one sense in the first proposition, and in another in the second, or, finally, because the terms of the conclusion are not taken in the same sense in the premises as in the conclusion: For we do not restrict the word ambiguity to those words alone that are manifestly equivocal, which scarcely ever mislead any one, but we comprise under it anything which may change the meaning of a word, especially when men do not easily perceive that change, because different things being signified by the same word, they take them for the same thing. On this subject, we may refer to what has been said towards the end of the First Part, where we have also spoken of the remedy which should be employed against the confusion of ambiguous words, by defining them so precisely that none can be deceived.

We shall content ourselves, therefore, with referring to some examples of this ambiguity, which sometimes deceive men of ability, such as those which we often find in words which signify some whole, which may be taken either collectively, for all their parts together, or distributively, for each of these parts.

In this way is to be resolved that sophism of the Stoics, who concluded that the universe was an animal endowed with reason, because *that which has the use of reason is better than that which has not;* "Now there is nothing," say they, "which is better than the universe; therefore, the universe has the use of reason." The minor of this argument is false, since it attributes to the universe that which belongs only to God, which is, that of being such that it is impossible to conceive anything better, or more perfect. But in limiting ourselves to creatures, although we may say that there is nothing better than the universe, taking it collectively, for the totality of all the beings that God has created, all that we can conclude from this at most is, that the universe has the use of reason in relation to some of its parts, such as are angels and men, and not that the whole together was an animal endowed with the use of reason. This would be the same kind of bad reasoning as to say—man thinks; now, man is composed of mind and body; therefore, mind and body think. For it is enough, in order that we may attribute thought to the whole man, that thinking belongs to one of the parts: and from this it does not at all follow that it belongs also to the other.

IX. Deriving a General Conclusion from a Defective Induction

When, from the examination of many particular things, we rise to the knowledge of a general truth—this is called induction. Thus, when we find, by the examination of many seas, that the water in them is salt, and of many rivers, that the water in them is fresh, we infer, generally, that the water of the sea is salt, and that of rivers fresh. The different experiments by which we have found that gold does not diminish in the fire, lead us to judge that this is true of all gold. And since no people have ever been found who do not speak, we believe confidently that all men speak, that is to say, employ sounds to express their thoughts. It is in this way that all our knowledge begins, since individual things present themselves to us before universals, although, afterwards, the universals help us to know the individual.

It is, however, nevertheless true, that *induction alone* is never a *certain means of acquiring perfect knowledge*, as we shall show in another place. [Part IV, chap. 6.] The consideration of individual things furnishes to our mind only the occasion of turning its attention to its natural ideas, according to which it judges of the truth of things in general. For it is true, for example, that I might never perhaps have been led to consider the nature of a triangle if I had not seen a triangle, which furnished me with the occasion of thinking of it. But it, nevertheless, is not the particular examination of all triangles which makes me conclude generally and certainly of all, that the space which they contain is equal to that of the rectangle of their whole base and a part of their side (for this examination would be impossible), but simply the consideration of what is contained in the idea of a triangle which I find in my mind.

Be this as it may, reserving the consideration of this subject for another place, it is enough to say here, that *defective inductions*, —those, that is to say, which are not complete, —*often lead us to fall into error*; and I shall content myself with referring to one remarkable example of this.

All philosophers had believed, up to the present time, as an undoubted truth, that a syringe being well stopped, it would be impossible to draw out the piston without bursting it, and that we might make water rise as high as we chose in pumps by suction. What made this to be so firmly believed was, that it was supposed to have been verified by a most certain induction derived from a multitude of experiments; but, both are found to be false, since new experiments have been made which have proved that the piston of a syringe, however well it may be stopped, may be drawn out, provided we employ a force equal to the weight of a column of water of more than thirty feet in height, of the diameter of the syringe; and that we cannot raise water, by suction in a pump, higher than thirty-two or thirty-three feet.

Chapter 20.   Of the Bad Reasonings Which Are Common in Civil Life and in Ordinary Discourse.

We have seen some examples of the faults which are most common in reasoning on scientific subjects; but, since the principal use of reason is not in relation to those kinds of subjects, which enter but little into the conduct of life, and in which there is much less danger of being deceived, it would, without doubt, be much more useful to consider generally what betrays men into the false judgments which they make on every kind of subject, —especially on that of morals, and of other things which are important in civil life, and which constitute the ordinary subject of their conversation. But, inasmuch as this design would require a separate work, which would comprehend almost the whole of morals, we shall content ourselves with indicating here, in general, some of the causes of those false judgments which are so common amongst men.

We do not stay to distinguish false judgments from bad reasonings, and shall inquire indifferently into the causes of each, —both because false judgments are the sources of bad reasonings, and produce them as a necessary consequence, and because in reality there is almost always a concealed and enveloped reasoning in what appears to be a simple judgment, there being always something which operates on the motive and principle of that judgment. For example, when we judge that a stick which appears bent in the water is really so, this judgment is founded on that general and false proposition, that what appears bent to our senses is so really, and thus contains an undeveloped reasoning.

In considering them generally, the causes of our errors appear to be reducible to two principles: the one internal—the *irregularity of the will*, which *troubles and disorders the judgment*; the other external, which lies in the *objects of which we judge*, and which deceive our minds by *false appearances*. Now although these causes almost always appear united together, there are nevertheless certain errors, in which one prevails more than the other; and hence we shall treat of them separately. . . .

Of the False Reasonings Which Arise From Objects Themselves.

We have already noticed that we ought not to separate the inward causes of our errors from those which are derived from objects, which may be called the outward, because the false appearance of these objects would not be capable of leading us into error, if the will did not hurry the mind into forming a precipitate judgment, when it is not as yet sufficiently enlightened.

Since, however, it cannot exert this power over the understanding in things perfectly evident, it is plain that the obscurity of the objects contributes somewhat to our mistakes; and, indeed, there are often cases in which the passion which leads us to reason ill is almost imperceptible. Hence it is useful to consider separately those illusions which arise principally from the things themselves:— . . .

IV. The false inductions by which general propositions are derived from some particular experiences, constitute one of the most common sources of the false reasonings of men. Three or four examples suffice them to make a *maxim* and a *common-place*, which they then employ as a principle for deciding all things.

There are many maladies hidden from the most skilful physicians, and remedies often do not succeed: rash minds hence conclude that medicine is absolutely useless, and only a craft of charlatans.

There are light and loose women: this is sufficient for the jealous to conceive unjust suspicions against the most virtuous, and for licentious writers to condemn all universally.

There are some persons who hide great vices under an appearance of piety; libertines conclude from this that all devotion is no better than hypocrisy.

There are some things obscure and hidden, and we are often grossly deceived: all things are obscure and uncertain, say the ancient and modern Pyrrhonists, and we cannot know the truth of anything with certainty.

There is a want of equality in some of the actions of men, and this is enough to constitute a common-place, from which none are exempt. "Reason," say they, "is so weak and blind, that there is nothing so evidently clear as to be clear enough for it; the easy and the hard are both alike to it; all subjects are equal, and nature in general disclaims its jurisdiction. We only think what we *will* in the very moment in which we *will* it; we will nothing freely, nothing absolutely, nothing constantly."

Most people set forth the defects or good qualities of others only by general and extreme propositions. From some particular actions we infer a habit: from three or four faults we conclude a custom; and what happens once a month or once a year, happens every day, at every hour, and every moment, in the discourses of men,—so little pains do they take to observe in them the limits of truth and justice. . . .

VI. But there are no false reasonings more common amongst men than those into which they fall, either by judging rashly of the truth of things from some authority insufficient to assure them of it, or by deciding the inward essence by the outward manner. We call the former the sophism of authority, the latter the sophism of the manner.

To understand how common these are, it is only necessary to consider that the majority of men are determined to believe one opinion rather than another, not by any solid and essential reasons which might lead them to know the truth, but by certain exterior and foreign marks which are more consonant to, or which they judge to be consonant to, truth, than to falsehood.

The reason of this is, that the interior truth of things is often deeply hidden; that the minds of men are commonly feeble and dark, full of clouds and false light, while their outward marks of truth are clear and sensible; so that, as men naturally incline to that which is easiest, they almost always range themselves on the side where they see those exterior marks of truth which are readily discovered.

These may be reduced to two principles, —the authority of him who propounds the thing, and the manner in which it is propounded. And these two ways of persuading are so powerful that they carry away almost all minds.

Wherefore God, who willed that the sure knowledge of the mysteries of faith might be attained by the simplest of the faithful, has had the condescension to accommodate himself to this weakness of the spirit of man, in not making this to depend on the particular examination of all the points which are proposed to faith; but in giving us, as the certain rule of truth, the authority of the church universal, which proposes them, which, being clear and evident, relieves the mind of the perplexities which necessarily arise from the particular discussion of these mysteries.

Thus, in matters of faith, the authority of the church universal is entirely decisive; and so far is it from being possible that it should be liable to error, that we fall into it only when wandering from its authority, and refusing to submit ourselves to it.

We may derive, moreover, convincing arguments in matters of religion from the manner in which they are advanced. When we see, for example, in different ages of the church, and principally in the last, men who endeavour to propagate their opinions by bloodshed and the sword; when we see them arm themselves against the church by schism, against temporal powers by revolt; when we see people without the common commission, without miracles, without any external marks of piety, and with the plain marks rather of licentiousness, undertake to change the faith and discipline of the church in so criminal a manner, it is more than sufficient to make reasonable men reject them, and to prevent the most ignorant from listening to them.

But in those things, the knowledge of which is not absolutely necessary, and which God has left more to the discernment of the reason of each one in particular, the authority and the manner are not so important, and they often lead many to form judgments contrary to the truth.

We do not undertake to give here the rules and the precise limits of the respect which is due to authority in human things, we simply indicate some gross faults which are committed in this matter.

We often regard only the number of the witnesses, without at all considering whether the number increases the probability of their having discovered the truth, which is, however, unreasonable; for, as an author of our time has wisely remarked, in difficult things, which each must discover for himself, it is more likely that a single person will discover the truth than that many will. Thus the following is not a valid inference: this opinion is held by the majority of philosophers; it is, therefore, the truest.

We are often persuaded, by certain qualities which have no connection with the truth, of the things which we examine. Thus there are a number of people who trust implicitly to those who are older, and who have had more experience, even in those things which do not depend on age or experience, but on the clearness of the mind.

Piety, wisdom, moderation, are without doubt the most estimable qualities in the world, and they ought to give great authority to those who possess them in those things which depend on piety or sincerity, and even on the knowledge of God, for it is most probable that God communicates more to those who serve him more purely; but there are a multitude of things which depend only on human intelligence, human experience, and human penetration, and, in these things, those who have the superiority in intellect and in study, deserve to be relied on more than others. The contrary, however, often happens, and many reckon it best to follow, even in these things, the most devout men.

This arises, in part, from the fact that these advantages of mind are not so obvious as the external decorum which appears in pious persons, and in part, also, from the fact that men do not like to make these distinctions. Discrimination perplexes them; they will have all or nothing. If they trust to a man in one thing, they will trust to him in everything; if they do not in one, they will not in any; they love short, plain, and easy ways. But this disposition, though common, is nevertheless contrary to reason, which shows us that the same

persons are not to be trusted to in anything, because they are not distinguished in anything; and that it is bad reasoning to conclude: he is a serious
man, therefore he is intelligent and clever in everything.

VII. It is true, indeed, that if any errors are pardonable, those into which we
fall through our excessive deference to the opinion of good men are among
the number. But there is a delusion much more absurd in itself, but which is
nevertheless very common, that, namely, of believing that a man speaks the
truth because he is a man of birth, of fortune, or high in office.

Not that any formally make these kinds of reasonings—he has a hundred
thousand livres a year; therefore he possesses judgment: he is of high birth;
therefore what he advances must be true: he is a poor man; therefore he is
wrong. Nevertheless, something of this kind passes through the minds of the
majority, and unconsciously bears away their judgment.

Let the same thing be proposed by a man of quality, and by one of no
distinction, and it will often be found that we approve of it in the mouth of
the former, when we scarcely condescend to listen to it in that of the latter.
Scripture designed to teach us this disposition of men, in that perfect represen-
tation which is given of it in the book of Ecclesiasticus.[2] "When a rich man
speaketh, every one holdeth his tongue, and look, what he saith they extol it
to the skies; but if the poor man speak, they say, 'What fellow is this?' " . . .

It is certain that complaisance and flattery have much to do with the
approbation which is bestowed on the actions and words of people of quality;
as also that they often gain this by a certain outward grace, and by a noble,
free, and natural bearing, which is sometimes so distinctive that it is almost
impossible for it to be imitated by those who are of low birth. It is certain,
also, that there are many who approve of everything which is done and said
by the great, through an inward abasement of soul, who bend under the
weight of grandeur, and whose sight is not strong enough to bear its lustre; as,
indeed, that the outward pomp which environs them always imposes a little,
and makes some impression on the strongest minds.

This illusion springs from the corruption of the heart of man, who, having
a strong passion for honours and pleasures, necessarily conceives a great
affection for the means by which these honours and pleasures are obtained.
The love which we have for all those things which are valued by the world,
makes us judge those happy who possess them; and, in thus judging them
happy, we place them above ourselves, and regard them as eminent and

2. Eccles. 13:23.

exalted persons. This habit of regarding them with respect passes insensibly from their fortune to their mind. Men do not commonly do things by halves; we, therefore, give them minds as exalted as their rank; we submit to their opinions; and this is the reason of the credit which they commonly obtain in the affairs which they manage.

But this illusion is still stronger in the great themselves, when they have not laboured to correct the impression which their fortune naturally makes on their minds, than it is in their inferiors. Some derive from their estate and riches a reason for maintaining that their opinions ought to prevail over those who are beneath them. They cannot bear that those people whom they regard with contempt should pretend to have as much judgment and reason as themselves, and this makes them so impatient of the least contradiction. All this springs from the same source, that is, from the false ideas which they have of their grandeur, nobility, and wealth. Instead of considering them as things altogether foreign from their character, which do not prevent them at all from being perfectly equal to all the rest of men, both in mind and body, and which do not prevent their judgment even from being as weak and as liable to be deceived as that of all others, they, in some sort, incorporate with their very essence all these qualities of grand, noble, rich, master, lord, prince, —they exaggerate their idea of themselves with these things, and never represent themselves to themselves without all their titles, their equipage, and their train.

They are accustomed from their infancy to consider themselves as of a different species from other men; they never mingle in imagination with the mass of human kind; they are, in their own eyes, always counts or dukes, and never simply men. Thus they shape to themselves a soul and judgment according to the measure of their fortune, and believe themselves as much above others in mind as they are above them in birth and fortune.

The folly of the human mind is such, that there is nothing which may not serve to aggrandize the idea which it has of itself. A beautiful horse, grand clothes, a long beard, make men consider themselves more clever; and there are few who do not think more of themselves on horseback or in a coach than on foot. It is easy to convince everybody that there is nothing more ridiculous than these judgments, but it is very difficult to guard entirely against the secret impression which these outward things make upon the mind. All that we can do is to accustom ourselves as much as possible to give no influence at all to those qualities which cannot contribute towards finding the truth, and to give it even to those which do thus contribute only so far as they really contribute to this end. Age, knowledge, study, experience, mind, energy, memory, accuracy, labour, avail to find the truth of hidden things, and these qualities, therefore, deserve to be respected; but it is always necessary to weigh with care, and then to make a comparison with the opposite reasons; for from separate individual things we can conclude nothing with certainty, since there are very false opinions which have been sanctioned by men of great mental power, who possessed these qualities to a great extent.

VIII. There is something still more deceptive in the mistakes which arise from the manner, for we are naturally led to believe that a man is in the right when he speaks with grace, with ease, with gravity, with moderation, and with gentleness; and, on the contrary, that a man is in the wrong when he speaks harshly, or manifests anything of passion, acrimony, or presumption, in his actions and words.

Nevertheless, if we judge of the essence of things by these outward and sensible appearances, we must be often deceived. For there are many people who utter follies gravely and modestly; and others, on the contrary, who, being naturally of a quick temper, or under the influence even of some passion, which appears in their countenance or their words, have nevertheless the truth on their side. There are some men of very moderate capacity, and very superficial, who, from having been nourished at court, where the art of pleasing is studied and practised better than anywhere else, have very agreeable manners, by means of which they render many false judgments acceptable; and there are others, on the contrary, who, having nothing outward to recommend them, have, nevertheless, a great and solid mind within. There are some who speak better than they think, and others who think better than they speak. Thus reason demands of those who are capable of it, that they judge not by these outward things, and hesitate not to yield to the truth, not only when it is proposed in ways that are offensive and disagreeable, but even when it is mingled with much of falsehood; for the same person may speak truly in one thing, and falsely in another; may be right in one thing, and wrong in another.

It is necessary, therefore, to consider each thing separately, that is to say, we must judge of the manner by the manner, and of the matter by the matter, and not of matter by the manner, nor of the manner by the matter. A man does wrong to speak with anger, and he does right to speak the truth; and, on the contrary, another is right in speaking calmly and civilly, and he is wrong in advancing falsehoods.

But as it is reasonable to be on our guard against concluding that a thing is true or false, because it is proposed in such a way, it is right, also, that those who wish to persuade others of any truth which they have discovered, should study to clothe it in the garb most suitable for making it acceptable, and to avoid those revolting ways of stating it which only lead to its rejection.

They ought to remember that when we seek to move the minds of people, it is a small thing that we have right on our side; and it is a great evil to have only right, and not to have also that which is necessary for making it acceptable.

If they seriously honour the truth, they ought not to dishonour it by covering it with the marks of falsehood and deceit; and if they love it sincerely, they ought not to attach to it the hatred and aversion of men, by the offensive way in which they propound it. It is the most important, as well as the most useful, precept of rhetoric, that it behooves us to govern the spirit as well as the words; for although it is a different thing to be wrong in the manner from being wrong in the matter, the faults, nevertheless, of the manner are often greater and more important than those of the matter.

In reality, all these fiery, presumptuous, bitter, obstinate, passionate manners, always spring from some disorder of the mind, which is often more serious than the defect of intelligence and of knowledge, which we reprehend in others. It is, indeed, always unjust to seek to persuade men in this way; for it is very right that we should lead them to the truth when we know it; but it is wrong to compel others to take as true everything that we believe, and to defer to our authority alone. We do this, however, when we propose the truth in this offensive manner. For the way of speaking generally enters into the mind before the reasons, since the mind is more prompt to notice the manner of the speaker than it is to comprehend the solidity of these proofs, which are often, indeed, not comprehended at all. Now the manner of the discourse being thus separated from the proofs, marks only the authority which he who speaks arrogates to himself; so that if he is bitter and imperious, he necessarily revolts the minds of others, since he appears to wish to gain, by authority, and by a kind of tyranny, that which ought only to be obtained by persuasion and reason.

This injustice is still greater when we employ these offensive ways in combating common and received opinions; for the judgment of an individual may indeed be preferred to that of many when it is more correct, but an individual ought never to maintain that his authority should prevail against that of all others.

Thus, not only modesty and prudence, but justice itself, obliges us to assume a modest air when we combat common opinions or established authority, otherwise we cannot escape the injustice of opposing the authority of an individual to an authority either public, or greater and more widely established, than our own. We cannot exercise too much moderation when we seek to disturb the position of a received opinion or of an ancient faith. This is so true, that St. Augustine extended it even to religious truths, having given this excellent rule to all those who have to instruct others:—

"Observe," says he, "in what way the wise and religious catholics taught that which they had to communicate to others. If they were things common and authorised, they propounded them in a manner full of assurance, and free from every trace of doubt by being accompanied with the greatest possible gentleness; but if they were extraordinary things, although they themselves very clearly recognised their truth, they still proposed them rather as doubts and as questions to be examined, than as dogmas and fixed decisions, in order to accommodate themselves in this to the weakness of those who heard them." And so if a truth be so high that it is above the strength of those to whom it is spoken, they prefer rather to keep it back for a while, in order to give them time for growth, and for becoming capable of receiving it, instead of making it known to them in that state of weakness in which it would have overwhelmed them.

3.

Four Sorts of Arguments

John Locke

[The following excerpt is from John Locke, *An Essay Concerning Human Understanding*, edited by A. C. Fraser (New York: Dover, 1959), Book IV, chap. xvii, sections 19–22. The notes are by A. C. Fraser.]

19. . . . It may be worth our while a little to reflect on *four sorts of arguments*, that men, in their reasonings with others, do ordinarily make use of to prevail on their assent; or at least so to awe them as to silence their opposition.

I. The first is, to allege the opinions of men, whose parts, learning, eminency, power, or some other cause has gained a name, and settled their reputation in the common esteem with some kind of authority. When men are established in any kind of dignity, it is thought a breach of modesty for others to derogate any way from it, and question the authority of men who are in possession of it. This is apt to be censured, as carrying with it too much pride, when a man does not readily yield to the determination of approved authors, which is wont to be received with respect and submission by others: and it is looked upon as insolence, for a man to set up and adhere to his own opinion against the current stream of antiquity; or to put it in the balance against that of some learned doctor, or otherwise approved writer. Whoever backs his tenets with such authorities, thinks he ought thereby to carry the cause, and is ready to style it impudence in any one who shall stand out against them. This I think may be called *argumentum ad verecundiam*.[1]

---

1. Locke is always chary of appeals to human authority, which in medieval reasonings had so much taken the place of a purely intellectual appeal. Yet, in many cases, one's judgment of the trustworthiness of the judgment of another person is the only available foundation in reason for an opinion of one's own.

20. II. Secondly, Another way that men ordinarily use to drive others, and force them to submit their judgments, and receive the opinion in debate, is to require the adversary to admit what they allege as a proof, or to assign a better. And this I call *argumentum ad ignorantiam*.[2]

21. III. Thirdly, A third way is to press a man with consequences drawn from his own principles or concessions. This is already known under the name of *argumentum ad hominem*.[3]

22. IV. The fourth is the using of proofs drawn from any of the foundations of knowledge or probability. This I call *argumentum ad judicium*. This alone, of all the four, brings true instruction with it, and advances us in our way to knowledge. For, 1. It argues not another man's opinion to be right, because I, out of respect, or any other consideration but that of conviction, will not contradict him. 2. It proves not another man to be in the right way, nor that I ought to take the same with him, because I know not a better. 3. Nor does it follow that another man is in the right way, because he has shown me that I am in the wrong. I may be modest, and therefore not oppose another man's persuasion: I may be ignorant, and not be able to produce a better: I may be in an error, and another may show me that I am so. This may dispose me, perhaps, for the reception of truth, but helps me not to it: that must come from proofs and arguments, and light arising from the nature of things themselves, and not from my shamefacedness, ignorance, or error.[4]

---

2. We are not bound in reason to accept our adversary's conclusion as proved, because we cannot offer better proof of another conclusion. For the question may be one which transcends man's experience and intelligence, intermediate between mere sense and Omniscience. "Malebranche having enumerated and showed the difficulties of the other ways whereby he thinks human understanding may be attempted to be explained, and how insufficient they are to give a satisfactory account of the ideas we have, treats this of 'seeing all things in God' on that account as the true, *because it is impossible to find a better*. Which argument, so far being only *argumentum ad ignorantiam*, loses all its force as soon as we consider the weakness of our minds, and the narrowness of our capacities, and have but humility enough to allow that there may be many things which we cannot fully comprehend, and that God is not bound in all he does to subject his ways of operation to the scrutiny of our thoughts, and confine himself to do nothing but what we must comprehend." (Locke's *Examination of Malebranche*, §2.)

3. This argument is legitimate when the question in dispute is not the truth of a proposition but the self-consistency of the person who proposes it. It becomes irrelevant, and therefore fallacious, when used as an *argumentum ad rem*. This and the two preceding arguments, when fallacious, may be regarded as modes of the fallacy of irrelevant reasoning.

4. The *argumentum ad judicium* suggests the reference to the limits and ultimate foundations of reason in man contained in the following section [i.e., chap. 17, sec. 23, not reprinted here. Eds.].

4

Kinds of Arguments and the Doctrine of Sophisms

Isaac Watts

[The following excerpt is from Issac Watts, *Logick: or, the Right Use of Reason*, 2d ed., 1796 (repr., New York: Garland, 1984), Part III, chap. ii, sec. 8, and Part III, chap. iii.]

Sect. VIII Of Several Kinds of Arguments and Demonstrations.

We proceed now to the Division of Syllogisms according to the middle term; and in this Part of our Treatise the Syllogisms themselves are properly called Arguments, and are thus distributed.

I. Arguments are called Grammatical, Logical, Metaphysical, Physical, Moral, Mechanical, Theological, &c. according to the Art, Science, or Subject whence the middle Term or Topic is borrowed. Thus if we prove that no Man should steal from his Neighbour because the Scripture forbids it, this is a theological Argument: If we prove it from the Laws of the Land, it is political; but if we prove it from the Principles of Reason and Equity, the Argument is moral.

II. Arguments are either certain and evident, or doubtful and meerly probable.

Probable Arguments are those whose Conclusions are proved by some probable Medium; as, This Hill was once a Church-Yard, or a Field of

Battle, because there are many human Bones found here. This is not a certain Argument, for human Bones might have been conveyed there some other Way.

Evident and certain Arguments are called Demonstrations; for they prove their Conclusions by clear Mediums and undoubted Principles; and they are generally divided into these two sorts.

1. Demonstrations *a Priori*, which prove the Effect by its necessary Cause; as, I prove the Scripture is infallibly true, because it is the Word of God, who cannot lye.

2. Demonstrations *a Posteriori*, which infer the Cause from its necessary Effect; as, I infer there hath been the Hand of some Artificer here, because I find a curious Engine. Or, I infer there is a God, from the Works of his Wisdom in the visible World.

The last of these is called *Demonstratio tou hoti* [literally, of the that (it is)], because it proves only the Existence of a Thing; the first is named *Demonstratio tou dioti* [literally, of the because], because it shews also the Cause of its Existence.

But Note, That tho' these two sorts of Arguments are most peculiarly called Demonstrations, yet generally any strong and convincing Argument obtains that Name; and it is the Custom of Mathematicians to call all their Arguments Demonstrations, from what Medium soever they derive them.

III. Arguments are divided into artificial and inartificial.

An artificial Argument is taken from the Nature and Circumstances of the Things; and if the Argument be strong it produces a natural Certainty, as; The World was first created by God, because nothing can create itself.

An inartificial Argument is the Testimony of another, and this is called *original*, when our Information proceeds immediately from the Persons concerned, or from Eye or Ear-Witnesses of a Fact: it is called *Tradition* when it is delivered by the Report of others.

We have taken Notice before, that Testimony is either divine or human. If the human Testimony be strong, it produces a moral Certainty; but divine Testimony produces a supernatural Certainty which is far superior.

Note; Arguments taken from human Testimony, as well as from Laws and Rules of Equity, are called moral; and indeed the same Name is also applied to every sort of Argument which is drawn from the free Actions of God, or the contingent Actions of Men, wherein we cannot arise to a natural Certainty, but content our selves with an high Degree of Probability, which in many Cases is scarce inferior to natural Certainty.

IV. Arguments are either direct or indirect. It is a direct Argument where the middle Term is such as proves the Question itself, and infers that very Proposition which was the Matter of Enquiry. An indirect or oblique Argument proves or refutes some other Proposition, and thereby makes the Thing enquired appear to be true by plain Consequence.

Several Arguments are called indirect; as, (1.) When some contradictory Proposition is proved to be false, improbable, or impossible: Or when upon Supposition of the Falshood or Denial of the original Proposition, some Absurdity is inferred. This is called a Proof *per impossibile*, or a *Reductio ad absurdum*. (2.) When some other Proposition is proved to be true which is less probable, and thence it follows that the original Proposition is true, because it is more probable. This is an Argument *ex magis probabili ad minus*. (3.) When any other Proposition is proved upon which it was before agreed to yield the original Question. This is an Argument *ex Concesso*.

V. There is yet another Rank of Arguments which have Latin Names; their true Distinction is derived from the Topics or middle Terms which are used in them, tho' they are called an Address to our Judgment, our Faith, our Ignorance, our Profession, our Modesty, and our Passions.

1. If an Argument be taken from the Nature or Existence of Things, and addrest to the Reason of Mankind, it is called *Argumentum ad Judicium*.

2. When it is borrowed from some convincing Testimony, it is *Argumentum ad Fidem*, an Address to our Faith.

3. When it is drawn from any insufficient Medium whatsoever, and yet the Opposer has not Skill to refute or answer it, this is *Argumentum ad Ignorantiam*, an Address to our Ignorance.

4. When it is built upon the profest Principles or Opinions of the Person with whom we argue, whether these Opinions be true or false, it is named *Argumentum ad Hominem*, an Address to our profest Principles. St. Paul often uses this Argument when he reasons with the Jews, and when he says, I speak as a Man.

5. When the Argument is fetch'd from the Sentiments of some wise, great, or good Men, whose Authority we reverence, and hardly dare oppose, it is called *Argumentum ad Verecundiam*, an Address to our Modesty.

6. I add finally, when an Argument is borrowed from any Topics which are suited to engage the Inclinations and Passions of the Hearers on the Side of the Speaker, rather than to convince the Judgment, this is *Argumentum ad Passiones*, an Address to the Passions; or if it be made publickly, it is called *ad Populum*, or an Appeal to the People.

After all these Divisions of Syllogism or Argument arising from the middle Term, there is one Distinction proper to be mentioned which arises from the Premisses. An Argument is called uniform when both the Premisses are derived from the same Springs of Knowledge, whether it be Sense, Reason, Consciousness, human Faith or divine Faith: But when the two Premisses are derived from different Springs of Knowledge, it is called a mixt Argument.

Whether the Conclusion must be called Human or Divine, when one or both Premisses are Divine, but the Conclusion is drawn by human Reason, I leave to be disputed and determined in the Schools of Theology.

Thus the second Chapter is finished, and a particular Account given of all the chief Kinds of Syllogisms or Arguments which are made use of among Men, or treated of in Logic, together with the special Rules for the Formation of them, as far as is necessary.

If a Syllogism agree with the Rules which are given for the Construction and Regulation of it, it is called a true Argument: If it disagree with these Rules, it is a Paralogism, or false Argument: But when a false Argument puts on the Face and Appearance of a true one, then it is properly called a Sophism or Fallacy, which shall be the Subject of the next Chapter.

Chap. III.   *The Doctrine of Sophisms*

From Truth nothing can really follow but what is true: Whensoever therefore we find a false Conclusion drawn from Premisses which seem to be true, there must be some Fault in the Deduction or Inference; or else one of the Premisses is not true in the Sense in which it is used in that Argument.

When an Argument carries the Face of Truth with it, and yet leads us into Mistake, it is a Sophism; and there is some Need of particular Description of these fallacious Arguments, that we may with more Ease and Readiness detect and solve them.

Sect. I Of Several Kinds of Sophisms, and their Solution.

As the rules of right Judgment and of good Ratiocination often coincide with each other, so the Doctrine of Prejudices, which was treated of in the second Part of *Logic*, has anticipated a great deal of what might be said on the Subject of Sophisms; yet I shall mention the most remarkable Springs of false

Argumentation, which are reduced by Logicians to some of the following Heads.

I. The first sort of Sophism is called *Ignoratio Elenchi*, or a Mistake of the Question; that is, when something else is proved which has neither any necessary Connection or Inconsistency with the Thing enquired, and consequently gives no Determination to the Enquiry, tho' it may seem at first Sight to determine the Question; as, if any should conclude that St. Paul was not a native Jew, by proving that he was born a Roman; or if they should pretend to determine that he was neither a Roman, nor Jew, by proving that he was born at Tarsus in Cilicia: These Sophisms are refuted by shewing that all these three may be true; for he was born of Jewish Parents in the City of Tarsus, and by some peculiar Privilege granted to his Parents, or his native City, he was born a Denizen of Rome. Thus there is neither of these three Characters of the Apostle inconsistent with each other, and therefore the proving of one of them true does not refute the others.

Or if the Question be proposed, Whether Excess of Wine can be hurtful to him that drinks it, and the Sophister should prove that it revives his Spirits, it exhilarates his Soul, it gives a Man Courage, and makes him strong and active, and then he takes it for granted that he has proved his Point. But the Respondent may easily shew that tho' Wine may do all this, yet it may be finally hurtful, both to the Soul and Body of him that drinks it to Excess.

Disputers when they grow warm are ready to run into this Fallacy: They dress up the Opinion of their Adversary as they please, and ascribe Sentiments to him which he doth not acknowledge; and when they have with a great deal of Pomp attack'd and confounded these Images of Straw of their own making, they triumph over their Adversary as tho' they had utterly confuted his Opinion.

It is a Fallacy of the same kind which a Disputant is guilty of when he finds that his Adversary is too hard for him, and that he cannot fairly prove the Question first propos'd; he then with Slyness and Subtilty turns the Discourse aside to some other kindred Point which he can prove, and exults in that new Argument wherein his Opponent never contradicted him.

The Way to prevent this Fallacy is by keeping the Eye fixt on this precise Point of Dispute, and neither wandering from it ourselves, nor suffering our Antagonist to wander from it, or substitute anything else in its Room.

II. The next Sophism is called *Petitio Principii*, or a Supposition of what is not granted; that is, when any Proposition is proved by the same Proposition in other Words, or by something that is equally uncertain and disputed: As if any one undertake to prove that the human Soul is extended thro' all the Parts of the Body, because it resides in every Member, which is but the same Thing in other Words. Or if a Papist should pretend to prove that his Religion is the only Catholick Religion, and is derived from Christ and his Apostles, because it agrees with the Doctrine of all of the Fathers of the Church, all the holy Martyrs, and all the Christian World throughout all Ages: Whereas this is a great Point in Contest, whether their Religion does agree with that of all the Antients, and the primitive Christians or no.

III. That sort of Fallacy which is called a Circle is very near akin to the *Petitio Principii*; as, when one of the Premisses in a Syllogism is questioned and opposed, and we pretend to prove it by the Conclusion: Or, when in a Train of Syllogisms we prove the last by recurring to what was the Conclusion of the first. The Papists are famous at this sort of Fallacy, when they prove the Scripture to be the Word of God by the Authority or infallible Testimony of their Church; and when they are called to shew the infallible Authority of their Church, they pretend to prove it by the Scripture.

IV. The next kind of Sophism is called *non Causa pro Causa*, or the Assignation of a false Cause. This the Peripatetic Philosophers were guilty of continually, when they told us that certain Beings, which were called substantial Forms, were the Springs of Colour, Motion, Vegetation, and the various Operations of natural Beings in the animate and inanimate World; when they informed us that Nature was terribly afraid of a Vacuum, and that this was the Cause why the Water would not fall out of a long Tube if it was turned upside down: The Moderns as well as the Antients fall often into this Fallacy when they positively assign the Reasons of natural Appearances, without sufficient Experiments to prove them.

Astrologers are overrun with this sort of Fallacies, and they cheat the People grosly by pretending to tell Fortunes, and to deduce the Cause of the various Occurrences in the Lives of Men, from the various Positions of the Stars and Planets, which they call Aspects.

When Comets and Eclipses of the Sun and Moon are construed to signify the Fate of Princes, the Revolution of States, Famine, Wars and Calamities of all kinds, it is a Fallacy that belongs to this Rank of Sophisms.

There is scarce any thing more common in human Life than this sort of deceitful Argument. If any two accidental Events happen to concur, one is presently made the Cause of the other. If Titius wronged his Neighbour of a Guinea, and in six Months after he fell down and broke his Leg, weak Men will impute it to the divine Vengeance on Titius for his former Injustice. This Sophism was found also in the early Days of the World: For when holy Job was surrounded with uncommon Miseries, his own Friends inferr'd, that he was a most heinous Criminal, and charged him with aggravated Guilt as the Cause of his Calamities; tho' God himself by a Voice from Heaven solv'd this uncharitable Sophism, and cleared his Servant Job of that Charge.

How frequent is it among Men to impute Crimes to wrong Persons? We too often charge that upon the wicked Contrivance and premeditated Malice of a Neighbour, which arose merely from Ignorance, or from unguarded Temper. And on the other hand, when we have a Mind to excuse ourselves, we practice the same Sophism, and charge that upon our Inadvertence or our Ignorance, which perhaps was design'd Wickedness. What is really done by a Necessity of Circumstances, we sometimes impute to Choice: And again, we charge that upon Necessity, which was really desired and chosen.

Sometimes a Person acts out of Judgment in Opposition to his Inclination; another Person perhaps acts the same Thing out of Inclination, and against his Judgment. 'Tis hard for us to determine with Assurance what are the inward Springs and secret Causes of every Man's Conduct; and therefore we should be cautious and slow in passing a Judgment, where the Case is not exceeding evident: And if we should mistake, let it rather be on the charitable than the censorious Side.

'Tis the same Sophism that charges Mathematical Learning with leading the Minds of Men to Scepticism and Infidelity, and as unjustly accuses the new Philosophy and paving the Way to Heresy and Schism. Thus the Reformation from Popery has been charged with the Murder and Blood of Millions, which in Truth is to be imputed to the Tyranny of the Princes and of the Priests, who would not suffer the People to Reform their Sentiments and their Practices according to the Word of God. Thus Christianity in the primitive Ages was charged by the Heathens with all the Calamities which befel the Roman Empire, because the Christians renounced the Heathen Gods and Idols.

The Way to relieve ourselves from these Sophisms, and to secure ourselves from the Danger of falling into them, is an honest and diligent Enquiry into the real Nature and Causes of Things, with a constant Watchfulness against all those Prejudices that might warp the Judgment aside from Truth in that Enquiry.

V. The next is called *fallacia Accidentis*, or a Sophism wherein we pronounce concerning the Nature and essential Properties of any Subject, according to something which is merely accidental to it. This is akin to the former, and is also very frequent in human Life. So if Opium or the Peruvian Bark has been used imprudently or unsuccessfully, whereby the Patient has received Injury, some weaker People absolutely pronounce against the Use of the Bark or Opium upon all Occasions whatsoever, and are ready to call them Poison. So Wine has been the accidental Occasion of Drunkenness and Quarrels; Learning and Printing may have been the accidental Cause of Sedition in a State; the Reading of the Bible by Accident hath been abused to promote Heresies or destructive Errors; and for these Reasons they have been all pronounced evil Things. Mahomet forbad his Followers the Use of Wine; the Turks discourage Learning in their Dominions; and the Papists forbid the Scripture to be read by the Laity. But how very unreasonable are these Inferences, and these Prohibitions which are built upon them!

VI. The next Sophism borders upon the former; and that is when we argue from that which is true in particular Circumstances to prove the same thing true absolutely, simply, and abstracted from all Circumstances; this is called in the Schools a Sophism *a dicto secundum quid ad dictum simpliciter;* as, That which is bought in the Shambles is eaten for Dinner; raw Meat is bought in the Shambles; therefore raw Meat is eaten for Dinner. Or thus, Livy writes Fables and Improbabilities when he describes Prodigies and Omens; therefore Livy's Roman History is never to be believed in any thing. Or thus, There may be some Mistake of Transcribers in some Part of Scripture; therefore Scripture alone is not a safe Guide for our Faith.

This sort of Sophism has its Reverse also; as, when we argue from that which is true simply and absolutely to prove the same thing true in all particular Circumstances whatsoever;[1] as, if a Traytor should argue from the sixth Commandment, Thou shalt not kill a Man, to prove that he himself ought not to be hanged: Or if a mad Man should tell me, I ought not to withold his Sword from him, because no Man ought to withold the Property of another.

These two last Species of Sophisms are easily solved by shewing the Difference betwixt Things in their absolute Nature, and the same Things surrounded with peculiar Circumstances, and considered in Regard to special

---

1. This is arguing from a moral Universality which admits of some Exceptions, in the same manor as may be argued from metaphysical or natural Universality, which admits of no exceptions.

Times, Places, Persons, and Occasions; or by shewing the Difference between a moral and a metaphysical Universality, and that the Proposition will hold good in one Case but not in the other.

VII. The Sophisms of Composition and Division come next to be mentioned.

The Sophism of Composition is when we infer any thing concerning Ideas in a compounded Sense, which is only true in a divided Sense. As when it is said in the Gospel that Christ made the Blind to see, and the Deaf to hear, and the Lame to walk, we ought not to infer hence that Christ performed Contradictions; but those who were blind before were made to see, and those who were deaf before made to hear, &c. So when the Scripture assures us the worst of Sinners may be saved, it signifies only that they who have been the worst of Sinners may repent and be saved, not that they shall be saved in their Sins. Or if anyone should argue thus, Two and three are even and odd; five are two and three; therefore five are even and odd. Here that is very falsly inferred concerning two and three in Union, which is only true of them divided.

The Sophism of Division is when we infer the same Thing concerning Ideas in a Divided Sense, which is only true in a compounded Sense; as, if we should pretend to prove that every Soldier in the Grecian Army put an hundred thousand Persians to Flight, because the Grecian Soldiers did so. Or if a Man should argue thus; five is one Number; two and three are five; therefore two and three are one Number.

This sort of Sophisms is committed when the Word *All* is taken in a collective and a distributive Sense, without a due Distinction; as, if any one should reason thus; All the musical Instruments of the Jewish Temple made a noble Consort: The Harp was a musical Instrument of the Jewish Temple; therefore the Harp made a noble Consort.

It is the same Fallacy when the universal Word *All* or *No* refers to Species in one Proposition, and to Individuals in another; as, All Animals were in Noah's Ark; therefore no Animals perished in the Flood: Whereas in the Premise all Animals signifies every kind of Animals, which does not exclude or deny the drowning of a thousand Individuals.

VIII. The last sort of Sophisms arises from our Abuse of the Ambiguity of Words, which is the largest and most extensive kind of Fallacy; and indeed several of the former Fallacies might be reduced to this Head.

When the Words or Phrases are plainly equivocal, they are called Sophisms of Equivocation; as, if we should argue thus, He that sends forth a Book into the Light, desires it to be read; He that throws a Book into the Fire, sends it into the Light; therefore, he that throws a Book into the Fire desires it to be read.

This Sophism, as well as the foregoing, and all of the like Nature are solved by shewing the different senses of the Words, Terms or Phrases. Here Light in the major Proposition signifies the publick View of the World; in the minor it signifies the Brightness of Flame or Fire, and therefore the Syllogism has four Terms, or rather it has no middle Terms, and proves nothing.

But where such gross Equivocations and Ambiguities appear in Arguments, there is little Danger of imposing upon ourselves or others. The greatest Danger, and which we are perpetually exposed to in Reasoning, is, where the two Senses or Significations of one Term are near akin, and not plainly distinguished, and yet they are really sufficiently different in their Sense to lead us into great Mistakes, if we are not watchful. And indeed the greatest Part of Controversies in the sacred or civil Life arise from the different Senses that are put upon Words, and the different Ideas which are included in them; as has been shewn at large in the first Part of *Logick*, Chapt. IV, which treats of Words and Terms.[2]

There is after all these, another sort of Sophism which is wont to be called an imperfect Enumeration, or a false induction, when from a few Experiments or Observations Men infer general Theorems and universal Propositions. But this is sufficiently noticed in the foregoing Chapter, where we treated of that sort of Syllogism which is called Induction.

2. [Watts is here referring to his own *Logick*, i.e., the work from which this passage has been excerpted. Eds.]

5

Of Fallacies

Richard Whately

[The following excerpt is from Richard Whately, *Elements of Logic*, 8th London edition, revised (repr., New York: Harper and Row, 1853), Bk. III, secs. 1–4 inclusive, sec. 13, part of sec. 14, and sec. 15.]

Of Fallacies

Introduction

Although sundry instances of Fallacies have been from time to time noticed in the foregoing Books, it will be worth while to devote a more particular attention to the subject.

By a Fallacy is commonly understood, "any unsound mode of arguing, which appears to demand our conviction, and to be decisive of the question in hand, when in fairness it is not." Considering the ready detection and clear exposure of Fallacies to be both more extensively important, and also more difficult, than many are aware of, I propose to take a logical view of the subject; referring the different Fallacies to the most convenient heads, and giving a scientific analysis of the procedure which takes place in each.

After all, indeed, in the practical detection of each individual Fallacy, much must depend on natural and acquired acuteness; nor can any rules be given, the mere learning of which will enable us to *apply* them with mechanical certainty and readiness: but still we shall find that to take correct general views of the subject, and to be familiarized with scientific discussions of it, will tend above all things, to *engender such a habit of mind*, as will best fit us for practice.

Indeed the case is the same with respect to Logic in general. Scarcely any one would, in ordinary practice state to himself either his own or another's reasoning, in syllogisms in Barbara at full length; yet a familiarity with logical principles tends very much (as all feel, who are really well acquainted with them) to beget a habit of clear and sound reasoning. The truth is, in this, as in many other things, there are processes going on in the mind (when we are practising anything quite familiar to us) with such rapidity as to leave no trace in the memory; and we often apply principles which did not, as far as we are conscious, even occur to us at the time.

It would be foreign, however, to the present purpose to investigate fully the manner in which certain studies operate in remotely producing certain effects on the mind: it is sufficient to establish the *fact*, that habits of scientific analysis (besides the instrinsic beauty and dignity of such studies) lead to practical advantage. It is on logical principles therefore that I propose to discuss the subject of Fallacies; and it may, indeed, seem to have been unnecessary to make any apology for so doing, after what has been formerly said, generally, in the defence of Logic; but that the generality of logical writers have usually followed so opposite a plan. Whenever they have to treat of any thing that is beyond the mere elements of Logic, they totally lay aside all reference to the principles they have been occupied in establishing and explaining, and have recourse to a loose, vague, and popular kind of language; such as would be the best suited indeed to an exoterical discourse, but seems strangely incongruous in a professional logical treatise. What should we think of a geometrical writer, who, after having gone through the Elements, with strict definitions and demonstrations, should, on proceeding to Mechanics, totally lay aside all reference to scientific principles—all use of technical terms—and treat of the subject in undefined terms, and with probable and popular arguments? It would be thought strange if even a Botanist, when addressing those whom he had been instructing in the principles and terms of his system, should totally lay these aside when he came to describe plants, and should adopt the language of the vulgar. Surely it affords but too much plausibility to the cavils of those who scoff at Logic altogether, that the very writers who profess to teach it should never themselves make any application of, or reference to, its principles, on those very occasions, when, and *when only*, such application and reference are to be expected. If the principles of any system are *well* laid down—if its technical language is judiciously framed—then, surely, those principles and that language will afford (for those who have once thoroughly learned them) the best, the most clear, simple, and concise method of treating any subject connected with that system. Yet even writers generally acute in treating of the Dilemma and of the Fallacies, have very much forgotten the Logician, and assumed a loose and rhetorical style of writing, without making any application of the principles they had formerly laid down, but, on the contrary, sometimes departing widely from them.[1]

The most experienced teachers, when addressing those who are familiar with the elementary principles of Logic, think it requisite, not indeed to lead them on each occasion, *through the whole detail* of those principles, when the process is quite obvious, but always to *put them on the road*, as it were to those principles, that they may plainly see their own way to the end, and take a scientific view of the subject: in the same manner as mathematical writers avoid indeed the occasional tediousness of going all through a very simple demonstration, which the learner, if he will, may easily supply; but yet always speak in strict mathematical language, and with reference to mathematical principles, though they do not always state them at full length. I would not profess, therefore, any more than they do to write (on subjects connected with the science) in a language intelligible to those who are ignorant of its first rudiments. To do so, indeed, would imply that one was not taking a scientific view of the subject, nor availing one's-self of the principles that had been established, and the accurate and concise technical language that had been framed.

The rules already given enable us to develope the principles on which all reasoning is conducted, whatever be the subject-matter of it, and to ascertain the validity or fallaciousness of any apparent argument, as far as the *form of expression* is concerned; that being alone the proper province of Logic.

But it is evident that we may nevertheless remain liable to be deceived or perplexed in argument by the assumption of *false or doubtful premises*, or by the employment of *indistinct or ambiguous terms*; and, accordingly, many logical writers wishing to make their systems appear as perfect as possible,

---

1. Aldrich (and the same may be said of several other writers) is far more confused in his discussion of Fallacies than in any other part of his treatise; of which this one instance may serve: after having distinguished Fallacies into those in the *expression*, and those in the *matter* ("*in dictione*," and "*extra dictionem*,") he observes of one or two of *these last*, that they are not properly called *Fallacies* as not being *syllogisms faulty in form*; ("syllogisimi forma peccantes;") as if any one, that was such, could be "Fallacia *extra dictionem*." [The reference is to Henry Aldrich (1647–1710) and his book *Artis Logicae Compendium*, 1691. For a discussion of Aldrich's importance, see Hamblin, 1970. Eds.]

have undertaken to give rules "for attaining clear ideas," and for "guiding the judgment;" and fancying or professing themselves successful in this, have consistently enough denominated Logic, the "Art of using the Reason;" which in truth it would be, and would nearly supersede all other studies, if it could of itself ascertain the *meaning* of every *term*, and the *truth* or *falsity* of every *proposition*; in the same manner as it actually can, the *validity* of every *argument*. And they have been led into this, partly by the consideration that Logic is concerned about the "three operations" of the mind—simple apprehension, judgment, and reasoning: not observing that it is not *equally* concerned about all: the last operation being alone its appropriate province; and the rest being treated of only in reference to that.

The contempt justly due to such pretensions has most unjustly fallen on the science itself; much in the same manner as Chemistry was brought into disrepute among the unthinking, by the extravagant pretensions of the Alchymists. And those logical writers have been censured, not (as they should have been) for *making* such professions, but for not *fulfilling* them. It has been objected, especially, that the rules of Logic leave us still at a loss as to the most important and difficult point in reasoning; *viz*. the ascertaining the sense of the terms employed, and removing their ambiguity: a complaint resembling that made (according to a story told by Warburton,[2] and before alluded to) by a man who found fault with all the reading-glasses presented to him by the shopkeeper; the fact being that he had never *learnt to read*. In the present case, the complaint is the more unreasonable, inasmuch as there neither is, nor ever *can possibly be*, any such system devised as will effect the proposed object of clearing up the ambiguity of terms. It is, however, no small advantage, that the rules of Logic, though they cannot, alone, ascertain and clear up ambiguity in any term, yet do point out in *which* term of an argument it is to be sought for: directing our attention to the *middle*-term, as the one on the ambiguity of which a fallacy is likely to be built.

It will be useful, however, to class and describe the different kinds of ambiguity which are to be met with; and also the various ways in which the insertion of false, or, at least, unduly assumed, premises, is most likely to elude observation. And though the remarks which will be offered on these points may not be considered as strictly forming a *part* of Logic, they cannot be thought out of place, when it is considered how essentially they are connected with the *application* of it.

2. In his *Div. Leg.* [William Warburton (1698–1779) in his *Divine Legation*. Eds.]

§1. The division of Fallacies into those in the words (IN DICTIONE,) and those in the matter (EXTRA DICTIONEM) has not been, by any writers hitherto, grounded on any distinct principle: at least, not on any that they have themselves adhered to. The confounding together, however, of these two classes is highly detrimental to all clear notions concerning Logic; being obviously allied to the prevailing erroneous views which make Logic the *art of employing the intellectual faculties in general*, having the *discovery of truth* for its object, and all kinds of knowledge for its proper subject-matter; with all that train of vague and groundless speculations which have led to such interminable confusion and mistakes, and afforded a pretext for such clamorous censures.

It is important, therefore, that rules should be given for a division of Fallacies into logical and non-logical, on such a principle as shall keep clear of all this indistinctness and perplexity.

If any one should object, that the division about to be adopted is in some degree arbitrary, placing under the one head, fallacies which many might be disposed to place under the other, let him consider not only the indistinctness of all former divisions, but the utter impossibility of framing *any* that shall be completely secure from the objection urged, in a case where men have formed such various and vague notions, from the very want of some clear principle of division. Nay, from the elliptical form in which all reasoning is usually expressed, and the peculiarly involved and oblique form in which fallacy is for the most part conveyed, it must of course be often a matter of doubt, or rather, of arbitrary *choice*, not only to which genus each *kind* of fallacy should be referred, but even to which kind to refer any *one individual* fallacy. For, since, in any argument, one premiss is usually suppressed, it frequently happens, in the case of a fallacy, that the hearers are left to the alternative of supplying *either* a premiss which is *not true*, or *else*, one which *does not prove* the conclusion. E.G. if a man expatiates on the distress of the country, and thence argues that the government is tyrannical, we must suppose him to assume *either* that "every distressed country is under a tyranny," which is a manifest falsehood, *or*, merely that "every country under a tyranny is distressed," which, however true, proves nothing, the middle-term being undistributed. Now, in the former case, the fallacy would be referred to the head of "extra dictionem"; in the latter to that of "in dictione." Which are we to suppose the speaker meant us to understand? Surely just whichever each of his hearers might happen to prefer: some might assent to the false premiss; others, allow the unsound syllogism; to the sophist himself it is indifferent, as long as they can but be brought to admit the conclusion.

Without pretending, then, to conform to every one's mode of speaking on the subject, or to lay down rules which shall be in themselves (without any call for labour or skill in the person who employs them) readily applicable to, and decisive on, each individual case, I shall propose a division which is at least perfectly clear in its main principle, and coincides, perhaps, as nearly as possible, with the established notions of Logicians on the subject.

§2. In every Fallacy, the conclusion either *does*, or *does not follow from the premises*. Where the conclusion does not follow from the premises, it is manifest that the fault is in the *reasoning*, and in that alone; these, therefore, we call Logical Fallacies,[3] as being properly, violations of those rules of reasoning which it is the province of Logic to lay down.

Of these, however, one kind are more *purely Logical*, as exhibiting their fallaciousness by the bare *form* of the expression, without any regard to the meaning of the terms: to which class belong: 1st. undistributed middle; 2. illicit process; 3d. negative premises, or affirmative conclusion from a negative premiss, and *vice versa:* to which may be added 4th, those which have palpably (*i.e. expressed*) more than three terms.

The other kind may be most properly called *semi-logical; viz.* all the cases of ambiguous middle-term except its non-distribution: for though in such cases the conclusion does not follow, and though the rules of Logic show that it does not, *as soon as the ambiguity of the middle term is ascertained*, yet the discovery and ascertainment of this ambiguity requires attention to the *sense of the term*, and knowledge of the subject-matter; so that here, Logic teaches us not *how to find* the Fallacy, but only *where to search* for it, and on what principles to condemn it.

Accordingly it has been made a subject of bitter complaint against Logic, that it presupposes the most difficult point to be already accomplished, *viz.* the sense of the terms to be ascertained. A similar objection might be urged against every other art in existence; *e.g.* against Agriculture, that all the precepts for the cultivation of land presuppose the possession of a farm; or against perspective, that its rules are useless to a blind man. The objection is indeed peculiarly absurd when urged against Logic, because the object which it is blamed for not accomplishing *cannot* possibly be within the province of *any one* art whatever. Is it indeed possible or conceivable that there should be any method, science or system that should enable one to know the full and exact meaning of every term in existence? The utmost that can be done is to

---

3. In the same manner in which we call that a *criminal* court in which crimes are *judged*.

give some general rules that may assist us in this work; which is done in the first two chapters of Book II.[4]

Nothing perhaps tends more to conceal from men their imperfect conception of the meaning of a term, than the circumstance of their being able fully to comprehend a *process of reasoning* in which it is involved, without attaching any distinct meaning at all to that term; as is evident when X Y Z are used to stand for terms, in a regular syllogism. Thus a man may be *familiarized* with a term, and never find himself *at a loss* from not comprehending it; from which he will be very likely to infer that he *does* comprehend it, when perhaps he does not, but employs it vaguely and incorrectly; which leads to fallacious reasoning and confusion. It must be owned, however, that many logical writers have, in great measure, brought on themselves the reproach in question, by calling Logic "the right use of reason," laying down "rules for gaining clear ideas," and such-like *alazoneia*,[5] as Aristotle calls it; (*Rhet.* Book I. Chap. ii).

§3. The remaining class (*viz.* where the conclusion does follow from the premises) may be called the Material, or Non-logical Fallacies: of these there are two kinds;[6] 1st. when the premises are such as ought not to have been assumed; 2d. when the conclusion is not the one required, but irrelevant; which Fallacy is commonly called "*ignoratio elenchi,*" because your argument is not the "elenchus" (*i.e.* proof of the *contradictory*) of your opponent's assertion, which it should be; but proves, instead of that, some other proposition resembling it. Hence, since Logic defines what contradiction is, some may choose rather to range this with the *logical* Fallacies, as it seems, so far, to come under the jurisdiction of that art. Nevertheless, it is perhaps better to adhere to the original division, both on account of its clearness and also because few would be inclined to apply to the Fallacy in question the accusation of being *inconclusive*, and consequently "illogical" reasoning; besides which, it seems an artificial and circuitous way of speaking, to suppose in all

4. The very author of the objection says, "This (the comprehension of the meaning of general terms) is a study which every individual must carry on for himself; and of which no rules of Logic (how useful soever they may be in directing our labours) can supersede the necessity." D. Stewart, *Phil.* Vol. II. chap. ii. s. 2. [The reference is to Dugald Stewart (1753–1828), *Elements of the Philosophy of the Human Mind*, vol. 2 (1814), chap. ii, sec. 2. Eds.]

5. [We have here replaced a Greek term by its transliteration, *alazoneia*, which means "false pretension" or "imposture." The reference in the text that follows immediately is to Aristotle's *Rhetoric*. Eds.]

6. For it is manifest that the fault, if there be any, must be either 1st. in the *premises*, or 2dly. in the *conclusion*, or 3dly. in the *connexion* between them.

cases an *opponent* and a *contradiction*; the simple statement of the matter being this—I am required, by the circumstances of the case, (no matter why) to prove a certain conclusion; I prove, not that, but one which is likely to be mistaken for it; in this lies the Fallacy.

It might be desirable therefore to lay aside the name of *"ignoratio elenchi,"* but that it is so generally adopted as to require some mention to be made of it. The other kind of Fallacies in the matter will comprehend (as far as the vague and obscure language of logical writers will allow us to conjecture) the fallacy of *"non causa pro causa,"* and that of *"petitio principii."* Of these, the former is by them distinguished into *"a non vera pro vera,"* and *"a non tali pro tali;"* this last would appear to mean arguing from a case *not parallel* as if it *were* so; which, in logical language, is, having the *suppressed* premiss false; for it is in *that* the *parallelism* is affirmed; and the *"non vera pro vera"* will in like manner signify the *expressed* premiss being false; so that this Fallacy will turn out to be, in plain terms, neither more nor less than falsity (or unfair assumption) of a premiss.

The remaining kind, *"petitio principii,"* ["begging the question,"] takes place when a premiss, whether true or false, is either plainly equivalent to the conclusion, or depends on it for its own reception. It is to be observed, however, that in all correct reasoning the premises must, virtually, imply the conclusion; so that it is not possible to mark precisely the distinction between the Fallacy in question and fair argument; since that may be correct and fair reasoning to one person, which would be, to another, "begging the question;" inasmuch as to one, the conclusion might be more evident than the premiss, and to the other, the reverse. The most plausible form of this Fallacy is arguing in a *circle*; and the *greater* the circle, the harder to detect.

§4. There is no Fallacy that may not properly be included under some of the foregoing heads: those which in the logical treatises are separately enumerated, and contra-distinguished from these, being in reality instances of them, and therefore more properly enumerated in the subdivision thereof; as in the scheme annexed [Table 5.1]. . . .

§13. On the non-logical (or material) Fallacies: and first, of "begging the question;" *Petitio Principii.*

The indistinct and unphilosophical account which has been given by logical writers of the fallacy of *"non causa,"* and that of *"petitio principii,"* makes it very difficult to ascertain wherein they conceived them to differ, and what, according to them, is the nature of each. Without, therefore, professing to conform exactly to their meaning, and with a view to distinctness only,

Table 5.1.

Fallacies

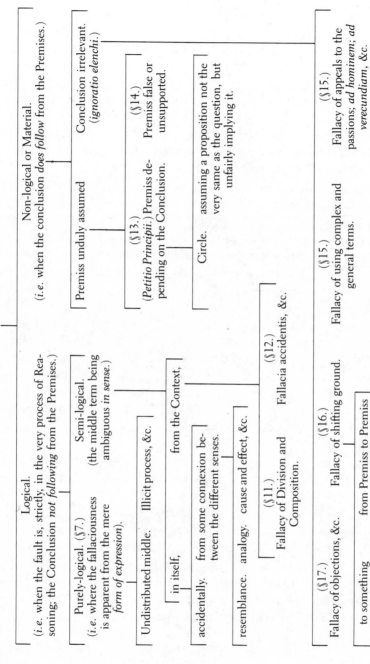

Fallacies

Logical.
(*i.e.* when the fault is, strictly, in the very process of Reasoning; the Conclusion *not following* from the Premises.)

Non-logical or Material.
(*i.e.* when the conclusion *does follow* from the Premises.)

Purely-logical. (§7.)
(*i.e.* where the fallaciousness is apparent from the mere *form of expression*).

Semi-logical.
(the middle term being ambiguous *in sense.*)

Premiss unduly assumed

Conclusion irrelevant.
(*ignoratio elenchi.*)

Undistributed middle.   Illicit process, &c.

(§13.)
(*Petitio Principii.*) Premiss depending on the Conclusion.

(§14.)
Premiss false or unsupported.

in itself,   from the Context,

Circle.   assuming a proposition not the very same as the question, but unfairly implying it.

accidentally.   from some connexion between the different senses.

resemblance.   analogy.   cause and effect, &c.

(§11.)
Fallacy of Division and Composition.

(§12.)
Fallacia accidentis, &c.

(§15.)
Fallacy of using complex and general terms.

(§15.)
Fallacy of appeals to the passions; *ad hominem; ad verecundiam,* &c.

(§17.)
Fallacy of objections, &c.

to something wholly irrelevant.

from Premiss to Premiss alternately.

(§16.)
Fallacy of shifting ground.

which is the main point, let us confine the name *"petitio principii"* to those cases in which the premiss either appears manifestly to be the same as the conclusion, or is actually proved from the conclusion, or is such as would naturally and properly so be proved; *i.e.* such as the persons you are address-ing[7] are not likely to know, or to admit, except as inferred from an admission of the conclusion; as *e.g.* if any one should infer the actual occurrence of the eclipses recorded in the Chinese annals, from an assumption of the authentic-ity of those annals. And to the other class may be referred all other cases, in which the premiss (whether the expressed or the suppressed one) is either proved false, or has no sufficient claim to be received as true.

Let it however be observed, that in such cases (apparently) as this, we must not too hastily pronounce the argument fallacious; for it may be perfectly fair at the *commencement* of an argument to assume a premiss that is not more evident than the conclusion, or is even ever so parodoxical, provided you proceed to prove fairly that premiss; and in like manner it is both usual and fair to *begin* by deducing your conclusion from a premiss exactly equivalent to it; which is merely throwing the proposition in question into the form in which it will be most conveniently proved.

Arguing in a circle, however, must necessarily be unfair; though it fre-quently is practised undesignedly; *e.g.* some Mechanicians attempt to prove, (what they ought to have laid down as a probable but doubtful hypothesis,) that every particle of matter gravitates equally; "why?" because those bodies which contain more particles ever gravitate more strongly, *i.e.* are heavier; "but (it may be urged) those which are heaviest are not always more bulky;" "no, but still they contain more particles, though more closely condensed;" "how do you know that?" "because they are heavier"; "how does that prove it?" "because all particles of matter gravitating equally, that mass which is specifically the heavier must needs have the more of them in the same space."

Of course the *narrower* the circle, the less likely it is to escape the detec-tion, either of the reasoner himself, (for men often deceive *themselves* in this way) or of his hearers. When there is a long circuit of many intervening propositions before you come back to the original conclusion, it will often not be perceived that the arguments really do proceed in a "circle:" just as when any one is advancing in a *straight line* (as we are accustomed to call it) along a plain on this earth's surface, it escapes our notice that we are really

7. For it should be remembered that of two propositions, the one may be more evident to some, and the other, to others.

moving along the *circumference of a circle*, (since the earth is a globe) and that if we could go on without interruption in the same line, we should at length arrive at the very spot we set out from. But this we readily perceive, when we are walking round a small hill.

For instance, if any one argues that you ought to submit to the guidance of himself, or his leader, or his party, &c., because these maintain what is right; and then argues that what is so maintained is right, because it is maintained by persons whom you ought to submit to; and that these are, himself and his party; or again, if any one maintains that so and so must be a thing morally wrong, because it is prohibited in the *moral portion* of the Mosaic-law, and then, that the prohibition of it does form a part of the *moral* (not the ceremonial, or the civil) portion of that law, *because* it is a thing *morally wrong*— either of these would be too narrow a circle to escape detection, unless several intermediate steps were interposed. And if the *form of expression* of each proposition be *varied* every time it recurs—the sense of it remaining the same—this will greatly aid the deception.

Of course, the way to expose the Fallacy, is to reverse this procedure: to narrow the circle, by cutting off the intermediate steps; and to exhibit the same proposition—when it comes round the second time—in the same words.

Obliquity and disguise being of course most important to the success of the *petitio principii* as well as of other Fallacies, the sophist will in general either have recourse to the "circle," or else not venture to *state* distinctly his assumption of the point in question, but will rather assert some other proposition which *implies* it;[8] thus keeping out of sight (as a dexterous thief does stolen goods) the point in question, at the very moment when he is taking it for granted. Hence the frequent union of this Fallacy with *"ignoratio elenchi:"* [*vide* §15.] The English language is perhaps the more suitable for the Fallacy of *petitio principii*, from its being formed from two distinct languages, and thus abounding in synonymous expressions, which have no resemblance in sound, and no connexion in etymology; so that a sophist may bring forward a proposition expressed in words of Saxon origin, and give as a reason for it, the very same proposition stated in words of Norman origin; *e.g.* "to allow every man an unbounded freedom of speech must always be, on the whole, advantageous to the State; for it is highly conducive to the interests of the commu-

8. Gibbon affords the most remarkable instances of this kind of style. That which he really means to speak of, is hardly ever made the subject of his proposition. His way of writing reminds one of those persons who never dare look you full in the face.

nity, that each individual should enjoy a liberty perfectly unlimited, of expressing his sentiments."

§14. The next head is, the falsity, or, at least, undue assumption, of a premiss that is not equivalent to, or dependent on, the conclusion; which, as has been before said, seems to correspond nearly with the meaning of Logicians, when they speak of "*non causa pro causa.*" This name indeed would seem to imply a much narrower class: there being one species of arguments which are *from cause to effect*; in which, of course, two things are necessary; 1st, the *sufficiency* of the cause; 2d, its establishment; these are the two premises; if therefore the *former* be unduly assumed, we are arguing from that which is *not* a sufficient cause as if it *were* so: *e.g.* as if one should contend from such a man's having been unjust or cruel, that he will certainly be visited with some heavy temporal judgment, and come to an untimely end. In this instance the sophist, from having assumed, in the premiss, the (granted) existence of a pretended cause, infers, in the conclusion, the existence of the pretended effect, which we have supposed to be the question. Or *vice versa*, the pretended effect may be employed to establish the cause; *e.g.* inferring sinfulness from temporal calamity. But when *both* the pretended cause and effect are granted, *i.e.* granted to *exist*, then the sophist will infer something from their pretended *connexion*; *i.e.* he will assume as a premiss, that "of these two admitted facts, the one is the cause of the other:" as Whitfield attributed his being overtaken by a hail-storm to his having not preached at the last town; or as the opponents of the Reformation assumed that it was the cause of the troubles which took place at that period, and thence inferred that it was an evil.

Many are the cases in which a *sign* (see *Rhet.* Part I.[9]) from which one might fairly infer a certain phenomenon, is mistaken for the *cause* of it: (as if one should suppose the falling of the mercury to be a cause of rain; of which it certainly is an indication) whereas the fact will often be the very reverse. E.G. a great deal of *money* in a country is a pretty sure proof of its wealth; and thence has been often regarded as the cause of it; whereas in truth it is an effect. The same, with a numerous and increasing *population*. Again, The *labour* bestowed on any commodity has often been represented as the cause of its value; though every one would call a fine pearl an article of value, even though he should meet with it accidentally in eating an oyster. Pearls are indeed generally obtained by laborious diving: but they do not fetch a high

9. [Whately here refers to his own *Elements of Rhetoric*, 1828. It was reissued by Southern Illinois University Press in 1963. Part I, chap. 2, sec. 3 deals with signs. Eds.]

price from that cause; but on the contrary, men dive for them *because* they fetch a high price.[10] So also exposure to want and hardship in youth, has been regarded as a cause of the hardy constitution of those men and brutes which have been brought up in barren countries of uncongenial climate. Yet the most experienced cattle-breeders know that animals are, *ceteris paribus*, the more hardy for having been well fed and sheltered in youth; but early hardships, by destroying all the tender, ensure the hardiness of the survivors; which is the cause, not the effect, of their having lived through such a training. So, loading a gun-barrel to the muzzle, and firing it, does not *give* it strength; though it *proves*, if it escape, that it *was* strong.

In like manner, nothing is more common than to hear a person state confidently, as from his own experience, that such and such a patient *was cured* by this or that medicine: whereas all that he absolutely *knows*, is that he took the medicine, and that he recovered.

Similar is the procedure of many who are no *theorists* forsooth, but have found by *experience* that the diffusion of education disqualifies the lower classes for humble toil. They have perhaps experienced really a deterioration in this last respect; and having a dislike to education, they shut their eyes to the increase of pauperism; *i.e.* of the habit of depending on parish-pay, rather than on independent exertions; which, to any unprejudiced eye would seem the most natural mode of explaining the relaxation of those exertions. But such men require us, on the ground that they are *practical* men, to adopt the results of their experience; *i.e.* to acquiesce in their crude guesses as to cause and effect, (like that of the rustic who made Tenterden-steeple the cause of Goodwin Sands,) precisely because they are *not* accustomed to reason.

I believe we may refer to the same head the apprehensions so often entertained, that a *change*, however small, and however in itself harmless, is necessarily a dangerous thing, as tending to *produce* extensive and hurtful innovations. Many instances may be found of small alterations being *followed* by great and mischievous ones;[11] but I doubt whether all history can furnish an instance of the greater innovation having been, properly speaking, *caused* by the lesser. Of course the first change will always *precede* the second; and many mischievous innovations *have* taken place; but these may all I think be referred to a mistaken effort to obtain some good, or get rid of some evil; not to the love of innovation for its own sake. The mass of mankind are,

10. *Pol. Econ.* Lect. IX., p. 253. [The reference here is to Whately's *Introductory Lectures on Political Economy*, 1832. Eds.]

11. "*Post hoc; ergo, propter hoc.*"

in the serious concerns of life, wedded to what is established and customary; and when they make rash changes, this may often be explained by the too long *postponement* of the requisite changes; which allows (as in the case of the Reformation) evils to reach an intolerable height, before any remedy is thought of. And even then, the remedy is often so violently resisted by many, as to drive others into dangerous extremes. And when this occurs, we are triumphantly told that experience shows what mischievous excesses are *caused* by once beginning to innovate. "I told you that if once you began to repair your house, you would have to pull it all down." "Yes; but you told me wrong; for if I had begun sooner, the replacing of a few tiles might have sufficed. The mischief was, not in the taking down the first stone, but in letting it stand too long."

Such an argument as any of these might strictly be called *"non causa pro causa;"* but it is not probable that the logical writers intended any such limitation (which indeed would be wholly unnecessary and impertinent,) but rather that they were confounding together *cause* and *reason;* the sequence of *conclusion* from *premises* being perpetually mistaken for that of *effect* from physical *cause.*[12] It may be better, therefore, to drop the name which tends to perpetuate this confusion, and simply to state (when such is the case) that the premiss is "unduly assumed;" *i.e.* without being either self-evident, or satisfactorily proved. . . .

§15. The last kind of Fallacy to be noticed is that of irrelevant conclusion, commonly called *ignoratio elenchi.*

Various kinds of propositions are, according to the occasion, substituted for the one of which proof is required. Sometimes the particular for the universal; sometimes a proposition with different terms: and various are the contrivances employed to effect and to conceal this substitution, and to make the conclusion which the sophist has drawn, answer, practically, the same purpose as the one he ought to have established. I say, "practically the same purpose," because it will very often happen that some *emotion* will be excited—some sentiment impressed on the mind—(by a dexterous employment of this Fallacy) such as shall bring men into the *disposition* requisite for your purpose, though they may not have assented to, or even stated distinctly in their own minds, the *proposition* which it was your business to establish.[13]

12. See Appendix, No. 1 article *Reason.* [The appendix of the *Elements of Logic* is devoted to discussing "certain terms which are peculiarly liable to be used ambiguously," "reason" being one of about fifty terms discussed. Eds.]

13. See *Rhetoric*, Part II. [Whately is referring to his own *Elements of Rhetoric.* Eds.]

Thus if a sophist has to defend one who has been guilty of some *serious* offence, which he wishes to extenuate, though he is unable distinctly to prove that it is not such, yet if he can succeed in *making the audience laugh* at some casual matter, he has gained practically the same point.

So also if any one has pointed out the extenuating circumstances in some particular case of offence, so as to show that it differs widely from the generality of the same class, the sophist, if he find himself unable to disprove these circumstances, may do away the force of them, by simply *referring the action to that very class*, which no one can deny that it belongs to, and the very name of which will excite a feeling of disgust sufficient to counteract the extenuation; *e.g.* let it be a case of peculation; and that many *mitigating* circumstances have been brought forward which cannot be denied; the sophistical opponent will reply, "Well, but after all, the man is a *rogue*, and there is an end of it;" now in reality this was (by hypothesis) never the question; and the mere assertion of what was never denied, *ought* not, in fairness, to be regarded as decisive; but practically, the odiousness of the word, arising in great measure from the *association of those very circumstances* which belong to *most of the class*, but which we have supposed to be *absent* in *this particular* instance, excites precisely that *feeling of disgust*, which in effect destroys the force of the defence. In like manner we may refer to this head, all cases of improper appeals to the passions, and every thing else which is mentioned by Aristotle as extraneous to the matter in hand (*exō tou pragmatos*).[14]

In all these cases, as has been before observed, if the fallacy we are now treating of be employed for the apparent establishment, not of the *ultimate* conclusion, but (as it very commonly happens) of a *premiss*, (*i.e.* if the premiss required be assumed on the ground that some proposition resembling it has been proved) then there will be a combination of this fallacy with the last mentioned.

For instance, instead of proving that "this prisoner has committed an atrocious fraud," you prove that "the fraud he is accused of is atrocious;" instead of proving (as in the well-known tale of Cyrus and the two coats) that "the taller boy had a right to force the other boy to exchange coats with him," you prove that "the exchange would have been advantageous to both:" instead of proving that "a man has not a right to educate his children or to dispose of his property, in the way *he thinks best*," you show that the way in which he educates his children, or disposes of his property is not *really the best*: instead of proving that "the poor ought to be relieved in this way rather

14. [Literally: "out of the thing, business or affair." Eds.]

than in that," you prove that "the poor *ought to be relieved:*" instead of proving that "an irrational-agent—whether a brute or a madman—can never be deterred from any act by apprehension of punishment," (as for instance, a dog, from sheep-biting, by fear of being beaten) you prove that "the beating of one dog does not operate as an *example* to *other* dogs," &c. and then you proceed to assume as premises, conclusions different from what have really been established.

A good instance of the employment and exposure of this Fallacy occurs in Thucydides, in the speeches of Cleon and Diodotus concerning the Mitylenæans; the former (over and above his appeal to the angry passions of his audience) urges the *justice* of putting the revolters to death; which, as the latter remarked, was nothing to the purpose, since the Athenians were not sitting in *judgment*, but in *deliberation*; of which the proper end is *expediency*. And to prove that they had a right to put them to death, did not prove this to be an *advisable* step.

It is evident, that *ignoratio elenchi* may be employed as well for the apparent *refutation* of your opponent's proposition, as for the apparent establishment of your own; for it is substantially the same thing, to *prove* what was not denied, or to *disprove* what was not asserted. The latter practice is not less common; and it is more offensive, because it frequently amounts to a personal affront, in attributing to a person opinions, &c. which he perhaps holds in abhorrence. Thus, when in a discussion one party vindicates, on the ground of general expediency, a particular instance of resistance to government in a case of intolerable oppression, the opponent may gravely maintain, that "we ought not to do evil that good may come:" a proposition which of course had never been denied; the point in dispute being "whether resistance in this particular case *were* doing evil or not." Or again, by way of disproving the assertion of the *"right* of private-judgment in religion," one may hear a grave argument to prove that "it is impossible every one can be *right in his judgment.*" In these examples, it is to be remarked, (as well as in some given just above,) that the fallacy of *petitio principii* is combined with that of *ignoratio elenchi*; which is a very common and often successful practice; *viz.* the sophist proves, or disproves, not the proposition which is really in question, but one which is so dependent on it as to proceed on the supposition that it is already decided, and can admit of no doubt; by this means his "assumption of the point in question" is so indirect and oblique, that it may easily escape notice; and he thus establishes, practically, his conclusion, at the very moment he is withdrawing your attention from it to another question. E.G. An advocate will prove, and dwell on the high *criminality* of a certain act, and the propriety of severely punishing it; assuming (instead of proving) the *commission*.

There are certain kinds of argument recounted and named by logical writers, which we should by no means universally call Fallacies; but which *when unfairly* used, and *so far as they are* fallacious, may very well be referred to the present head; such as the "*argumentum ad hominem*," ["or personal argument."] "*argumentum ad verecundiam*," "*argumentum ad populum*," &c. all of them regarded as contradistinguished from "*argumentum ad rem*;" or, according to others (meaning probably the very same thing) "*ad judicium*." These have all been described in the lax and popular language before alluded to, but not scientifically: the "*argumentum ad hominem*," they say, "is addressed to the peculiar circumstances, character, avowed opinions, or past conduct of the individual, and therefore has a reference to him only, and does not bear directly and absolutely on the real question, as the '*argumentum ad rem*' does:" in like manner, the "*argumentum ad verecundiam*" is described as an appeal to our reverence for some respected authority, some venerable institution," &c. and the "*argumentum ad populum*," as an appeal to the prejudices, passions, &c. of the multitude; and so of the rest. Along with these is usually enumerated "*argumentum ad ignorantiam*," which is here omitted as being evidently nothing more than the employment of *some* kind of Fallacy, in the widest sense of that word, toward such as are likely to be deceived by it.

It appears then (to speak rather more technically) that in the "*argumentum ad hominem*" the conclusion which actually is established, is not the *absolute* and *general* one in question, but *relative* and particular; *viz.* not that "such and such is the fact," but that "*this man* is bound to admit it, in conformity to his principles of reasoning, or in consistency with his own conduct, situation," &c.[15] Such a conclusion it is often both allowable and necessary to

15. The "*argumentum ad hominem*," will often have the effect of shifting the *burden of proof*, not unjustly to the adversary. (See *Rhet.* Part I, chap. iii., sec. 2. [Whately's *Elements of Rhetoric*, Eds.]) A common instance is the defense, certainly the readiest and most concise, frequently urged by the sportsman, when accused of barbarity in sacrificing unoffending hares or trout to his amusement: he replies, as he may safely do, to most of his assailants, "why do you feed on the flesh of the harmless sheep and ox?" and that this answer presses hard, is manifested by its being usually opposed by a *palpable falsehood*; *viz.* that the animals which are killed for food are sacrificed to our *necessities*; though not only men *can*, but a large proportion (probably a great majority) of the human race actually *do*, subsist in health and vigour without flesh-diet; and the earth would support a much greater human population were such a practice universal.

When shamed out of this argument they sometimes urge that the brute creation would overrun the earth, if we did not kill them for food; an argument, which, if it were valid at all, would not justify their feeding on *fish*; though, if fairly followed up, it *would* justify Swift's proposal for keeping down

establish, in order to silence those who will not yield to fair general argument; or to convince those whose weakness and prejudices would not allow them to assign to it its due weight. It is thus that our Lord on many occasions silences the cavils of the Jews; as in the vindication of healing on the Sabbath, which is paralleled by the authorized practice of drawing out a beast that has fallen into a pit. All this, as we have said, is perfectly fair, provided it be done plainly, and *avowedly*; but if you attempt to *substitute* this partial and relative conclusion for a more general one—if you triumph as having established your proposition absolutely and universally, from having established it, in reality, only as far as it relates to your opponent, then you are guilty of a Fallacy of the kind which we are now treating of; your conclusion is not in reality that which was, by your own account, proposed to be proved. The fallaciousness depends upon the *deceit*, or attempt to deceive. The same observations will *apply* to "*argumentum ad verecundiam*," and the rest.

---

the excessive population of Ireland. The true reason, *viz.* that they eat flesh for the gratification of the palate, and have a taste for the pleasures of the table, though not for the sports of the field, is one which they do not like to assign.

6

On Fallacies

John Stuart Mill

[The following excerpt is from John Stuart Mill, A *System of Logic, Ratiocinative and Inductive* (London: Routledge and Sons, 1892), Book V, "On Fallacies," chaps. 1 and 2 inclusive.]

Chapter I.   Of Fallacies in General

§I. It is a maxim of the schoolmen, that 'contrariorum eadem est scientia:' we never really know what a thing is, unless we are also able to give a sufficient account of its opposite. Conformably to this maxim, one considerable section, in most treatises on Logic, is devoted to the subject of Fallacies; and the practice is too well worthy of observance, to allow of our departing from it. The philosophy of reasoning, to be complete, ought to comprise the theory of bad as well as of good reasoning.

We have endeavoured to ascertain the principles by which the sufficiency of any proof can be tested, and by which the nature and amount of evidence needful to prove any given conclusion can be determined beforehand. If these principles were adhered to, then although the number and value of the truths ascertained would be limited by the opportunities, or by the industry, ingenuity, and patience, of the individual inquirer, at least error would not be embraced instead of truth. But the general consent of mankind, founded upon all their experience, vouches for their being far indeed from even this negative kind of perfection in the employment of their reasoning powers.

In the conduct of life—in the ordinary business of mankind—wrong inferences, incorrect interpretations of experience, unless after much culture of the thinking faculty, are absolutely inevitable: and with most people after the highest degree of culture they ever attain (unless where the events of their daily life supply an immediate corrective), such erroneous inferences are as frequent if not more frequent than correct inferences, correct interpretations of experience. Even in the speculations to which the highest intellects systematically devote themselves, and in reference to which the collective mind of the scientific world is always at hand to aid the efforts and control the aberrations of individuals, it is only from the more perfect sciences, from those of which the subject-matter is the least complicated, that opinions not resting upon a correct induction have at length, generally speaking, been expelled. In the departments of inquiry relating to the more complex phenomena of the universe, and especially those of which the subject is man, whether as a moral and intellectual, a social, or even as a physical being; the diversity of opinions still prevalent among instructed persons, and the equal confidence with which those of the most contrary ways of thinking cling to their respective tenets, are a proof not only that right modes of philosophising are not yet generally adopted on those subjects, but that wrong ones are; that philosophers have not only in general missed the truth, but have often embraced error; that even the most cultivated portion of our species have not yet learned to abstain from drawing conclusions for which the evidence is insufficient.

The only complete safeguard against reasoning ill, is the habit of reasoning well; familiarity with the principles of correct reasoning, and practice in applying those principles. It is, however, not unimportant to consider what are the most common modes of bad reasoning; by what appearances the mind is most likely to be seduced from the observance of true principles of induction; what, in short, are the most common and most dangerous varieties of Apparent Evidence, whereby men are misled into opinions for which there does not exist evidence really conclusive.

A catalogue of the varieties of apparent evidence which are not real evidence, is an enumeration of Fallacies. Without such an enumeration, therefore, the present work would be wanting in an essential point. And while writers who included in their theory of reasoning nothing more than ratiocination, have, in consistency with this limitation, confined their remarks to the fallacies which have their seat in that portion of the process of investigation: we, who profess to treat of the whole process, must add to our directions for performing it rightly, warnings against performing it wrongly in any of its parts: whether the ratiocinative or the experimental portion of it be in fault, or the fault lie in dispensing with ratiocination and induction altogether.

§2. In considering the sources of unfounded inference, it is unnecessary to reckon the errors which arise, not from a wrong method, or even from ignorance of the right one, but from a casual lapse, through hurry or inattention, in the application of the true principles of induction. Such errors, like the accidental mistakes in casting up a sum, do not call for philosophical analysis or classification; theoretical considerations can throw no light upon the means of avoiding them. In the present treatise our attention is required, not to mere inexpertness in performing the operation in the right way, (the only remedies for which are increased attention and more sedulous practice,) but to the modes of performing it in a way fundamentally wrong; the conditions under which the human mind persuades itself that it has sufficient grounds for a conclusion which it has not arrived at by any of the legitimate methods of induction—which it has not, even carelessly or overhastily, endeavoured to test by those legitimate methods.

§3. There is another branch of what may be called the Philosophy of Error, which must be mentioned here, though only to be excluded from our subject. The sources of erroneous opinions are two-fold, moral and intellectual. Of these, the moral do not fall within the compass of this work. They may be classed under two general heads; Indifference to the attainment of truth, and Bias: of which last the most common case is that in which we are biased by our wishes; but the liability is almost as great to the undue adoption of a conclusion which is disagreeable to us as of one which is agreeable, if it be of a nature to bring into action any of the stronger passions. Persons of timid character are the more predisposed to believe any statement, the more it is calculated to alarm them. Indeed, it is a psychological law, deducible from the most general laws of the mental constitution of man, that any strong passion renders us credulous as to the existence of objects suitable to excite it.

But the moral causes of our opinions, though real and most powerful, are but remote causes: they do not act immediately, but by means of the intellectual causes; to which they bear the same relation that the circumstances called, in the theory of medicine, *predisposing* causes, bear to *exciting* causes. Indifference to truth cannot, in and by itself, produce erroneous belief; it operates by preventing the mind from collecting the proper evidences, or from applying to them the test of a legitimate and rigid induction; by which omission it is exposed unprotected to the influence of any species of apparent evidence which occurs spontaneously, or which is elicited by that smaller quantity of trouble which the mind may be not unwilling to take. As little is Bias a direct source of wrong conclusions. We cannot believe a proposition only by wishing, or only by dreading, to believe it. The most violent inclination to find a set of propositions true will not enable the weakest of mankind to believe them without a vestige of intellectual groups, without any, even apparent, evidence. It can only act indirectly, by placing the intellectual grounds of belief in an incomplete or distorted shape before his eyes. It makes him shrink from the irksome labour of a rigorous induction, when he has a misgiving that its result may be disagreeable; and in such examination as he does institute, it makes him exert that which *is* in a certain measure voluntary, his attention, unfairly, giving a larger share of it to the evidence which seems favourable to the desired conclusion, a smaller to that which seems unfavourable. And the like when the bias arises not from desire but fear. Although a person afraid of ghosts believes that he has seen one on evidence wonderfully inadequate, he does not believe it altogether without evidence; he has perceived some unusual appearance, while passing through a church-yard: he saw something start up near a grave which looked white in the moonshine. Thus every erroneous inference, though originating in moral causes, involves the intellectual operation of admitting insufficient evidence as sufficient; and whoever was on his guard against all kinds of inconclusive evidence which can be mistaken for conclusive, would be in no danger of being led into error even by the strongest bias. There have been minds so strongly fortified on the intellectual side, that they *could* not blind themselves to the light of truth, however really desirous of doing so; they could not, with all the inclination in the world, pass off upon themselves bad arguments for good ones. If the sophistry of the intellect could be rendered impossible, that of the feelings, having no instrument to work with, would be powerless. A comprehensive classification of all those things which, not being evidence, are liable to appear such to the understanding, will, therefore, include all errors of judgment arising from moral causes, to the exclusion only of errors of practice committed against better knowledge.

To examine, then, the various kinds of apparent evidence which are not evidence at all, and of apparently conclusive evidence which do not really amount to conclusiveness, is the object of that part of our inquiry into which we are about to enter.

The subject is not beyond the compass of classification and comprehensive survey. The things, indeed, which are not evidence of any given conclusion, are manifestly endless, and this negative property, having no dependence upon any positive ones, cannot be made the groundwork of a real classification. But the things which, not being evidence, are susceptible of being mistaken for it, are capable of a classification having reference to the positive property which they possess, of appearing to be evidence. We may arrange them, at our choice, on either of two principles; according to the cause which makes them appear evidence, not being so: or according to the particular kind of evidence which they simulate. The Classification of Fallacies which will be attempted in the ensuing chapter, is founded upon these considerations jointly.

Chapter II.   Classification of Fallacies

§1. In attempting to establish certain general distinctions which shall mark out from one another the various kinds of Fallacious Evidence, we propose to ourselves an altogether different aim from that of several eminent thinkers, who have given, under the name of Political or other Fallacies, a mere enumeration of a certain number of erroneous opinions; false general propositions which happen to be often met with; *loci communes* of bad arguments on some particular subject. Logic is not concerned with the false opinions which men happen to entertain, but with the manner in which they come to entertain them. The question for us is not, what facts men have at any time erroneously supposed to be proof of certain other facts, but what property in the facts it was which led them to this mistaken supposition.

When a fact is supposed, although incorrectly, to be evidentiary of, or a mark of, some other fact, there must be a cause of the error; the supposed evidentiary fact must be connected in some particular manner with the fact of which it is deemed evidentiary, must stand in some particular relation to it, without which relation it would not be regarded in that light. The relation may either be one resulting from the simple contemplation of the two facts side by side with one another, or it may depend upon some process of our own mind, by which a previous association has been established between them. Some peculiarity of relation, however, there must be; the fact which can, even by the wildest aberration, be supposed to prove another fact, must stand in some special position with regard to it; and if we could ascertain and define that special position, we should perceive the origin of the error.

We cannot regard one fact as evidentiary of another unless we believe that the two are always, or in the majority of cases, conjoined. If we believe A to be evidentiary of B, if when we see A we are inclined to infer B from it, the reason is because we believe that wherever A is, B also either always or for the most part exists, either as an antecedent, a consequent, or a concomitant. If when we see A we are inclined not to expect B, if we believe A to be evidentiary of the absence of B, it is because we believe that where A is, B either is never, or at least seldom, found. Erroneous conclusions, in short, no less than correct conclusions, have an invariable relation to a general formula, either expressed or tacitly implied. When we infer some fact from some other fact which does not really prove it, we either have admitted, or if we maintained consistency, ought to admit, some groundless general proposition respecting the conjunction of the two phenomena.

For every property, therefore, in facts, or in our mode of considering facts, which leads us to believe that they are habitually conjoined when they are not, or that they are not when in reality they are, there is a corresponding kind of Fallacy; and an enumeration of Fallacies would consist in a specification of those properties in facts, and those peculiarities in our mode of considering them, which give rise to this erroneous opinion.

§2. To begin, then; the supposed connexion, or repugnance, between the two facts, may either be a conclusion from evidence (that is, from some other proposition or propositions) or may be admitted without any such ground; admitted, as the phrase is, on its own evidence; embraced as self-evident, as an axiomatic truth. This gives rise to the first great distinction, that between Fallacies of Inference, and Fallacies of Simple Inspection. In the latter division must be included not only all cases in which a proposition is believed and held for true, literally without any extrinsic evidence, either of specific experience or general reasoning; but those more frequent cases in which simple inspection creates a *presumption* in favour of a proposition; not sufficient for belief, but sufficient to cause the strict principles of a regular induction to be dispensed with, and creating a predisposition to believe it on evidence which would be seen to be insufficient if no such presumption existed. This class, comprehending the whole of what may be termed Natural Prejudices, and which I shall call indiscriminately Fallacies of Simple Inspection or Fallacies *a priori*, shall be placed at the head of our list.

Fallacies of Inference, or erroneous conclusions from supposed evidence, must be subdivided according to the nature of the apparent evidence from which the conclusions are drawn; or (what is the same thing) according to the particular kind of sound argument which the fallacy in question simulates. But there is a distinction to be first drawn, which does not answer to any of the divisions of sound arguments, but arises out of the nature of bad ones. We may know exactly what our evidence is, and yet draw a false conclusion from it; we may conceive precisely what our premisses are, what alleged matters of fact, or general principles, are the foundation of our inference; and yet, because the premisses are false, or because we have inferred from them what they will not support, our conclusion may be erroneous. But a case, perhaps even more frequent, is that in which the error arises from not conceiving our premisses with due clearness, that is, (as shown in the preceding Book,) with due fixity: forming one conception of our evidence when we collect or receive it, and another when we make use of it; or unadvisedly and in general unconsciously substituting, as we proceed, different premisses in the place of those with which we set out, or a different conclusion for that which we undertook to prove. This gives existence to a class of fallacies which may be justly termed Fallacies of Confusion; comprehending, among others, all those which have their source in language, whether arising from the vagueness or ambiguity of our terms, or from casual associations with them.

When the fallacy is not one of Confusion, that is, when the proposition believed, and the evidence on which it is believed, are steadily apprehended and unambiguously expressed, there remain to be made two cross divisions, giving rise to four classes. The Apparent Evidence may be either particular facts, or foregone generalizations; that is, the process may simulate either simple Induction, or Deduction: and again, the evidence, whether consisting of facts or general propositions, may be false in itself, or, being true, may fail to bear out the conclusion attempted to be founded upon it. This gives us, first, Fallacies of Induction and Fallacies of Deduction, and then a subdivision of each of these, according as the supposed evidence is false, or true but inconclusive.

Fallacies of Induction, where the facts upon which the induction proceeds are erroneous, may be termed Fallacies of Observation. The term is not strictly accurate, or rather, not accurately coextensive with the class of fallacies which I propose to designate by it. Induction is not always grounded upon facts immediately observed, but sometimes upon facts inferred: and when these last are erroneous, the error is not, in the literal sense of the term, an instance of bad observation, but of bad inference. It will be convenient, however, to make only one class of all the inductions of which the error lies in not sufficiently ascertaining the facts on which the theory is grounded; whether the cause of failure be malobservation, or simple non-observation, and whether the mal-observation be direct, or by means of intermediate marks which do not prove what they are supposed to prove. And in the absence of any comprehensive term to denote the ascertainment, by whatever means, of the facts on which an induction is grounded, I will venture to retain for this class of fallacies, under the explanation already given, the title, Fallacies of Observation.

The other class of inductive fallacies, in which the facts are correct, but the conclusion not warranted by them, are properly denominated Fallacies of Generalization: and these, again, fall into various subordinate classes, or natural groups, some of which will be enumerated in their proper place.

When we now turn to Fallacies of Deduction, namely, those modes of incorrect argumentation in which the premisses, or some of them, are general propositions, and the argument a ratiocination; we may of course subdivide these also into two species, similar to the two preceding, namely, those which proceed on false premisses, and those of which the premisses, though true, do not support the conclusion. But of these species, the first must necessarily fall within some one of the heads already enumerated. For the error must be either in those premisses which are general propositions, or in those which assert individual facts. In the former case it is an Inductive Fallacy, of one or the other class; in the latter it is a Fallacy of Observation: unless, in either case, the erroneous premiss has been assumed on simple inspection, in which case the fallacy is *a priori*. Or, finally, the premisses, of whichever kind they are, may never have been conceived in so distinct a manner as to produce any clear consciousness by what means they were arrived at; as in the case of what is called reasoning in a circle: and then the fallacy is of Confusion.

There remain, therefore, as the only class of fallacies having properly their seat in deduction, those in which the premisses of the ratiocination do not bear out its conclusion; the various cases, in short, of vicious argumentation, provided against by the rules of the syllogism. We shall call these, Fallacies of Ratiocination.

We have thus five distinguishable classes of fallacy, which may be expressed in the following synoptic table (Table 6.1):

Table 6.1.

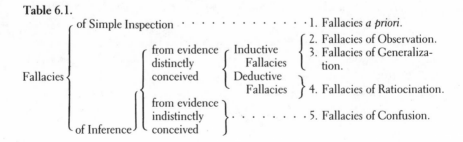

§3. We must not, however, expect to find that men's actual errors always, or even commonly, fall so unmistakeably under some one of these classes, as to be incapable of being referred to any other. Erroneous arguments do not admit of such a sharply-cut division as valid arguments do. An argument fully stated, with all its steps distinctly set out, in language not susceptible of misunderstanding, must, if it be erroneous, be so in some one, and one only, of these five modes: or indeed of the first four, since the fifth, on such a supposition, would vanish. But it is not in the nature of bad reasoning to express itself thus unambiguously. When a sophist, whether he is imposing upon himself or attempting to impose upon others, can be constrained to throw his sophistry into so distinct a form, it needs, in a large proportion of cases, no further exposure.

In all arguments, everywhere but in the schools, some of the links are suppressed; *a fortiori* when the arguer either intends to deceive, or is a lame and inexpert thinker, little accustomed to bring his reasoning processes to any test: and it is in those steps of the reasoning which are made in this tacit and half-conscious, or even wholly unconscious manner, that the error oftenest lurks. In order to detect the fallacy, the proposition thus silently assumed must be supplied; but the reasoner, most likely, has never really asked himself what he was assuming: his confuter, if unable to extort it from him by the Socratic mode of interrogation, must himself judge what the suppressed premiss ought to be in order to support the conclusion. And hence, in the words of Archbishop Whately, 'it must be often a matter of doubt, or rather, of arbitrary choice, not only to which genus each *kind* of fallacy should be referred, but even to which kind to refer any *one individual* fallacy; for since, in any course of argument, one premiss is usually suppressed, it frequently happens in the case of a fallacy, that the hearers are left to the alternative of supplying *either* a premiss which is *not true*, or *else* one which *does not prove* the conclusion: *e.g.*, if a man expatiates on the distress of the country, and thence argues that the government is tyrannical, we must suppose him to assume *either* that "every distressed country is under a tyranny," which is a manifest falsehood, *or*, merely that "every country under a tyranny is distressed," which, however true, proves nothing, the middle term being undistributed.' The former would be ranked, in our distribution, among fallacies of generalization, the latter among those of ratiocination. 'Which are we to suppose the speaker meant us to understand? Surely' (if he understood himself) 'just whichever each of his hearers might happen to prefer: some might assent to the false premiss; others allow the unsound syllogism.'

Almost all fallacies, therefore, might in strictness be brought under our fifth class, Fallacies of Confusion. A fallacy can seldom be absolutely referred to any of the other classes; we can only say, that if all the links were filled up which should be capable of being supplied in a valid argument, it would either stand thus (forming a fallacy of one class), or thus (a fallacy of another); or at furthest we may say, that the conclusion is most *likely* to have originated in a fallacy of such and such a class. Thus in the illustration just quoted, the error committed may be traced with most probability to a fallacy of generalization; that of mistaking an uncertain mark, or piece of evidence, for a certain one; concluding from an effect to some one of its possible causes, when there are others which would have been equally capable of producing it.

Yet, though the five classes run into each other, and a particular error often seems to be arbitrarily assigned to one of them rather than to any of the rest, there is considerable use in so distinguishing them. We shall find it convenient to set apart, as Fallacies of Confusion, those of which confusion is the most obvious characteristic; in which no other cause can be assigned for the mistake committed, than neglect or inability to state the question properly, and to apprehend the evidence with definiteness and precision. In the remaining four classes I shall place not only the comparatively few cases in which the evidence is clearly seen to be what it is, and yet a wrong conclusion drawn from it, but also those in which, although there be confusion, the confusion is not the sole cause of the error, but there is some shadow of a ground for it in the nature of the evidence itself. And in distributing these cases of partial confusion among the four classes, I shall, when there can be any hesitation as to the precise seat of the fallacy, suppose it to be in that part of the process in which, from the nature of the case, and the known infirmities of the human mind, an error would in the particular circumstances be the most probable.

After these observations we shall proceed, without further preamble, to consider the five classes in their order.

PART II

Contemporary Theory and Criticism

Introduction

The chapters that follow address the general question of what fallacies are, whether there is or can be an intellectually respectable theory of fallacies and, if there can be, what shape that theory should take.

Revising the Standard Treatment

Hamblin's Criticisms

It is only a slight exaggeration to say that serious work on the fallacies in the second half of the twentieth century begins with the publication in 1970 of Charles Hamblin's watershed book, *Fallacies*. Because Hamblin's book is once again in print[1] and because we assume that serious students of the fallacies will consult the original, we have not excerpted it in this volume. We think it useful, however, to offer a brief synopsis of it here.

Hamblin's *Fallacies* opens with a chapter entitled "The Standard Treatment," in which he purports to examine "the typical or average account as it appears in the typical short chapter or appendix of the average modern textbook" (1970, 12). His judgment on what he claims to find there is harsh: "what we find in most cases, I think it should be admitted, is as debased, worn-out and dogmatic a treatment as could be imagined—incredibly tradition-bound, yet lacking in logic and historical sense alike, and almost without connection to anything else in modern Logic at all" (1970, 12).

He supports this judgment by running through a list of about twenty fallacies (or categories thereof) and canvassing some of what is said about each in the textbooks more or less current at the time he wrote. The canvass relies heavily on a half-dozen or so books—by Copi, Schipper and Schuh, Black, Cohen and Nagel, Oesterle, Joseph, Fearnside and Holther[2]—with

---

1. *Fallacies* was first published in 1970 by Methuen. It was reissued (with a preface by John Plecnik and John Hoaglund) in 1986 by Vale Press (P.O. Box 6519, Newport News, Virginia 23606) and is now available from that source.

2. In a footnote on page 13, Hamblin lists "the recent books I have especially consulted." He does not list Fearnside and Holther or Joseph (who are frequently cited in chapter 1), but does list Salmon's *Logic* (which is cited only once, on p. 46). Joseph's *An Introduction to Logic* is from the beginning of

frequent mentions of Aristotle and occasional references to J. S. Mill and to Whately as historical background.

The justice of Hamblin's harsh assessment has not gone unchallenged.[3] But just or not, Hamblin's book was instrumental in giving rise to a lively and serious literature aimed at filling a gap Hamblin believed he'd identified when he wrote: "The truth is that nobody, these days, is particularly satisfied with this corner of logic. The traditional treatment is too unsystematic for modern tastes. Yet to dispense with it, as some writers do, is to leave a gap that no one knows how to fill. We have no theory of fallacy at all, in the sense in which we have theories of correct reasoning or inference" (1970, 11).

In the remaining chapters of *Fallacies*, Hamblin offered a now classic history of fallacy theory beginning with Aristotle (chapter 2), tracing the development of the Aristotelian tradition through to the late Middle Ages (chapter 3), detailing the introduction and development of the '*ad*' arguments (chapter 4), as well as looking at the Indian tradition (chapter 5), and the history of the formal fallacies (chapter 6).

In the last three chapters of *Fallacies* (7–9), Hamblin attempts to break new ground by sketching a more adequate framework for a rigorous theory of fallacies—a framework that, as Hamblin sees it, should be grounded in formal dialectics.[4]

Of the papers that follow, the first four attempt to present coherent accounts of the nature of fallacy and of the shape that a theory of fallacy should take. All of them can and should be read against the background of the critique that Hamblin offered of the Standard Treatment.

---

the century—the first edition is 1906, the second revised edition 1916—and is not therefore a "recent book," but is referred to six times in the chapter.

The editions cited by Hamblin are as follows: Max Black, *Critical Thinking: An Introduction to Logic and Scientific Method*, 2d ed. (Englewood Cliffs, N.J.: Prentice-Hall, 1952); Irving Copi, *Introduction to Logic*, 2d ed. (New York: Macmillan, 1961); Morris Cohen and Ernest Nagel, *An Introduction to Logic and Scientific Method* (London: Routledge and Kegan Paul, 1934); Ward Fearnside and William Holther, *Fallacy, the Counterfeit Argument* (Englewood Cliffs, N.J.: Prentice-Hall, 1959); H. W. B. Joseph, *An Introduction to Logic*, 2d rev. ed. (Oxford: Clarendon, 1916); John Arthur Oesterle, *Logic: The Art of Defining and Reasoning* (Englewood Cliffs, N.J.: Prentice-Hall, 1963); Wesley Salmon, *Logic* (Englewood Cliffs, N.J.: Prentice-Hall, 1963); Edith Schipper and Edward Schuh, *A First Course in Modern Logic* (London: Routledge and Kegan Paul, 1960).

3. See Ralph Johnson 1990. Johnson's criticisms were challenged in Douglas Walton 1991d. See also Johnson's reply to Walton in Johnson 1991.

4. For a critique of Hamblin's positive views, see John Woods and Douglas Walton (1989, chap. 1, pp. 1–10).

Johnson

In " 'The Blaze of her Splendors': Suggestions About Revitalising Fallacy Theory,"[5] Ralph Johnson argues against conceptions of fallacy modeled on the formula that "a fallacious argument is one which *seems to be valid* but is *not* so."[6] In light of the difficulties occasioned by such a conception of the nature of fallacy, and after a review of "The Standard Critique" of fallacy theory, Johnson proposes the following definition of fallacy: "A fallacy is an argument which violates one of the criteria/standards of good argument and which occurs with sufficient frequency in discourse to warrant being baptized."

He then proposes to "spell out the criteria which determine a good argument." In Johnson's account there are three principal criteria: the premises must be *relevant*, they must furnish *sufficient* evidence to support the conclusion, and they must be *acceptable*: "On this account then there are three basic fallacies: irrelevant reason, hasty conclusion and problematic premise. Other fallacies can then be seen as species belonging to one of the three basic types." What Johnson provides, then, is a revised conception of fallacy, and a theoretic framework arising out of that revised framework into which the traditional list of fallacies can be fitted.

Finocchiaro

In "Six Types of Fallaciousness," Maurice Finocchiaro attempts to develop an overall approach to fallacy that departs considerably from the standard treatment and its traditional list of fallacies. A main feature of his approach "involves the realization that the study of fallacies is part of what Johnson and Blair call 'the theory of criticism' . . . , or what I have elsewhere called the problem of the evaluation of reasoning." Finocchiaro construes this somewhat narrowly: "fallaciousness is essentially the failure of one proposition to follow from others: that is, an argument is fallacious if and only if the conclusion does not follow from the premises. Starting with this basic definition, I plan to explore the main reasons why a conclusion might not follow from premises, and each such reason will yield a distinct type of fallaciousness."

In the portion of his paper that we have excerpted here, Finocchiaro develops a typology of six types of flaw that result in fallacious or logically defective arguments: *formal* (invalidity: a defect Finocchiaro pictures as typi-

5. Excerpted and updated by the author from Ralph Johnson 1987.
6. These words are from Hamblin (1970, 12), but there is a variety of similar definitions cited by Johnson. They all echo Aristotle's initial explanation of a sophistical refutation (*Soph. Ref.* 164a20–b27).

cally brought to light through the construction of a counterexample), *explanatory* (a flaw that is brought out by producing another argument from the same premises for a different conclusion and that appears as of equal strength as the original; this is something, Finocchiaro says, that occurs primarily in explanatory contexts—hence the label he uses for it), *presuppositional* (occurring when an argument can be constructed in the context, whose conclusion is the denial of a presupposed assumption), *positive* (where it can be shown that some proposition derivable from the premises is actually inconsistent with the conclusion drawn), *semantical* (involving equivocation), and *persuasive* (e.g., begging the question).

In working through the excerpt from Finocchiaro, the reader should take pains to note the extent to which he links his fallacy types to strategies of criticism that can be developed in the context of dialectical interchange. This feature is essential to Finocchiaro's approach, which as we saw views the study of fallacies as part of the theory of criticism. Moreover, the reader should not be misled by what appears to be an aprioristic cast to the presentation as excerpted. In the broader context of Finocchiaro's published work it is clear that the categories or types he lists here are grounded in his study of the critical strategies actually deployed in the writings of Galileo.[7] Moreover, in Finocchiaro's more recent work, he relates his typology to the empirical findings of Harvard psychologist David Perkins, with fascinating results.[8]

Van Eemeren and Grootendorst

Hamblin's suggestion (in chapter 7 of *Fallacies*, 245ff.) that the preferred criteria for evaluating arguments are dialectical criteria and his attempt (in chapter 8) to provide a grounding for fallacy theory in formal dialectic, have been broadly echoed in greater or lesser degree in the literature since 1970. Finocchiaro,[9] Walton,[10] Rescher,[11] Freeman,[12] Barth and Krabbe,[13] Blair

7. This is apparent not only from the final sections of "Six Types of Fallaciousness" omitted here for lack of space, but also from Finocchiaro's *Galileo and the Art of Reasoning* (Dordrecht: D. Reidel, 1980).

8. Maurice A. Finocchiaro, "Two Empirical Approaches to the Study of Reasoning," *Informal Logic* 16 (1994): 1–21.

9. In Finocchiaro 1987, as we've just seen.

10. See for example Douglas Walton 1989a or "What is Reasoning? What is an Argument?" *Journal of Philosophy* 87 (1990): 399–419.

11. See Nicholas Rescher, *Dialectics: A Controversy-Oriented Approach to the Theory of Knowledge* (Albany: State University of New York Press, 1977).

12. James Freeman, *Dialectics and the Macrostructure of Arguments* (Dordrecht: Foris, 1991).

13. E. M. Barth and Erik C. W. Krabbe, *From Axiom to Dialogue: A Philosophical Study of Logics and Argumentation* (Berlin: de Gruyter, 1982).

and Johnson[14] are just a few of those who have stressed the importance of dialogal or dialectical context and/or structure for the study of arguments and of fallacies. We include here a presentation of one of the most prominent variants of such an approach to fallacies, the pragma-dialectical theory (PDA). For this volume van Eemeren and Grootendorst have crafted a succinct general outline of their view entitled "The Pragma-Dialectical Approach to Fallacies."[15] Their lucid presentation obviates any need to provide the reader with extended explanatory or introductory remarks. We call your attention only to the following points: in PDA, argumentative discourse is conceived of as a rule-governed activity that has distinct stages; essential ingredients of PDA are the identification of those stages (there are four) and the careful and explicit formulation of idealized rules for the conduct of such discourse (in the simplified version presented here, there are ten such rules); fallacies are understood as violations of those rules. Van Eemeren and Grootendorst believe that this theoretical framework permits them to illuminate the traditional informal fallacies as "faux pas of communication—as wrong moves in argumentative discourse." In addition to the theoretical discussion in Part II, van Eemeren and Grootendorst present an example of the application of PDA to the *ad hominen* fallacy in Part III of this volume.

Willard

In A *Theory of Argumentation*, communication theorist Charles Willard discussed fallacies in a book devoted to the thesis that "*argument* is a form of interaction in which two or more people maintain what they construe to be incompatible positions," a book in which "the theoretical context is a communication theory."[16] In chapter 10 of that book ("Fallacy Theory"), Willard made a case for limiting the use of the word "fallacy" in his interactional theory to "a relatively narrow designation of logical mistakes whose source of authority is Logic."[17]

> Other terms are better suited to label procedural and interpersonal errors and (thus) the sources of authority for criticism. This narrows

14. J. Anthony Blair and Ralph H. Johnson, "Argumentation as dialectical," *Argumentation* 1 (1987): 41–56.

15. Their theory is also available in book form. See van Eemeren and Grootendorst 1984 and, more recently, 1992a.

16. Charles Arthur Willard, A *Theory of Argumentation* (Tuscaloosa: University of Alabama Press, 1989), 1.

17. Ibid., 237.

the term perhaps more than informal logicians want to narrow their field, but the breadth of the term is not the best way to justify broadening Informal Logic's borders. Nor is a broad sense of fallacy helpful to Argumentation theorists who want to know how fallacy theory fits into argument criticism.[18]

Willard noted, but refused to endorse, a broader construction of the term "fallacy" that he took to be common among informal logicians. In "Failures of Relevance: A Rhetorical View"—written specially for this volume— Willard returns to the issue of the relationship between informal logic's conception of fallacies, on the one hand, and the categories and conceptualizations current in "rhetoric" or communication theory, on the other. Here he argues that as informal logicians work through their (broader) notion of fallacy and add the qualifications needed to make what they say about fallacies plausible, they are led to a conception in which "all pragmatic fallacies become fallacies of relevance" and where what they are talking about is the fit between messages, situations, and intentions that is the focal point of the best recent work in rhetoric and communication theory.

Is a Theory of Fallacies Possible at All?

Massey

Hamblin had claimed that at the time he wrote, there was "no *theory* of fallacy at all;" his aim, however, was not to dispense with fallacies as a topic within logic, but to produce an acceptable theory that would fill the gap in logic which he thought the Standard Treatment filled so inadequately. A more radical challenge to the standard treatment of fallacies emerged in the mid-seventies in the work of Gerald Massey (1975a, 1975b), who argued for the stronger thesis that a theory of fallacies is an impossibility. Massey's case depends on two crucial ideas. The first is the conception (which Massey cites Hamblin as authority for) that fallacies are arguments that seem to be valid, but are not; from this, Massey concludes that a *theory* of fallacy is possible only if a *theory* of invalid argument is possible. The second crucial idea is what has come to be called *the asymmetry thesis*: the thesis that logic can

18. Ibid., 237.

supply methods for proving that particular arguments are valid, but that apart from the "trivial logic-indifferent method"[19] there is no method for proving invalidity that has theoretical legitimacy. The latter claim is based on two ideas:

(a) an argument is invalid if and only if there is no valid argument form that it instantiates.
(b) from that fact that one is unable to find a valid form which an argument instantiates, it does not follow that no such form exists, because
   (i) someone more clever than you might be able to come up with an ingenious translation that yields a valid argument form, and
   (ii) even if it is somehow impossible to get a valid argument form by translating the argument into any of the formal languages you know and respect, there might be hitherto undreamt of formal languages congenial to you such that translation into them would yield a valid argument form.

Massey is not denying that we can intuitively recognize invalid arguments. His claim is rather that there is no *method* for proving invalidity that has *theoretical* legitimacy. We have excerpted the core of Massey's 1981 paper, "The Fallacy behind Fallacies,"[20] where he makes his case in context and in detail.

Govier

In 1987, Trudy Govier published "Four Reasons There are No Fallacies?"—a paper that dealt among other things with Massey's asymmetry thesis and its implications.[21] For this volume, Govier has prepared an updated version of the sections of that paper bearing on Massey's claim that arguments cannot be proved invalid. We reproduce it under the title "Reply to Massey."

Govier challenges Massey on two main fronts. First, she argues that invalidity is neither a necessary nor a sufficient condition of fallaciousness. Second, she insists on a distinction between semantic validity and formal validity. She

19. Massey recognizes the case in which one proves an argument invalid by showing that its premises are true but its conclusion false. He calls this *the trivial logic-indifferent* method of proving invalidity.

20. Gerald Massey 1981.

21. Trudy Govier 1987. An earlier version of this paper appeared under the title "Who Says There are No Fallacies?" *Informal Logic Newsletter* 5 (1982): 2–10.

concedes that Massey may have demonstrated that there is no formally adequate way of showing an argument to be formally invalid. But she objects to
"the move from *not having a formally adequate method* to *not having any
theoretically adequate method.*" Govier writes: "Anyone who thinks that respectable nonformal theories are possible will not accept this move and will not
move to the final conclusion either."

Woods

In a paper written specially for this volume and entitled "Fearful Symmetry,"
John Woods embraces the formalizing tendencies that Govier objected to and
carries them even further than Massey did—with surprising results. Massey
is able to maintain the asymmetry thesis because he concedes that "one can
recognize a correct translation of a natural-language argument into a formal
language, thereby establishing that the argument instantiates a particular
argument form."[22] Only on the basis of such a recognition is it possible to
appeal to the principles of logic to validate the arguments that purportedly
instantiate valid argument forms.

Woods zeroes in on the move in which we go from "arguments on the
hoof" (natural language arguments) to their reconstructions in formalized
languages. Woods maintains that those moves, though intuitively unexceptional, lack *theoretical* justification. There are specific reasons why this is so;
we lack both a theoretically adequate understanding and a set of proof procedures for two of the tasks that must be accomplished in order to reconstruct a
natural argument in the formalized languages of propositional logic or of
quantification theory: (1) the task of filtering out semantic entailments that
don't depend on logical form, and (2) the task of deciding what is and isn't
logically "simple" in arguments on the hoof. To accomplish these tasks, we
would need what Woods calls a "dressing theory"—and such a theory is not
available. Without a dressing theory, we cannot have a theory of reconstruction. Without a theory of reconstruction, we cannot have a theory of validity
for natural language arguments. Ergo, we cannot have a theory of validity for
natural language arguments. This result Woods calls the *symmetry thesis:*
There is no theory of validity or invalidity for natural language arguments.

What is the upshot? In Woods's view, formal logic continues to have a
coherently formulable program (it need not concern itself with arguments on
the hoof, but only with formalized—what used to be called artificial—

---

22. See 164 below. To be fair, Massey says that this concession is "for the sake of argument."

languages). What about informal logic? If it is to be a *theory* of the validity or invalidity of natural language arguments, it doesn't exist. "The informal logician . . . is simply out of business."

Other Developments

There are at least three points of view not represented by theoretical pieces in Part II. They include the views of Douglas Walton,[23] Jaakko Hintikka,[24] and the broader views of John Woods concerning the pedagogical and critical role of fallacies.[25] However, the approaches associated with these three names will be represented in the analyses of particular fallacies to be found in Part III.

23. See note 10.
24. See Jaakko Hintikka 1987 and Jaakko Hintikka and James Bachman, *What If . . . ? Toward Excellence in Reasoning* (Mountain View, Calif.: Mayfield, 1991).
25. Views developed, for example, in Woods 1988 and 1992.

7

The Blaze of her Splendors: Suggestions About Revitalizing Fallacy Theory*

Ralph H. Johnson

[The following is excerpted from the article of the same title by R. H. Johnson, that originally appeared in *Argumentation* 1 (1987): 239–53. Copyright 1987 by D. Reidel Publishing Company. Reprinted by permission of Kluwer Academic Publishers. Minor changes have been made by the author.]

> The genius of a man's logical method should be loved and reverenced as his bride, whom he has chosen from all the world. He need not condemn the others; on the contrary he may honor them deeply, and in doing so he only honors her more. But she is the one that he has chosen, and he knows he was right in making that choice. And having made it, he will work and fight for her, and will not complain that there are blows to take, hoping that there may be as many and as hard to give, and will strive to be the worthy knight and champion of her from *the blaze of whose splendors* he draws his inspiration and courage.
>
> —C. S. Peirce, "The Fixation of Belief"

These words of Peirce's on the choice of a logical method are perhaps florid, not to say sexist. But if we can transcend the latter and suffer the former, it's a useful metaphor. It fits my situation because, although I am not wedded to Fallacy Theory, it was my first love. And she has taken her share of blows of

---

* I am indebted to my colleague J. A. Blair, for many helpful comments and criticisms on an earlier draft.

late. However, her honor is worth fighting for. My purpose then in this paper is to review the main criticisms of Fallacy Theory that are responsible for her tarnished image and then see what can be done to restore her, if not to a position of blazing splendor, then at least matronly respectability.

Let me start with a list of the sorts of questions I have in mind:

Are there fallacies? Or are fallacies nothing but a *feu de follet*, existing as another contributor to this volume has claimed on another occasion "only in the mind of the interpreter?" (Finocchiaro 1981, 15). Has the concept of fallacy been rendered obsolete by developments in logic in the twentieth century, thus becoming a remnant of folk logic in much the same way that some claim the concept of belief is a vestige of folk psychology?[1] Even if the idea of fallacy should prove useful pedagogically, would that fact alone be sufficient to warrant retaining it? These are some of the questions I should like to address in this paper.

In particular, I shall defend the view that there are indeed distinguishable fallacies and that Fallacy Theory (or FT as I shall refer to it) when properly presented constitutes a viable theory of criticism.

I first examine various ways of defining fallacy. I then look at four important criticisms of FT and examine possible responses. Finally, I present an outline of a viable approach to fallacy theory.

What is a Fallacy?

Whether or not there are any fallacies is at least partly a conceptual issue: that is, the answer to this question will depend in part on how one conceives fallacy. This fact may explain the rather widespread disagreement about the existence and nature of fallacies, never mind the disparate conceptions of fallacy afoot. There are at least three different, though clearly related, notions or conceptions of fallacy.

Standard Definitions of Fallacy

It has become customary to date recent serious research into fallacies to the publication of *Fallacies* by Hamblin in 1970. In that work, Hamblin provides a solid historical account of the origin of fallacies, as well as insightful

---

1. See Stephen P. Stich, *From Folk Psychology to Cognitive Science* (Cambridge: MIT Press, 1983).

criticism of what he calls "The Standard Treatment."[2] It should come as no surprise then that the most common conception of fallacy is that cited by Hamblin.

(F1)   A fallacy is an argument which appears to be valid but is not (Hamblin 1970, 12)

(This is the conception of fallacy that Massey adopts in both of his articles, about which more in a moment.)[3] Hamblin's definition is, it is no surprise, of Aristotelian provenance. In *Sophistical Refutations*, Aristotle writes: "Let us now discuss sophistic refutations, i.e., arguments which appear to be refutations but are really fallacies instead. . . . That some reasonings are genuine, while others seem to be but are not, is evident (164a20).[4] This then is the first and by far the most common way of defining or conceptualizing fallacy. Before looking at it critically, I want to table the other conceptions I came across.

A second conception of fallacy is that given in Black:

(F2)   A fallacy is an argument that seems to be sound without being so in fact.[5]

Black uses *soundness* where Hamblin had *validity*, making this conception somewhat broader. An argument could be fallacious in this sense but not in the first, if for example the premises seemed to be true but were false.

A third definition is that given by Joseph:

(F3)   A fallacy is an argument which appears to be conclusive but is not.[6]

This definition is interesting in that it does not use the terminology of formal deductive logic, avoiding both the terms *valid* and *sound* and instead substituting *conclusive*.

2. See Hamblin (1970). For a fuller account of my views on the Standard Treatment, see R. H. Johnson (1990). My criticisms were challenged by Douglas Walton (1991d); see my reply in R. H. Johnson (1991).

3. Gerald Massey (1975a; 1981). I shall refer to the first article as "Good Arguments" and the second as "Fallacy." For my views on Massey, see R. H. Johnson (1989).

4. Aristotle, *On Sophistical Refutations & On Coming To Be and Passing Away*, translated by E. S. Forster (Cambridge: Harvard University Press, 1955), 11.

5. Max Black, *Critical Thinking*, 2d ed. (Englewood Cliffs, N.J.: Prentice-Hall, 1952), 230.

6. H. W. B. Joseph, *An Introduction to Logic* (Oxford: Clarendon Press, 1906), 525.

The reader will no doubt have noted the pattern common to these three definitions:

(F*)   A fallacy is an X which appears to be Y but is not in fact Y.

X ranges over terms like *argument, reasoning,* and *inference;* Y ranges over terms like *conclusive, persuasive, sound,* and *valid.* Since the Y term ranges over predicates denoting desirable features of discourse and X ranges over acts of reasoning, we might suggest the following schematization of the concept of fallacy as the one that extracts the essence of the idea as historically articulated:

(FS)   A fallacy is reasoning which appears to be good but is not.

What we learn from this exercise (and what shall emerge as an important idea) is that the conception of fallacy belongs to the theory of criticism.

There is something else to be learned from (FS); that is, one can see why it is that people disagree about whether there are fallacies or not, since the standard ways of defining fallacy are "subjective." By that I mean that whether there is fallacy becomes, on these accounts, a matter of *appearance.* For it is not at all unthinkable that a defective argument might appear to one individual to be good reasoning, while to some other individual that same reasoning appears to be quite bad. It will follow then that for the first there is fallacy (because the conditions of the definition are satisfied) but for the second there is not. Small wonder, then, that doubts have arisen about FT.

In similar fashion it becomes intelligible why critics of fallacy theory often wish to point out that what is fallacious in one context is not so in another. Just as what is green under one lighting configuration will not appear to be so under another.

The lesson I draw from these reflections is not that there are no fallacies, nor yet that the concept of fallacy is incoherent, but rather that if we wish the term "fallacy" to do serious logical duty, then it cannot be defined that way. I shall offer a more extended critique in the next section, calling attention to additional problems with the definitions already cited.

Critique of Standard Definitions

What, then, are the additional problems with (F1)? There are at least two. First, (F1) uncritically assumes the vantage point of formal, deductive logic.

The key term in this definition is "valid," and I assume that most will unpack this term in one of the customary ways sanctioned by formal logic; i.e., an argument is valid when the conclusion follows necessarily from the premises—or something akin to this. In this way of defining fallacy, validity is made the standard against which arguments are to be measured. But I would argue that this standard is too limiting, for it can sensibly be applied only to deductive arguments. It turns out then that a serious problem with this conception of fallacy is the underlying *assumption* it makes about argumentation: that all argumentation is deductive in nature.

This assumption, aptly termed "deductive chauvinism,"[7] has been challenged by many in the last fifteen years so that if anyone wishes to continue to hold this conception he or she incurs some obligation to defend the theory of argument which is presupposed.[8]

The first problem had to do with the applicability of (F1); the second problem concerns its utility. If "valid" takes its usual meaning, then it seems to follow that only those who have grasped that meaning will be able to use it. That is, to use the term "fallacy" as thus defined one must be able to think (and say in appropriate circumstances): "That argument appears to be valid but it is not." Such a person needs to have much savvy in validity-judgments. This means that a good portion of the intellectual community will be disenfranchised.

Yet a third problem emerges from Massey's critique, which claims that there cannot be any theory of fallacy because there is not a theory of invalidity, and that is a condition of there being a theory of fallacy (given this definition).[9] I am inclined to grant the point that there cannot be a theory of invalidity, and for largely the reasons cited by Massey. The conclusion that I draw is not that there cannot be a theory of fallacy, but rather that "fallacy" should not be defined in terms of validity/invalidity.

Similar problems are to be expected then with (F2), if "sound" has its customary meaning of true premises plus a valid inference. The one important difference here would be the tacit concession that there might well be other sources of fallacy than the apparent validity of an invalid argument. For presumably, by this definition, an argument with a false premise is fallacious, if

7. I first heard this term used by Merrilee Salmon at the Carnegie-Mellon Conference on Logic and Liberal Learning, at Carnegie-Mellon University, June 1979. See also *Informal Logic Newsletter* 2, no. 1 (1979): 10.

8. See, for example, Govier's development of this point in "Who says there are no fallacies?" *Informal Logic Newsletter* 5, no. 1 (1982): 2–10.

9. See Massey (1981, 494), reprinted below, 163–64.

that premise is the reason why the argument appears to be sound. Whether we really want to commit ourselves to this account of fallacy is an open question.[10]

There are problems with Joseph's definitions, too, though it is free of some of the problems that afflict the previous definitions. We would want to know, first, why an argument must be conclusive in order to be a good argument? It would seem that an argument might well be inconclusive and yet be "good." So defining goodness as conclusiveness runs the same kind of risk of being unduly restrictive as the other two definitions incur. Further, we would need to know just how the notion of "conclusive" gets unpacked. Does it reduce, perhaps, to soundness?

On reflection then it seems that none of these standard ways of defining "fallacy" is entirely satisfactory. The core we can extricate, once the definitions are purged of undue recourse to formal logic, is that a fallacy is an argument that falls short of the appropriate logical standard. Some of the discontent with FT may well stem from the problems in traditional ways of conceiving fallacy. It would be possible to repair these defects by developing a better conception of fallacy. But before going into that possibility, I want to look at some of the other standard criticisms of FT. These are not directed at the concept but rather at its deployment.

Criticisms of Fallacy Theory

Not only is there such a thing as "The Standard Treatment" of fallacy (as outlined by Hamblin). There has also come to exist what might be termed "The Standard Critique" of FT. I would like now to have a look at four prominent yet distinct lines of criticism of FT and make some response to each. In doing so, I will be defending FT, but I do not wish this to be construed as suggesting that the critiques are without merit. Indeed, each has some validity. Fallacy theorists have often been among their own worst enemies, exhibiting what Massey calls "an exaggerated fascination with taxonomies" (Massey 1981, 489).[11] Nor can it be denied that many who

10. There is an additional and intriguing question here about the categories in terms of which premises are best appraised. The assumption in the tradition of formal logic is that the appropriate standard is *truth*. But that view needs to be reevaluated, so Blair and I have argued in "Argumentation as dialectical," *Argumentation* 1 (1987): 41–56.

11. Massey has the right idea here but aims at the wrong target. It is not the textbook authors that exhibit this morbid fascination with taxonomy; they simply table their own lists. An observant reader cannot but notice the difference.

endorse FT have been slipshod in their own presentations of this or that fallacy. In spite of these problems, I believe FT is worth saving.

It might be good to look at the problems in historical perspective. In the first place, even though it is customary to trace interest in fallacy back to Aristotle in *Sophistical Refutations,* in fact the twentieth century has witnessed very little activity in the area of fallacy theory, at least when other research outposts in logic are compared; viz., modal logic, deontic logic, many-valued logic, etc. Formal deductive logic so dominated the research program of logic in this century that it is only in the last twenty-five years or so that FT has shown any signs of vitality and been able to attract the interest of researchers.[12] In this set of circumstances, it hardly comes as a surprise that there has yet to emerge a clearly defined research program or paradigm to guide research. There are signs that this situation has begun to change in the last decade and so it may well be that some of the long-standing problems with FT will receive attention. Furthermore the criticisms I am about to recount do not seem to me to be directed against FT per se, but only against individual accounts. I hope to show that none of these lines of criticism individually, and not even the lot of them taken severally, is enough to subvert the hope that FT might be placed on solid ground.

The first line of criticism I wish to mention is the charge of incompleteness. Some critics are content to mouth the shibboleth that goes back to De Morgan: since the ways of error are infinite, no list of the mistakes or fallacies can be complete.[13] In response it may be said that even if it is the case (and this is far from obvious) that the ways the human mind can go wrong are infinite, still it would not follow that we could not have completeness in some important sense. For it could be that (a) the ways of going wrong in *argumentation* (a subdomain of intellectual activities) are finite; or that (b) the ways of going wrong in argumentation are infinite, but they fall into a pattern. Indeed, I am inclined to think that (b) is true and hence that it is possible to give some semblance of completeness to the account of fallacy. But we shall see. Thus to use a possibly contentious analogy: the ways of going wrong in grammar and syntax are vast (perhaps infinite) but that has not stood in the way of one or another author's constructing a helpful list of

12. For documentation, see Ralph H. Johnson and J. Anthony Blair, "The Recent Development of Informal Logic" in Blair and Johnson (1980, 6–11).

13. The standard reference here is A. De Morgan, *Formal Logic* (1847) 2d ed., edited by A. E. Taylor (London: Open Court, 1926), 276. Also quoted on this very point: Joseph, *Introduction to Logic,* 569; and M. R. Cohen and E. Nagel, *Introduction to Logic and Scientific Method* (London: Routledge and Kegan Paul, 1934), 382.

errors. On the other hand, it must be acknowledged that FT will never be able to demonstrate completeness in the sense of Post, or other senses of completeness that may occur in formal systems.

A second line of criticism is that made by Finocchiaro to the effect that there probably are no common errors in reasoning and that fallacies exist only in the mind of the interpreter (Finocchiaro 1981). But there are common errors in reasoning, as anyone who has spent any amount of time analyzing ordinary responses to reasoning knows.[14] For example, people will often attack a distorted and weakened form of an opponent's position; or they will engage in an irrelevant attack on the individual rather than the position (*ad hominem*); or they will introduce a side issue (red herring). In addition to these evidences, cognitive psychologists have been studying the sorts of mistakes that commonly occur when people engage in inductive inferences: i.e., generalizing from a sample that is too small and not representative.[15] It is hard to believe that these mistakes do not exist in fact but are creations that exist only in the mind of the critic.

Indeed though we must grant the possibility that the critic is sometimes responsible for the mistake, i.e., in the critic's reconstruction the mistake is introduced, yet it seems entirely too paradoxical to suggest, as Finocchiaro seems to, that ordinary reasoners do not make mistakes and that mistakes in reasoning are confined to those who reason about that reasoning.

Another line of criticism of FT is that presented by McPeck. Following Toulmin, McPeck claims that each field has its own logic and hence that what is fallacious in one context might not be so in another: "A principle of reason in business or law might be fallacious in science or ethics."[16] Whatever *prima facie* validity this conjecture may possess seems to fade as one looks for examples of, say, a principle of reason that is valid in law but not in science. Is it, for example, legitimate to attack the person rather than his or her position in the field of business but not legitimate in science? Is it legitimate to distort someone's position in law but not in ethics? Short of being presented with examples of this conjecture, I am not inclined to take it

---

14. If it should occur to someone that I have here been guilty of begging the question, that would seem to present some problems for Finocchiaro's views. For an account of errors in everyday reasoning, see D. N. Perkins, Richard Allen, and James Hafner, "Difficulties in everyday reasoning," in *Thinking: the Expanding Frontier*, edited by William Maxwell (Philadelphia: Franklin Institute Press, 1983).

15. Richard Nisbett and Lee Ross, *Human Inference: Strategies and Shortcomings of Social Judgment* (Englewood Cliffs, N.J.: Prentice-Hall, 1980).

16. John McPeck, *Critical Thinking and Education* (Oxford: Martin Robinson, 1981), 72.

as much of a threat. On the other hand, if it can be shown for example that such examples exist, then FT will have been confronted with a very serious challenge.

The remaining significant line of criticism I wish to discuss is that of Paul, who objects to the way in which fallacies are taught: i.e., atomistically and without any real sense of how in the actual give-and-take of a dialectical exchange, the charge of fallacy is rarely if ever fatal.[17] I think it is best to concede Paul's point—FT is often taught poorly. But his is surely not a sufficient basis for discarding it. Rather it may be viewed as a call to improve our methods of teaching fallacy.

In light of the foregoing it should be apparent that I prefer to retain FT, and I will now spell out both the presuppositions of FT and a conception of fallacy that I believe are not vulnerable to the lines of criticism we have been discussing.

The Revitalization of Fallacy Theory

In light of the criticisms and problems we have seen in FT, and given the rather low esteem in which it is held by many logicians, what would be required to revitalize FT and to make it an intellectually respectable theory of logical criticism?

It will require three changes. First, it will require a revision of our conception of fallacy. Second, the presuppositions of FT must be identified and shown to be defensible. Third, some strictures need to be developed about the way in which FT is taught. In the space that remains I can do little more than indicate in broad terms how I would go about the task of discharging these obligations.

First, revision of the concept of fallacy requires, in my view, three steps.

(i) We should retain the historical nucleus of the idea of fallacy as a logically bad *argument*;
(ii) At the same time, the concept should be purged of its subjective and psychological nuances; i.e., we should delete reference to matters of appearance, and

17. Richard Paul, "Teaching Critical Thinking in the 'Strong' Sense," *Informal Logic Newsletter* 4 (1984): 2–7.

(iii) we should introduce the notion of frequency; because a fallacy is not just any mistake in argument, but one that occurs with some frequency.

In line with these, I propose the following definition of fallacy

(F#)   A fallacy is an *argument* that violates one of the criteria/standards of good argument and that occurs with sufficient frequency in discourse to warrant being baptized.

The above definition appears to be a significant departure from the concept as defined and used in the tradition. For the term *fallacy*—deriving from the Latin *fallax*—has always carried with it the notion of possible deception. Yet if we go back to Aristotle's terminology in *Sophistical Refutations*, we will find a precedent for our proposal. There, one of the terms that is translated *fallacy* is "paralogismos," which literally means "something that goes against reason or logic." Hence in proposing to define fallacy as a violation of logical standards (with no mention of potential deception) we are in harmony with at least one important strand in Aristotle's thought.

Let me move on then to the second task and set forth what I take the governing presuppositions of FT to be. They are four in number:

1. That people do make logical mistakes in reasoning and argumentation;
2. That at least one important category of these mistakes can be described as nonformal;
3. That nonformal mistakes can be identified according to type;
4. That such mistakes in reasoning occur with sufficient frequency to warrant the utility of a list of such mistakes.

A full defense of FT would require lines of reasoning to support each of these four propositions. I trust the reader will forgive me if I do not undertake that task here, and move on instead to discuss the next step in the revitalization of FT.

The next step in revitalizing fallacy theory would be to spell out the criteria that determine a good argument.[18]

What are we looking for in a good argument? First the premises must be *relevant* to the conclusion. If it can be shown that one of the premises is irrelevant to the conclusion then it has been shown that the argument is not a good one. Do people with some degree of frequency produce arguments in

18. It should be understood here that I am referring to nonformal criteria.

which a premise is irrelevent to the conclusion? I think so. And we call that sort of malfeasance a *non sequitur.* We say, "That doesn't follow."[19]

Suppose now that the premises of an argument are relevant to the conclusion; is that enough? Hardly, for the premises must furnish *sufficient* evidence to support the conclusion. It might for example be relevant to the determination of guilt or innocence that the alleged murderer can be placed at the scene of the crime, but that would hardly be sufficient evidence to convict. Do people with some degree of frequency produce arguments in which the premises taken together are insufficient to yield the conclusion? I think so. People get a notion in their heads, cast about for a few bits of isolated evidence to support it, and then settle comfortably into their position. We promote intuitions and half-truths based on partial evidence to the status of truths without bothering to consider the full body of evidence that bears on the issue. This malfeasance in the argumentative process occurs often enough to warrant a name. Then why not give it a name? Call it jumping to a conclusion or hasty conclusion.

Suppose now that we judged that the premises are both relevant and sufficient. (Grant that these are difficult judgments to make and will often have to be made tentatively and provisionally.) Are we then obligated to accept the conclusion? Not necessarily, for we still have to decide whether we are going to accept the premises as stated. We need to be prepared to press such questions as: Is this a reasonable claim? Is it in need of defense itself? Is it true? If the answer to any of these is no and if we can articulate the thinking behind the no, then we have reason to reject the argument as it stands. This fault occurs frequently enough to be worth baptizing; give it a name: call it *problematic premise.*

On this account then there are three basic fallacies: irrelevant reason, hasty conclusion, and problematic premise. Other fallacies can then be seen as species belonging to one of the three basic types.[20]

---

19. Is there a formal way of reaching a verdict about relevance—surely a fundamental concept in argument criticism? Notwithstanding the herculean efforts of researchers like Alan Ross Anderson and Nuel D. Belnap, Jr. (*Entailment: the Logic of Relevance* [Princeton, N.J.: Princeton University Press, 1975]) and more recently, Walton (*Topical Relevance in Argumentation* [Amsterdam: Benjamins, 1982]) no formal procedure exists that yields the verdict. The difficulties are compounded by the need for translating from ordinary language into the symbolism of the artificial language. Yet it surely does not follow that there is nothing we can do to educate our students in the intelligent use of this important concept.

20. Thus, for example, the fallacy known as the improper appeal to authority will be an instance of hasty conclusion—if some but not enough evidence is presented to show that the person cited is an authority; of irrelevant reason, in case the issue or question is one that does not by nature allow for an appeal to authority.

In asking these three basic questions: "Is it relevant? Is it sufficient? Is it acceptable?" we pose three questions phrased in everyday English language, using concepts with which most people have some familiarity: relevance, sufficiency, acceptability. The point of a fallacy approach to argument analysis is to provide students with experience deploying these concepts and thereby improve their capacity to wield them. The fallacy labels are simply devices, the means to an end and not the end itself.

In deciding which instantiations to baptize and which not, I suggest that we be led by perceived frequency. That is, we should admit a (new) fallacy to the inventory just when it can be "shown" that this fallacy occurs with sufficient frequency to make it worth our while to have a label handy. On this account, the function of the inventory is purely heuristic and critical—to enable the individual to call to mind frequent violations of the criteria.

The approach to fallacy I have just outlined is, I believe theoretically defensible, coherent, and capable of providing a solid foundation for a fallacy approach to argument analysis and evaluation. It is not open to the charges that Massey makes against the standard textbook treatments of fallacy: it exhibits no gross exaggeration with taxonomy; it is not aimless or directionless (at least as Johnson and Blair have presented it in *Logical Self-Defense*).[21]

There is no denying that the fallacy approach is subject to abuse, especially to the sort Paul discusses in his article, but then the formal approach is subject to abuse—as Massey has demonstrated (Massey 1981, 493). I conclude this section then by presenting the strictures that I maintain a fallacy approach must adhere to in order to avoid such abuse.

1. Each fallacy must be presented with the identity conditions: i.e., the conditions that make it clear that it is fallacious and that at the same time differentiate it from other fallacies. Thus while *ad hominem* and straw man are both fallacies of relevance, their identity conditions are different.[22]
2. Any charge of fallacy must be thoroughly defended by arguing that the identity conditions for the occurrence of that fallacy are satisfied.
3. The charge of fallacy must be viewed as an initial critical probing of the argument under consideration rather than as a definitive, categorical refutation of it.

21. See Johnson and Blair (1993).

22. See Johnson and Blair, *Logical Self-Defense*, 85 and 90. The existence of such identity conditions creates problems for McPeck's position regarding "the absence of definitive criteria for distinguishing fallacious from non-fallacious propositions" (McPeck, *Critical Thinking and Education*, 53).

4. The point must continually be stressed that even if the argument is fallacious, it doesn't mean that the conclusion is false. Students having located this or that problem in the reasoning can then be confronted with the question: How might the arguer repair the argument over this charge?
5. The point must be made repeatedly that FT is a means to an end: that the point of having a label or name is simply to help people remember a certain kind of defective move that occurs in argumentation. The student must learn to dispense with the label when he or she goes public and be able to make the points in language which the arguer can understand.

If fallacy is defined in the way presented here, if the assumptions initialled earlier are defensible and if the strictures itemized above are followed, then it seems to me that FT can be a viable theory of criticism.

8

Six Types of Fallaciousness: Toward a Realistic Theory of Logical Criticism

Maurice A. Finocchiaro

[The following is excerpted from the article by the same title by M. A. Finocchiaro that originally appeared in *Argumentation* 1 (1987): 263–82. Copyright 1987 by D. Reidel. Reprinted by permission of Kluwer Academic Publishers.]

Like Mt. Everest and the moon, fallacies are challenging simply because they exist. Though it is not exactly true that if they did not exist someone would have to invent them, they do seem to possess the uncanny power deriving from the principle that likes attract each other, and so a number of authors have recently complained about such things as "the fallacy behind fallacies" (Massey 1981), the prevalence of "some fallacies about fallacies" (Grootendorst 1987), and "how philosophers' charges of fallacy are often themselves fallacious" (Finocchiaro 1981, 22).

Be that as it may, the phenomenon of error in general, and of fallacies in particular, is too much a part of the human condition for us to give up the study of them simply because this study, like any other human activity, is itself liable to error and to fallacy. So, instead of trying to articulate and classify the various errors (be they actual, potential, or imaginary) that characterize the study of fallacies, it is preferable to begin by briefly mentioning a number of approaches that are possible and that are to some extent followed by different scholars. This is especially true in the present context, where the only appropriate attitude is one of live and let live.

Methodological Considerations

It is useful to distinguish three main approaches to the study of fallacies, the third being the one to be pursued here. In the first, one takes the essential problem to be that of devising various formalisms of either classical or non-classical mathematical logic that are meant to represent the various fallacies which philosophers have named and discussed. Here fallacies are taken to be self-subsisting entities that have their own abstract existence independently of human thinking. This is the approach which is perhaps best exemplified by the work of Woods and Walton.[1] The full description and evaluation of this approach is admittedly a long story and cannot be attempted here. Thus, with all due respect to the practitioners of this approach, and with the proviso that if they were not doing this I would be tempted to do it myself, allow me to state briefly my disagreement. I find this approach excessively abstract and formalistic and insufficiently empirical and practical, and I believe that at the root of this approach lie two things: a mathematical-formalist bias, and an obsession with philosophers' conceptualizations of fallacies rather than with the actual fallacious thinking by ordinary people. At the opposite end of the methodological spectrum we find the empirical approach of experimental psychologists.[2] No less than the formalist approach, this second one would deserve extended discussion as well as rigorous pursuit in the spirit of both methodological pluralism and the economic maximization and exploitation of resources at one's disposal.[3] Here I can only dogmatically state the reasons for my skepticism. Partly I feel that it represents an empiricist excess; in part it displays a curious "value-free" attitude, as if the attribution of fallacies to people's thinking were not an evaluative enterprise; it also tends to be uncritical vis-à-vis the epistemological basis of the logical theories it uses to define

1. See, for example, Woods and Walton, "Towards a Theory of Argument," *Metaphilosophy* 8 (1977): 298–315; Woods and Walton (1982a); and Walton (1981; 1985b). Their individual and joint publications are too numerous to list here, as one can see from the partial list in Walton (1985b, 293–95). In all fairness it should also be mentioned that some of their work is not at all formalist but comes close to the third approach mentioned below, an example being Walton (1987c).

2. See P. C. Wason and P. N. Johnson-Laird, *Psychology of Reasoning* (Cambridge: Harvard University Press, 1972); R. E. Nisbett and L. Ross, *Human Inference* (Englewood Cliffs, N.J.: Prentice-Hall, 1980); and J. St. B. T. Evans, *The Psychology of Deductive Reasoning* (London: Routledge, 1982).

3. I am referring to such methodological suggestions as the pluralism advocated by Paul Feyerabend, *Against Method* (London: NLB, 1975), and the at least temporary "normal-science" closed-mindedness of Kuhn's theory of scientific revolutions; see T. S. Kuhn, *The Structure of Scientific Revolutions*, 2d enlarged ed. (Chicago: University of Chicago Press, 1970).

the fallacies experimentally attributed to humans;[4] and finally it faces some internal problems of a sort suggesting that its experimental results are not really phenomena of reasoning, but rather involve other cognitive activities like perception.[5]

Elements of the third alternative approach have been emerging for some time. One clue can be traced at least as far back as Strawson's *Introduction to Logical Theory* and his notion of "the logician's second-order vocabulary";[6] I would include "fallacy" terminology here, since it ordinarily occurs when someone wants to comment about some logical feature of a first-order expression of reasoning. This means that the best place to begin in the study of fallacies, or at least a crucial phenomenon to examine, is allegations that fallacies are being committed. An analogous, though slightly different suggestion is made by Grootendorst (1987, 335) when he says that "*fallacy* is a theory-dependent concept. That is, something is only a fallacy within the framework of a properly articulated theory of fallacies." My point amounts to a slight twist on this. I am saying that fundamentally we have a fallacy only within the framework of a given practitioner's conception of the argument he is commenting upon. That is, we have "theory" in the sense of reflection upon practice.

A second feature of this approach involves the realization that the study of fallacies is part of what Johnson and Blair call the "theory of criticism,"[7] or what I elsewhere have called the problem of the evaluation of reasoning (Finocchiaro 1981). What this amounts to is that a fallacy-allegation or fallaciousness-claim is to be treated as a special case of criticism or evaluation and thus studied in the context of criticism or evaluation in general. Moreover, we can thus easily incorporate an important element of the dialectical

---

4. Cohen is perhaps the leading exponent of this sort of criticism, which may be found in L. J. Cohen (1982). A different type of methodological criticism may be found in M. A. Finocchiaro, "The Psychological Explanation of Reasoning: Logical and Methodological Problems," *Philosophy of the Social Sciences* 9 (1979): 277–91, and M. A. Finocchiaro, *Galileo and the Art of Reasoning: Rhetorical Foundations of Logic and Scientific Method* (Dordrecht: Reidel, 1980), to which a reply was attempted by P. C. Wason, "Realism and Rationality in the Selection Task," in J. St. B. T. Evans, *Thinking and Reasoning: Psychological Approaches* (London: Routledge, 1983).

5. Here I am referring to the work of J. St. B. T. Evans, *The Psychology of Deductive Reasoning*, and *Thinking and Reasoning: Psychological Approaches*, though it must be said in all fairness that this methodological point represents *my* interpretation of his criticism, a matter elaborated in more detail, if still insufficiently, in Finocchiaro, "An Historical Approach to the Study of Argumentation," in F. H. van Eemeren, R. Grootendorst et al. (1987a), 81 n. 4.

6. P. F. Strawson, *Introduction to Logical Theory* (London: Methuen, 1952), 15.

7. R. H. Johnson and J. A. Blair, "The Recent Development of Informal Logic," in Blair and Johnson (1980); see also Johnson and Blair (1985).

approach, since the fallaciousness of an argument is not seen as an objectively verifiable fact but rather as the result of the intersubjective interaction of the persons engaged in dialogue.[8] Finally, this point is beginning to be appreciated even by scholars who are otherwise proponents of the formalist approach, as shown by what is undoubtedly the most comprehensive available account of *ad hominem* argument, namely a work by Walton (1985b) where he properly treats both an *ad hominem* argument and the claim that a given argument is *ad hominem* as types of criticism.[9]

Besides being sensitive to the second-order vocabulary, and oriented toward the evaluation of argument, a proper approach must, I believe, recognize the negativity of the evaluations expressed by "fallacy" second-order terminology. In other words, fallaciousness-claims are obviously an unfavorable type of evaluation of an argument. This point is so obvious that its significance is easily missed. And yet when the nature of positive logical evaluation is compared to the nature of negative logical evaluation, certain asymmetries emerge.[10] The existence, origin, and avoidability of these asymmetries is a fascinating problem in itself and deserves much more discussion than it has so far received in the literature. In the present context it will have to suffice to note that negative evaluations are more frequent, much lengthier, much fuller of complexities, and much more interesting than positive evaluations of arguments. Hence we can take advantage of this phenomenon by studying the wealth of data that exist when our task is conceived in the manner mentioned above, that is, given that the study of fallacies is conceived in terms of the various ways in which one can find logical fault with arguments.

8. See Grootendorst who, in illustrating the dialectical approach by means of the example of the argument from authority, says that "another difference is that in other approaches the expert's expertise is seen as an objectively verifiable fact, whereas in the dialectical analysis it is regarded as the intersubjective agreement of the discussants" (1987, 339).

9. Unfortunately he is not always consistent in this, though I am not sure whether at the root of this inconsistency lies his formalist bent; for more details, see Finocchiaro, "Review of Walton's *Arguer's Position,*" *Philosophy and Rhetoric* 20 (1987): 63–65.

10. See Massey (1981); Finocchiaro, *Galileo and the Art of Reasoning*; Finocchiaro (1981); and Richard Montague's remarks in "Formal Logic and Natural Language Argumentation (A symposium)," edited by J. F. Staal, *Foundations of Language* 5 (1969): 256–84. Though Massey's articles on fallacies are commonly viewed, perhaps even by himself, as undermining what is sometimes called informal logic, it seems to me that this is not so, any more than my own (Finocchiaro 1981) points in the direction of what is claimed by someone like Govier, "Who Says There are No Fallacies?" *Informal Logic Newsletter* 5, no. 1 (1982): 2–10. I believe that the full import and significance of Massey's thesis for informal logic remains to be appreciated and exploited. See also Bencivenga (1979); George (1983); Massey (1975a; 1975b); and Massey, "The Pedagogy of Logic," *Teaching Philosophy* 4 (1981): 303–36.

The next issue that needs to be decided in such an approach is how literal one wants to be about studying fallacies. That is, should we examine only those reflective judgments that use the particular term "fallacy"? This might seem advisable since semantic intuition suggests that a fallacy is a particular type of logical error, or if you will, that to charge a fallacy is to express a special kind of second-order negative evaluation; the point here would be that there is something especially seriously wrong with an argument that commits a fallacy, or alternatively that to characterize an argument as a fallacy is to devalue it to an especially low degree. To this one might reply that what we are exploring is not the semantics of "fallacy" but the logic of fallacy, and so to be too literalistic would be self-defeating. Moreover, even a semantics of "fallacy" would have to admit other cognate terms like "fallacious" and "falla-ciousness," as when one says that such and such an argument is fallacious; but once the term "fallacious" is allowed inside the field, then we are really in the domain of the general theory of logical error or general theory of negative evaluation, since this term does not seem to possess the finality and annihilat-ing connotation that the word "fallacy" does. Finally, when one characterizes an argument as a fallacy (in the literal sense), he must be able to specify what special kind of fallacy it is, because otherwise the claim only means that there is something wrong with the argument, and this would bring us back to questions of degrees of fallaciousness, varieties of logical error, and so on; now, if one cannot be literalistic about fallacy, without being literalistic about particular nameable special cases of fallacy, then the literalistic approach is simply too narrow and constricted, and ultimately it leads to studying philoso-phers' "fallacy" talk, rather than negative judgments of arguments by ordinary experienced arguers.[11]

Finally, mindful of the above-mentioned criticism of the first two ap-proaches, the one we are proposing tries to steer a middle course between abstract theory and uncritical experimental data. To what extent we are successful is, of course, something that the reader must judge for himself. A good, if short, example of a balanced, negative, evaluative, and reflection-oriented examination of a particular type of logical criticism is Govier's (1985) study of the technique of criticism by logical analogy.[12] In my own

11. It is interesting that in one of his latest papers on the topic, presented at the First International Congress on Argumentation (Amsterdam, 3–6 June 1986), Douglas Walton argued for a weakening of the literalistic, finalistic conception of fallacy. Whether this involves a movement away from the earlier formalistic approach for which he is famous and toward the one advocated here, is difficult to say; see Walton (1987c).

12. See T. Govier, "Logical Analogies," *Informal Logic* 6 (1985): 27–33.

exposition, to emphasize this attempt at a balanced synthesis of the other two approaches, I shall proceed in a bidirectional sort of way by alternating and counterposing theoretical and empirical considerations (sections 2 and 3 respectively),[13] and then by alternating within the latter what may be called the element of data collection and the element of analysis of data; this is aimed at ensuring both that my theorizing is not empty and that my "observing" is not blind.

Theoretical Considerations

Let us then proceed to an abstract conceptualization of *fallacious* arguments, or types of logical *fallaciousness*. I focus on these terms in part because they are cognate to the word fallacy but are weaker, in accordance with the preceding considerations. I could have chosen the term "invalidity,"[14] but only at the risk of confusion and deviance, given the traditional definition of validity. The term "unsound" would have also violated well-established conventions and created confusion, though admittedly the phrase "unsound inference" is less ambiguous and confusing than the attribute "unsound argument," and in fact it comes close to the notion of fallaciousness I am trying to articulate. The word "incorrectness" would be too weak as a description of the logical error involved, and too inclusive of all sorts of nonlogical error. By contrast the notion of fallaciousness seems quite inclusive of all the various degrees of logical error; it also seems to exclude automatically nonlogical errors, for, though it is very proper to speak of a fallacious belief (and thus apply the label to a single proposition, rather than to an argument), when this is done there is a connotation that the incorrectness of the belief is due largely to the impropriety of the reasons on which it is based.

It seems to me that fallaciousness is essentially the failure of one proposition to follow from others: that is, an argument is fallacious if and only if the conclusion does not follow from the premises. Starting with this basic definition, I plan to explore the main reasons why a conclusion might not follow from premises, and each such reason will yield a distinct type of fallaciousness. Notice that to formulate the problem this way immediately places us

---

13. Only section 2 is reprinted in this volume [Eds.].

14. This is the term I used in *Galileo and the Art of Reasoning*, 424–31, a term that misled me in the sense that I did not realize fully the pertinence of the theory of invalidity elaborated there to the theory of fallacy.

into the Strawsonian second-order level, or into what might be called the level of "reasoning about reasoning."[15] For we are then trying to think of the various ways in which we would go about justifying the claim that a particular conclusion does not follow from particular premises.

It might seem that this is a hopeless task since we are talking about the absence of a relationship between premises and conclusion, the relationship of consequence, and this relation either holds or it does not, and there is only one way of characterizing this absence. However, we are not trying to describe the different absences, but to catalogue the different grounds for the absence.

The typology we want should be analogous to, but different from and richer than, the twofold classification commonly discussed in elementary textbooks about how the justification of a claim may fail, or how the conclusion of an argument may turn out to be untenable: that is, the conclusion may not follow from the premises, or at least one of the premises may not itself be true. The difference is that we have already excluded the latter flaw, as textbooks themselves frequently are quick to do. The standard justification for this exclusion is that the individual truth or falsity of a proposition involves questions of its relationship to the world, and hence falsity of premises is a material, nonformal, or nonlogical flaw. However, it can be easily argued that the examination of the correspondence between a proposition and the world ordinarily reduces to the examination of the relationship between this proposition and others. Even if one accepts this, the intended distinction could still be made in terms of whether or not the proper relationship holds among the *given* propositions, that is, the statements explicitly made in the argument; we could then say that an argument is logically flawed if and only if the *stated* conclusion does not follow from the *stated* premises. But, assuming we are dealing with natural language argumentation, the question of whether or not the consequence holds usually cannot be decided without subjecting to various transformations the conclusion as originally stated and the premises as originally stated. This really amounts to an examination of the relationship between the original propositions and others, and though the latter may be relatively general principles involving various logical and linguistic concepts, they obviously have to be learned, and so it is not clear that logical evaluation as ordinarily understood can remain faithful to the idea of restricting oneself to relationships among the originally given propositions. However, what I want to conclude from this discussion is not that logical flaws or logical evaluations do not essentially involve questions of the interre-

15. Cf. Finocchiaro, *Galileo and the Art of Reasoning*, 301.

lations of propositions, but rather that we cannot totally exclude other propositions of an appropriate sort. Since what I am here calling fallaciousness is by definition the basic logical flaw of reasoning, then it is also true to say that fallaciousness must indeed involve interrelationships among propositions, but not merely among the propositions explicitly stated. So I am conceiving the failure of the conclusion to follow from the premises quite generally, in such a way that the failure may originate from the way that these propositions relate among themselves and/or to others.

Let us being with an analysis of the most familiar case of fallaciousness, invalidity. That is, it may be that the conclusion of an argument does not follow from the premises because it is possible for the premises to be true while the conclusion is false. Such possibility would normally be shown by constructing an argument with the same form or structure as the original one, but having obviously true premises and an obviously false conclusion. Such an argument is called a counterexample. So in this first type of fallaciousness the conclusion does not follow because an appropriate counterexample exists. Other well-known ways of describing the situation would be to say that the conclusion does not follow because it does not follow *necessarily*, or because it does not follow in virtue of the *form* of the argument, or because it does not follow ("analytically") in virtue of the meaning of the terms involved, or because it does not follow in virtue of the rules of *deductive* inference. Correspondingly, this first type of fallaciousness could be labeled formal, analytic, or deductive fallaciousness, or as we said earlier simply invalidity.

A second reason why one might be entitled to say that the conclusion does not follow from the premises is that it may not follow any more likely than some other specifiable proposition. In other words, in such a situation the critic produces another argument which has the same premises as the original argument but a different conclusion, and which appears of equal strength as the original. This occurs primarily with explanatory arguments whose conclusion is an explanation of what is stated in the premises, and the criticism amounts to providing an alternative explanation. Occasionally it may happen that the explanandum occurs because of both factors mentioned in the two conclusions, but the point is that a given explanation has no force if there is no reason to prefer it to some other alternative. This may be called explanatory fallaciousness; since it is obviously reminiscent of inductive incorrectness, it may also be called inductive fallaciousness. Still, since the connection between explanation and induction is problematic, it may be advisable to avoid the latter label.

These first two types of fallaciousness are relatively well known, and so what we have done here is primarily to embed well-known facts into a (presumably) novel conceptual framework. Our other types involve a greater departure from well-trodden paths.

To appreciate the third type of fallaciousness we need to underscore the fact that we are dealing with natural language argumentation as it occurs in ordinary circumstances, and that such arguments are always incompletely stated and have many missing assumptions or tacit presuppositions. With this in mind, it is easy to see that a reason why the conclusion does not follow from the premises may be that one of the presuppositions is false. What does this falsity mean in this context? I believe it really amounts to the existence of some ("sound") argument constructible in the context, whose conclusion is the denial of the presupposed assumption. Even the groundlessness of such a presupposition would create trouble for the original argument, at least as long as such a groundlessness is not merely asserted but demonstrated, that is, as long as one gives contextually sound arguments to show that there seems to be no good reason to assert the assumption in question. This third type may be called presuppositional fallaciousness.

Let us notice now that a pattern is beginning to emerge here. In fact, the first type was grounded on the construction of an appropriate counterexample, the second on the production of an alternative explanation, the third on the construction of a presuppositional criticism, and all three of these entities are arguments different from but appropriately related to the original. This pattern allows us to define a fourth type of fallaciousness where the conclusion does not follow because what does follow from the premises is some specifiable proposition inconsistent with it. Such a proposition would naturally be called a counterconclusion, and the new argument a counterargument. Normally such a counterargument will have as premises not only the premises of the original argument, but other propositions which are independently justifiable or contextually acceptable. For lack of a better term, this type may be called positive fallaciousness, to underscore the fact that the criticism here contributes something positive since it shows what does follow from the premises, and not merely what does not.

The fifth type of fallaciousness may be called semantical, and is meant to take care of equivocations. This is the case when the conclusion does not follow because the premises contain a term which has two meanings such that, if it is used in one sense, one of the premises is false (though they would imply the conclusion), whereas if the term is used in the other sense, the premises do not imply the conclusion (though admittedly the previously problematic premise becomes true); in short, in the context the conclusion cannot follow from true premises. The discussion below will show that semantical fallaciousness is very intimately related to presuppositional fallaciousness, since the semantical ambiguity in question is normally not a self-subsisting property of a term, but rather something that needs to be argued in the context on the basis of the inferential relationships affecting the term. Nevertheless, it is useful to have a special term for this phenomenon.

Finally, our sixth and last type refers to the flaw of begging the question and circularity. This too will be seen to involve presuppositional fallaciousness, but could be given the special name of persuasive fallaciousness. In such cases the conclusion does not *follow* from the premises because it *is* one of the premises.

We have thus defined six types of fallaciousness: formal, explanatory, presuppositional, positive, semantical, and persuasive. They all involve arguments whose conclusion may be said not to follow from the premises, and thus logical evaluations of the relationships among propositions; moreover, in each case the reason for the fallaciousness involves the construction of some other argument, or some other part of the original argument, to make the point.

9

The Pragma-Dialectical Approach to Fallacies

Frans H. Van Eemeren and Rob Grootendorst

Thanks to Hamblin's book *Fallacies* (1970), it is now common knowledge that the Standard Treatment of fallacies suffers from serious theoretical and practical defects. Many generally recognized fallacies clearly fall outside the scope of the standard definition of a fallacy as an argument that seems valid but is not valid: in some cases because there is not the slightest question of there being an argument (*many questions, ad baculum*); in other cases because, logically speaking, the argument in question is not invalid at all (*circular reasoning*); in still other cases (*ad verecundiam, ad populum*) because it would be missing the point completely to identify the error as one of invalidity.[1]

In our own efforts to offer an alternative to the Standard Treatment we started from the consideration that there is no reason to assume from the outset that all the fallacies are essentially logical errors. We were convinced that the single-minded preoccupation with the logical aspects of arguments should be rigorously abandoned. For the informal fallacies it had, after all, only led to largely unsatisfactory and unsystematic *ad hoc* analyses. In our opinion, the fallacies could be better understood if they were treated as faux pas of communication—as wrong moves in argumentative discourse. Viewed from

---

1. One of the most constructive reactions to Hamblin's devastating criticism of the Standard Treatment is provided by the works of Woods and Walton (1982a, 1989). Their remedy is to call on more sophisticated modern logics than just syllogistic, propositional, and predicate logic: every fallacy gets, so to speak, its own logic. Among the other constructive reactions are Finocchiaro (1981, 1987) and Hintikka (1987).

this perspective, a fallacy is a hindrance or impediment to the resolution of a disagreement, and the specific nature of each of the fallacies depends on the exact manner in which it interferes with the resolution process. This was our starting point in setting about to develop a general and comprehensive approach to argumentation that covers the whole domain of the fallacies.

Some Basic Characteristics of the Pragma-Dialectical Approach

Argumentation, being a phenomenon of verbal communication, should be studied as an integral part of the conduct of argumentative discourse. Its quality and possible flaws are to be measured against criteria that are appropriate for determining the reasonableness of such discourse. The study of argumentation should therefore be construed as a special branch of linguistic pragmatics in which descriptive and normative perspectives on argumentative discourse are methodically integrated. Contrary to what some formal and informal logicians seem to think, this study cannot be based, unilaterally, on mere intellectual idealization; and contrary to what some discourse and conversation analysts seem to think, neither can it be based on mere empirical observation.[2] Both the limitations of the nonempirical regimentation exemplified in normative modern logic and the limitations of the noncritical explanation exemplified in contemporary descriptive linguistics are to be systematically overcome. This calls for the development of an integrating and coherent research program in which normative and descriptive insights are to be closely interwoven.

The pragma-dialectical research program is based on the assumption that, on the one hand, a philosophical ideal of reasonableness must be developed and, starting from this ideal, a theoretical model for acceptable argumentative discourse. On the other hand, argumentative reality must be investigated empirically, so that it becomes clear how argumentative discourse is in fact conducted. Then the normative and the descriptive dimensions must be linked together by developing instruments that make it possible to analyze

---

2. Biro and Siegel (1992) are among the most outstanding protagonists of a purely normative approach; whereas C. A. Willard, *Argumentation and the Social Grounds of Knowledge* (Tuscaloosa: University of Alabama Press, 1983), and *A Theory of Argumentation* (Tuscaloosa: University of Alabama Press, 1989), is a prominent advocate of a purely descriptive approach.

argumentative practice from the perspective of the projected ideal of reasonable argumentative discourse. Finally, the problems that occur in practice must be systematically diagnosed and it must be determined how they can be tackled methodically. The pragma-dialectical research program therefore includes a philosophical, a theoretical, an empirical, an analytical, and a practical component.

In the implementation of the pragma-dialectical research program, the study of argumentation is approached with four basic metatheoretical premises, each of which represents a point of departure from other contemporary perspectives. It is characteristic of the pragma-dialectical approach that the subject matter under investigation is being externalized, functionalized, socialized and dialectified. What do these meta-theoretical labels mean?

Externalization

Making an argument pragmatically presupposes a standpoint and at least the potential for opposition to that standpoint. In order to find out whether or not a person's opinions make sense and whether or not his reasoning holds water, he must submit them to public scrutiny. While beliefs, inferences, interpretation, and so on certainly underlie argumentation (and other discursive activities), the way in which the argument is expressed and proceeds is channeled by a system of public commitment and accountability. The motives people have for holding a position may sometimes be different from the grounds they will offer and accept in its defense. What is at stake in the study of argumentation is not so much the psychological dispositions of the arguers, but the positions to which the parties can be held committed in the discourse, whether these positions have been expressed directly or indirectly. This is why the pragma-dialectical approach to argumentation concentrates on externalized commitments.

Socialization

In approaches that are merely concerned with argument "as a product" arguments are typically seen as an externalization of an individual thought process, abstracting elements of reasoning such as "major premise," "minor premise," and "conclusion" from the communicative process in which they occur. Then, the central question becomes one of assessing whether and how these elements hold together to validate the arguer's position. But argumentation does not consist in a single individual privately drawing a conclusion: it is part of a discourse procedure whereby two or more individuals try to arrive at an agreement. The collaborative way in which the protagonist of a standpoint in the fundamentally dialogical interaction responds to the—real or projected—questions, doubts, objections, and counterclaims of an antagonist is reflected in the argumentation. This is why in the pragma-dialectical approach argumentation is put in the social context of a problem-solving process.

Functionalization

Not only in formal and informal logical approaches to arguments, but also in studies of fallacies and practical argumentation, argumentation is often described in purely structural terms. Although structural descriptions have much to recommend them, they tend to ignore the functional rationale of the structural design of the discourse. Argumentation arises in response to, or anticipation of, disagreement, and particular lines of justification are fitted to realize this purpose in a particular case. The need for argumentation, its structure, and the requirements of justification are all adapted to the opposition, doubts, objections, and counterclaims that have to be met. An adequate description and evaluation of argumentation can only be given if the purpose for which the argumentation is put forward in the interaction is duly taken into account. This is why the pragma-dialectical approach to argumentation concentrates on its function in managing the resolution of disagreements.

Dialectification

Discourse and conversation analysts generally restrict themselves to describing argumentation as it occurs, without regard for how it ought to occur if it is to be appropriate for resolving a difference of opinion. The argumentation is appropriate only if it is capable of accommodating the critical reactions of a rational judge. In order to determine whether this is the case, the argumentation is to be viewed as part of a critical discussion conducted in accordance with a problem-valid and conventionally valid discussion procedure.[3] The problem-validity of a discussion procedure depends on its efficiency in achiev-

3. For the notions of problem-validity and conventional validity, see E. M. Barth and E. C. W. Krabbe, *From Axiom to Dialogue: A Philosophical Study of Logics and Argumentation* (Berlin: De Gruyter, 1982), 21–22; and for a similar distinction R. Crawshay-Williams, *Methods and Criteria of Reasoning: An Inquiry into the Structure of Controversy* (London: Routledge and Kegan Paul, 1957), 175.

ing a resolution to the disagreement and its efficacy in furthering the resolution process while avoiding "false" resolutions. The conventional validity depends on the intersubjective acceptability of the procedure. The procedure provides a set of standards for rational judgment. This is why in the pragma-dialectical approach argumentation is put in the dialectical perspective of a critical discussion.

In the pragma-dialectical approach, externalization, socialization, functionalization, and dialectification of the notion of argumentation are realized by making use of pragmatic insight from discourse and conversation analysis and dialectical insight from critical rationalist philosophy and dialogical logic.[4] Dialectification is achieved by viewing argumentation in the perspective of a regulated critical discussion aimed at resolving a difference of opinion. Functionalization is realized by defining argumentation as a complex speech act that can only serve its purpose adequately if certain identity and correctness conditions are fulfilled. Socialization is a result of putting argumentation in the collaborative context of an interaction between two or more discussants. Finally, externalization is accomplished by identifying argumentation with the specific commitments created by the performance of the speech act of arguing in a certain context of disagreement.[5] As a matter of course, notions referring to other components of argumentative discourse, such as standpoints, are treated similarly.

Fallacies and the Rules for Critical Discussion

In the pragma-dialectical approach, argumentation is treated as part of a reasonable argumentative discourse aimed at resolving a difference of opinion. In implementing the research program, it should therefore be clarified what this involves. For this purpose, in the theoretical component, the

4. The pragmatic insight we are referring to is primarily gained from J. L. Austin, *How to Do Things with Words* (Cambridge: Harvard University Press, 1962); and J. R. Searle, *Speech Acts: An Essay in the Philosophy of Language* (Cambridge: Cambridge University Press, 1969) and *Expression and Meaning: Studies in the Theory of Speech Acts* (Cambridge: Cambridge University Press, 1979); and H. P. Grice, "Logic and conversation," in *Syntax and Semantics*, vol. 3, *Speech Acts*, edited by P. Cole and J. L. Morgan (New York: Academic Press, 1975), 43–58. Among the providers of fundamental dialectical insight are Crawshay-Williams, *Methods and Criteria*, and Barth and Krabbe, *From Axiom to Dialogue*; also K. R. Popper, *Objective Knowledge: An Evolutionary Approach* (Oxford: Clarendon Press, 1972), and *Conjectures and Refutations: The Growth of Scientific Knowledge* (London: Routledge and Kegan Paul, 1974).

5. For a more elaborate exposition, see van Eemeren and Grootendorst (1984, 7–18).

critical-rationalist philosophy of reasonableness is given shape in an ideal model of a critical discussion.[6] The model specifies the various stages that are to be distinguished in the resolution process and the verbal moves that are integral parts of each of these stages. The principles authorizing the distribution of the verbal moves over the consecutive stages are accounted for in a set of rules for the performance of speech acts. Taken together, these rules constitute a theoretical definition of a critical discussion.

The four stages that are analytically distinguished in the resolution process are the confrontation stage, the opening stage, the argumentation stage, and the concluding stage. In the confrontation stage a difference of opinion presents itself through the confrontation between a standpoint and (real or imagined) nonacceptance of this standpoint. In the opening stage the parties to the dispute are identified as well as their apparent premises—procedural or otherwise. In the argumentation stage the party that acts as the protagonist defends his standpoint methodically against the critical reactions of the antagonist. In the concluding stage the parties establish what the result of the discussion is. By specifying a critical discussion in this way, a heuristic, analytical, and critical framework is created for dealing with argumentative discourse.

In a critical discussion, the protagonist and the antagonist of the standpoint at issue must in all stages of the discussion observe all the rules that are instrumental to resolving the dispute. For the elucidation of the pragma-dialectical analysis of fallacies aimed for in this article we offer the simplified and nontechnical version of the rules introduced in van Eemeren and Grootendorst (1992a), where the rules are reduced to a succinct recapitulation of ten basic rules:[7]

1. Parties must not prevent each other from advancing standpoints or casting doubt on standpoints.
2. A party that advances a standpoint is obliged to defend it if the other party asks him to do so.

6. For a critical-rationalist philosophy of reasonableness, see both works of Popper referred to in note 4.

7. In van Eemeren and Grootendorst (1984), a full exposition has been given of the pragma-dialectical version of these rules. There, the rules that are constitutive for a critical discussion are stated in terms of the speech acts to be performed by the parties who are engaged in the resolution process. It is worth noting that observance of the rules can only constitute a sufficient condition for resolving a difference of opinion in conjunction with the fulfillment of the appropriate "higher-order conditions" pertaining to the attitudes and dispositions of the discussants and the circumstances of discussion. See F. H. van Eemeren, R. Grootendorst, S. Jacobs, and S. Jackson, *Reconstructing Argumentative Discourse* (Tuscaloosa: University of Alabama Press, 1993).

3. A party's attack on a standpoint must relate to the standpoint that has indeed been advanced by the other party.

4. A party may defend his standpoint only by advancing argumentation relating to that standpoint.

5. A party may not falsely present something as a premise that has been left unexpressed by the other party or deny a premise that he himself has left implicit.

6. A party may not falsely present a premise as an accepted starting point nor deny a premise representing an accepted starting point.

7. A party may not regard a standpoint as conclusively defended if the defense does not take place by means of an appropriate argumentation scheme that is correctly applied.

8. In his argumentation, a party may only use arguments that are logically valid or capable of being validated by making explicit one or more unexpressed premises.

9. A failed defense of a standpoint must result in the party that put forward the standpoint retracting it, and a conclusive defense of the standpoint must result in the other party retracting his doubt about the standpoint.

10. A party must not use formulations that are insufficiently clear or confusingly ambiguous and he must interpret the other party's formulations as carefully and accurately as possible.

In principle, each of these ten discussion rules constitutes a separate and different standard or norm for critical discussion. Any infringement of one or more of the rules, whichever party commits it and at whatever stage in the discussion, is a possible threat to the resolution of a difference of opinion and must therefore be regarded as an incorrect discussion move. In the pragma-dialectic approach, fallacies are analyzed as such incorrect discussion moves in which a discussion rule has been violated. A *fallacy* is then defined as a speech act that prejudices or frustrates efforts to resolve a difference of opinion and the use of the term "fallacy" is thus systematically connected with the rules for critical discussion.

In this approach, as soon as fallacies in argumentative discourse are discussed, the discourse is treated as if it were aimed at resolving a difference of opinion. In practice, a discourse will hardly ever be completely resolution-oriented—nor completely non–resolution-oriented, for that matter. For a realistic appreciation of the scope of the pragma-dialectical approach to fallacies, it is important to note that the norms provided by the rules for critical discussion apply only where and insofar as the discourse concerned is indeed aimed at resolving a difference of opinion.[8] Although it is often clear, or can be reasonably assumed, that this is—or is not—the case, it is not always obvious. This is one of the reasons why a discourse can only be fully and methodically screened for fallacies if it is first adequately analyzed.

As it occurs in practice, even a discourse that is clearly argumentative will in many respects not correspond to the ideal model of a critical discussion— or at least not explicitly, completely, and immediately. In many cases, the how's and why's of the divergent forms of argumentative reality can be easily explained with the help of some empirical insight and in a great many cases the differences can even be explained away. At any rate, it would certainly not do if all verbal behavior that does not seem to agree with the model was automatically declared defective just like that. The discourse as it has been brought to the fore can only be evaluated adequately if one has first accurately determined what it actually conveys.

An analysis undertaken from a pragma-dialectical perspective is aimed at reconstructing all those and only those elements in the discourse that are pertinent to the resolution process. Such a resolution-oriented reconstruction concentrates on identifying the speech acts that play a potential part in bringing a difference of opinion to an adequate conclusion. In this endeavor, speech acts that are immaterial to the resolution process are ignored, implicit elements are made explicit, indirect speech acts are restated as direct speech acts, and unintentional swerves from the resolution path are rearranged.[9] By pointing out which speech acts are relevant in the consecutive stages of the resolution process, the ideal model of a critical discussion gives specific heuristic direction as to which speech acts are to be considered in the reconstruction process. Thus, the model is a valuable tool for accomplishing a systematic analysis.

It is, of course, crucial that the proposed analysis of a discourse in terms of a critical discussion is indeed justified. The reconstruction should be faithful to the commitments that may rightly be ascribed to the actors on the basis of their contributions to the discourse. In order not to "overinterpret" the speech act potential of the discourse, a sensitivity must be maintained to the details of the presentation, the general rules for communication, and the specific

8. The pragma-dialectical identification of fallacies is in fact always conditional: only if it is a correct interpretation that the discourse is aimed at resolving a difference of opinion can it be maintained that a fallacy has occurred.

9. For the transformations of deletion, addition, substitution, and permutation carried out in a pragma-dialectical reconstruction, see van Eemeren, Grootendorst, Jackson and Jacobs, *Reconstructing Argumentative Discourse*, chap. 4.

contextual constraints inherent in the speech event concerned.[10] In those exceptional cases where there is really no clue whatsoever as to whether a speech act is intended to contribute to the resolution process, it is the most charitable solution to opt for a "maximally dialectical analysis" and interpret the utterance as a constructive move in a critical discussion, thus deciding for an analysis "for reason's sake."[11]

When it comes to the detection of fallacies, the pragma-dialectical analysis proceeds in a number of steps. An utterance must first be interpreted as a particular kind of speech act. After it has been established that the speech act concerned has indeed been performed in a context of discourse aimed at resolving a difference of opinion, it must be determined whether the performance of this speech act agrees with the rules for critical discussion. If the speech act proves to be a violation of one of the norms pertaining to a particular stage of the resolution process, it must be determined what kind of violation it entails. Which specific criterion for satisfying the norm has not been met? Only after this question has been answered can it be determined which fallacy has been committed.

Overview of Violations of Rules for Critical Discussion

There are many things that can go wrong in resolving a difference of opinion by argumentative discourse. We shall now turn our attention to a discussion of the most important violations of the rules for a critical discussion. The list of violations we will explain is by no means complete, but it gives one a fair impression of the great variety of fallacious moves that might be detected in the various stages of an argumentative discourse that has been analyzed as a critical discussion.

Rule 1 can be violated—at the confrontation stage—in various ways, both by the protagonist and the antagonist. A discussant can impose certain restrictions on the standpoints that may be advanced or called into question; he can also deny a certain opponent the right to advance the standpoint he likes to

10. At this juncture, insight from conversation and discourse analysis can be beneficial. The empirical research augmenting the analyst's intuitions so as to go beyond a naive reading of the discourse may vary from quantitative measuring to qualitative studies. See van Eemeren, Grootendorst, Jackson and Jacobs, *Reconstructing Argumentative Discourse*.

11. See F. H. van Eemeren, "For Reason's Sake: Maximal Argumentative Analysis of Discourse," in F. H. van Eemeren, R. Grootendorst, J. A. Blair, and C. A. Willard (1987a, 201–16).

advance or to criticize the standpoint he likes to criticize. Violations of the first kind mean that certain standpoints are in fact excluded from the discussion or that particular standpoints are declared sacrosanct, so that the opponent is prohibited from casting doubt on them and they are rendered immune to criticism. Violations of the second kind are directed to the opponent personally and aim at eliminating him as a serious partner in the discussion. This may be done by putting pressure on him by threatening him with sanctions (*argumentum ad baculum*) or by playing on his feelings of compassion (*argumentum ad misericordiam*), but also by discrediting his expertise, impartiality, integrity, or credibility (*argumentum ad hominem*).

Rule 2 can be violated—at the opening stage—by the protagonist by *evading* or *shifting the burden of proof*. In the first case, he attempts to create the impression that there is no need to defend his standpoint and no point in calling it into question by presenting it as self-evident, giving a personal guarantee of the rightness of the standpoint (special variant of *argumentum ad verecundiam*) or immunizing the standpoint against criticism. In the second case, the protagonist challenges the opponent to show that the protagonist's standpoint is wrong (special variant of *argumentum ad ignorantiam*) or that the opposite standpoint is right.

Rule 3 can be violated—at all stages—by the protagonist or the antagonist in a "mixed" discussion (in which both parties have a standpoint to defend) by imputing a fictitious standpoint to the other party or distorting the other party's standpoint (*straw man*). The first effect can be achieved by emphatically advancing the opposite as one's own standpoint or by creating an imaginary opponent; the second by taking utterances out of context, oversimplification (ignoring nuances or qualifications), or exaggeration (absolutization or generalization).

Rule 4 can be violated—at the argumentation stage—by the protagonist in two ways: first, by putting forward argumentation that does not refer to the standpoint under discussion as advanced at the confrontation stage (*irrelevant argumentation* or *ignoratio elenchi*); second, by defending the standpoint using nonargumentative means of persuasion. Among the latter are playing on the emotions of the audience (special variant of *argumentum ad populum*) and parading one's own qualities (special variant of *argumentum ad verecundiam*). If the audience's positive or negative emotions (such as prejudice) are exploited, *pathos* replaces *logos*; for this reason, such violations of Rule 4 are sometimes called *pathetic fallacies*. If the protagonist attempts to get his standpoint accepted by the opponent just because of the authority he has in the eyes of the audience because of his expertise, credibility, integrity, or other qualities, *ethos* replaces *logos*; for this reason, such violations of Rule 4 are sometimes called *ethical fallacies*.

Rule 5 can be violated—at the argumentation stage—by the protagonist by *denying an unexpressed premise* or by the antagonist by *distorting an unexpressed premise*. By denying an unexpressed premise ("I never said *that*"), the protagonist in effect tries to evade the responsibility assumed in his argumentation by denying his commitment to an unexpressed premise that is correctly reconstructed as such. The antagonist is guilty of the fallacy of distorting an unexpressed premise if he has produced a reconstruction of a protagonist's unexpressed premise that goes beyond the pragmatic optimum to which the protagonist can actually be held, given the verbal and nonverbal context of the discussion.

Rule 6 can be violated—at the argumentation stage—by the protagonist by falsely presenting something as a common starting point or by the antagonist by denying a premise representing a common starting point. By falsely presenting something as a common starting point, the protagonist tries to *evade the burden of proof*; the techniques used for this purpose include falsely presenting a premise as self-evident, wrapping up a proposition in a presupposition of a question (*many questions*), hiding away a premise in an unexpressed premise, and advancing argumentation that amounts to the same thing as the standpoint (*petitio principii*, also called *begging the question* or *circular reasoning*). By denying a premise representing a common starting point, the antagonist in fact denies the protagonist the opportunity of defending his standpoint *ex concessis*, which is a denial of a *conditio sine qua non* for all successful argumentation.

Rule 7 can be violated—at the argumentation stage—by the protagonist by relying on an inappropriate argumentation scheme or using an appropriate argumentation scheme incorrectly. The various violations can be classified according to the three main categories of argumentation schemes: symptomatic, similarity, and instrumental argumentation. Symptomatic argumentation is being used incorrectly if, for instance, a standpoint is presented as right because an authority says it is right (special variant of *argumentum ad verecundiam*) or because everybody thinks it is right (populistic variant of *argumentum ad populum* and, as such, also a special variant of *argumentum ad verecundiam*), or if a standpoint is a generalization based upon observations that are not representative or not sufficient (*hasty generalization* or *secundum quid*). Similarity argumentation is being used incorrectly, if, for instance, in making an analogy, the conditions for a correct comparison are not fulfilled (*false analogy*). And, finally, instrumental (or causal) argumentation is being used incorrectly if, for instance, a descriptive standpoint is being rejected because of its undesired consequences (*argumentum ad consequentiam*); a cause-effect relation is inferred from the mere observation that two events take place one after the other (*post hoc ergo propter hoc*); or it is unjustifiably suggested that by taking a proposed course of action one will be going from bad to worse (*slippery slope*).[12]

Rule 8 can be violated—at the argumentation stage—by the protagonist in a variety of ways. Some logical invalidities occur with a certain regularity and are often not immediately recognized. Among them are violations that have to do with confusing a necessary condition with a sufficient condition (or vice versa) in arguments with an "If . . . , then . . ." premise (*affirming the consequent, denying the antecedent*); other violations amount to erroneously attributing a (relative or structure-dependent) property of a whole to its constituent parts or vice versa (*fallacies of division* and *composition*).

Rule 9 can be violated—at the closing stage—by the protagonist by concluding that a standpoint is true just because it has been successfully defended (*making an absolute of the success of the defense*) or by the antagonist by concluding from the fact that it has not been proved that something *is* the case, that it is *not* the case, or from the fact that something has not been proved *not* to be the case, that it *is* the case (*making an absolute of the failure of the defense* or special variant of *argumentum ad ignorantiam*). In making an absolute of the success of the defense, the protagonist makes a double mistake: first, he ascribes to the common starting points the unjustified status of established facts whose truth is beyond discussion; and, second, in doing so, he erroneously invests his successful defense with an objective rather than (inter)subjective status. In making an absolute of the failure of the defense, the antagonist makes a double mistake as well: first, he confuses the roles of antagonist and protagonist; and, second, he erroneously assumes that a discussion must always end in a victory for either a positive or a negative standpoint, so that not having the positive standpoint automatically means adopting the negative standpoint, and vice versa, thereby ignoring the possibility of entertaining a zero standpoint.

Rule 10 can be violated—at all stages—by the protagonist or the antagonist by misusing unclarity (*fallacy of unclarity*) or misusing ambiguity (*fallacy of ambiguity, equivocation, amphiboly*). Various sorts of unclarity can occur: unclarity resulting from the structuring of the text, from implicitness, from

---

12. For a discussion of the three main categories of argumentation schemes, see van Eemeren and Grootendorst (1992a, 94–102).

indefiniteness, from unfamiliarity, from vagueness, and so on. Again, there are various sorts of ambiguity: referential ambiguity, syntactic ambiguity, semantic ambiguity, and so on. The fallacy of ambiguity is closely related to the fallacy of unclarity; it can occur on its own but also in combination with other fallacies (such as the fallacies of *composition* and *division*).

Comparison with Other Approaches

This brief overview may suffice to show that the pragma-dialectical analysis of the traditional fallacies as violations of the rules for critical discussion is more systematic than the Standard Treatment. Instead of being given *ad hoc* explanations, all the fallacies fall under one or more of the rules for critical discussion. A comparison between the violations of the pragma-dialectical rules and the traditional categories also shows that the pragma-dialectical analysis is more refined. Fallacies that were only nominally lumped together are now either shown to have something in common or they are clearly distinguished, and genuinely related fallacies that were separated are brought together. Distinguishing two variants of the *argumentum ad populum* as a violation of Rule 4 or 7 makes, for instance, clear that these variants are, in fact, *not* of the same kind. Analyzing one particular variant of the *argumentum ad verecundiam* and one particular variant of the *argumentum ad populum* as a violation of the *same* Rule 7 makes clear that seen from the perspective of resolving a difference of opinion these variants *are* of the same kind.

The overview also reveals that the pragma-dialectical approach makes it possible to analyze thus far unrecognized and unnamed "new" obstacles to resolving a difference of opinion: *declaring a standpoint sacrosanct* (violation of Rule 1), *evading the burden of proof* by *immunizing a standpoint against criticism* (violation of Rule 2) or *falsely presenting a premise as self-evident* (violation of Rule 6), *denying an unexpressed premise* (violation of Rule 5), *denying an accepted starting point* (violation of Rule 6), *falsely presenting something as a common starting point* (violation of Rule 6), *making an absolute of the success of the defense* (violation of Rule 9), and so on.

Rather than considering the fallacies as belonging to an unstructured list of nominal categories, which happen to have come down to us from the past, as in the Standard Treatment, or considering all fallacies to be violations of one and the same (validity) norm, as in the logico-centric approaches, the pragma-dialectical approach differentiates a functional variety of norms. A whole series of norms other than just logical validity are taken into account, depending on the rule that has been violated. The logical norm of validity gets its proper (and limited) place in the argumentation stage.

The pragma-dialectic approach is both broader and at the same time more specific than the traditional logico-centric approaches, including the Standard Treatment. The scope is broader because at any stage of a critical discussion all possible violations of a discussion rule are treated as fallacies—not just the "logical" errors. The greater specificity ensues from the fact that fallacies are systematically linked to the (non)resolution of a difference of opinion, which at the same time makes it possible to explain why something is a fallacy.

Analyzing fallacies systematically from the perspective of a well-defined theory of argumentation, set up as a set of rules, is not a unique feature of the pragma-dialectical approach but it is also promoted in the formal dialectics of Barth and Krabbe (1982).[13] The first attempt to analyze a fallacy, *ad hominem*, within a formal-dialectical framework is reported in Barth and Martens (1977).[14] According to Barth and Martens, a theory of rational argumentation must be consequently envisaged as a finite set of production rules for generating rational arguments. Each individual rule states a sufficient condition for the rationality of a generated argument: all (and only) arguments that can be generated by one or more of these rules are rational arguments. Fallacies can be analyzed—"unmasked" in the words of Barth and Martens—as argumentative moves that can *not* be generated by the production rules (Barth and Martens 1977, 96).[15]

A first difference with the pragma-dialectical rules is that the latter are not formulated as production rules for generating rational arguments, but as conditions for resolving differences of opinion. Each pragma-dialectical rule refers to a necessary condition for resolving a difference of opinion. Only observing all the rules constitutes a sufficient condition. A second difference is that the pragma-dialectical rules are not primarily about the use of logical constants in a formal dialogue; they are rather about the performance of

13. In several aspects, the pragma-dialectical approach links up with formal dialectics. Maintaining the term *dialectics* points to the agreement in general objectives, replacing *formal* by *pragma* (from *pragmatic*) to the differences in orientation. See note 3 above.

14. In fact, in Barth and Martens (1977), *ad hominem* is not treated as a fallacy but as an admissible discussion move "ex concessis."

15. Barth and Martens do not undertake any attempt to analyze the various fallacious variants of *ad hominem*. This is no wonder: Lorenzen's dialogue rules on which their analysis is based relate, after all, only to the use of logical constants such as "if . . . then . . . ," "and," "or," "not," "all," and "none."

speech acts in the various stages of a critical discussion aimed at resolving a difference of opinion. All aspects of a critical discussion fall within the scope of the pragma-dialectical theory, not only the logical aspects. Owing to their more encompassing pragmatic orientation toward the performance of speech acts, the pragma-dialectical rules link up better with real-life argumentative discourse and are also better equipped for dealing adequately with the awkward informal fallacies.[16]

Where the peculiarities of ordinary argumentative discourse are, in the logico-approaches, either completely ignored or treated as "infirmities" of natural language, the pragma-dialectical approach takes all these phenomena, notably implicitness and indirectness, systematically into account.[17] In principle, the rules for critical discussion provide all the norms that play a role in resolving a difference of opinion. The logico-centric approaches make use of just one norm: formal validity, in one sense or another. The pragma-dialectical rules amount to ten different norms that not only cover formal (in)validity but also many other things that can go wrong in argumentative discourse.[18]

16. The crucial difference between the opponent's concessions in a formal dialogue and the protagonist's arguments in a critical discussion shows how much more distant formal dialectics is from argumentation in ordinary discourse. See van Eemeren and Grootendorst (1984, 13–15).

17. Interpretation problems in the literature on fallacies are generally ignored or trivialized. Furthermore, no distinction is made between norms defining the various types of fallacy and criteria for deciding whether a certain verbal move is indeed to be regarded as a perpetration of a particular type of fallacy.

18. For a more detailed illustration of our position, see our treatment of the *argumentum ad hominem* in Part III of this volume.

10

Failures of Relevance: A Rhetorical View

Charles Arthur Willard

This essay will be a rhetorical exercise. It will try to define areas of collaboration between informal logic and rhetoric. It will *not* try to define these fields by their irreducible principles, then ask what is left in common among their nouns. Instead it will ask how the two fields might define themselves so as to engage in common ventures.

One venture concerns what has been called—since John Dewey's time—the *crisis of liberal democracy.* The most familiar version of this crisis concerns the low state of public discourse—its commodification, its reduction to the techniques of public relations and advertising. These corruptions suggest a common pedagogical project—one in keeping with Dewey's view of the classroom as a public sphere in microcosm. Many would call this pedagogy *criticism*: the analysis and appraisal of public discourse. And criticism, for many, is necessarily interdisciplinary. Ralph Johnson (1987) has said that fallacy theory *is* a theory of criticism; in this essay I show that it is a coupling point—a common issue agenda—that brings rhetoric and informal logic together.

Another venture is a precondition of the common pedagogy—and a classic case of disciplinary convergence. Fallacy theory, it seems to me, is groping its way toward a theory of *relevance.* Where Hamblin, for instance, once recognized that not all *ad hominems* are invalid, but added that it wasn't clear when they are and why, Woods and Walton (1977a; Walton 1987a) are clarifying the fallacy's relevance conditions by focusing on pragmatic inconsistencies between claims and actions. This pragmatic focus is arguably a rhetorical turn. Rhetoric, as an art and discipline, is *about* relevance—about the *fit* between discourse and context and between intention and utterance. So we have, as Humphrey Bogart said, "the beginning of a beautiful friendship." And my aim here is to sketch a rhetorical view of fallacies that will take this friendship a step further.[1]

I am using the word *relevance* to mean *pertinence, aptness, applicability,* or *connection* (and thus ignoring the technical issues that divide, say, Grice's relevance maxim, Sperber and Wilson's propositional theory, and Jacobs and Jackson's view of pragmatic relevance).[2] *Relevance*, for my purposes, is a general term for the *fit* between discourse and context and intention and utterance. And the determination of relevance, as Johnson argues,[3] requires the study of argumentation in actual situations.

The new importance of relevance may not be immediately apparent, for fallacy theory is in considerable ferment. The confrontation between the Standard Treatment and The Standard Critique is still something of a ritual kill in the literature. There is little agreement about how to explain exceptions to fallacies or cases in which acts condemned by one theory might be endorsed by another. And some fallacies (*post hoc, division*) have not been—and perhaps cannot be—treated as failures of relevance.

Still, the range of phenomena seen as germane to fallaciousness has steadily grown. Syllogistic, propositional, and predicate logics have given way to inductive logic, plausible reasoning, and game theory (Woods and Walton 1982a). Procedural flaws now figure coequally with informal logical errors.[4] And some believe that dialectical glitches—rule breaches—should replace inferential errors entirely (Hintikka 1987). Informal logic thus seems to be moving away from the focus on *arguments that seem valid but aren't* toward

---

1. In *A Theory of Argumentation* (Tuscaloosa: University of Alabama Press, 1989), I advocated reserving the term *fallacy* for logical mistakes and using the vocabulary of pragmatics and argumentation to describe the moral and procedural errors fallacy theorists have lately been addressing. My thinking had to do with properly identifying the sources of authority for critics' claims. Still I concede that any number of pragmatic antics—strategic moves inside organizations, propaganda ploys, and advertising techniques—may be profitably characterized as fallacious; and I concede that there may be pedagogical reasons for developing a fallacy theory relevant to the messages most common in daily life.

2. See the discussion in John Woods, "Apocalyptic Relevance," *Argumentation* 6 (1992): 189–202; and Scott Jacobs and Sally Jackson, "Relevance and Digressions in Argumentative Discussion: A Pragmatic Approach," *Argumentation* 6 (1992): 161–76.

3. Fallacies, for Johnson, are failures of either relevance, acceptability of premises, or sufficiency.

4. Frans H. van Eemeren and Rob Grootendorst (1989). The most comprehensive statement of the pragma-dialectical view appears in van Eemeren and Grootendorst (1992a).

a view of fallaciousness as context-dependent. The *ad hominem* is the most famous case (depending on details, personal attacks may be relevant to matters at hand), but a recent special issue of *Argumentation*[5] describes relevance (defined in a dozen or so ways) as the pivotal failure in (to name a few) the *ad misericordiam, ad populum, ad baculum, ad ignorantiam,* and *ad verecundiam* as well as an array of procedural errors, rule violations, and collaborative malfunctions.

Rhetoric and Philosophy

I will begin with some remarks about the historically uneasy relations between philosophy and rhetoric. This may serve both to clarify the term *rhetoric* and to specify the range of concerns in a rhetorical view of fallacies. Then I will take something of a Darwinian approach to a single fallacy—the *ad populum*—to trace its evolution from a primitive proscription of persuasion to a more nuanced stance toward public discourse.

Discourse across disciplinary boundaries always runs the risk of misunderstanding. We may be wrong in thinking that we are speaking the same language—and end up like a mental health project involving psychiatrists, psychologists, and sociologists who thought they had a common view of *aggression*. After analyzing their data, however, they decided that the only thing they could agree on was that *aggression* is a "nice word."[6]

Some informal logicians might not even agree that *rhetoric* is a nice word. They may see it as trivial grandiloquence, or as a loose label for the shenanigans of demogogues: pandering, manipulating, exploiting. Others may think that persuasion violates Kant's injunction against treating people as means. And still others may equate rhetoric with the domineering master narratives feared by poststructuralists.

These qualms go back to Plato, who called rhetoric a "knack akin to cookery," yet thought it so dangerous that he restricted its use to the Philosopher Kings, who were to know the truth and then employ the means necessary to dupe the public. The Athenians were too primitive to grasp the truth, so the Philosopher Kings were to serve up what can fairly be called false consciousness in service of the truth. Plato, to put it mildly, was no populist.

5. *Argumentation* 6 (1992).
6. Julie Thompson Klein, *Interdisciplinarity* (Detroit: Wayne State University Press, 1990), 127.

Aristotle had an equally unflattering view of "the depraved character of the audience," but he fathered a very different tradition. "Rhetoric," he wrote, "is the counterpart of dialectic," the next resort in politics and law when reasonable discussion ends in disagreement.[7] It is an art used by everyone, since human affairs turn on uncertainties, and an art open to ethical governance. Rhetoric, in this view, is the theory, practice, and criticism of persuasion; and many in the communication field, though there are few Aristotelians among them, still accept that general view—including within it studies of the literary structure of scientific argument, or the study of the constitution of discourses. In this view, the morality of rhetoric comes down to pragmatic motives and foreseeable side effects: Hitler and Churchill, Goebbels and Gandhi were equally rhetoricians, but not equally moral. Totalitarianism and liberalism are equally rhetorics, but not equal rhetorics.

The theory, practice, and criticism of persuasion is a pivotal part of any viable attempt to reform public discourse; and fallacy theory may play an important role. Or at least fallacy theory of a certain kind: it won't do to hold public discourse up to hyperbolic ideals of pristine logic, or to hold the present accountable for a nostalgic vision of antiquity. Fallacy theory needs to be less gestural—less Platonic, if you will—and more attuned to the contexts in which discourse functions.

This pragmatic or rhetorical turn might be traced in any number of fallacies, but for brevity I will focus on the *ad populum*. This fallacy has obvious pertinence to public discourse. And it is apt for the disciplinary background it conjures up. For reasons that will be clear, how we read the *ad populum* is a litmus test of whether philosophers and rhetoricians can fraternize. I will start by describing a rhetorical version of the *ad populum* and then turn to the views of fallacy theorists that are (arguably) converging with it.

A Reformulation of the *Ad Populum*

A rhetorical view of the *ad populum* might locate the fallacy in the use of emotional appeals or aesthetic images that distract the persuadee from reflective thinking about the arguments being made. There is evidence, for in-

7. Aristotle, *Rhetoric*, translated by W. Rhys Roberts, in *The Works of Aristotle*, edited by David Ross (Oxford: Clarendon Press, 1966), 1354a1.

stance, that aesthetic effects disrupt counterarguing.[8] Music and visual imagery in television commercials divert attention from argumentatively weak messages yet leave enduring general impressions. And there is evidence that when persuadees find a topic personally irrelevant, they are vulnerable to *peripheral route persuasion*.[9] It is *easier* to accept influence from ethos, slogans, or other oversimple decision heuristics than to engage in issue-relevant thinking.

Notice that distraction and peripheral route persuasion are not *masquerading* as sound argumentation. It isn't that they *appear to be valid but are not* but that they distract attention from matters the analyst takes to be relevant. It isn't that they are logical errors but that they disrupt counterargument. Both crimes are matters of degree. The *ad populum* in the first degree functions solely by peripheral route persuasion. For instance, a catchy jingle for Gatorade ("I want to be like Mike") overlayed on stunning basketball feats by Michael Jordan ends with the conclusion "Drink Gatorade." It is a flawless practical syllogism (and arguably defensible on the Ciceronian grounds that the young should emulate exemplars), but there is circumstantial evidence against it. Aside from the obvious—it is a paid endorsement—there is the question of how all that Gatorade comes to sit so noticeably on the benches of sports teams. If we find a pattern developing in this larger context, we may want to say an organization is taking a fallacious stance toward its messages.

The point isn't that ethos appeals are always or even usually fallacious. Endorsements—even for pay—may be probative evidence. Status appeals may be *rational* reasons for buying designer ties. But neither sort of reason is likely to be the *only* reason. The rhetorical analyst might thus assess not a lone message but the whole package of messages made available to the consumer.

At first glance, this focus on organizational practices—and families of messages rather than lone messages—strays rather far from what the reader might take to be the philosophical thrust of fallacy theory. And it may seem too cavalier about matters of degree, for it might have had nothing bad to say about "I want to be like Mike" had it found a less incriminating pattern of organizational behavior. The *ad populum*, as I said, brings the uneasy relations between philosophy and rhetoric to the surface. So it may be instructive

8. R. A. Osterhouse and T. C. Brock (1970), "Distraction Increases Yielding to Propaganda by Inhibiting Counterarguing," *Journal of Personality and Social Psychology* 15 (1970): 344–58.

9. R. E. Petty and J. T. Cacioppo, "The Elaboration Likelihood Model of Persuasion," in *Advances in Experimental Social Psychology*, vol. 19, edited by L. Berkowitz (New York: Academic Press, 1986).

to look at some permutations of the *ad populum*. It has become, I claim, more and more a rhetorical fallacy as fallacy theorists have successively revised it.

The *ad populum* fallacy can be put so hyperbolically that it proscribes persuasion. In Plato's *Gorgias*, for instance, the crime is audience-adaptation—making one's claims consistent with an audience's beliefs rather than arguing from true premises. If arguing from true premises is one's standard, then one condemns wholesale two of the most famous definitions of rhetoric—Aristotle's "faculty of observing in any given case the available means of persuasion," and Donald Bryant's adjusting ideas to people and people to ideas.[10]

But arguing from true premises is a flawed standard. As Aristotle says, public issues turn on uncertainties. They are open to dispute. There are more true believers than true premises in public life, so truth is a faulty ideal—one that encourages dogmatism and underwrites fanaticism. It is certainly a barrier to *argument*, for most argumentation theorists would say that one requirement for good public argument is that the arguers sincerely put their ideas at risk. Even Aristotle's dialectic required that the arguers begin with their interlocutors' premises.

Another version of the *ad populum* refers to "fallacious attempts to justify a claim on the basis of its supposed popularity. The fact that many members of a given group hold some belief is offered as evidence that this belief is true. Class or national, religious, or professional identity is substituted for the evidence that would be genuinely relevant to the truth of the claim."[11] Some textbooks call this the *bandwagon* technique.

But is the bandwagon always shady? Is it specious or irrational, for instance, to claim that a car is a best-seller? Over time, sales may be probative evidence—plausibly relevant evidence and perhaps the best evidence—about a product's quality. Consumer loyalty isn't an infallible sign, but it is one sign of a corporate track record. And in the case of knowledge claims, a consensus theory of truth implies that the prevailing consensus in a discipline is "genuinely relevant to the truth of the claim." And, finally, in public discourses, disciplinary identification is essential if "the evidence that would be genuinely relevant to the truth of the claim" is arcane. In a world of

10. Donald C. Bryant, "Rhetoric: Its Function and Its Scope," *Quarterly Journal of Speech* 39 (1953), 422.

11. Stephen Toulmin, Richard Rieke, and Alan Janik, *An Introduction to Reasoning* (New York: Macmillan, 1979), 174.

enormous, highly specialized literatures, citizens and public decision-makers *must* do just what Toulmin, Rieke, and Janik proscribe. As Stich and Nisbett argue, deference to authority is often the rational thing to do. [12]

For Copi, the *ad populum* fallacy lies in "arousing the feelings and enthusiasms of the multitude."[13] This proscribes, apparently, *any* emotively based technique;[14] and it is thereby open to the objection that it would lead to perverse readings of, say, the Sermon on the Mount, Churchill's war speeches, Gandhi's pleas for nonviolence, and Martin Luther King's "I Have a Dream" speech. How, without resorting to cost-benefit analysis, does one argue for social justice without appealing to a sense of justice? And do fallacy theorists really want to condemn (say) Kennedy's "Ich bin ein Berliner" or the swell of crowd approval it sparked? If not every case of "arousing the feelings and enthusiasms of the multitude" is equally wicked, then Copi is making his point badly.

Douglas Walton, however, thinks that the "overwhelming difficulty" with Copi's view is that emotional appeals may not be arguments: "We have pretty well exclusively gone over into the psychology or sociology of rhetoric and propaganda" (Walton 1985b). But what, exactly, is wrong with that? Psychologism is a flaw if fallacy theory is to be entirely text-focused—if, that is, arguments are nothing more than words on a printed page. But arguments in real situations are enthymematic: they rely on the presuppositions and taken-for-granted realities of the interlocutors; they benefit from conversational structure; and they take their meanings from the intentions of the speakers. Since utterances are characteristically open to multiple interpretations, we often need situational details to choose the most accurate description. To know what speakers are saying, we often need to know what they intend to be saying.

But while psychologism is ethnographically useful, a rhetorical analysis needn't be psychologistic. While one can focus on the relationships between a speaker's intentions and the message she creates, one can also focus on the relationships between message designs and their meanings and effects. Instead of studying cognitive processes, communication researchers can "focus on analyzing communicative tasks and the methods by which they are accomplished. The evidence to which such analyses must be held accountable is

---

12. S. Stich and R. Nisbett, "Expertise, Justification, and the Psychology of Inductive Reasoning," in *The Authority of Experts*, edited by Thomas L. Haskell (Bloomington: Indiana University Press, 1984).

13. Irving Copi, *Introduction to Logic*, 4th ed. (New York: Macmillan, 1972), 79.

14. Keith Emerson Ballard, *Study Guide for Copi: Introduction to Logic*, 4th ed. (New York: Macmillan, 1972), 38.

primarily observations of what people do, not assessments of what (or how) they think while they do what they do."[15]

Barbara O'Keefe's research suggests the existence of *message design logics* (MDLs) that reflect systematic differences in the assumptions people make about communication—about what it is, what it can do, and how it works. The differences are manifested in people's uses of different communication-constituting concepts (different implicit theories) that yield different patterns of message organization and interpretation. She terms these MDLs *Expressive, Conventional*, and *Rhetorical*—labels that represent not merely a classificatory device for deriving coding schemes but a grammar that explains the production of particular message characteristics. Unsurprisingly, they comprise developmentally progressive stages (the more complex subsuming their simpler precursors) corresponding to constructivism's orthogenetic view of development.

In the *Expressive Design Logic*, "language is a medium for expressing thoughts and feelings." Communication is a process by which one expresses what one thinks or feels so that others can know what one thinks or feels. The Expressive thinks that the only function of communication is expression. The only possible relations between one's intentions and one's messages are *either* that the message expresses one's current mental state "fully and honestly," or the message distorts—lies or edits—the whole truth about one's current state. "A desire to conduct communication as full and open disclosure of current thoughts and feelings, concern for the fidelity of messages, and a deep concern with deceptive communication are thus characteristic of an Expressive view of message function."[16]

Expressives are rather literal in their creation and understanding of messages: they don't see that expression can serve multiple goals; the idea of messages strategically designed to elicit particular reactions is "foreign and mysterious"; and " they interpret messages as independent units rather than as threads in an interactional fabric, and so seem to disregard context."[17] The symptomology diagnostic of expressiveness, indeed, is messages with pragmatically pointless content, e.g., a lack of editing, lengthy expressions of the speaker's wants, even if the listener has already heard them or can do nothing about them, marked redundancies, noncontingent threats, and insults. Sec-

---

15. Barbara J. O'Keefe, "Developing and Testing Rational Models of Message Design," *Human Communication Research* 18 (1992), 644.

16. Ibid.

17. Barbara J. O'Keefe, "The Logic of Message Design," *Communication Monographs* 55 (1988): 80–103.

ond, Expressives' "semantic and pragmatic connections between Expressively generated messages and their contexts and among elements with Expressive messages tend to be idiosyncratic and subjective rather than conventional and intersubjective. When one asks of an Expressive message, why did the speaker say this now, the obvious answer is generally: because the immediately prior event caused the speaker to have such-and-so reaction or to make such-and-so mental association, and the speaker then said what he or she was thinking."[18]

The *Conventional Design Logic* sees communication as a cooperative, rule-governed game. The Conventional view thus subsumes the Expressive: "language is a means of expressing propositions, but the propositions one expresses are specified by the social effect one wants to achieve"—one accommodates to conventional methods, much as speech act theory suggests. One plays the game, obeys the rules, and fulfills one's obligations. Competence is a matter of appropriateness: one succeeds insofar as one occupies the correct position in a situation, and uses one's conventional resources for obligating the interlocutor, behaves competently as a communicator, and is dealing with an equally competent and cooperative interlocutor.

Conventional messages generally have an identifiable core action being performed that is characterizable as a speech act. These messages, O'Keefe says, generally allude to the felicity conditions of the core speech act, the structure of rights and obligations that give force to the act being performed, or the mitigating circumstances or conditions that bear on the structure of rights and obligations in the situation (e.g., excuses). Just as the connections among message elements involve classic pragmatic coherence relations, the connections between messages and their contexts display a conventional basis for coherence. In contrast to Expressive messages, which are characteristically psychological and reactive in their relation to context, conventional messages bear a conventionalized and rule-following relation to context. If one asks of a conventional message, why did the speaker say this now, the answer is generally that this is the normal and appropriate thing to say under the circumstances.[19]

About the *Rhetorical Design Logic*, O'Keefe's thinking is closely allied with that of Erving Goffman.[20] Communication is seen as the creation and

18. O'Keefe, "The Logic of Message Design."
19. Ibid.
20. See, for example, Erving Goffman, *The Presentation of Self in Everyday Life* (New York: Anchor, 1959); *Encounters* (Indianapolis: Bobbs-Merrill, 1961); *Behavior in Public Places* (New York: Free Press, 1963); *Interaction Ritual* (New York: Doubleday, 1967); *Strategic Interaction* (Philadelphia: University of Pennsylvania Press, 1969); and *Relations in Public* (New York: Basic Books, 1971).

negotiation (Goffman's "dramaturgical enactment") of situations and selves. Rules, roles, and relations are seen as mutable rather than fixed. The Rhetorical is alert to the subtleties of verbal behavior as clues to character, attitude, and definitions of situation. She wants a "depth interpretation" of the behavior, intentions, and expectations of others; and she will systematically exploit her depth interpretations to negotiate and enact the social reality best suited to her (and others') purposes. The Rhetorical MDL thus values careful listening, psychological analysis, and adaptation to others in the creation of intersubjective understandings. Different speakers may adopt different voices and thereby talk different realities in order to achieve a consensus about the reality in which they are engaged—to negotiate, that is, a common vocabulary or a common drama in which to play.

Rhetorical messages seek negotiation, interpersonal harmony, and consensus. They are designed to achieve specific goals, so they contain strategies designed to achieve intersubjective effects (e.g., explicit definitions of context, roles, rules, and options). In their connections to context, Rhetorical messages are proactive rather than reactive. Thus, O'Keefe says, if we ask why a speaker is saying *this now*, the likely answer is that the speaker is pursuing such-and-such a goal. And if we wonder about the organizing principle that unites all the elements of a rhetorical message, the answer, generally, is that these elements are "steps in a plan," "moments in a coherent narrative," "displays in a consistent character," or all three. Rhetorical messages get their coherence, in other words, from intersubjectively available, goal-oriented schemes.

Differences between the design logics are most striking when people need to manage conflicting goals, e.g., cases where one wants to criticize yet offer face protections to another person. The Expressive believes that the purpose of communication is the clear expression of thoughts, so the rule is, *be tactful*—edit the message or be less than frank. The Conventional will *be polite* by using off-the-record communications and conventional politeness forms such as apologies, hedges, excuses, and compliments.[21] The Rhetorical assumes that communication creates situations and selves; the solution: *be someone else*, by transforming one's social self or identity, by taking on a different character in social interaction. The rhetorical solution is create a new drama, or new characters, so as to minimize the conflict of interest.

---

21. P. Brown and S. Levinson, "Universals in Language Use: Politeness Phenomena." In *Questions and Politeness*, edited by E. N. Goody (Cambridge: Cambridge University Press, 1974).

So one doesn't need a whiff of psychology to analyze "I want to be like Mike," but one does need organizational details—matters of audience analysis and product positioning, the theories behind the message, the marketing strategy, and the track record—the other, similar messages. And one needs to analyze the message itself; and here, of course, is one point where Walton would disagree. If one restricts *argument* to propositions, then most mass messages are not arguments. Television commercials join words with the whole array of aesthetic images—music, electronic effects, drama, comedy, layout design, and even dance—to create persuasive effects. They are seeable as arguments if we adopt Toulmin's view: "I want to be like Mike" is *a claim on our attention and belief*. The rhetorical theorist attaches great importance to the idea of a claim on our attention. "I want to be like Mike" may be a valid claim on our belief, but an entirely fallacious one on our attention.

So what is at stake in keeping definitions of *argument* narrow? Disciplinary purity? Clarity? Simplicity? These concerns may be behind some attempts to keep argument narrow (e.g., Frege's followers want to keep the subject matter of logic free of psychology), but they are less important to informal logicians and only of anthropological importance to rhetoricians. If one concedes that argument has aesthetic and social dimensions, the term *argument* hasn't suddenly vanished into chaos. It has become broader and more complex, but this may merely prove that we are finally getting it right.

The deeper issue is the hope for a clear-cut vision of *rationality*. In the first half of this century, scholars in many fields observed a distinction between *conviction*, seen as a state of mind achieved by rational, logical means, and *persuasion*, seen as a manipulation of emotions. This *conviction-persuasion duality* came from faculty psychology. It figured in the Enlightenment rhetorics—of Hugh Blair, Joseph Priestley, George Campbell, and Richard Whately—as a means of using logic and reason to constrain the emotions. Right rhetoric was to be *scientific*, in all the eighteenth-century meanings of the term. It was *not* to be style, belles lettres, elocution, or appeals to mysticism. *Persuasion* was an unfortunate human frailty; *conviction* was the rational ideal to which rhetoric might aspire. And it is this rational ideal that seems to be at stake.

In one sense, this is a penny-ante stake. The interdependence of reason and emotion is now taken for granted in the social sciences. Faculty psychology is a historical curiosity. But in another sense, many readers may concede that wishes contaminate thinking, yet hope to create a pedagogy that attenuates the contamination. For them, rationality is an idealization. The conviction-persuasion duality is a *goal*.

But the goal of a pristine rationality—translated into public discourse—has a bad track record. The pristine becomes the concrete, the operationalized. It is precisely this idealization that has ensconced cost-benefit analysis at the center of political and legal decision-making. Cost-benefit analysis is as close as modernity has come to a "philosophy of the public sphere." It claims to be a theory of rationality that rules out fuzzy values and visceral feelings. Yet it is a despicable thing if we credit (say) environmentalists and advocates of distributive justice; worse, I argue, it is a closed discourse that admits of critique only in its own terms, thus insulating its premises from effective critique.

For another thing, the image of pristine logic uncontaminated by human frailties is a poor idealization of rationality. Anyone can be rational in a hypothetical state of grace—with the luxury of reflection, freed from prejudice, social pressures, time limits, and information shortages. But we live our lives shackled to these frailties. People must be rational, not in their armchairs but *amid* the swirl of society, the clamor of competing advocates. They care about epistemic issues, not in the abstract but in situations, pressed by time, coerced by their emotions, biases, and interdependencies with others. They scarcely need to be told that subjectivism is a deficient epistemological doctrine: they know that subjectivity is a painfully vulnerable personal position, a frightful obstacle to interpersonal and institutional success. Daily life is underdetermined by data. Communication is irretrievably social. Prejudices masquerade as facts. The struggle to distinguish good from bad authority, to know when it is right to acquiesce to a community consensus, is continually renewed.

The astonishing thing is that people succeed—badly provisioned in bad conditions. They muddle through, sometimes heroically, in circumstances so divergent from idealized pictures that we often can't explain their success. Idealizations of rationality ought to capture these successes. And instead of demanding that one be free of prejudice and the other human foibles, and free of organizational distortions and social influence, a theory of rationality should explain how one grapples with all of these things.

We have come rather far from the blanket prohibition of persuasion with which the *ad populum* began—but not perhaps far enough, for one might concede many of my points without conceding that the rhetorical *ad populum* lies at the end of the road fallacy theorists are traveling. I in fact think that some fallacy theorists have finished traveling the road (though some are a little further back). But to prove my point, I need to borrow from Hintikka to describe my own version of "The Fallacy of Fallacies."

I have elsewhere argued that fallacy textbooks have a habit of stating the fallacies as general, all-encompassing rules, and then trimming them back: broad labels are introduced with extreme examples.[22] As these are often caricatures, caveats and exceptions are added that both winnow the rule and collapse it to issues of relevancy. Kahane thus defines the *ad hominem* as "an attack on the man," then moves to a clear-cut, extreme example (Senator Randolph's "a small band of braless bubbleheads") and *then*, considering exceptions, collapses the fallacy to a failure of relevance: "It's often quite hard to decide whether an attack of a man is fallacious or not. In particular, we need to assess the *relevance* of the attack to the issue at hand."[23] The rule *seems* clearer than it is. Its apparent precision—indeed, scientific appearance—turns out to be a front for more modest claims.

The *ad populum* gets whittled down more dramatically. The best-selling text, in fact, presents examples of the *ad populum* that differ in kind from their rule. The rule, remember, refers to fallacious attempts "to justify a claim on the basis of its supposed popularity." The examples, however, are of propagandists justifying taxes by conjuring images of *real* Americans with "pioneer spirit," and of advertisers who associate their products with images of "the ideal American." Somehow, we have gotten from the bandwagon to Weberian ideal types. And then, finally, after mentioning appeals to conformity and snobbery, the rule boils down to asking an audience to trust a product or idea "not on account of any demonstrated merits but simply because other people supposedly do so."[24] For those who still doubt that fallacy theory has come as close to the rhetorical end of the road as I claim, I invite them to reread this last quotation and then look again at my description of the rhetorical *ad populum*. We have reached, it seems to me, Point Omega.

And it isn't all that bad. Fallaciousness *never did* reside solely in logical form. There *never were* plausible exceptionless rules. The most credible fallacy theories *always did* focus on the fits between messages, situations, and intentions. The rhetorical turn was an accomplished fact long ago. It began when the first fallacy theorists noticed that situational fit determined rele-

22. Willard, A *Theory of Argumentation*, 232.

23. Howard Kahane, *Logic and Contemporary Rhetoric* (New York: Wadsworth, 1971), 27–28. See also Kahane's 6th edition of this work (1992), 57–58.

24. Toulmin, Rieke, and Janik, 174–75.

vance. As Toulmin, Rieke, and Janik say: "Arguments that are fallacious in one context may turn out to be quite solid in another context. So we shall not be able to identify any intrinsically fallacious forms of argument."[25] That, it seems to me, is the most striking claim in the recent literature, for if nothing is intrinsically fallacious, then context is pivotal and all pragmatic fallacies become failures of relevance.

25. Ibid., 157.

11

The Fallacy Behind Fallacies

Gerald J. Massey

State of the Subject

Discover its natural habitat and you learn much about an animal. The same holds for matters logical. Just by determining where it is dealt with you come to know a great deal about a topic. Take, for instance, fallacy. Rarities aside (even prothonotary warblers are sometimes sighted in Maine), you do not come across treatments of fallacy in journals or scholarly treatises or advanced textbooks. Rather, introductory textbooks, especially those that propound so-called *informal logic*, constitute their natural habitat. What, then, should this distributional fact about discussions of fallacy lead us to expect?

Let us begin with the obvious. Textbooks are parasitic upon journals and scholarly tomes, and properly so. Cut off from their natural source of nourishment, textbooks are likely to suffer from conceptual malnutrition. Some of its symptoms: aimless or directionless thinking, exaggerated fascination with taxonomies, and shoddy reasoning. Alas but not unexpectedly, textbook treatments of fallacy exhibit all three symptoms.

Consider, for example, aimless or directionless thinking. Chapters or units on fallacy contrast markedly with those on sentential logic or quantifiers or even syllogistics. However maladroit in other respects, treatments of these latter topics appear organized and unified. Why? Because a highly articulated, well-understood theory underpins them. But there is no theory to underpin or give structure to treatments of fallacy. Consequently these treatments appear as a hodgepodge or miscellany of "fallacies" individuated by historical accident and sometimes related only by possession of a common pejorative label.

A possible explanation suggests itself. Perhaps the science of fallacy has yet to emerge from its natural history phase. At this early stage progress consists largely in collecting specimens and organizing them in suggestive ways. Note how this explanation accounts in one swoop for the predilection (obsession) of informal logicians to add to the already thick catalogue of documented fallacies as well as for their preoccupation with classificatory schemes.

Richness of classification and poverty of theory are directly related. As evidence thereof, compare the taxonomic wealth of neo-Aristotelian logic with the classificatory austerity of the logic of sentence connectives and quantifiers. The myriad and intricate schemes for classifying fallacies suggest that there is little theory behind the science of fallacy. This suggestion misleads only by implying that there is any theory at all behind it. The unvarnished truth is this: *there is no theory of fallacy whatsoever!* I will return to this claim shortly.

The third symptom of conceptual malnutrition is shoddy reasoning.

Formal Fallacies

So-called *formal fallacies* appear to falsify my claim that there is no theory whatsoever behind treatments of fallacy.[1] Why? Because formal fallacies are rooted in inference patterns proscribed by logical theory. For example, the inference pattern or argument form (1)

(1) $p \supset q$

    $\underline{q\qquad}$

    p

---

1. Curiously, none of the fallacies treated by Kahane (*Logic and Contemporary Rhetoric* [Belmont, Calif., 1971]) are formal fallacies.

is rejected as invalid by truth-functional logic on the sensible ground that some instantiations of it have true premises but a false conclusion. The formal fallacy called *affirmation of the consequent* is defined relative to the invalid pattern (1). But exactly how?

A naive account might go like this. Argument form (1) is invalid, so any argument of that form is invalid. Hence any such argument will be said to commit the affirmation-of-the-consequent fallacy. This naive account gains plausibility from such textbook examples of affirmation of the consequent as (2).

(2)   If Philadelphia is the capital of Pennsylvania, then Pittsburgh is not.
      Pittsburgh is not the capital of Pennsylvania.

      Philadelphia is the capital of Pennsylvania.

Argument (2) is clearly invalid (its premises are true but its conclusion is false). But is it invalid because it instantiates (1)? Surely not, for then any argument that instantiates (1) would be invalid. Yet (3),

(3)   If something has been created by God, then everything has been created by God.
      Everything has been created by God.

      Something has been created by God.

an argument that instantiates (1), is valid. The naive account, therefore, must be wrong.

It is easy to see where the naive account goes astray. The cardinal principle that undergirds the application of formal logic to natural languages is (4).

(4)   Arguments that instantiate valid argument forms are valid. (Principle of Logical Form)

In tandem with principle (5),

(5)   Translations of valid arguments are valid, and translations of invalid arguments are invalid. (Translation Principle)

the principle of logical form enables one to show natural-language arguments valid thus. First, one translates the natural-language argument into a formal language like sentential logic. The translation principle guarantees that the natural-language argument and its formal translation stand or fall together with respect to validity. Then one inspects the form of the formal argument for validity. If it proves valid, the principle of logical form allows one to conclude that the original natural-language argument is valid.

The naive account of formal fallacy uncritically supposes that proofs of argument invalidity go like proofs of argument validity. That is, it supposes that one proves an argument invalid by showing that it instantiates some invalid argument form. This is a mistake, a very elementary one, yet so common as virtually to escape notice.

There are three mutually reinforcing sources of the mistake. The first is common practice. Philosophers, logicians, and their students routinely do pretend to convict arguments of invalidity by producing invalid forms that the arguments instantiate. Introductory textbooks aid and abet this pernicious practice. After each installment of theory, they proffer exercises that require the student to prove certain arguments invalid. How? By translating them (as fully as possible) into the formal language at hand and then showing that the theory just imbibed declares the form of the resulting argument invalid. The method *seems* to work but only because authors choose their examples judi-ciously, supplying only intuitively invalid arguments when they want a ver-dict of invalidity.[2] But what confusion must greet the industrious student who applies the method to exercises appended to later chapters! Intuitively valid arguments accredited as valid by the next theory installment turn out to be invalid! Only lethargy protects students from this trauma.

The second source of the mistake is a simple confusion. Most textbook authors take pains to distinguish argument forms from arguments but subse-quently disregard their own distinction. For example, in an otherwise unusu-ally rigorous book on informal logic, Fogelin becomes careless about the

---

2. Most authors are altogether insensitive to the radical disability of the invalid-form method of showing argument invalidity. Copi, in his textbook (*Introduction to Logic*, 4th ed. [New York, 1972]) is a happy but not wholly blameless exception. What Copi calls *refutation by logical analogy* (see 268–75) is essentially the aforementioned discredited method. However, at each relevant juncture Copi appends a footnote to his account of refutation by logical analogy, the intent of which footnote is to restrict application of the method, in theory anyway, only to arguments for which it will yield the right verdict (see 185, 268, and 338). These footnotes stipulate that refutation by logical analogy works only if certain conditions obtain, e.g., that the only logical relations that obtain among the unanalyzed statements be those asserted or implied by the premises. But as the establishment of these conditions is equivalent to the problem of showing arguments to be invalid, the footnotes do not circumvent the basic failing of the method, even in theory. In practice as well as in the body of the text, Copi ignores his own footnoted injunction.

difference between arguments and argument forms at the point where he first mentions formal fallacies.[3] This carelessness causes him to endorse the fallacious method of showing invalidity discussed above. The endorsement takes the form of Fogelin's false claim that truth-table techniques constitute a *"decision procedure* for determining the validity of every argument involving conjunction, disjunction, negation, and conditionals."[4] Truth tables do provide a decision procedure for sentential argument-form validity; they do not constitute one for argument validity.

The third source of the mistake is uncritical application of the seductive principle (6).

(6)   Valid arguments instantiate valid argument forms. (Converse Principle of Logical Form)

The converse principle of logical form gives teeth to the widely held thesis that argument validity is at bottom a matter of form. Still it does not bite so deeply as its adherents seem to believe. The converse principle does not circumscribe or specify the argument forms that underpin validity. Yet those who implicitly accept it act as if the principle guarantees that proper analysis of intuitively valid arguments will yield valid argument forms of some standard logical system, typically quantification theory. Hence, when close analysis fails to isolate such a form, they feel justified in certifying the argument invalid. Far from legitimating the fallacious method of showing arguments invalid, the converse principle of logical form confers on it only unmerited respectability.

The Asymmetry Thesis

In his informative treatise on fallacy, Hamblin succinctly describes a *fallacious argument* as an argument that seems valid without being so (Hamblin 1970, 12). It is with fallacies so defined that I will hereafter be concerned.

Note first that fallacious arguments are invalid. Hence a theory of fallacy presupposes a theory of invalidity. Therein lies the rub. But as I claimed

3. Robert J. Fogelin, *Understanding Arguments: An Introduction to Informal Logic* (New York, 1978), 312.
4. Ibid., 134.

above and have argued for elsewhere, a theory of invalidity has yet to be developed (Massey 1975a; 1975b). It is not surprising, then, that treatments of fallacy eschew theory. There is no theory on which they could be based.

My claim about the non-existence of a theory of invalidity is so strong as to strike most philosophers as absurd or at least implausible. Everyone agrees that to show it has true premises but a false conclusion is to show that an argument is invalid. I call this *the trivial logic-indifferent method* of proving invalidity. This trivial method of showing invalidity is clearly independent of logical theory. Of course logical theory sometimes proves useful in the enterprise of establishing truth-value but that hardly makes this trivial method of showing invalidity a matter of logic. Physics is sometimes relevant to the determination of truth-value too, but no one would deny for this reason that the trivial method is indifferent to physical theory.[5]

Apart from the trivial logic-indifferent method, I claim, there is *no method whatsoever of establishing invalidity* that has theoretical legitimacy. To falsify this claim a single counterinstance would suffice. To date my critics have failed to produce any.

What positive evidence can be marshaled for my claim, which Bencivenga (1979, 249) has dubbed the *asymmetry thesis* as a reminder that our ability to prove invalidity is markedly more circumscribed than our ability to prove validity? Suppose one accepts both the principle of logical form and its converse, i.e., principles (4) and (6). (My case becomes even stronger when the converse principle of logical form is rejected.) Then an argument is invalid if and only if there is no valid argument form that it instantiates. For the sake of argument I concede that one can recognize a correct translation of a natural-language argument into a formal language, thereby establishing that the argument instantiates a particular argument form. If such translation yields a valid argument form, the principle of logical form allows you to conclude that the original argument is valid. But, suppose it yields an invalid argument form? That fact alone entails nothing about the goodness of the original argument. Suppose further that every translation you can come up with into every formal language you know and respect yields an invalid argument form. What may you then infer about the invalidity of the original argument? Nothing! Why? First, someone more clever than you might have been able to come up with an ingenious translation that yields a valid argument form. Second, even if it were somehow impossible to get a valid argument form by translating the argument into any of the formal languages you know and respect, or even into any of the extant formal languages you

5. This point seems to have been insufficiently appreciated by Bencivenga (1979, 249).

would respect if you knew them, there might be hitherto undreamt of formal languages congenial to you such that translation into them would yield a valid argument form.

Let us look at these two considerations more closely. To appreciate that the first is not just a skeptic's quibble, consider arguments (7) and (8).

(7)   John took a walk by the river.
      John took a walk.

(8)   Tom, Dick and Harry are partners.
      Tom and Harry are partners.

Davidson deserves credit for showing how to translate (7) into standard predicate logic in such a way as to get a valid argument form.[6] (Davidson's translation turns on quantification over events, something that some philosophers find objectionable, but that is another matter.) *Ante* Davidson, no one seemed able to supply such a translation, and so argument (7) was deemed invalid. To appease intuition which views the argument favorably, pre-Davidsonian philosophers regarded (7) as an enthymeme rendered valid by a suppressed premise relating to the predicate "took a walk by the river" to the logically unrelated predicate "took a walk." (I have discussed the disingenuousness and ultimate futility of this enthymematic ploy at length elsewhere.[7]

Similarly, before 1940 philosophers judged argument (8) invalid, unless enthymematic, for want of a formal-language translation that yields a valid argument form. But when the combined talents of Leonard and Goodman produced such a translation into mereological predicate logic, they reversed their verdict.[8] Leonard and Goodman's ingenuity enabled philosophers to treat (8) as a robust argument that stands validly on its own feet rather than as an anemic enthymeme propped up by suppressed premises.

The above examples show that more than skeptical fancy underlies the concern that failure to furnish valid-form translations may reflect badly on the translators rather than on the natural-language arguments translated. But you might object that through my choice of examples I have stacked the deck against good logical sense. After all, my examples (7) and (8) represent intu-

6. Donald Davidson, "The Logical Form of Action Sentences," in *The Logic of Decision and Action*, edited by Nicholas Rescher (Pittsburgh, 1968).

7. See Massey 1975a and 1975b as well as my "Tom, Dick, and Harry, and All the King's Men," *American Philosophical Quarterly* 13 (1976): 89–107.

8. Henry Leonard and Nelson Goodman, "The Calculus of Individuals and its Uses," *Journal of Symbolic Logic* 5 (1940): 45–56. Cf. my "Tom, Dick and Harry," passim.

itively good arguments. When such arguments are at issue, does not prudence dictate that failure to come up with valid-form translations should result at most in provisional findings of invalidity? On the other hand, when intuitively bad arguments like (9)

(9)   If Harrisburg is the capital of Pennsylvania, then Pittsburgh is not.
       Pittsburgh is not the capital of Pennsylvania.
       _____
       Harrisburg is the capital of Pennsylvania.

are at issue, universal failure to find valid-form translations should count as conclusive evidence of their invalidity for anyone who has not succumbed to skepticism.

A bona fide *theory* of invalidity would offer a principled account of why universal failure to find a valid-form translation of (9) shows it invalid whereas exactly the same failure in the case of an intuitively valid argument warrants only suspension of judgment. The method of showing invalidity advocated in the preceding paragraph amounts to unprincipled appeal to intuition. An account of invalidity that decides particular cases by how intuition views them forfeits all rights to the title "theory of invalidity." There is nothing wrong with such appeal to intuition, but it must not be allowed to masquerade as theory.

The second consideration mentioned above rises out of the *apparently unfinished state of contemporary logic* reflected in the fact that no philosophers would be so foolish as to claim that the family of formal languages they know and respect exhausts all possible systems that they would find congenial. This open-endedness of logic suffices itself to ground the asymmetry thesis. For even if it could somehow be established that no translation of an argument into extant formal systems yields a valid argument form, how could one hope to prove the same result about all *possible* systems?

But one might object that all sciences are unfinished, and so any asymmetry to which the apparent unfinished state of logic gives rise must be replicated in all the other sciences. Indeed, the objection might be put this way: Because physics is unfinished, pronouncements about what things are physically impossible must be deemed provisional. Similarly, in view of its unfinished state, verdicts of invalidity handed down by contemporary logic are subject to reversal wrought by theoretical advance.

The foregoing objection incorporates several misconceptions. Chief among them is the belief that the asymmetry thesis amounts to nothing more than the empiricist caution not to chisel in granite the deliverances of even the most entrenched contemporary theories. But the asymmetry thesis does not attribute to invalidity verdicts the kind of provisionality demanded by second-order induction over the fates of past scientific claims. If invalidity verdicts suffered from only the general dubiety that infects all human judgments, validity and invalidity verdicts would enjoy perfect parity. But whereas logical theory underwrites validity verdicts, the case for invalidity verdicts (where the trivial logic-indifferent method is inapplicable) rests at bottom on intuitive judgments of invalidity altogether unsupported by theory.

A popular tune of the 1940s urges us to accentuate the positive and eliminate the negative. Applied to fallacy and invalidity, the advice is sound. For, does our general inability to prove invalidity hamstring us in any way, either in composing arguments ourselves or in assessing those of others? Not if we accentuate the positive. All of us try to advance good arguments. Validity, of course, is one element of the goodness sought. If we devise a seemingly good argument only to find its validity challenged, we can call upon logical theory which will usually establish its validity to everyone's satisfaction.

But suppose none of the arguments we devise for some proposition p strike us as valid. What then? Do we need a theory of invalidity to discredit them? By no means! That these arguments seem upon careful reflection to be invalid is reason enough to abandon them and to look elsewhere for a good argument for p. It is much the same with arguments propounded by others. When appropriate, we can invoke logical theory to validate those arguments that appear good to us. Those that upon close scrutiny seem invalid are best set aside unless and until their composers or admirers supply cogent evidence of their validity. In short, the asymmetry inherent in showing validity and invalidity is exactly counterbalanced by a pragmatic asymmetry in burden of proof. Consequently, the asymmetry thesis does not generate any special difficulties for the practical use of logic.

Fallacies, Rules, and Inferential Practice

It is customary among logicians to name formal fallacies after the logical rules they violate.[9] For instance, argument (10)

9. This nomenclature wholly succeeds only when the logical rules have been formulated in such a way that an argument form is invalid if and only if at least one rule is violated. Because formulations of

(10)   All bachelors are rich.

   All unmarried adult males are rich.

   All unmarried adult males are bachelors.

is said to embody the *fallacy of undistributed middle term* because it violates the syllogistic rule that prescribes that the middle term be distributed at least once.

The aforesaid practice runs roughshod over the distinctions between arguments, argument forms, and their respective notions of validity. Note that as measured against the classical standard of argument validity, viz., joint impossibility of truth of premises with falsity of conclusion, (1) qualifies as a valid argument because its conclusion is necessarily true.[10] And since we have taken fallacies to be *invalid* arguments that seem valid, it follows that (10) is no argument at all. What is "fallacious" in the sense of being invalid is not (10) but rather argument form (11)

(11)   All H are G

   All F are G

   All F are H

which (10) instantiates.

But suppose we take (11) to be a *rule of inference* rather than an argument form. (It is of course a *bad rule* because it sometimes authorizes a falsehood to be inferred from truths.) Suppose further that someone advanced argument (10) *by applying* rule (11) to its premises. Then we might sensibly speak of (10) as a fallacy, specifically as a fallacy of undistributed middle term, in the *new sense* of being an argument generated by application of invalid rules. It seems to me that just such an account lies behind many presentations of fallacies.

Note that a fallacy in this new sense need not be an invalid argument. Strictly speaking, what is denominated fallacious or defective is not the

---

syllogistic rules typically meet this condition, syllogistic fallacies get their names from the rule or rules violated. In his treatise, Hamblin avers that unless the rules are so formulated that no more than one rule can be violated by a given argument form, the resulting classification of fallacies will be pointless (Hamblin 1970, 201). He seems to think that fallacies are insufficiently individuated when a single argument form may embody several. But it is enough for the individuation of fallacies that the *sets* of forms embodying each fallacy be distinct. (Hamblin's treatment also suffers somewhat from failure to keep distinct argument validity and argument-form validity. For example, he asserts that syllogistic rules define the set of valid syllogistic arguments rather than the valid syllogistic argument forms.)

   10. Relevance logicians, for example, would substitute a much more stringent standard of validity.

argument itself but the way it was constructed through application of rules. Even valid arguments like (3), (7), (8), and (10) will be fallacious if bad rules figured in their production.

This rule-based account of fallacy presupposes two things: that sense can be made of the notion of application of rules in inferential practice, and that the sense thus given enables one to ascertain which rules people have actually applied in composing particular arguments. In advance of someone's producing such accounts, one can only speculate about the shapes they are likely to assume. Here are my speculations.

The rules of reasoning that a person P accepts are reflected in P's inferential practice, i.e., in the arguments that P advances (the positive inferential corpus) as well as in the ones that P refuses to advance (the negative inferential corpus). That is, the rules P accepts constitute a theoretical explanation of P's total inferential behavior. Hence the rules actually accepted by P are determined by the best explanation of P's inferential behavior. For example (and with considerable simplification), if P's positive inferential corpus contains numerous cases that fit scheme (12)

(12) $p \supset q$

$\underline{p}$

q

while P's negative inferential corpus, when rectified for extraneous factors, contains virtually no cases that fit (12), we would say that P accepts *modus ponens*. Similarly, if we found that P's positive inferential corpus conforms to schema (1) whereas P's negative inferential corpus resists the same schema, we would say that P accepts the rule of *affirmation of the consequent*. But at this stage of human evolution it is unlikely that anyone accepts affirmation of the consequent. To accept affirmation of the consequent would amount not merely to a simple fallacy but to nearly certain suicide. Exposés of fallacies are not needed to eliminate affirmers of the consequent; evolutionary pruning does the job much more decisively.

But to know what rules P *accepts* is a long way from knowing what rules P *has actually applied* to construct a particular argument. Consider, for example, a person Q who accepts *modus ponens* and who advances (13).

(13)   If Philadelphia is the capital of Pennsylvania, then Pittsburgh is not.
       Philadelphia is the capital of Pennsylvania.

       Pittsburgh is not the capital of Pennsylvania.

Mere instantiation of an accepted rule schema by an argument does not mean that Q applied the rule to construct the argument. There might be other rules in Q's rule repertoire (the rules Q accepts) that would yield exactly the same argument. Again, one must look to the best explanation, i.e., to the rules in Q's repertoire that most efficiently yield the given argument. In the example, it is likely that Q's rule repertoire uniquely fixes *modus ponens* as the rule Q applied to get (13). Probably such unique determination of rules applied is rare; typically, Q's rule repertoire would contain several comparably efficient routes to a given argument. (The matter is analogous to the annotation of a Fitch-style natural deduction. Typically, the same deduction can be annotated in several ways.)

Suppose now that Q advances (9). That Q must be alive to advance any argument virtually eliminates *affirmation of the consequent* as the rule Q applied to construct (9). Suppose further and realistically that Q's rule repertoire contains no route to the conclusion of (9) from its premises? Where, then, does (9) come from?

To answer the previous question we need a pathology. Let Δ be the subset of Q's positive inferential corpus that contains all and only those arguments in the corpus that cannot be accounted for by Q's rule repertoire. Again we look for a best explanation, this time for the simplest set of rules F that, in conjunction with Q's rule repertoire, generates Δ. Unlike those in Q's rule repertoire, the rules in F are not accepted by Q. Rather, they may be described as rules that Q occasionally employs but does not accept. Because the typical member of F is an invalid rule like affirmation of the consequent or denial of the antecedent, F may be called Q's *pathological repertoire*. (Similarly, the typical member of Q's rule repertoire is a valid rule like *modus ponens* or simplification.) We might even call the members of F *fallacies*.

In the end, then, we explain the arguments in Δ as fallacious, i.e., as arguments constructed by Q through application of fallacies. Which fallacies? Those belonging to the simplest and most direct route in F to the given argument. For example, the likeliest explanation makes (9) a case of Q's affirming the consequent, i.e., an argument generated by application of rule (1) which belongs to F.

A careless and forgetful reader might object that I have traveled a long and circuitous path to reach the same conclusion that someone who merely examined (9) in isolation would reach, viz, that (9) exhibits the fallacy of affirmation of the consequent by virtue of instantiating (1). The objection would make fallacy purely a matter of form, the fundamental mistake that I have tried to expose in the previous sections. Fallacy is rather a matter of the generative limitation of accepted rules which are in turn a matter of theoretical explanation of inferential practice. Fallacies, therefore, are perhaps of more interest to psychologists and psychiatrists than to logicians and philosophers. Indeed, a recent magazine article on psychotherapy enumerates ten "negative" ways of thinking that distort reality.[11] Among them are found four familiar textbook-variety fallacies. Perhaps the topic of fallacy has at last found its natural place.[12]

11. David D. Burns, M.D., "How to Break Out of your Bad Moods," *Self* (June 1980): 121–31.
12. In writing this paper I profited from discussions with Barbara Alpern and Robert Brandom.

12

Reply to Massey

Trudy Govier

[The following is excerpted from "Four Reasons There Are No Fallacies?," chap. 9 of Trudy Govier, *Problems in Argument Analysis and Evaluation* (Dordrecht: Foris, 1987). Copyright 1987 by Foris. Reprinted by permission.]

Reacting to the proliferations of texts and courses on informal fallacies, a number of people have recently voiced concern about the lack of rigor and consensus in this area. Some have gone so far as to argue that there are no informal fallacies, that there is no way to show any argument invalid, that fallacies exist only in the pages of textbooks and the minds of logicians, or that fallacies are products of uncharitable interpretation.[1] Such revisionist views raise important questions.

By definition, a fallacy is a mistake in reasoning, a mistake which occurs with some frequency in real arguments and which is characteristically deceptive.[2] This means, not that a person who uses a fallacious argument necessar-

---

1. Karel Lambert and William Ulrich, *The Nature of Argument* (New York: Macmillan, 1980) argue there are no informal fallacies. Maurice Finocchiaro (1981) suspects fallacies occur only in textbooks. Gerald J. Massey (1975a; 1975b; 1981) claims fallacy theory falls apart because we can never demonstrate formal invalidity. Daniel Dennett, *Brainstorms* (Montgomery, Vt.: Bradford Books, 1978) and L. Jonathan Cohen (1979 and 1982) adopt principles of interpretation that would eliminate or virtually eliminate fallacies.

2. For similar definitions, see Woods and Walton (1982a): "A fallacy is a pitfall of reasoning that exhibits a general and recurring tendency to deceive and to deceive successfully, to trick even the entirely serious and honest arguer" (6). See also C. Kirwan, *Logic and Argument* (London: Duckworth, 1978), 269: "in logical parlance fallacies are not false propositions but incorrect arguments (non sequiturs) which seem to be correct and fallacy is not falsity but incorrectness." S. F. Barker, in

ily intends to deceive his audience but that the fallacious argument itself is deceptive, in the sense that it strikes many people as cogent, though it is not.[3] An arguer may recognize his fallacious argument as fallacious and intend to deceive others, or he may think that it is a cogent argument and use it in all sincerity. Since a fallacy in the logical sense is a mistake in reasoning, in order to commit one a person must be reasoning. Colloquially, false beliefs are often termed fallacies, but traditional logic usage restricts the term to reasoning errors, a usage followed here. In order to commit a fallacy, a person must reason from one or more claims to others. In the present context, this is to say that a person who commits a fallacy must be arguing. Furthermore, not just any mistake in reasoning counts as a fallacy. A fallacy is a mistake which is of a kind: it is repeatable, and repeated in other contexts.[4] A mistake in reasoning which is idiosyncratic and unlikely to be repeated does not qualify as a fallacy, even though it is a mistake in reasoning.

There is, then, a tacit empirical claim in saying that an argument involves a fallacy. Indeed, some who are skeptical about fallacies base their skepticism on empirical considerations. They agree that such moves as *post hoc* and *ad hominem* would be mistakes were they ever to occur, but believe that real arguments seldom or never include them. Saying that a fallacy is deceptive and that it is a mistake of a kind which occurs relatively often commits the critic to empirical claims as well as logical ones. If one invents a mistake in reasoning and invents an example in which it occurs, one will not thereby have invented or discovered a fallacy.

Thus we can see that there are many potential problems about fallacies. To

---

the first edition of *Elements of Logic* (New York: McGraw Hill, 1965), 174, says "A *fallacy* is a logical mistake in reasoning. . . . When there are premises and a conclusion that, through some logical error, is mistakenly thought to be proved by them, then and only then is there a fallacy in the logical sense." For empirical evidence that people commit a variety of inductive fallacies, see *Human Inference: Strategies and Shortcomings of Social Judgment*, by social psychologists R. Nisbett and Lee Ross (Englewood Cliffs, N.J.: Prentice-Hall, 1980).

3. In "A Comment on Fallacies and Argument Analysis" (*Informal Logic Newsletter* 5 (1983): 22–23), T. Carroll contends that a similar definition of mine makes deception an essential element of fallacy in such a way that the arguer must intend to deceive the audience if he or she is to be arguing fallaciously. This criticism fails to distinguish between deceptiveness as a tendency to deceive and actual deception. Actual deception is not required; nor is intent to deceive. What is required is that fallacious arguments will themselves tend to deceive in the sense that people will tend to mistake them for good arguments. Compare my "Who Says There Are No Fallacies?" (*Informal Logic Newsletter* 5 [1984]: 2–10). The present essay is an amended and extended version of that article.

4. Carroll, "A Comment on Fallacies," points out that my definition is slightly at odds with the usage in which "infrequently occurring fallacies" is an acceptable expression. If there is an element of stipulation in my account I am willing to accept it, and believe it does no harm.

say that an argument exemplifies one or another fallacy commits a critic to an interpretation of an arguer as reasoning in some specific way; to a logical judgment that the reasoning embodies a mistake; to a classification of that mistake as being one of a type; and, implicitly, to the empirical claim that the mistake is of a type repeated elsewhere and is deceptive in that people tend not to recognize it as a mistake.

These points are no doubt of very considerable pedagogical significance. Identifying and diagnosing a fallacy is no simple matter. Given the complexities involved, and given the additional problem that actual arguments may, on different interpretations or even on the same one, illustrate several distinct fallacies at once, there may be important reasons against teaching critical skills by first focusing on fallacies. Combine these features with the point that the counterfeit presumes the real, so that fallacies presuppose pertinent concepts of good argument, and it is easy to understand why many people object to teaching argument or critical thinking through fallacies analysis. However, while recognizing the importance of these points, we need not grant wholesale revisionist claims. From the fact that the identification of fallacies is a complicated matter it does not follow that there are no fallacies at all. Like the a priori elimination of evil, the a priori elimination of fallacies has a certain charm and appeal, but departs from common sense.

In several provocative articles, Gerald Massey has argued that it is not possible to prove an argument invalid. He linked this conclusion with the theory of fallacies. In 1975, in "Are There Any Good Arguments that Bad Arguments Are Bad?" Massey defended an asymmetrical account about proofs of validity and invalidity.[5] Given an argument in natural language, if we paraphrase it correctly into the symbols of a correct formal system, and show it to be valid according to the rules of that system, we know that the argument is valid. Thus, formal logic can be used to demonstrate the formal validity of arguments couched in natural languages. But for demonstrations of invalidity, Massey argued, matters are not so simple. Suppose that we paraphrase an argument into the symbols of a correct logical system and find that it turns out to be an invalid argument in that system. We do not know that there is no other system such that it would turn out to be valid in that one. The question of whether the paraphrase is the only logically revealing one remains open, as does the question of the possibility of a correct logical

5. See note 1 for full references.

system in which a logically revealing paraphrase of the argument would turn out to be valid.

> The reason for the marked asymmetry between showing validity and showing invalidity should now be apparent. To show that an argument is *valid* it *suffices* to paraphrase it into a demonstrably valid argument form of some (extant) logical system; to show that an argument is *invalid* it is *necessary* to show that it cannot be paraphrased into a valid argument form of *any* logical system, actual or possible. (Massey 1975a, 66)

Massey's account was welcomed by some informal logicians who thought this took the formalists down a peg or two. The account could be taken as showing that *formal analysis presupposes nonformal judgment as to the appropriacy of a paraphrase and the correctness of the logical system to which the argument is referred.* (For informalists, this will be the right moral to derive from the story.) We might see Massey as an ally, witting or unwitting, of those who advocate a nonformal approach to the analysis of arguments. He allowed in his paper that we can show arguments invalid in a logically trivial way by showing that the premises are true and the conclusion false and also, in subsequent discussion, that we may often have reasons for, or intuitions regarding, the inadequacy of arguments (Massey 1975b, 50). However, Massey remains adamant that such "low level" nonformal judgments do not amount to a theory of invalidity and that judgments of invalidity remain unfounded, theoretically. *Massey would require formal grounding for theoretical security.*

Judgments of invalidity might come to be properly grounded, were a logical grammar of a special kind to be found. In such a case, we would have assurance that some particular paraphrase of an argument was the correct one, and that the rules according to which that paraphrase came out as invalid were the right rules to apply: "the egregious asymmetry between proving validity and proving invalidity will persist until one or more programmes, such as Natural Logic, have been successfully implemented" (Massey 1975b, 50). Any alliance between informal logicians and Massey is premature and would not be to his taste. For him a theory is a formal theory, and a judgment without a theory is only a very slight improvement on no judgment at all.

An informal logician who sought consolation in Massey's 1975 paper would be disappointed by his later "The Fallacy Behind Fallacies" (Massey

1981). Here Massey criticizes both informal and formal logicians for their attempts to teach students to find fallacies. He explicitly links his view to his earlier account of validity and invalidity.

> In his informative treatise on fallacy, Hamblin succinctly describes a *fallacious argument* as an argument that seems valid without being so. It is with fallacies so defined that I will hereafter be concerned. Note first that fallacious arguments are invalid. Hence a theory of fallacy presupposes a theory of invalidity. Therein lies the rub. But, as I claimed above and have argued for elsewhere, a theory of invalidity has yet to be developed. It is not surprising, then, that treatments of fallacy eschew theory. There is no theory on which they could be based. (Massey 1981, 494; this volume, 163–64)[6]

Essentially, Massey employs the following argument:

(1)   Whatever else fallacies are, they are invalid arguments.

So,

(2)   To show that an argument is a fallacy, we must first show that it is invalid.

And,

(3)   There is no formally adequate method of showing that an argument is invalid.

So,

(4)   We cannot show that an argument is invalid in any theoretically adequate way.

Therefore,

(5)   There is no adequate theory underlying fallacies.

6. Massey assumes without question that invalidity is a necessary condition of fallaciousness. Discussions by Woods and Walton (1976b) and Abate (1979) have shown problems with this view.

Fallacy analysis is sloppy and in a theoretical mess, because it presupposes well-founded judgments of formal invalidity and these cannot be made, "whereas logical theory underwrites validity verdicts, the case for invalidity verdicts (where the trivial logic-indifferent method is inapplicable) rests at bottom on intuitive judgments of invalidity altogether unsupported by theory" (Massey 1981, 496; this volume, 167).

Let us examine Massey's argument. The first premise, linking fallaciousness and invalidity, would strike many people as obvious. However, it poses problems. First, *invalidity is not a necessary condition of fallaciousness*, provided that begging the question is a fallacy. Many arguments which beg the question are formally valid, and in some what explains their begging the question is the very same thing that makes them formally valid: they contain a premise which is logically equivalent to the conclusion.[7] Unless Massey has an unorthodox view about begging the question, this poses a problem for his account. We cannot begin our account of fallacies by assuming that all fallacious arguments are invalid unless we are prepared to rule out question begging as a fallacy from the very start. The problem can be extended to other fallacies with a dialectical component, such as straw man. An argument such as:

(1)   Indeterminists hold that human actions are entirely random.
(2)   Entirely random actions are not responsible actions.
(3)   Indeterminists hold that humans are responsible for their actions.

So,

(4)   Indeterminists hold an inconsistent position regarding human action.

Therefore,

(5)   Indeterminists hold a false view.

can no doubt be represented as a deductively valid argument. With some manipulation, it can be represented as formally valid. Nevertheless, due to

---

7. By dialectical conditions, I refer to states of knowledge and belief of the audience to whom the argument is addressed. An argument is question-begging if it contains a premise that the audience would not accept unless it already accepted the conclusion. I assume here that the common view that begging the question is a fallacy should not be rejected without prior reason.

the content of the first premise, the argument may commit the straw man fallacy. This has to do with the accuracy of that premise as an account of the indeterminist position. Given that a straw man argument might be cast as a deductively valid argument, and given that straw man has long been thought to be a fallacy,[8] we have another reason for questioning whether invalidity is a necessary condition of fallaciousness. Some traditional fallacies can appear even in deductively valid arguments, because they have to do with general features pertaining to content (as we saw with *ad hominem*, above) or because they have dialectical aspects.

Nor is invalidity sufficient for fallaciousness. It cannot be sufficient, if invalidity is deductive invalidity and there are any nonfallacious, strong inductive arguments. By all but the most adamant deductivists, it is allowed that there are some cogent arguments that are not deductive. If there is even one cogent inductive argument, then that is a nonfallacious argument that is deductively invalid. Hence, deductive invalidity is not a sufficient condition for fallaciousness. In fact, for different reasons, neither Hamblin nor Massey presume that invalidity would be sufficient for fallaciousness; both make the standard presumption that fallacious arguments must seem valid when they are not. Some invalid arguments would not even seem valid and would thus fail, on this view, to be fallacious. Invalidity in the deductive sense is neither necessary nor sufficient for fallaciousness.

The terms "valid" and "invalid" are used in a number of different senses even by logicians. The following three are pertinent here:

(1) An argument is valid if its premises are properly connected to its conclusion and provide adequate reasons for it. It is invalid otherwise. (Umbrella validity)
(2) An argument is valid if its premises deductively entail its conclusion, that is, given the truth of those premises, the falsity of the conclusion is a logical impossibility. It is invalid otherwise. (Semantic validity)
(3) An argument is valid if its conclusion is formally derivable from its premises using the rules of a correct logical system. It is invalid otherwise. (Formal validity)

In any theory of argument other than deductivism, it is only umbrella validity which is of general relevance for argument appraisal. Given a pluralistic

8. Here again, I assume that the common view that straw man is a fallacy is to be accepted until compelling reasons are advanced against it.

theory, the fact that an argument is semantically or formally invalid is, by itself, quite insufficient to establish the claim that the argument is fallacious.[9] An inductively strong argument is semantically and formally invalid, but that does not show that it is fallacious.

Thus, premise (1) in Massey's argument does not hold. Premise (2) gets its support from (1) and is therefore unsupported. Premise (3) is what Massey argues for in his 1975 paper. There is no formally adequate way of showing an argument to be formally invalid, because given its invalidity according to some system, the possibility remains open of its turning out to be formally valid according to some other system. This may be granted if by "formally adequate method" we mean "method which is formal and which does not presuppose any significant preformal judgments." If we grant premise (2) for the sake of argument and grant premise (3) as understood, there is still a gap in the inference from (2) and (3) to (4). The problem is in moving from *not having a formally adequate method* to *not having any theoretically adequate method*. This move reveals Massey's formalist predilections. Anyone who thinks that respectable nonformal theories are possible will not accept this move and will not move to the final conclusion either.

Massey's work is extremely important. It reveals the consequences of taking an entirely formalist account of validity and argument appraisal to its limits. Many share Massey's beliefs about the relationship between fallaciousness and invalidity and many endorse his formalist account of validity and the idea that any theory worth its salt is a formal one. For such people, Massey's work leaves an important and profound problem.

From the perspective of a pluralistic theory of argument and a nonformalist concept of theoretical adequacy, Massey's argument against the fallacies is far from conclusive. His point about invalidity is important and telling against insensitive formalization. It shows the need to attend to the workings of an argument, to detect the linkage which is supposed to be there, to distinguish between those features of the argument which are relevant to its logical appraisal and those which are not. We need a paraphrase which captures all of the logically relevant features. The formal invalidity of a particular paraphrase shows nothing unless we are sure that paraphrase has accurately captured the original argument.

Massey is unwilling to assume that ordinary human beings, ordinary philosophers, or even ordinary logicians have a preformal capacity to make these

---

9. Further information is always needed—at the very least we need interpretive grounds for regarding the argument as deductive. Compare Woods and Walton (1976b).

judgments about what is and what is not relevant to the deductive appraisal of an argument. He appears to use "valid" and "invalid" solely in a formal sense, to such a degree that he makes such comments as:

> . . . consider arguments (7) and (8).
>
> (7)   John took a walk by the river.
>   John took a walk.
>
> (8)   Tom, Dick and Harry are partners.
>   Tom and Harry are partners.
>
> Davidson deserves credit for showing how to translate (7) into stan-dard predicate logic in such a way as to get a valid argument form. (Davidson's translation turns on quantification over events, some-thing that some philosophers find objectionable, but that is another matter.) *Ante* Davidson, no one seemed able to supply such a trans-lation, and so argument (7) was deemed invalid. (Massey 1981, 494–95; this volume, 165)

This passage illustrates Massey's tendency to conflate semantic and formal validity and to attribute this conflation to other logicians and philosophers. Before Davidson's logical discoveries, arguments (7) and (8) were semanti-cally valid but were (perhaps) not known to be formally valid.

Massey's problem arises only within a strictly formalist framework. If we are willing to grant that people understand arguments and are capable of appreciating how these arguments work so as to be able to construct correct formal paraphrases, the problem does not arise. Granting that we understand an argument and see what sort of connection it depends on, we can some-times show an invalid argument to be invalid by paraphrasing it into the terms of a formal system and employing the standards of that system.[10] If we are not willing to grant that people sometimes understand arguments well enough to do this, Massey's point will hold. But then, in such a view, more than fallacies are in trouble, because this view entails that people lack the mental ability to identify the formal characteristics of natural arguments.

---

10. I say sometimes because the argument might depend on a term such as "property" that is not formalized and not formalizable.

13

Fearful Symmetry

John Woods

> First we must settle what a name is and what a verb is, and then what a
> negation, an affirmation, a statement and a sentence are.
> —Aristotle, *De Interpretatione*

In its ancient and persisting sense, fallacies are invalid arguments that do not
appear to be so. Thus Aristotle, in the *Sophistical Refutations*.[1] Straightaway
this sets the general parameters on what to count as a fallacy theory.

> *Def. FT:* T is a theory of fallacies iff it is the union of two subtheories T'
> and T", where T' is a theory of invalidity and T" is a theory of
> *not appearing to be invalid.*

Apart from some desultory and suggestive remarks about confusions occasioned by properties of language—for example, by lexical and syntactic
ambiguity—Aristotle has no contribution to make to T". What is more, no
self-styled fallacy theorist since Aristotle has done conspicuously better with
T" than he. It is easy to find authors, ancient and modern, for whom the
necessity to produce T" seems not to have been recognized, never mind that
they affirm the Aristotelian conception of fallacy. It follows from *Def. FT*,
whatever else we may think of it, that the *Sophistical Refutations* contains no
fallacy theory. Even so, in the transition from this work to the *Prior Analytics*
something momentous happened. Aristotle invented formal logic. And it is

---

1. *Soph. Ref.* 164a23.

tempting to think that, with that done, Aristotle made substantial headway with T'.

Although it contains no developed logical theory, the *Sophistical Refutations* advances a definition of validity. Aristotle speaks of syllogisms as finite sequences of propositions, the terminal member of which is necessitated by the preceding members (and by no proper subset of them), provided also that the terminal member does not repeat a preceding member.[2] By these lights, there are three logically independent ways in which an argument fails to qualify as a syllogism. It is not a syllogism if it contains a redundant premise; it is not a syllogism if a premise occurs as conclusion, and it is not a syllogism if its premises fail to necessitate its conclusion, that is, if it is invalid.[3] Fledgling though it is, the early doctrine of the syllogism presupposes the standard semantic conception of validity and invalidity:

> *Def.* V: An argument is valid if it is not in any sense possible both that its premises are true and its conclusion false.

> *Def.* I: An argument is invalid if it is in some sense possible both that its premises are true and its conclusion false.

One might think, therefore, that the *Sophistical Refutations* embeds a theory of invalidity and that it is *Def. I*. Such was not Aristotle's view. A theory of invalidity not only specifies what it is to be invalid (as *Def. I* does), but it also provides proof procedures for invalidity. A proof procedure for invalidity is a general method of demonstrating with respect to an invalid argument that it is invalid. There are no proof procedures in the *Sophistical Refutations*, whether for invalidity or validity.[4]

It is often complained that Aristotle's examples of fallacies are defective. They are said to be trivial, examples of arguments that would "fool no one," as witness

Happiness is the end of life.
The end of life is death.
Therefore, happiness is death.

2. It follows that the conclusion of a syllogism cannot be a logical truth. A logical truth follows from the null set of premises, which is a proper subset of any nonempty set of premises necessitating it.

3. It is more faithful to Aristotle's own account to define fallacies as arguments that are not *syllogisms* in the sense here specified, but that appear to be syllogisms. Even so, sometimes an argument will be a fallacy when it is invalid (for that is one way of failing to be a syllogism) and yet appears not to be. I shall confine my discussion to fallacies of this kind.

4. Nor for syllogisms.

Such complaints are true twice-over. Aristotle's examples are trivial and they are defective. What critics seem to have missed is that their defectiveness follows from their triviality. Aristotle's examples are examples of transparently invalid arguments. It follows that they cannot be examples of fallacies, for no fallacy is a transparently invalid argument.

Aristotle is left in an odd position. He completely fails to exemplify his own definition of fallacy. This may seem an unconscionable omission. For not only does Aristotle give no proof procedures for fallaciousness, it would seem that we now have a proof that no proof procedures for fallaciousness are possible. For, to produce an example of a fallacy it is necessary to produce a text or a piece of discourse that is recognized as invalid and yet is not recognized as invalid (since, if it were, it would not fail to appear invalid). On the face of it, a proof procedure that purports to establish that an argument A is a fallacy must demonstrate that A is invalid and that there is no demonstration that it is invalid, for otherwise there is no *fallacy*. And this, it may be thought, is a burden no proof procedure should be expected to shoulder. We may take it, in any case, as a minimum condition on the *exemplification* of a fallacy that at first sight people will not take it to be so. It is a tough condition. It bids the exemplifier to produce examples in such a way as to (1) overwhelm the antecedent confidence that there is nothing wrong with them and (2) to explain how it came to pass that the misplaced confidence was acquired in the first place.

It turns out to be wonderfully opportune that Aristotle's mature logic, the logic of the *Prior Analytics*, is a theory of logical forms. It enables the fallacy theorist to fulfil his obligation to produce T'. Might it not also be the case that it enables him to produce T'', a theory of not appearing to be invalid? Could we not say that arguments on the hoof, that is, arguments just as they come in natural speech, frequently disguise their logical forms? If so, one way of discharging our obligations with regard to T'' is to establish methods that reveal the logical forms of arguments on the hoof. This would be done by way of a theory of reconstruction. A fallacy would be an unreconstructed argument whose invalidity is revealed after reconstruction. A set of proof procedures for a fallacy would then look something like this. It would contain proof procedures for the invalidity of logical forms, and it would contain procedures for proving that a fallacious argument's invalidity cannot be proved prior to a reconstruction that discloses its logical form. It is an attractive idea, or so it is for an appropriately austere conception of proof.[5] Definitions lie in wait.

---

5. The question of what to count as a proof of invalidity is of central importance for the present idea. Counterexamples suggest themselves. It would seem that some arguments on the hoof with true

Def. V*: An argument is valid iff it has a valid logical form.

Def. I*: An argument is invalid iff it possesses an invalid logical form.[6]

What makes *Def.* V* and *Def.* I* so attractive is the promise they give for finding proof procedures for validity and invalidity. Since proof procedures are available for the validity and invalidity of logical forms, there will be proof procedures for the validity and invalidity of arguments on the hoof provided that there are also procedures for determining the logical forms of English on the hoof. Such procedures are equated with the rules for reconstructing English arguments in a set of logical forms.

As we see, the concept of reconstruction bears a good deal of the weight of our definitions, and it bears all of the weight of the idea that proof procedures for logical forms are also proof procedures for the validity and invalidity of arguments in natural speech. Reconstruction will fail this latter condition unless the following is true.

BRP: The rules of reconstruction have the *backward reflection property* with respect to validity and invalidity; that is, an argument is valid if its reconstruction under these rules is a valid logical form, and similarly for an argument's invalidity.

We need, obviously, to say something further about reconstruction as the exposure of logical form. For ease of exposition, and because my space is

---

premises and false conclusions are arguments that fail to appear invalid, yet under conditions that contradict the idea that their invalidity cannot be proved prior to reconstruction. Let A be such an argument and let its conclusion be a common misconception. Then A will be recognizably fallacious prior to reconstruction if (1) the premises appear to be true and there is good reason to think that they are true; (2) the conclusion is a common misconception and hence does not appear to be false; and (3) the misconception is *corrigible* and is so independently of any strategy for A's reconstruction. A would be a fallacy because, though invalid, its invalidity is not apparent until after a misconception is corrected.

Have we not succeeded in sketching a method for proving the invalidity of arguments such as A prior to reconstruction? And have we not done so in ways that account for their not appearing invalid prior to the application of this method of proof?

I shall not quibble over the word "proof." Proof or not of A's invalidity, ours is not a proof in any sense in which a proof turns on general procedures for recognizing and correcting misconceptions. I take it as given that such procedures we do not have. So there is no proof in the requisite sense that A is an invalid argument, even where there isn't the slightest doubt that A *is* invalid.

6. The definitions, of course, are symmetrical. They jointly provide that validity and invalidity are contraries.

limited, I shall assume the reader's acquaintance with the so-called translation rules from English to such familiar systems of logic as the propositional calculus (PC) and quantification theory (QT).

I find the expression "translation rules" unfortunate. It is not intended that such rules preserve meaning. It is required only that they reconstruct English arguments on the hoof in ways that ensure that they have the backward reflection property with respect to target properties such as validity and invalidity.[7] Let us consider the simplest kind of case—the reconstruction of English arguments in PC. As is well known, the reconstruction rules for PC restrict English arguments to finite sequences of sentences that are either simple indicative sentences or compounds of these and one or more of the English conjunctions, "not," "and," "or," "if . . . then," and "if and only if." These conjunctions in turn are reconstructed as the connectives of PC: $\neg$, $\wedge$, $\vee$, $\supset$, $\equiv$ respectively. Each simple indicative English sentence is reconstructed as an atom of PC, a different atom for each simple sentence. Compound sentences of English are reconstructed as molecular formulae of PC, that is, as concatenations of atoms and connectives. Thus, the argument

(1)   If the cat is on the mat then the dog is in the manger.
(2)   The cat is on the mat.
(3)   The dog is in the manger.

is reconstructible in PC as

(a) $p \supset q$
(b) p
(c) q

which is a valid logical form. If our reconstruction rules have the backwards reflection property for validity then the fact that there is a proof of the validity of (a)–(c) is itself a proof of the validity of (1)–(3).

Similarly, the argument

(4)   If the cat is on the mat then the dog is in the manger.
(5)   The dog is in the manger.
(6)   The cat is on the mat.

---

7. In particular, that "$\supset$" doesn't give the meaning of "if . . . then" is nothing to be concerned about. The "paradoxes" of material implication are a red herring.

is reconstructible in PC as

(d)   p ⊃ q
(e)   q
(f)   p

which is an invalid form. If the reconstruction rules have the backward reflection property for invalidity then the fact that there is a proof of the invalidity of (d)–(f) constitutes a proof of the invalidity of (4)–(6).

Consider now a third argument.

(7)   The thing is red.
(8)   The thing is colored.

Transparently valid by our semantic definition of validity (*Def. V*), it is reconstructible in PC as

(g)   p
(h)   q

which is a provably invalid form. This is a setback. It suggests that we make do with our earlier semantic definition of invalidity (*Def. I*). So we should, but in saying so there are confusions to be avoided. It was never intended that any argument valid by *Def. V** should not also be valid by *Def. V*, or that any argument invalid by *Def. I** should not also be invalid by *Def. I*. Intended or not, *Def. I** does give us an invalid argument that is not invalid by *Def. I*. So why not abandon *Def. I** in favor of *Def. I?* The answer is that if we did that we would lose proof procedure for invalidity. What is wanted is either a further definition that gives promise of proof procedures and is consistent with *Def. I*, or a principled reason for saying that our valid argument (7)–(8) does not reconstruct as (g)–(h) in PC. If we can do this latter thing, we will have removed our counterexample to *Def. I**, and the promise of proof procedures for the invalidity of arguments on the hoof will have been revived.

Of course, this is precisely what *is* done to exclude our counterexample. Sets of simple indicative sentences are said not to be eligible as inputs to the reconstruction rules of PC unless they meet a further condition:

SI: Sentences eligible for reconstruction must be themselves pairwise semantically inert, if simple, or compounds of simple and semantically inert sentences otherwise.

A set of simple sentences satisfies SI if for no two of them does either imply the other, or is the one inconsistent with the other. Sentences (7) and (8) jointly fail this condition. Hence the argument (7)–(8) is unreconstructible in PC; it has no form in PC, hence no invalid form.

In this, we learn an important lesson about the reconstruction of English in PC. As we now see, English on the hoof must be "dressed" before it can be reconstructed.[8] Not only are arguments restricted to those whose members are either simple indicative sentences or conjunction-concatenations thereof, they must contain only those simple sentences that also fulfill the semantic inertia condition, *SI*. *SI* together with the requirement of simplicity constitutes a dressing of English prior to application of the reconstruction rules.

Let us now examine the argument

(9)   All men are mortal.
(10) Socrates is a man.
(11) Socrates is mortal.

Transparently valid, it has (or appears to have) a reconstruction in PC which is provably invalid:

(l)   r
(m)   s
(n)   t.

Once again, *Def. I** is imperiled, not only because it gives a result that contradicts a result given by *Def.* V but also because it gives a result that contradicts a result given by *Def. V**. For our argument also has a valid reconstruction in QT, namely,

[a] $(x)(Fx \supset Gx)$
[b] Fa
[c] Ga

Perhaps we are going on too much about these apparent incompatibilities. True, (9)–(11) has a valid reconstruction in QT and an invalid reconstruction in PC. It is, so to speak, QT-valid and PC-invalid. Hardly inconsistent on

8. It is a gory metaphor. In the fateful passage from range to abbatoir to table, beef on the hoof is "dressed" before it is submitted to the final cut (reconstruction) in the meat department of Safeway.

their face, why not acknowledge the system-relativity of validity and invalidity and accept both these claims? There are two good reasons not to acquiesce in the system-relativity of validity and invalidity. One is that every logical form of PC is also a logical form of QT. This makes our acquiescence inconsistent; (9)–(11) is now QT-valid and QT-invalid (because invalid in PC). The other reason for not taking the present line is that reconstruction procedures for PC and QT alike are carefully designed to have the backward reflection property with respect to validity and invalidity. This being so, then, in particular, any PC-invalid argument is invalid and any QT-valid argument is valid. (9)–(11) is precisely such an argument. So it is valid and invalid, a genuine inconsistency.

We might recall that the claim that (9)–(11) has a reconstruction in PC was hedged. We said that it did or appeared to have such a reconstruction. We would now be well served if we could present a convincing reason for overriding the appearance that (9)–(11) reconstructs in PC. It all depends on (9). Is (9) a simple sentence of English? If it is, then the argument of which it is a premise has an invalid reconstruction in PC. What, then, are the truth conditions of the open sentence ". . . is a simple sentence of English"? In asking this question it again becomes apparent that if *Defs.* V* and I* are to serve their intended purposes we must have a theory of reconstruction for English constructions and that this theory must contain a dressing theory. We might expect that a theory of dressing for English will include the following theorem:

SSE: A sentence is a simple sentence of English iff it contains neither any sentence as a proper part nor any conjunction of English.

By this test (9), "All men are mortal," is a simple sentence of English, and (9)–(11) is an invalid argument. If this is to be resisted, we require an independent reason for rejecting SSE. It might occur to us that it is significant that the QT reconstruction of (9), "$(x)(Fx \supset Gx)$" is transparently not simple by an obvious analogue of SSE. Would that be reason enough to say that "All men are mortal" is implicitly the sentence

(9*)   For all x, if x is a man then x is mortal,

which, by SSE, is transparently complex? If so, then (9) is complex and (1)–(n) is not a reconstruction of (9)–(11), much less an invalid one. In fact, if (9) is implicitly (9*) then (9)–(11) will have no reconstruction in PC.

This is not a promising development. Talk of implicit sentential identities offends on account of its looseness. We have no truth conditions for such identities. Synonymy beckons, of course, but it beckons to no avail. Either synonymy is a theoretically intractable notion, as Quine avers, or it is not. If it is, we have embedded an illegitimate theoretical notion in our dressing theory. If it is not, the concept may be all right, but the claim that (9) is synonymous with (9*) is not all right. Existential import is the culprit. With (9) having it and (9*) not, prospects for synonymy collapse.

I admit that we might nevertheless grasp the nettle and insist that the quantifier "all" precludes (9)'s simplicity. If that were our decision we would need to replace *SSE* with

> *SSE**: A sentence is a simple sentence of English iff it fulfills the conditions of SSE and it contains no quantifiers.

By this test, the awkwardness of attributing implicit identity to sentences in the absence of truth conditions is averted. "All men are mortal" will qualify as complex thanks to the presence of the quantifier "all." Fine for the present case, and a welcome result—since (9)–(11) will have no reconstruction in PC—SSE* will not do for the likes of "All things are identical to themselves," which judges it complex when that is about the last thing it would appear to be.[9]

Help awaits. It is offered by Massey in a series of justly celebrated papers.[10] Massey proposes that *Def. I** must yield to

> *Def. I'*: An argument is invalid iff there is no valid logical form that it possesses.

By this test, (9)–(11) is invalid in PC and valid in QT, hence valid. This is tantamount to claiming that there is a deep asymmetry between validity and invalidity. It is this: whereas some reconstruction policies have the backward reflection property with respect to validity, none has it with respect to invalidity. Insofar as a theory of invalidity incorporates reconstruction principles that reflect invalidity backward it is inconsistent. If it does not reflect invalidity backward it will not be a theory of invalidity for natural language arguments.

---

9. Further cautions need to be sounded. Does "The man walked carefully" contain the sentence "The man walked"? And is the sentence "Grandfather drove a horse and buggy" made complex by virtue of the conjunction "and"?

10. Gerald Massey (1975a; 1975b; 1981).

Jointly, there is no such thing as an adequate formal theory of argument invalidity on the hoof.[11]

A startling result, it should not be embraced carelessly. We must insist on being told why it is precisely that no reconstruction procedures will have the backward reflection property for invalidity if *Def. I'* is true. The answer is that whereas arguments invalid by *Def. I'* have the property of having no forms that validate it, arguments having that property will not have it by virtue of any form they have. For suppose otherwise. Then there will be arguments whose form is such that there is no form that validates it. Any such argument will be invalid in virtue of its possession of that form, and any reconstruction procedures exposing that form will have the backward reflection property with respect to invalidity.

It is important to see that *Def. I'*, does not itself preclude an argument's being invalid by virtue of some form that it possesses. All that is required is that if such a form, F, exists then possession of it must preclude the having of any valid form. *Def I'* is moot on the question of whether F exists. The asymmetry thesis is not moot. For the asymmetry thesis to be true in its weakest formulation, *Def. V** has to be true, *Def. I'* has to be true, and it must also be true that even if F exists and some arguments have F, there must be some arguments on the hoof that don't have F and yet satisfy *Def. I'*. So much for truth. For the asymmetry thesis to be *interesting*, the class of such arguments must be large, much larger and more heterogeneous than any class of arguments valid by *Def. V* and invalid by *Def. I'*.[12] For it to be *maximally* interesting it needs to be shown that the property of having no valid form is never instantiated by virtue of any form that an argument has. It may be doubted that theoretical resources exist for showing this latter claim to be true, but I shall not doubt it here (but see below).

Let us, then, tentatively pledge ourselves to *Def. I'* and to the strong asymmetry thesis. Doing so is deeply consequential. No invalidity is invalidity of form. That being so, there is no such thing as a formal fallacy. To be a formal fallacy an argument would have to satisfy condition

---

11. It is ironic that the asymmetry reflected in *Def. V** and *Def. I'* is reversed at the level of our semantic definitions, *Def. V* and *Def. I*. To show (semantic) *in*validity it suffices to find premises that are true and a conclusion that is false. To show (semantic) validity it is necessary to show that no possibility exists that the premises are true and the conclusion is false. So at this level it will in general be easier to make a case for invalidity than for validity. I thank Hans Hansen for instruction on this point.

12. For example: "The thing is red; therefore the thing is colored."

FF: A is a formal fallacy iff it is a *formally* invalid argument that appears not to be.

If the asymmetry thesis is strongly sound, nothing fulfills *FF* and, if fallacies there are, they will satisfy some such condition as

IF: A is an informal fallacy iff . . . and, if invalid, A is not formally invalid (for there is no such thing as formal invalidity).

There are those who would rejoice in the collapse of the distinction between formal and informal fallacies. It is a naive rapture. Even waiving, for now, the weightiness of the task of filling the dots in *IF*, informal logicians are denied the intuitive comforts of such commonplaces as "informal fallacies are made distinctive by the fact that they stand apart from formal fallacies such as affirming the consequent and denying the antecedent." If there is to be a coherent distinction between these and those others thought to be distinctively different from them, it cannot be that the former are formal fallacies and the latter not.

Whatever the accumulating difficulties for informal logicians, the strong asymmetry thesis is ruinous for any theorist who holds that there is a category K of arguments *made* formally fallacious by concurrent fulfilment of the conditions of invalidity and appearing not to be. If invalidity is an informal property, no system of formal logic can qualify as its theory in the context of natural language argumentation. This leaves open the possibility that an informal theory of invalidity would still be constructible. Informal definitions there surely are, as witness *Def. I*. But *Def. I*, as we have seen, is no theory; it lacks the general wherewithal for proof.

Let us now recur to argument (9)–(11), and let us recall the difficulties it gave us for the dressing theory of English with respect to the property of sentential simplicity. When we left off, we found ourselves doubting whether we had a competent theoretical understanding of simplicity; we thought that we might not have at hand the requisite truth conditions. The requirement that simple sentences also be pair-wise semantically inert occasions similar difficulties, only worse. For it now falls to our dressing theory that it specify for any pair Φ, Ψ of simple sentences offered for reconstruction in PC, truth conditions for the open sentences $\ulcorner \Phi$ implies $\Psi \urcorner$ and $\ulcorner \Phi$ is inconsistent with $\Psi \urcorner$. The dressing theory, thus, must be a logic of implication and consistency for simple sentences of English. Since those sentences are inputs to the dressing theory and since dressing is prior to reconstruction, the logic will have to make do without logical forms, which are the output of reconstruction. This will be an informal logic, if anything is. But, denied the fulcrum of logical forms, it is greatly to be doubted whether this logic will be able to produce general proof procedures. It will be quite true that "the thing is red," and "the thing is colored" will fail the pairwise semantic inertia test, but what will prove it so, and what will prove it so for any pair of sentences which are so? Does anything deserve the name of logic in the absence of such proof procedures? I harbor grave doubts about this. Of course, proof procedures aren't always and only the manipulation of logical forms. Axiomatic set theory fixes and achieves high standards of proof, but insofar as set theory trades in theorems that are not formally valid, its proof procedures are not simply manipulations of syntax. If a system of logic is to do well with proofs detached from a domain of logical forms, it will require what it manifestly has not been shown to have, namely, a susceptibility to theoretical treatment by way of finite stocks of (so-called) nonlogical axioms or axiom-schemata.

Consequences of more immediate significance press for recognition. If what I have been saying is so then we have nothing that counts as a theory of reconstruction for English. The problem is especially acute in the dressing theory. We lack a theoretically adequate understanding of simplicity and semantic inertia, each indispensable to the determination of the logical forms of English. This is a disaster. An argument, Δ, presses in upon us. It is this.

1. For any argument of English, A, having a logical form is, by *Def.* V* a condition on its validity.
2. Being dressed is a condition on A's having a logical form.
3. Having an informal logic is a condition on a dressing theory for A (by the pairwise semantic inertia condition).
4. No theory is a logic if it lacks proof procedures.
5. Informal logic, so-called, lacks proof procedures.
6. Hence, informal logic does not exist.
7. Hence, there is no dressing theory for A.
8. Hence, there is no reconstruction theory for A.
9. Hence, there is no theory of validity for A.

Just pages ago, we wondered whether the asymmetry thesis is true in ways that make it maximally interesting. It would be maximally interesting iff the property of having no valid forms were never a property that an argument had by virtue of any form that it has. We said that it is open to question whether resources exist to show this true, and with appropriate diffidence we subscribed to the strong asymmetry thesis only tentatively. As we now see, it doesn't matter whether our subscription deserved the tentativeness we give it. Argument Δ easily extends to give for invalidity the same result that it gives for validity. Whether or not the asymmetry thesis is true enough to be interesting, it is displaced by a more fearsome claim. It is the *symmetry thesis*.

> ST: There is no theory of validity *or* invalidity for natural language arguments.

It is not a happy result. It compromises the ambitions of any formal logician naive enough to think that a theory of logical forms could be grafted onto natural languages in ways that disclose the logical structures that they "really" have. Formal logicians, if ever there were any doubt of it previously, must approach language with considerable circumspection. With the connivance of neologism and other *ad hoc* devices language needs to be contrived with artifice enough to avert the discouraging difficulties of dressage. Language thus will have to be rigged and gerrymandered in ways that serve, for example, the objectives of extensional science, including mathematics. Suitably rigged, a theory of logical forms may qualify as a theory of validity and invalidity for such "languages." It can be said, in fact, that a condition on the rigging is that the asymmetry thesis will turn out, at best, to be not *very* interesting when applied to results of the rigging.

It is clear, in any event, that the business of rigging a language is the engineering of radical departures from the real thing. No lexicon of any natural language will long survive the process, what with predicate vagueness banned outright, adverbs all but barred, adjectival constructions crimped, and on and on. Whatever the prospects for success with respect to these much-circumscribed ambitions, the formal logician has a coherently formulable programme. The informal logician, on the other hand, is simply out of business.[13]

13. Research for this chapter was supported by a Research Grant from the Social Sciences and Humanities Council of Canada and by an appointment in the second half of 1992 as Visiting Professor in the Institute for Discourse Analysis and the Study of Argumentation at the University of Amsterdam. I am most grateful to SSHRC and to DASA for their support. I also thank Hans Hansen, Frans H. van Eemeren, Rob Grootendorst, and Francisca Snoek Henkemans for their helpful comments.

PART III

Analyses
of
Specific Fallacies

Introduction

The papers that follow present analyses or discussions of specific fallacies; all have been written especially for this volume. We believe that they are representative of the best work currently being done on fallacies. Whatever justice there may have been to Hamblin's complaints about the Standard Treatment in 1970,[1] those complaints do not apply to the work represented here.

Overview

These papers illustrate a number of things that are true of current thinking and writing about the fallacies.

First, these are not brief sketches offered in textbooks that invite students to apply fallacy labels in mechanical ways. Rather, they are attempts either (1) to provide a theoretical elucidation of the nature of the fallacy under consideration, or else (2) to solve a theoretical problem that arises in connection with the fallacy.

Second, in most of these pieces the authors draw on a theoretical background to accomplish the task they have undertaken. This appeal to theoretical underpinnings takes at least two different forms. In some cases (e.g., van Eemeren and Grootendorst, Bachman, Freeman) the authors draw on an explicit theory of the nature of argumentation, reasoning and/or of fallacy to provide a context for locating and illuminating the fallacy under consideration. In other cases (e.g., Woods, Krabbe, Brinton), the authors draw on specific theoretical notions or apparatuses drawn from allied disciplines in order to clarify problematic aspects of the fallacy they are writing about.

Third, as a group these papers demonstrate the variety of theories and theoretical techniques that are currently being put to use in elucidating both the nature of particular fallacies and the problems arising in connection with them. In 1970, Hamblin had complained that "we have no *theory* of fallacy at all, in the sense in which we have theories of correct reasoning or infer-

---

1. See Hamblin (1970, 12): "as debased, worn-out and dogmatic a treatment as could be imagined, incredibly tradition-bound, yet lacking in logic and historical sense alike, and almost without connection to anything else in modern Logic at all."

ence" (11). Some might take the fact that there is still no common theoretical approach in place to be evidence that the niche Hamblin wanted to see filled remains as empty today as it was in 1970. But the situation is not, we believe, that simple, and there are three reasons why it is not. (a) Even in the absence of a single theory or paradigm that dominates the study of fallacies, there is in fact a considerable and robust theoretical literature today that did not exist in 1970. (b) There is a strand or echo that turns up in more than half the pieces here—the appeal to dialogue or dialectic as the appropriate context for understanding at least the informal fallacies, an appeal which Hamblin himself endorsed. (Among the papers that follow, see van Eemeren and Grootendorst, Walton, Krabbe, Bachman, Freeman, Pinto; see also the works cited in notes 9–14 of the Introduction to Part II above.) It might be argued, therefore, that there are signs in the current literature that a common theory is beginning to emerge. (c) At least two of the authors here (Woods, Pinto) question whether a *theory* of the fallacies is possible, but think that sufficient resources and motivation nevertheless exist for a fruitful deployment of the traditional fallacy labels.

Fourth, most of the papers that follow are very sensitive to the fact that no simplistic formula can capture the difference between, say, a fallacious appeal to authority and one that is not fallacious. Charles Willard's paper in Part II made much of the fact that appropriate use of many of the traditional fallacy labels is highly sensitive to contextual factors. This kind of problem occurs with respect to almost all the traditional "informal fallacies" and there are two different linguistic strategies that have been taken in face of it. One is illustrated by van Eemeren and Grootendorst, who want to reserve the traditional label *argumentum ad hominem* for *objectionable* cases of criticizing a person in the context of argumentative discourse. In short, they build the idea of fallacy into the very concept of *ad hominem*. The other linguistic strategy is illustrated by Brinton, who recommends we use *ad hominem* for a particular sort of attack on a person, whether that attack constitutes a fallacy or not; his problem then becomes distinguishing between the objectionable or fallacious uses of *ad hominem* and the acceptable ones. Whichever linguistic strategy one adopts, the substantive problems remain the same: one must trace or illuminate the subtle differences between dialectical or argumentative moves that are fallacious or objectionable and superficially similar moves that are not objectionable. These problems are widely recognized in the contemporary literature, as in the sample of papers here, and constitute the motivation of a good deal of the theoretical work on fallacies that is currently taking place.

There is a more or less traditional list of prominent fallacy labels, whose number is in the neighborhood of eighteen to twenty.[2] And, of course, contemporary authors are free to create new labels[3] or new schemes.[4] The papers that follow deal with a proper subset of the fallacies from the traditional list. All would be classed today as "informal fallacies,"[5] since what is at issue in them is not a violation of the "rules" of formal logic. In selecting topics for inclusion, considerations of space made it impractical to deal with every fallacy on the traditional list. Our aim has therefore been twofold:

(a) to include a representative sample of the major fallacies or fallacy labels currently in use, and
(b) to choose examples that would permit us to illustrate the variety of different approaches taken in the theoretical discussions of fallacies in the current literature.

Summary of Individual Selections

Ad Hominem (Alan Brinton)

We offer two different, indeed opposed, analyses of the *ad hominem*. The first is by Alan Brinton, and pictures the *ad hominem* as a type of argument that, in real life, is usually not fallacious; the disciplinary background of Brinton's

2. John Woods refers to "the traditional eighteen fallacies or so, as disclosed in a punning, joking, and yes, at times even witless Standard Treatment" and takes to calling them "the gang of eighteen" (Woods 1992, 24). In Hamblin's account of the Standard Treatment (1970, chap. 1), there were thirteen individual fallacies drawn from Aristotle, the four *ad* fallacies usually attributed to Locke, and (44–48) four additional categories of fallacies: (1) the "other 'arguments *ad*' . . . more rarely mentioned" (*ad baculum*, *ad populum*, *ad odium*, etc.), (2) formally invalid syllogisms (comprising a number of faults that have traditional names found, for example, in Whately; see Hamblin 1970, 196ff.), (3) fallacies of scientific method (including the genetic fallacy, hasty generalization, as well as some less well known variants due to Salmon and to Cohen and Nagel), (4) a grab-bag category called "Miscellaneous" (that includes the pathetic fallacy and Moore's famous naturalistic fallacy, among others). A good sense of the emergence and history of the major fallacy labels can be gleaned from the Introduction to Part I of this volume and from chapters 2 to 6 of Hamblin.

3. As Michael Scriven does (1987, 333–49).

4. As Maurice Finocchiaro does in "Six Types of Fallaciousness," excerpted in Part II of this volume.

5. As opposed to formal fallacies. Hamblin (1970, 195) says that the concept of "formal fallacies" dates from Whately, though he suggests (1970, 205) that Whately's use of "formal fallacy" may not map all that neatly onto twentieth-century distinctions between formal and informal fallacies.

analysis lies in rhetoric. The other analysis is by van Eemeren and Groot-endorst, and portrays the ad hominem as typically a violation of the rules appropriate to argumentative discourse and as therefore almost always a fallacy; this second analysis is an example of a pragma-dialectical analysis of a fallacy.

In the first half of his paper, Brinton develops a conception of *ad hominem* as a type of argument, not as a type of fallacy. Not all arguments or rhetorical strategies directed against some person are to count as *ad hominems*.

> The *ad hominem* is directed toward a person or persons, but in the following way. For some particular person, say Jones, to qualify as a victim of an *ad hominem* argument, there must be some proposition (or point of view, etc.), say *p*, of which Jones is regarded as an advocate. The typical object of *ad hominem* attack is Jones's advocacy of *p*. . . . A normal, nonfallacious case of *ad hominem* argument . . . will consist in bringing alleged facts about Jones to bear in an attempt to influence hearers' attitudes toward Jones's-advocacy-of-*p*. That is to say, the conclusion of a logically healthy *ad hominem* in this case will be about Jones's advocacy of *p*; it will not be about *p* itself.

The conception offered here differs from the conception of the *ad hominem* as essentially a type of argument in which the *truth* of a proposition is attacked via an attack on a person who advocates that proposition. *Such* arguments are indeed virtually always fallacious, but Brinton maintains that "this logical phenomenon is not typical of the *ad hominem*; it is to be found mainly in textbook examples (or in logically hard-hearted textbook interpretations of real-life examples)."

When real-life *ad hominems* go awry, it is likely to be for very different reasons: either because negative information about the person is *irrelevant* to that person's advocacy of *p* (e.g., "I refuse to listen to Senator Jones's proposals for amending the New Bank Bill; he cheats on his wife"), or because of a failure in *degree of support* (e.g., "Candidate Jones has no right to moralize about the family; he was once seen arguing with his wife").[6]

In the second part of his paper Brinton develops a notion drawn from

---

6. Still another kind of failure occurs when the assertions made about the person are false or doubtful.

Aristotle's *Rhetoric* to explain why *ad hominem* arguments are *good* arguments when they don't suffer from the failures listed above. *Ad hominem* arguments call into question the *ethos* (character) of an advocate—where *ethos* is something that can be analyzed in terms of good sense (*phronesis*), good moral character (*arete*) and good will (*eunoia*). Assessing *ethos* is important because, especially in deliberative contexts, we must decide *whose* opinions and judgments to take seriously, to consider, to follow up on—and *ethos* is an apt ground on which to base such a decision. Brinton argues that *ad hominems* are appropriate, especially in deliberative contexts, because "the ordinary *ad hominem* may in general be understood to be an assault on the rhetorical ethos of a speaker whose *ethos* would otherwise be regarded as more of a persuasive factor than the adhominist believes reasonable. It is a legitimate form of argument and is logically acceptable in many, perhaps most, of its actual occurrences."

Ad Hominem:
Van Eemeren and Grootendorst's Pragma-Dialectical Analysis

Van Eemeren and Grootendorst begin by criticizing what they take to be the Standard Treatment of *ad hominem* as a fallacy of relevance. They find this problematic because (a) reconstructing fallacies of relevance as arguments "usually requires stretching a point or two" and (b) the notion of logical relevance is left undefined and its connection with logical validity remains unexplained.

Instead of appealing to an unanalyzed or unclarified notion of relevance, van Eemeren and Grootendorst think that the fallacies of relevance can be analyzed as violations of the rules for critical discussion. In particular, "the *argumentum ad hominem* is a violation of the first rule for critical discussion: 'Parties must not prevent each other from advancing standpoints or casting doubt on standpoints.' " They maintain that all three variants on the *ad hominem*—the abusive, the circumstantial, and the *tu quoque*—violate the first rule because "they all amount to a party claiming that the other party has no right to speak."

Finally, van Eemeren and Grootendorst compare the pragma-dialectical approach to *ad hominem* with the Standard Treatment. In the Standard Treatment some *ad hominems* depend on premises that are relevant, and some do not; hence in the Standard Treatment there is a problem of determining which *ad hominems* are fallacious and which are not. In the pragma-dialectical approach, this problem does not arise since there are no exceptions: "If the criterion for one of the variants of the *argumentum ad hominem* is fulfilled, a personal attack is always a violation of the first rule for critical discussion. It is therefore, without any exception, a fallacy." Van Eemeren and Grootendorst maintain that even when *ad hominem* is a response to a misuse of expertise or authority by an opponent, it is still not a correct discussion move, since "two wrongs do not make a right."

For a fuller understanding of the content and rationale of the first rule for critical discussion, the reader may consult "The Pragma-dialectical Approach to Fallacies," Chapter 9 of this volume.

Begging the Question (Douglas Walton)

In a paper that appeared in *Journal of Philosophy* in 1990,[7] Walton calls for a redefinition of logic that extends its scope beyond that of formal logic. The extension consists in including in logic what he calls "logical pragmatics" or "the study of the uses of logical reasoning in a context of argument."[8] He sums up his conception as follows:

> *Formal logic* abstracts from the content of the premises and conclusion of an argument, calling them propositions. *Informal logic* must interpret the uses of these propositions as speech acts in a context of dialogue, seeing them as moves that incur or relinquish commitments, e.g., assertions, denials, retractions, questioning moves, etc.
>
> Formal logic has to do with forms of argument (syntax) and truth values (semantics). At any rate, that is the traditional conception. Informal logic (or more broadly, argumentation, as a field) has to do with the uses of argumentation schemes in a context of dialogue, an essentially pragmatic undertaking. . . .[9]
>
> . . . If the study of fallacies is to be part of logic, clearly logicians make no headway in working toward its primary goal unless the pragmatic study of the uses of reasoning in argument (informal logic) is included as a legitimate part of the subject.[10]

7. Douglas N. Walton, "What is Reasoning? What is an Argument?" *Journal of Philosophy* 87 (1990): 399–419.

8. Ibid., 417.

9. Ibid., 417–18.

10. Ibid., 419.

Walton's contribution to this volume exemplifies this approach to the study of fallacies. In Chapter 16 he lays down two requirements for committing the fallacy of begging the question: "(i) there must be a circular sequence of reasoning, where the conclusion to be established is either identical to one of the premises, or the premise in question depends on the conclusion, and (ii) the circular sequence of reasoning must be used illicitly in a context of dialogue (conversation) to escape the proper fulfillment of a legitimate burden of proof in that context."[11]

He then proceeds to show that whether or not a sequence of reasoning is circular can be determined only by reference to the context of dialogue in which that reasoning occurs. Moreover, Walton maintains, circular reasoning itself is not always fallacious or illegitimate. There is a problem, then, in determining when circular reasoning is fallacious and when it is not. The key to determining this is the concept of *evidential priority*: "meaning that the premises are being used as evidence to support the conclusion in such a way that each premise must be capable of being established without having to depend on the prior establishment of the conclusion." Issues of evidential priority can only be settled with reference to specific contexts of dialogue, since what is required to establish a premise depends on what assumptions and concessions the participants in a dialogue are prepared to make.

Walton lays out the concept of evidential priority and the restrictions on the use of circular reasoning in abstract fashion, and then shows how the ideas thus developed can be used to analyze the example of begging the question offered in the opening paragraph of the paper. He claims that this sort of analysis "can be applied to more subtle, problematic and lengthy cases with good results," and he summarizes the three steps that must be taken to conduct such an analysis successfully. Walton concludes by remarking: "As

11. A brief note on burden of proof is in order. In a dialogal situation, one or the other party has the burden of proof with respect to any given claim that is advanced in the dialogue. In general, someone introducing or making a claim has the burden of proof with respect to that claim—has, as it were, an obligation to show that the claim is justified. One can shift the burden of proof with respect to a claim by providing a cogent *prima facie* argument in support of that claim. In such an event, the burden of proof shifts to the other party. In a court of criminal law, the initial burden rests with the prosecution: they have an obligation to show that the accused is guilty, and they lose if they fail to discharge that obligation. But if the prosecution makes a *prima facie* case for the guilt of the accused, then the burden of proof shifts to the defense; the defense now has an obligation either to find fault with the case made by the prosecution or else to make a case for the innocence of the accused. (The principle that "you are (presumed) innocent until you are proven guilty" expresses this point about the burden of proof in a criminal trial.)

noted, such an evaluation has formal elements. But it is also very much a matter of pragmatic analysis of the context of dialogue in a given case."

Appeal to Force (John Woods)

The discussion of *appeal to force* in Woods's chapter fits nicely into the framework outlined in his 1992 "Who Cares about the Fallacies?" In that earlier essay, Woods had suggested that "the fallacies are idealized caricatures that are also symptoms of the sorts of things that can go wrong with those skills that make up our rational survival kits." He added

> the fallacies that the tradition has thrown up are a highly idealized, vivid symptomatology of basic rational misperformance. . . .
> . . . . It follows from this that the importance of the fallacies is derivative. They owe their importance to the importance of survival and to the contribution thereto made by those skills with which they are associated by caricatured misperformance. (1992, 25)

Woods offered a list "without any pretense of completeness" of those survival skills. Its seventh and final member was "the rudiments of cost-benefit protections of self-interest, including measures for conflict resolution." A few pages later, referring back to this seventh survival skill, he said, "Elementary routines of cost-benefit analysis are needed for the protection of self-interest. This is prudence, . . . the recognition of where one's interests lie and of what will and won't conduce to their realization. Whereupon the *ad baculum* enters the picture: 'Your money or your life!' " (1992, 28).

Moreover, in the 1992 paper Woods had argued against what he saw as premature attempts to provide a unified or integrated theory of the fallacies. He proposed an adequacy condition that any unified theory of the fallacies should meet: "An integrated theory of the fallacies should preserve the fallacies in as much of their difference as reflects the difference in the rational survival skills of whose misperformance they are idealized symptomatic caricatures" (1992, 43). If we accept such a condition, Woods argued

> we would have committed ourselves to the analysis of the fallacies in the context of the rational exercise of deduction, induction, analogy, dialectic, prudential reasoning, conflict resolution, and much, much more besides. . . . It is better, I suggest, to have something theoretically interesting at hand before taking on the daunting task of unifica-

tion. Better, too, is the present course of tolerant methodological pluralism and, yes, of "a different [type of] logical system[12] for each different
[type of] fallacy." (1992, 43)

It seems to us that the approach that Woods takes toward *appeal to force* in
this volume exemplifies the approach sketched in his 1992 paper. Woods
works through seven types of case that, in one way or another, might be
construed as arguments that appeal to force—arguments that enjoin belief or
action on the ground of some threat or bribe. The first two cases amount to
wholly implausible or practically unworkable parodies of argument; the third
("Accept *P* or I'll punch your nose") is a workable argument that is objectionable because the arguer is "suborning dialectal insincerity" in the arguee. The
fourth through the seventh cases (Risk Aversion Strategies, the Stick Up,
Negotiations, Veiled Threats) are the ones Woods is interested in investigating. And he explores each by sketching the concrete context of reasoning or
dialogue (prudential reasoning, cost-benefit analysis, collective bargaining)
within which such arguments occur and attempting to judge them according
to norms appropriate to those contexts.

The main value of Woods's analyses lies, we think, in a sharpened appreciation of the opportunities and pitfalls that await us in the regions of practical thinking that he explores. But the reader should not overlook the concluding summary in which Woods articulates his main conclusions in five lucid
theses.

Appeal to Ignorance (Erik Krabbe)

Like Walton and van Eemeren and Grootendorst, Krabbe wants to illuminate the issues surrounding fallacies by considering arguments dialectically,
i.e., by viewing allegedly fallacious arguments in the context of the dialogues
in which they occur. Krabbe's specific concern is with the *ad ignorantiam* or
appeal to ignorance—with arguments that proceed from the fact that the
negation of a proposition isn't known or hasn't been proved, to the conclusion that the proposition itself is true. He opens his essay by placing the *ad
ignorantiam* in historical context and outlines the structure of the analyses
that will follow.

He next considers two varieties of *ad ignorantiam* argument that would

12. The reference to a different logical system for each different fallacy is presumably an allusion
to complaints made by van Eemeren and Grootendorst (1989, 101).

constitute a fallacious use of this argument form. One variant considered is a dialectical move that amounts to an objectionable attempt to shift the burden of proof:[13] the person defending a claim challenges the opponent to prove that the claim is false. Krabbe shows that such a move is objectionable by showing that the dialogue rule that would license it would be an inadvisable rule (i.e., would not serve the legitimate goals of a persuasion dialogue). The next variant considered involves a principle for evaluating the outcome of a dialogue—a principle that holds that if a participant has not successfully defended *not-p*, then she or he is obliged to (provisionally) accept *p*. Krabbe concludes that to follow such a rule is to commit a fallacy, since the rule is rash.

The rules considered and rejected are rules that would license *all* arguments that "appeal to ignorance." But from the fact that *not all* arguments of this sort are *good* it doesn't follow that all arguments of this sort are bad. Krabbe next considers cases in which a proponent in a dialogue utilizes an appeal to ignorance, and asks what implications this has for the opponent. Krabbe maintains that if an opponent wants to object to such an appeal, the burden of proof lies on the opponent to show that the appeal to ignorance is defective or weak in the case at hand. This is so, says Krabbe, because there are a number of kinds of case in which it *is* reasonable to argue from the fact that a proposition hasn't been shown false to the conclusion that the proposition is true.[14] In other words, "the appeal to ignorance in dialogue in itself does not constitute a fallacy."[15]

These conclusions, says Krabbe, do not complete the study of *ad ignorantiam*, but rather enable us to pose the problems concerning *ad ignorantiam* in a fruitful way. Krabbe's concluding section outlines a research agenda for a study of the appropriateness, strengths, and weaknesses of various kinds of "ignorance premises" in the context of persuasive dialogues.

Appeal to Popularity (James Freeman)

In discussing the appeal to popularity, Freeman is interested in one species of the traditional fallacy of *ad populum*—the bandwagon appeal (arguing for a claim on the ground that it is widely believed) as opposed to grandstanding

13. See note 11 above on burden of proof.

14. A second reason is given as well: that the proponent presumably intends the appeal to ignorance to be a good reason, and therefore the opponent should at least give him a hearing or else explain why she does not think this is worthwhile.

15. The context is one in which Krabbe is conceding that *ad ignorantiam* is (always?) inappropriate in an argumentative text, as contrasted with a dialogue.

(attempting to win popular assent by arousing the emotions and enthusiasms of the multitude). He begins by addressing the question of whether this type of argument should be defined as one which claims that widespread belief provides *conclusive* support for a claim, or rather as one that claims merely that it provides *sufficient* support. He opts for broader definition of the appeal to authority "as an argument that claims that because many, most, or all people accept a certain belief or approve a certain course of action, we have sufficient reason to accept that belief as true or that course of action as right."

Now Freeman wants to maintain that appeals to popularity are "basically hasty conclusion fallacies": "The data concerning the popularity of a belief is simply not sufficient to warrant accepting the belief. The logical error in appeal to popularity lies in its inflating the value of popularity as evidence." In such a reading, appeals to popularity are *always* fallacious.

This creates a problem, however, since something which at least superficially resembles the popularity of a claim is widely recognized as a legitimate source of warrant—namely, that fact that a claim is "common knowledge." This leads to the question: "What does it mean to say that a claim is a matter of common knowledge or that common knowledge vouches for a claim? More trenchantly, what more does this mean beyond saying that many, most, all people accept that claim? If it does not mean more than that, and popularity is never sufficient to warrant acceptance, then it would seem that common knowledge is not a proper source of presumption."

Freeman develops a solution by considering the problem in the context of critical dialogue and applying technical or semitechnical concepts that have been developed for clarifying such dialectical situations. The principal concepts he deploys are those of *presumption* ("to say that there is a presumption in favor of a statement means that in the absence of counterevidence or counterindications, we may accept that statement") and the concept of the obligations that fall on the proponent and the challenger in a dialectical exchange. The issue then becomes one of whether a proponent can create a presumption in favor of a proposition by claiming that that proposition is widely believed or that it is common knowledge. In oversimplified form, Freeman's answer is that such a move is not open to the proponent: "It is the challenger's role to recognize that being a matter of common knowledge creates a presumption for a claim and that a particular claim is a matter of common knowledge. Hence whether a statement is a matter of common knowledge is a question for the challenger to decide from her perspective." This blocks the appeal to common belief or to common knowledge as an *argument* that can be deployed by a proponent, while at the same time preserving common knowledge as a source of presumption in favor of a claim when the challenger is prepared to acknowledge the status of that claim as common knowledge.

Freeman fleshes out his story with an account of how a claim can gain the status of common knowledge for a challenger. The details of this account make it plain why it is dialectically inefficacious for a proponent to claim that a proposition is common knowledge unless the challenger is already prepared to concede this. Freeman's conclusion is that appeals to popularity are always fallacious, but that "appeals to common knowledge, at least appeals by the challengers to the common knowledge included in their own background knowledge, are not appeals to popularity."

Appeal to Authority (James Bachman)

Bachman—who coauthored *What If . . . ? Toward Excellence in Reasoning* with Jaakko Hintikka[16]—employs Hintikka's interrogative model of reasoning to contextualize the issues associated with appeal to authority.

As we saw above, Walton conceived the study of *argumentation* as dealing with "the uses of argumentation schemes in a context of dialogue, an essentially pragmatic undertaking"; but one that relies on formal logic to provide an elaboration of the forms of (valid) argument. Somewhat analogously, Hintikka's interrogative model conceives of *reasoning* as made up of two kinds of steps or moves that constitute "the fundamental ingredients of rational inquiry": interrogative steps and logical inference steps.

In the interrogative model, the inference steps are required to be deductive and (with a qualification to be mentioned in a moment) their appropriateness is a matter of the rules of deductive logic. The interrogative steps are those "that seek or gather information for an inquiry or argument," and such information-seeking is "modeled as an activity of addressing questions to sources." The sources of information are called "oracles"; they may be, but need not be, human persons.

Applying the model to an ordinary oral or written expression of inquiry (called a "sketch") consists in (1) *analyzing* the sketch (disentangling and identifying the interrogative and inference moves), (2) *evaluating* the sketch so analyzed, and (3) *constructing* a new or enhanced inquiry based on the prior analysis and/or evaluation of a sketch. Of principal interest here is the evaluation phase in the application of the model.

16. (Mountain View, Calif.: Mayfield, 1991).

Evaluation of the moves in an inquiry, whether they be interrogative moves or inference moves, is on the basis of *definitory rules for correctness* and *strategies for effectiveness.* "The former define the steps admissible in correct reasoning, while the latter suggest ways to make creative use of the steps allowed by the definitory rules."

In the evaluation of *inference* moves, the *definitory* rules "that characterize valid deductive inference" hold center stage, though there is scope even here for noting the efficiency or appropriateness of the deductive strategies employed. It is in the evaluation of *interrogative* moves, however, that *strategic* considerations become crucial. (There is at least one definitory rule for interrogations, which requires that the presuppositions of any question be established before the question is asked; violation of this rule constitutes the fallacy of many questions.)

In this model of reasoning, appeal to authority—far from being a fallacy—is an essential ingredient of inquiry. Accepting the answers to the questions we put to an "oracle" is, after all, a case of appeal to the authority of that oracle, and inferences must always begin from such answers. But the very indispensability of appeal to authority, together with the fact that the "oracles" to which we appeal are not infallible, makes it all the more important that our interrogative strategies be effective and appropriate. In the interrogative model, issues surrounding the traditional concerns about appeal to authority are reconceptualized as issues dealing with strategies for effective questioning. Bachman's paper presents an overview of such strategy issues as they are viewed from the perspective of the interrogative model. He then develops the idea that "many traditional fallacies do not so much indicate crimes against the definitory rules of reasoning as problems that arise in choosing and deploying strategies for successfully seeking and gathering information through questioning." Following up on this idea, he attempts to highlight hitherto unnoticed interconnections among issues traditionally parceled out under the headings of *appeal to authority, abusive ad hominem,* and *begging the question.*

Equivocation (Lawrence Powers)

Powers's paper "Equivocation" contains both (i) a defense of his controversial "one fallacy theory"[17] and (ii) a lucid exposition of the main varieties of

17. In the second paragraph of his paper, Powers describes the theory as controversial. It's worth noting that in *Soph. Ref.* 177b8–10, Aristotle says, "It is evident also that not all refutations depend on ambiguity as some people say they do."

equivocation (or of what Aristotle would have called the fallacies dependent on language).

(i) The defense of the "one fallacy theory" depends on the acceptance of three ideas:

(1) that fallacies are arguments that are not good but appear to be so
(2) that arguments whose surface grammar does not appear to exemplify a valid argument form do not appear to be good
(3) that an argument can, in the relevant sense, appear to be good even though it is readily seen through.

By deploying these ideas appropriately, Powers thinks he can defend the claim that "there is no clear way to make an argument appear to have a goodness it really lacks except by playing with ambiguities."

The first of these ideas—Powers's definition of fallacy—comes close to a common (though controverted) definition:

(DF) Fallacies are arguments that appear to be valid but are not.

In DF, invalidity (and, if validity is equated with formal validity, failure to have valid logical form) is a necessary condition of fallacy. In Powers's account, however, arguments that exhibit no valid logical form are typically disqualified from counting as fallacies (since typically such arguments don't appear to have any forms other than invalid ones and therefore, in Powers's account, don't appear to be good).[18]

Readers who would resist Powers's conclusion are quite likely to dispute (3). But before rejecting Powers's thesis out of hand, such readers should consider two things. First, (3) is necessary basically to defend the legitimacy of the examples that are used in the paper to illustrate the various forms of equivocation;[19] as Powers points out, the truly interesting fallacious arguments will not be so readily seen through. Second, Powers is attempting to use an objective, rather than a subjective, criterion of appearance: in his

18. Powers's definition of fallacy differs subtly from DF. In fact, one of the standard objections to DF—that question-begging arguments are valid but are fallacies nonetheless (see, for example, the objections to DF in Govier's paper in Part II of this volume)—does not apply to Powers's definition. This objection to DF is not one that would matter to Powers, however, since "the One Fallacy Theory holds that there is no such fallacy as begging the question."

19. And many of these, it should be remembered, are quite traditional examples of fallacies; some of them go back to Aristotle.

account, what makes an argument appear good seems to be that in some respect it exemplifies a valid logical form.[20]

(ii) Powers's review of the varieties of equivocation is rooted in Aristotle's account of fallacies dependent on language in *On Sophistical Refutations*. Though it does not repeat the Aristotelian account in every detail, it is a lucid summary and updating of the tradition Aristotle initiated and should prove valuable to modern readers struggling with many of the obscurities in *Sophistical Refutations*.

Post Hoc Ergo Propter Hoc *(Robert Pinto)*

On the basis of a review of the literature on *post hoc,* Pinto concludes that three distinguishable species of *post hoc* reasoning have been recognized:

1. *Causal interpretation of particular events* (concluding that particular event A caused a particular event B from the fact that A preceded B)
2. *Inference from correlation to cause* (concluding that there is a causal relation between two event types from the fact that those event types are positively correlated)
3. *Causal generalization from one sequence of events* (concluding that there is a causal relation between two event types A and B from the fact that a single instance of A was followed by an instance of B).

Pinto then asks whether all *post hoc* reasoning is fallacious. He argues first that our inferences from correlation to cause need not be fallacious, so long as the kind of doxastic attitude that we entertain toward the causal conclusion is appropriate to the extent and character of the correlational evidence on which it is based. Next, he produces three cases of the causal interpretation of particular events which, he claims, are nonfallacious instances of *post hoc* reasoning and which justify a fair degree of confidence in their causal conclusion.

Next, he poses the question of whether it is possible to state necessary and/or sufficient conditions for distinguishing fallacious from nonfallacious instances of *post hoc* reasoning. He argues that any strictly "local" rule—anything like an algorithm—for distinguishing fallacious from nonfallacious

---

20. Indeed, in this way Powers may succeed in meeting an objection that Johnson raises against attempts to define fallacies as "arguments which appear to be X but are not," to wit, the objection that such definitions render the concept of fallacy too subjective. (See Johnson's essay, Chapter 7 of this volume.)

cases will hold only *ceteris paribus* and will always be liable to being overridden by other considerations.

Finally, he asks how a fruitful use of fallacy labels such as *post hoc ergo propter hoc* is possible in the absence of any general theory that can distinguish fallacious from nonfallacious cases. He answers that there is an entrenched critical practice that anchors our talk about such fallacies and renders it illuminating.

14

The *Ad Hominem*

Alan Brinton

The literal meaning of "*ad hominem*" is simply "toward the person." Arguments "toward," about, or against persons are, of course, plentiful in both public and private discourse. They fill the editorial pages of newspapers and enliven nearly every public controversy and political campaign. But it does not seem advisable to classify every argument or rhetorical strategy directed against or toward some person as *ad hominem*, at least not for fallacy theorists. The sort of arguments that merit the distinction of being set apart under the label *ad hominem* are, I suggest, logically interesting and sometimes logically problematic in a way in which someone's arguing that, say,

> (1) Jones is not a fit candidate for public office, since he is a known embezzler

is not. (1) is an example of a perfectly ordinary and unexceptional argument type. It belongs to the class of arguments that draw an evaluative conclusion on the basis of one or more factual claims. The fact that the conclusion is about a person's character is merely "accidental"; from a logical point of view, argument (1) is only coincidentally about a person. It is of a kind with

> (2) The Mitsuzuki is not a fit car to drive, since it has a history of rolling over on sharp curves.

The bare bones of the *ad hominem* are, as I conceive of it, as follows. The *ad hominem* is directed toward a person or persons, but in the following way.

For some particular person, say Jones, to qualify as a victim of *ad hominem* argument, there must be some proposition (or point of view, etc.), say *P*, of which Jones is regarded as an advocate. The typical *object* of *ad hominem* attack is Jones's advocacy of *P*. We may somewhat artificially distinguish three elements, any one of which might be the focus of attention at some time during the life of an *ad hominem*. In this case they are *Jones*, *Jones's advocacy-of-P*, and *P* itself. A normal, nonfallacious case of *ad hominem* argument, in relation to these particular elements, will consist in bringing alleged facts about Jones to bear in an attempt to influence hearers' attitudes toward Jones's advocacy-of-*P*. That is to say, the conclusion of a logically healthy *ad hominem* in this case will be about Jones's advocacy of *P*; it will not be about *P* itself.[1]

---

1. My attention in what follows is focused on ordinary run-of-the-mill *ad hominems* and what they (as well as more exotic *ad hominems*) have in common. This is why I speak of the "bare bones" of the *ad hominem*.

Various types of *ad hominem* argument have been identified by different writers. Four kinds in particular have been discussed by informal logicians: the *ad hominem* "abusive," the *ad hominem* "circumstantial," "poisoning the well," and the *tu quoque*. The *ad hominem* abusive is generally distinguished in terms of the making of disparaging personal remarks about one's opponent in argument in order to discredit the opponent's point of view; the ad hominem circumstantial is usually characterized as attempting to show that, given certain alleged facts about one's opponent's background, behavior, prior commitments, or other circumstances, it is inconsistent for that opponent to accept (or reject) a particular point of view. "Poisoning the well" is said to consist in attacking the motives of one's opponents in advocating their claims. And the *tu quoque* ("you, too") is identified as a tactic of responding to criticism by pointing out that a critic of one's behavior is no less guilty of comparable misdeeds.

The conceptions of these four, especially of the "circumstantial" *ad hominem*, are, however, by no means very clear or very consistent in the literature. Nor are they clearly distinguishable as four separate subspecies. Cases of "poisoning the well" seem arguably to all be cases of the "circumstantial" *ad hominem*, as do cases of *tu quoque*. Most characterizations of "*ad hominem* abusive" are, moreover, loose enough to cover most of the examples usually given under each of the other three headings. All negative *ad hominems* are in fact "abusive" in that all attack the character of their victim, either directly or by implication; accordingly, a case can be made for regarding the *ad hominem* "abusive" as most fundamental, if such distinctions are to be invoked at all. (It should also be mentioned, however, though the matter will not be pursued, that there is no good reason, from a logical point of view, to refuse recognition as genuine *ad hominems* to argument strategies which commend or vindicate rather than attack.)

There are, in addition, extraordinary *ad hominem* strategies that are beyond the purview of the present discussion, for example the dastardly *petitio circumstantial ad hominem principii* Freudian strategy of dismissing potential critics of his theory and its empirical supports as in "Thus we shall not be so very greatly surprised if a woman analyst who has not been sufficiently convinced of the intensity of her own desire for a penis also fails to assign an adequate importance to that factor in her patients" (*The Outline of Psychoanalysis*, trans. James Strachey [New York: Norton, 1949]). Also deserving mention here as significant in the higher regions of *ad hominem* studies is the work of Henry Johnstone on the role of the *ad hominem* in philosophical argument, for example in "Philoso-

These are very bare bones; and some qualifications are needed. "Advocacy of a proposition" is meant rather loosely. Expressions of moral indignation, for example, are meant to be included, as are recommendations. In fact, expressions of emotion or recommendations are much more likely and more common objects of *ad hominem* attack than is advocacy of a proposition in the narrower sense, in the sense of asserting that some statement is true. I will assume that expressions of emotion or recommendations can be paraphrased into propositional terms, however, which are adequate for the purposes of analysis. Jones's moralizing, for example, can be represented in terms of Jones's advocacy of specific claims and of a certain point of view.

Despite the fact that many logic textbooks still classify them under the rubric of "fallacies," not all arguments *ad hominem* are fallacious. The legitimacy of the *ad hominem* as a type of argument is (and always has been) accepted in practice by nearly everyone and is nowadays even generally acknowledged by the authors of logic textbooks whose tables of contents seem to indicate otherwise. It is with care, therefore, if at all, that we should speak of "the *ad hominem* fallacy." My approach, as will already be apparent, will be to regard *argumentum ad hominem* as a kind of argument rather than as a kind of logical offense, and then to ground my account in normal, logically sound cases rather than in fallacious, logically deviant ones.[2] The following are typical examples of ordinary logically acceptable *ad hominems*:

> (3) Candidate Jones has no right to moralize about the family, since he cheats on his wife.

> (4) I won't bother reading Henrietta Jones's 800-page tome, *The Theory of Evolution Disproved*. Jones has no scientific credentials and is motivated solely by her religious assumptions.

---

phy and *Argumentum ad Hominem*," *Journal of Philosophy* 49 (1952), and "Philosophy and *Argumentum ad Hominem* Revisited," *Revue Internationale de Philosophie* 24 (1970). See also Douglas Walton (1985b).

2. Despite the acknowledgment in a nice section "Fallacies in the Law" that not all ad hominem arguments are fallacious, Copi and Cohen (1990) persist in listing argument *ad hominem* under the rubric of "fallacies" and in saying that the label "names a fallacious attack" (97). The same is true in their treatment of argument *ad verecundiam* and other forms of argument that are clearly not by their very nature fallacious. More than just terminology is at stake here. Whatever the intentions of textbook authors might be, this sort of practice encourages students to identify *ad hominems*, *ad verecundiams*, etc., in terms of the characteristics that identify them as kinds of argument or argument strategies, and *not* in terms of logical defects. Students are implicitly encouraged to identify an argument type by name, but then to take the name itself as imputing fallaciousness.

(5) We refuse to take King Jones's assurances seriously, since he has "wickedly broken through every moral and human obligation," etc.

(6) Don't believe Joan Jones's story about experiences with the Mafia; she's delusional and a habitual liar.

(7) Boo! Sit down, Senator Jones, Chair of the Senate Banking Committee! We're not listening to your proposals for amending the New Bank Bill. You can't even balance your own checkbook.

(8) I wouldn't accept career advice from soon-to-retire Assistant Professor Jones, if I were you; he hates the idea of being outdone by any of his students, and he resents your successes in particular.

(9) The Reverend Jones says that *P*, but her own theological system entails that *not-P*.

In each of these cases, relevant alleged facts are brought to bear in an attempt to in some way or other affect hearers' attitudes toward Jones's advocacy-of-*P*: Jones's expressions of moral sentiment, Jones's tender of a voluminous written attack on a scientific theory, Jones's offering of assurances, Jones's recommending of policies, Jones's giving of advice, Jones's purporting to give information about the past, Jones's asserting of some theological proposition. In each case, acceptance of the respective allegations may rightly affect hearers' attitudes toward Jones's advocacy as well as (and by way of) affecting hearers' attitudes toward Jones. In some sense or other in the typical *ad hominem*, doubt is cast upon an advocate's credibility and thereby, and in conclusion, upon his or her advocacy or endorsement of some proposition or position.

I will be going on to suggest that classical rhetorical theory provides some very helpful resources for the further elaboration of this view of the nature of *ad hominem* argument. Before we turn in that direction, however, it will be worth considering the sense or senses in which it might be meaningful to speak of an "*ad hominem* fallacy." In what ways, from a logical point of view, can *ad hominem* argument go wrong?

Is There an *Ad Hominem* Fallacy?

There is one, near-comic way in which things can go wrong so as to give a clear sense to the idea of a specifically *ad hominem* fallacy. The healthy *ad hominem* is directed toward the first two "elements" identified earlier: toward a person and toward that person's advocacy of some proposition P. But it is possible, though not typical, that a deviant adhominist extends the attack to P itself. This is what some textbook authors seem to think is characteristic of *ad hominem* argument. (10) is a farcical example; (11) is an only near-farcical example from real life (from a student essay).

> (10) Calvin claims that 2 + 2 = 4; but Calvin is a juvenile Deconstructionist. So 2 + 2 must equal 5.

> (11) To me personally this view Hobbes takes is off base, because he had his own motives for wanting this type of government. For if he could persuade the masses to this, surely he would be recognized by the power in control and gain some sort of special status. . . . Hobbes in my opinion was a self-interested egoist looking out for his own self gain.

Hobbes's motives are, of course, irrelevant to the question whether his political theory is "off base." It is not a *particular* irrelevancy, however, that is in question here; it is the general inappropriateness of extrapolating from what might be legitimate critique of Hobbes and even of his advocacy of his theory to an intellectual rejection of the theory itself. If King Jones said, "I refuse to take my advice from Hobbes, brilliant thinker though he is, since he's a self-interested egoist looking out for his own self-gain," there would be no such problem. It is the misapplication of the *ad hominem* to the "propositional content" (as we might say) of P which is generally problematic. It is when adhominizing goes wrong in this way, in terms of a clearly identifiable *structural* failure, that it makes the most sense to speak of a specifically *ad hominem* fallacy. But whether it is *useful* to do so is another question. This sort of failure does occur, but it is a not very common logical crudeness almost on a level with "Since this cake is so tasty, each of the ingredients must be tasty." In any case, this logical phenomenon is not typical of the *ad hominem*; it is to be found mainly in textbook examples (or in logically hard-hearted textbook interpretations of real-life examples).

There are two other general, and much more common, ways in which *ad hominem* argument may go wrong. They correspond to two familiar questions in the evaluation of arguments, "Are the premises true?" and "Do they support the conclusion?" In the first place, the assertions (accusations, say) made about Jones, the adhominee, may be false (or at least doubtful). Second, the assertions made about Jones may fail to provide adequate grounds for the proposed shift in hearers' attitudes toward Jones's advocacy-of-P. The former is not a *logical* failure, though it is certainly one of the more common ways in which *ad hominem* argument fails. Falsehood or dubiousness of premises is a defect in argument, but not a logical defect. A fallacy, in the logician's sense, is a logical defect.

The more significant logical failures of an argument *ad hominem* against Jones (advocate of P) are failures of the latter sort, failures having to do with the relationship between (a) adhominizing claims made about Jones and (b) proposed shifts in attitude toward Jones's advocacy-of-P. At least two kinds of such failures are distinguishable, (1) failures in degree of support and (2) failures of relevance. The following is a clear example of a failure in *degree of support*:

> (12) Candidate Jones has no right to moralize about the family; he was once seen arguing with his wife.

Evidence of disharmony within Jones's own family has *some* bearing on his moral authority as an advocate of family values; how much it has may be in general debatable, and in this case we have at best only slight evidence of it. "Candidate Jones has no right to moralize about the family, since he beats the hell out of his wife once a week and sexually abuses his children" would, on the other hand, be a rather good *ad hominem*. Failure in degree of support is, as its name suggests, a matter of degree. *Ad hominem* argument is, of course, probabilistic argument. It can be very strong, as in Examples (3)–(6) above; moderately strong, as it appears to me to be in (7)–(9); and so on down to its being terribly weak, as in (12). To speak of an *"ad hominem* fallacy" with respect to failures in degree of support, however, is at best a risky proposition. Speaking in those terms suggests that we have in view some particular, identifiable move in argument that is logically objectionable. But a failure in degree of support is not a particular, identifiable move in argument.

A fairly clear example of a failure of *relevance* is (13):

> (13) I refuse to listen to Senator Jones's proposals for amending the New Bank Bill; he cheats on his wife.

I say "fairly clear," because what is known about Jones's character in general may indeed have *some* relevance to his fitness to take the lead in suggesting amendments to a bill which, we may suppose, is meant in part to deal with ethical problems (even if they are problems relating to banking). It is a *particular* relevance which is in question here; and that is generally so with respect to failures of relevance in standard cases of *ad hominem* argument (whose "conclusion" has to do with what sort of attitude ought to be taken toward Jones's advocacy-of-*P*). But, as is illustrated by (13), this sort of relevance is also debatable and a matter of degree. The relevance of "premises" (claims about Jones) to "conclusions" (recommended shifts in attitude toward Jones's advocacy-of-*P*) in standard *ad hominem* argument is generally a matter of degree. Hardly ever, except in blatantly stupid or highly artificial cases, is there an utter absence of relevance. In the case of failures of particular relevance, then, it again seems inapt to speak of an "*ad hominem* fallacy."

I have been whittling away at the idea that it is useful to speak at all of a specifically "*ad hominem* fallacy." One other tactic often identified as *ad hominem* ought to be whittled off as well. It is the personal attack as a diversionary strategy, as in

(14) Well, Socrates Jones, your arguments seem to have me on the ropes; but don't you think you need a wet nurse to follow you around wiping your driveling nose?

Personal insults, ridicule, and the like are significant strategies in argumentation; but they are not logical mistakes and are thus also not aptly referred to as "fallacious."

A Rhetorical View of the *Ad Hominem*

Mainstream logicians have often been handicapped in dealing with a variety of logical phenomena discussed under the rubric of the "informal fallacies" by a strong predisposition to restrict their attention to the propositional content of argument and to be too narrowly preoccupied with the truth values of propositions. Among the ways in which the so-called informal fallacies are problematic are ways in which they involve the "senders" and "receivers" of arguments. Arguments *ad hominem, ad verecundiam, ad populum, ad misericordiam,* and *ad baculum,* for example, address themselves in one way or another to speakers (or givers of arguments) or to hearers. But an argument is an argument, and what counts from the mainstream logician's point of view is what goes on among the propositions that make it up. To cast aspersions on the character of an opponent in argument, for example, or to work on the emotions of recipients of argument, seems to be to overstep the bounds of fair and objective arguing and argument assessment. This is the reasonable sounding point of view by which mainstream logicians have tended to be logically impaired in their approach to much of the subject matter of this volume. On account of this impairment, they have been loath to give up the assumption that arguments *ad hominem, ad misericordiam*, etc., are by their very nature fallacious.

Theorists of rhetoric, on the other hand, from the first Sophistic down to the present day, have taken a more inclusive view of the nature of argument. They have at various times and in various ways focused their attention on many of the same phenomena with which mainstream logicians have lately struggled under the rubric of " informal fallacies." Granting that logicians have been on the whole a more scrupulous bunch than rhetoricians, one still might suspect that theorists known for their more intimate involvement with the realities of public argumentation and persuasion might have something to offer to our understanding of these troublesome logicial phenomena. They do, indeed, with respect to the *ad hominem*.

Conveniently enough, the rhetorical conceptions of the first great systematic theorist of rhetoric (to whose authority we might appeal, were appeals to authority in order) are useful for further explicating the view of the *ad hominem* that I have been proposing. Aristotle defines rhetoric as "the faculty of observing in any given case the available means of persuasion" (1355b).[3] It is with persuasive public speaking that Aristotle, like other classical rhetoricians, is concerned in the *Rhetoric*. Of kinds of public oratory, he takes *deliberative* speaking to be the most fundamental. *Deliberation*, as students of Aristotle's *Nicomachean Ethics* know, is reasoning about what to do rather than about what to believe. Deliberative rhetoric, as characterized by Aristotle, is a process whereby decisions are made about public policy and courses of action (See Book I, 1357a and chaps. 4–8). Its end is right choice and right practice (*orthopraxy*) rather than right belief (*orthodoxy*). It is in deliberative contexts, we may observe, that ordinary "garden-variety" *ad hominems* are perhaps most common, as we might suspect and as is suggested by even a casual survey of textbook examples.

Aristotle's *Rhetoric* introduces a distinction, which figures prominently in subsequent classical rhetorics, between three "modes of rhetorical argument":

---

3. Quotations from Aristotle's *Rhetoric* will be from *The Rhetoric and The Poetics of Aristotle*, translated by W. Rhys Roberts (New York: Modern Library, 1984).

the appeals to *logos, pathos,* and *ethos* (1356a). *Logos* in this context is roughly equivalent to what modern logicians focus their attention on as the "propositional content" of argument, the ordinary giving of premises in support of conclusions. Aristotle's detailed discussion of *pathos* (in Book II) is concerned with arousing and manipulating the emotions of hearers. But it is his discussion of rhetorical *ethos* that relates most directly to our present topic.

It is at the start of Book II of the *Rhetoric* that Aristotle comments about *ethos* in a way most germane to our subject. Rhetoric, he says there, "exists to affect the giving of decisions" (1377b). He has pointed out much earlier that the influence of a speaker's *ethos* is most important (and most appropriate, we may infer) "where exact certainty is impossible and opinions are divided" (1356a). The idea surely is that people willingly and out of necessity (and reasonably, we might add) look to the judgment of certain sorts of individuals in discussions about public action and policy: they allow certain individuals to take the lead, to determine the direction in which discussion proceeds; they trust certain persons as advisers; they recognize certain individuals as having political savvy or moral insight; and so on. This is consonant with Aristotle's observation in the *Nicomachean Ethics* that "the unproved assertions or opinions of experienced and elderly people, or of prudent men, are as much deserving of attention as those which they support by proof; for experience has given them an eye for things, and so they see correctly."[4]

The concern about *ethos* in chap. 1 of Book II of the *Rhetoric* is with audience *attitudes* toward a speaker. Aristotle there analyzes rhetorical *ethos* into three aspects:

> There are three things which inspire confidence in the orator's own character—the three, namely, that induce us to believe a thing apart from any proof of it: good sense (*phronesis*, prudence), good moral character (*arete*), and goodwill (*eunoia*). False statements and bad advice are due to one or more of the following three causes. Men either form a false opinion through want of good sense; or they form a true opinion, but because of their moral badness do not say what they really think; or finally, they are both sensible and upright, but not well disposed to their hearers, and may fail in consequence to recommend what they know to be the best course. (1738a)

4. *The Nicomachean Ethics of Aristotle,* translated by H. Rackham (London: Heinemann, 1926), 1143b; see also 1176a.

Now I suggest that, although Aristotle is speaking as a rhetorician in this passage and is accordingly concerned with what kind of *impressions* hearers have, rather than with the real authority or credibility of speakers, he is in fact identifying the sorts of considerations which bear on the real authority or credibility of speakers or of participants in debates about public policy. For opponents to question the judgment, the moral character, or the motives of fellow deliberators is not in itself either rhetorically or logically inappropriate. Analogously, while it makes sense for me to consult with persons of prudence, moral insight, and goodwill in making important and difficult personal decisions, and to give a careful hearing and weight to their opinions, signs of poor practical judgment, of dishonesty, or of malice toward me are grounds for discounting advice or refusing a hearing to a purported adviser.

Ad hominem argument, I am suggesting, is most commonly to be found in deliberative contexts of one sort or another, or in contexts which are sufficiently like them, or which at least involve a deliberative component (such as deciding whether to give Henrietta Jones's *Evolution Refuted* a reading or to trouble ourselves about inquiring into Joan Jones's reports about the Mafia). *Ad hominem* attacks are typically responsive to or anticipatory of implicit or explicit appeals *ad verecundiam*. They occur most commonly in contexts in which a speaker or arguer's authority or credibility as an advocate for some point of view or course of action is asserted or assumed. That is to say, the ordinary *ad hominem* may in general be understood to be an assault on the rhetorical *ethos* of a speaker or writer whose *ethos* would otherwise be regarded as more of a persuasive factor than the adhominist believes reasonable. It is a legitimate form of argument and is logically acceptable in many, perhaps most, of its actual occurrences.

15

Argumentum Ad Hominem: A Pragma-Dialectical Case in Point

Frans H. Van Eemeren and Rob Grootendorst

Fallacies of Relevance in the Standard Treatment

In the Standard Treatment of fallacies, the *argumentum ad hominem* is generally analyzed as a fallacy of relevance.[1] This category also includes *ad baculum, ad ignorantiam, ad misericordiam, ad populum,* and *ad verecundiam.* It gives the impression that it serves primarily as a depository, for it accommodates precisely those fallacies for which the Standard Treatment has no adequate solution because they are beyond the scope of the definition of a fallacy as an argument that seems valid but is not so.

In the common examples of fallacies of relevance there is no sign of any argument in the logical sense. Reconstructing them as prototypical arguments with two premises and a conclusion, usually requires stretching a point or two. Even then, not much is explained. Naturally, it only makes sense to claim that an argument is fallacious because its premises are "logically irrelevant" if the notion of logical relevance is first defined. In the Standard Treatment, no effort is made to that effect.

The Standard Treatment gives a logical overtone to the notion of relevance by suggesting that in a fallacy of relevance the irrelevancy of the premises for the conclusion is a matter of logic.[2] If this logico-centric approach is to be

---

1. For the Standard Treatment of fallacies, see Hamblin (1970, chap. 1).

2. See, e.g., N. Rescher, *Introduction to Logic* (New York: St. Martin's Press, 1964), 78; Copi and Cohen (1990, 3); and, for a more recent example, T. E. Damer, *Attacking Faulty Reasoning*, 1st ed. (Belmont, Calif.: Wadsworth, 1987), 99.

taken seriously, not only the logical validity of arguments will have to be tested, but also their logical relevance. But the notion of logical relevance is left undefined and its connection with logical validity remains unexplained.[3] Is the relevance of the premises to the conclusion in a logically valid argument always guaranteed? Can the argument be valid even though the premises are not relevant to the conclusion? Or is it also possible for the premises to be relevant while the argument is invalid?

In the absence of any further clarification, the Standard Treatment makes it hard to determine whether we are dealing with a fallacy of relevance. The "explanatory comments" that are provided are confined to the observation that the premises are not germane, do not really support the truth of the conclusion, or something of the sort.[4] In practice, the problem is circumvented by selecting only examples that are, as it were, dripping with irrelevance, so that the question of the relation between relevance and validity does not so easily arise.

Argumentum ad Hominem as a Violation of a Rule for Critical Discussion

In our opinion, a satisfactory alternative to the Standard Treatment of the argumentum ad hominem and other so-called fallacies of relevance can only be achieved if the preoccupation with the logical validity of arguments is abandoned. In the pragma-dialectical approach, we have done this by placing the fallacies in the perspective of a critical discussion aimed at resolving a difference of opinion. The fallacies of relevance are then analyzed as violations of the rules for critical discussion.[5]

The argumentum ad hominem is a violation of the first rule for critical discussion: "Parties must not prevent each other from advancing standpoints or casting doubt on standpoints." This discussion rule is designed for the confrontation stage, where the protagonist and the antagonist of a standpoint

3. In A Practical Study of Argument, 2d ed. (Belmont, Calif.: Wadsworth, 1988), Trudy Govier does give a definition of relevance, and her approach is certainly much more thorough than the Standard Treatment, but on some crucial points she is still so firmly tied to the logico-centric approach that she fails to provide a satisfactory analysis of ad hominem as a fallacy of relevance. See van Eemeren and Grootendorst (1992b).

4. See, e.g., Rescher, Introduction to Logic, 81, and Copi and Cohen (1990, 98).

5. For the theoretical framework of the pragma-dialectical approach, see Chapter 9, this volume.

enter into a difference of opinion. Naturally, the rule also applies to a difference of opinion that arises when the argumentative support for a standpoint
meets with doubt or other criticism. The premise concerned is then to be
considered as a substandpoint.

The first discussion rule aims at ensuring that any difference of opinion
can be expressed without hindrance. It may seem odd, but in order to
promote the possibility that differences of opinion can be resolved, the open
confrontation between the parties needs to be stimulated. Therefore, in a
critical discussion the parties have a principal right to advance any standpoint
they wish and to challenge any standpoint they wish.[6] This implies that any
potential obstacles to expressing standpoints or criticizing standpoints are to
be cleared away. As a consequence, neither party is allowed to prevent the
other party from entering into an unimpeded confrontation by ruling him out
as a serious discussion partner. And this is precisely what is attempted in the
argumentum ad hominem.[7]

All three variants of the *argumentum ad hominem* are violations of the first
rule for critical discussion. In effect, they all amount to a party claiming that
the other party has no right to speak. In the *abusive* variant, this party
undermines the other party's credentials by denigrating his intelligence, experience, or good faith. In the *circumstantial* variant, he does so by suggesting
that the other party is not capable of making an impartial judgment because
he is driven by personal interests. And in the *tu quoque* variant the other
party's credentials are being reduced by denouncing an inconsistency in his
opinions or behavior.

This brief explanation not only suffices to show that the three variants of
the *argumentum ad hominem* are all offenses against a fundamental norm
for argumentative discourse aimed at resolving a difference of opinion: it
also gives some indications of the criteria for determining with which variant of the *argumentum ad hominem* we are dealing in a given case.[8] The

6. It goes without saying that this does not automatically mean that a party is always obliged to
continue the discussion after a confrontation has taken place. It may, for instance, become clear at
the opening stage of the discussion that the antagonist is not prepared to comply with the rules for
critical discussion, so that there is no chance that the difference can be resolved.

7. The party that is personally attacked may, of course, always decide to enter into a confrontation about the premise that is expressed in the *argumentum ad hominem*, but then we are dealing
with an entirely different case: instead of being taken aback by the *argumentum ad hominem*, the
person who is attacked voluntarily engages in another discussion in which this premise is the
standpoint at issue.

8. This is not to say that there are no problems left. Interpretation procedures are, for instance,
required to determine whether a speech act fulfills the criterion of an *abusive argumentum ad*

general criterion that applies to all three variants is, of course, whether a party has said something that is calculated to undermine the other party's position as a credible discussion partner. For the *abusive* variant, the criterion is whether something negative is said of the other party's personal characteristics: his intelligence, expertise, and so on. For the *circumstantial* variant, the criterion is whether the attention is drawn to the other party's particular interests in adopting a specific position: financial gain, social success, and so on. The criterion for the *tu quoque* variant is whether an inconsistency is pointed out in the other party's words or actions: he himself does something that he condemns in others, now he says this but yesterday he said that, and so on.

The Pragma-Dialectical Approach versus the Standard Treatment

In the Standard Treatment, an *argumentum ad hominem* is a fallacy because the premises of the argument are irrelevant to the conclusion, except in those cases where the premises *are* relevant to the conclusion—unless they turn out not to be relevant on further reflection. The criteria applied in this endeavor are usually not only implicit and intuitive, but also highly arbitrary and *ad hoc*. It looks as if each case must be assessed individually to see whether there are mitigating circumstances that render the personal attack less blameworthy than it appears. Invariably, some examples are presented of personal attacks in which the *ad hominem* is after all not a fallacy.

The pragma-dialectical approach offers a systematic solution to the problem of the many exceptions to the rule that an *argumentum ad hominem* is a fallacy. The solution is very simple: there are no exceptions. If the criterion for one of the variants of the *argumentum ad hominem* is fulfilled, a personal attack is always a violation of the first rule for critical discussion. It is therefore, without any exception, a fallacy.

An *argumentum ad hominem* that is a countermove against the misuse of expertise or authority by the opponent is by some authors considered as a

---

hominem, that something negative is said about the opponent. As we explained in van Eemeren and Grootendorst (1992b), this is not a major problem in the case of an *abusive argumentum ad hominem*.

correct use of the *argumentum ad hominem*.[9] However, the discussion is then rather directed toward gaining victory in a dispute than toward resolving the difference of opinion. Since the move, therefore, falls outside the scope of the rules for critical discussion, it is no *argumentum ad hominem* in the pragma-dialectical sense.[10] If the countermove were part of a critical discussion, it would be fallacious and indeed an *argumentum ad hominem*. That the fallacy is a reaction to another fallacy, an *argumentum ad verecundiam*, does not make it a correct discussion move: two wrongs do not make a right.

The fact that the term *argumentum ad hominem* is sometimes used in a neutral way for a personal attack and sometimes refers to the fallacy which occurs when such an attack is incorrect is one of the reasons why the analysis of "exceptions" in the Standard Treatment gives the impression of being merely *ad hoc*.[11] It may seem as if the same discussion move is in one case permitted and not in another, so that it is in some cases a fallacy and in other cases not. What the two moves have in common is that something negative is said about a person, but on a closer inspection they prove to be very different. Because the term *argumentum ad hominem* is more often used to make a negative rather than a neutral judgment, the standard meaning seems to bear the connotation of "fallacy," whereas the exceptional cases (in which *ad hominem* argumentation *is* allowed) seem to represent deviations. Unfortunately, when an author uses the term *argumentum ad hominem* it is not always clear whether he is dealing with a justified exception. To avoid this kind of obscurity, we use the ordinary expression *personal attack* for the neutral case and the technical term *argumentum ad hominem* for the fallacy of an incorrect personal attack.

In the pragma-dialectical analysis of the *argumentum ad hominem*, unlike in the Standard Treatment, no reference is made to the relevance of the premises of an argument for its conclusion. The reason for this is that an *argumentum ad hominem* is not fallacious because it is an argument with irrelevant premises. Viewed within a pragma-dialectical perspective, the relevance of a discussion move depends on its contribution to the

9. See, e.g., Woods and Walton, "Ad Hominem" (1989, 55–73).

10. In our opinion, there is no point in calling such a move a fallacy because it is not part of a clearly conceptualized goal-directed enterprise whose standards are defined in a well-delineated normative framework; if such a framework were developed, however, say in ethics, it would make sense to speak of "ethical" fallacies. A similar case could be made for "epistemological" fallacies.

11. One of the other reasons is the one-sided concentration on the premise-conclusion relation in arguments.

resolution of a difference of opinion.[12] In a critical discussion, an *argumentum ad hominem* is, in fact, always highly relevant, but in a negative sense: it hinders, or sometimes even prevents, the resolution of a difference of opinion.[13]

12. The pragma-dialectical approach also recognizes fallacies of relevance, but they are either violations of the third rule or the seventh rule for critical discussion (van Eemeren and Grootendorst (1992a, 124–31, 158–68). Among the violations of rule 7 that produce a fallacy of relevance are the cases in which the arguer defends his standpoint by wrongly launching a personal attack on a third party who is absent or even dead: "Frege's logical views are not to be taken seriously because he was anti-Semitic." In the pragma-dialectical sense, such an attack on a third party is not an *argumentum ad hominem*, but if such a case of incorrect symptomatic argumentation hinders the resolution of a difference of opinion by falsely presenting something (being anti-Semitic) as a sure sign of something else (having no serious logical views), it is a fallacy of relevance. We owe the observation concerning attacks on a third party to Hans Hansen, who would like to maintain the *ad hominem* terminology for such cases by envisaging a distinction between first-, second-, and third-person *ad hominems* (personal communication).

13. We owe the notion of negative relevance to Govier, A *Practical Study of Argument*, 98–99, who contrasts negative relevance with positive relevance and irrelevance.

16

The Essential Ingredients of the Fallacy of Begging the Question

Douglas N. Walton

What could be called the classic case used to illustrate the fallacy of begging the question is the following story (Fearnside and Holther, 1959, 167).

Case 1:

> In a picture by the famous French comedian Sacha Guitry some thieves are arguing over division of seven pearls worth a king's ransom. One of them hands two to the man on his right, then two to the man on his left. "I," he says, "will keep three." The man on his right says, "How come you keep three?" "Because I am the leader." "Oh. But how come you are the leader?" "Because I have more pearls."

In this case, it is not hard to see how the sequence of circular reasoning is used by the one thief to attempt to silence the objections or questioning of the other two. Insead of giving an independent line of argumentation to support his contention by genuinely meeting the requirement of burden of proof, the first thief tries to bamboozle his fellow perpetrators by using circular reasoning. If they were satisfied by his argumentation, then they were pretty gullible. Most of us easily see what's going on, at least in general outline. We see that the circular argument is a tactic of argumentation used by the one participant in the persuasion dialogue to unfairly and deceptively get the best of the others.

Case 1 shows, at least intuitively, what the fallacy of begging the question is, and what it is not. To beg a question is not just to postpone the answering of a question in a dialogue, or to fail to answer it by giving a relevant reply. Increasingly, the phrase is used by the news media in this incorrect and misleading way.[1] To commit the fallacy of begging the question, two requirements must be met, in a given case: (i) there must be a circular sequence of reasoning, where the conclusion to be established is either identical to one of the premises, or the premise in question depends on the conclusion, and (ii) the circular sequence of reasoning must be used illicitly in a context of dialogue (conversation) to escape the proper fulfillment of a legitimate burden of proof in that context.[2] These requirements are met by the argumentation of the first thief in case 1.

However, there remains disagreement on how this fallacy is to be precisely analyzed. Some, like Biro (1977; 1984) see it as an epistemic failure. Some, like Sanford (1972; 1977; 1981) see it as a failure to increase rational belief. Some, like De Morgan see it as a purely formal failure.[3] Others like Aristotle, see it as a kind of fallacy that can take different forms in different contexts of argumentation; e.g., taking one form in demonstrative arguments, and another form in dialectical arguments.[4]

As usual, in philosophy, there is something to be said for all these conflicting points of view. But consideration of another case tends to tilt a burden of proof more in favor of Aristotle's and against De Morgan's.

The Case of God and the Virtues

The following case, first put forward by Robinson (1971b, 113), shows that determining whether an argument begs the question is not (generally) possible by any straightforward operation or test on the given premises and conclusion. Instead, to make such a determination, a context of dialogue has to be supplied.

1. See Walton (1991a, 11–12).
2. Ibid.
3. Augustus De Morgan, *Formal Logic* (London: Taylor and Walton, 1847).
4. See Hamblin (1970, 74–77).

Case 2:

> God has all the virtues.
> Therefore, God is benevolent

As Barker (1976, 245) pointed out, this argument is an enthymeme—the missing premise "Benevolence is a virtue" needs to be filled in.[5] Once this has been done, it seems that the argument is suspiciously circular, and could perhaps be offered as an example of the fallacy of begging the question. But is this evaluation so clear or straightforward?

To see that it is not, consider two contexts for case 2 that could be filled in.

Case 2a:

> Shirley, a nonbeliever, says to Bob, a believer, "how can you prove that God is benevolent? He looks pretty nonbenevolent in some parts of the Old Testament, striking sinners down, and so forth." Bob responds by advancing the argument of case 2, above.

In case 2a, Shirley would surely have the right to object that Bob's argument begs the question. For as she might say, "Given that benevolence is one of the virtues (as presumed in case 2), your major premise 'God has all the virtues' takes for granted what you are supposed to prove; namely, that God is benevolent. Hence your argument begs the question." Bob could possibly respond to this charge, but surely as an allegation it is a fair and good one, in this case.

Case 2b:

> Bob and Ed are both fervent believers in a religion that takes as its holy scripture the Book of Zog. Ed says to Bob: "Gosh, Bob, I am starting to have doubts whether God is benevolent. Aren't there some passages in the Book of Zog that suggest that nonbelievers will be reincarnated as toads or lizards?" Bob replies: "Yes, Ed, but don't you remember it explicitly says, in the Gospel of Charlene, and then again in the Gospel of Barry, that God has all the virtues!" Ed replies: "Oh, heavens! Of course, you are right. God is benevolent, for sure."

5. See Walton (1991a, 304).

In case 2b, Bob's argument, as stated in its bare form in case 2, is sufficient to convince Ed to accept the conclusion. The argument is noncircular, as used in case 2a, because there is independent evidence (or what purports to be evidence, and is acceptable to Ed as evidence) that the conclusion is true.[6] Here *independent evidence* means a line of argument or backing that does not require or depend on prior presumption of the conclusion as true or acceptable.

We could sum up the difference between cases 2a and 2b as follows. In case 2a, as schematized on the left of Figure 1, no evidence for the premise, P is given, other than provided by C, the conclusion.

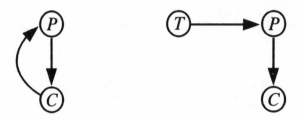

Figure 1

However, in case 2b, schematized on the right of Figure 1, textual evidence for P is given, evidence that could be established or argued for independently of C. The evidence invoked is an appeal to authority, which could be legitimate if both Bob and Ed accept the book of Zog as an authoritative source. Hence we are entitled to perceive the argumentation in case 2b as non–question-begging, even though it contains an appeal to authority that could be questioned. By contrast, in case 2a, the context strongly suggests that the argument could be circular, unless Bob can come up with some independent evidence for his conclusion.

Our study of these cases indicates that begging the question is not simply a function of the given premises and conclusion of a (localized) argument. Instead, it is at least partly a function of the context of dialogue surrounding that argument. We need to know the conflict of opinions that is at issue, and something about the positions (points of view) of the participants at the given stage of the argumentation.

Formal elements are involved, because the analysis of the case requires, to begin with, an argument diagram of the premises and conclusion of some specific argument in the case. And considerations of the kinds of linkages

6. For analysis of comparable cases see Colwell (1989) and Walton (1991a, 274).

between such propositions (whether deductive or otherwise), will clearly be an important factor. But that is not all that is involved. The case has also revealed how the context of dialogue surrounding this argument diagram structure is also of crucial importance in judging whether the circle in the reasoning really constitutes an instance of the fallacy of begging the question or not.

Circular Reasoning Is Not Always Fallacious

Another important point to be made is that it is possible to have circular argumentation without the fallacy of begging the question having been committed. In the following case, from Walton (1985a, 263) for example, the sequence of questions and replies in the dialogue is circular.

Case 3:

> When asked to prove that the economy in a certain state is in a slump, an economist replies: "A lot of people are permanently leaving the state. Things are very poor in the building industry, for example, because there is no need for new housing." Next question: "How can you be sure such a lot of people are permanently leaving the state?" The economist's answer: "Well, the state of the economy is poor. People just don't seem to be able to get jobs, with the economy being so slow at the moment. And when this happens, people leave permanently."

The economy is depressed because people are permanently leaving, it is claimed. But, at the same time, it is also claimed that people are permanently leaving because the economy is depressed.

But in this case, despite the circular reasoning involved, it would be premature and unjustified to claim that the economist has committed the fallacy of begging the question. For he could quite reasonably reply: "I am just pointing out the feedback loop inherent in human collective (economic) behavior. It's like the situation of a diabetic who, as he becomes more overweight, builds up more insulin in his blood, which makes him eat more, and consequently store up more fat. The process is circular, but there is no fallacy in it. That's the way reality sometimes is." Similarly in mathematical reasoning, proving conclusion A from starting point B, and then proving B from A, could be a quite legitimate equivalence proof. From the circular reasoning alone, it doesn't follow that a fallacy has been committed.

One might reply that in case 3, the economist is only explaining economic behavior, and not really arguing from one proposition to another, or reasoning in a circle. But it is far from evident that this is so. The economist's circular sequence certainly does seem to be a chain of reasoning, and the fact that it does have an explanatory power, or could even partly be an explanation, does not exclude its being a sequence of argumentation. It could well be, as it would appear to be from the text and context of discourse, that the economist is trying to present evidence to his interviewer, to argue for the conclusions that people are leaving the state, and that the economy is poor in this state. If so, his argumentation is not (at least, as the case stands) of a kind that gives sufficient evidence that shows he has committed the fallacy of begging the question.

What sort of additional evidence would be needed in a case like this, where there is circular reasoning, to pin down a charge of begging the question? What is needed is evidence that the context of dialogue is one in which successful argumentation must meet a requirement of *evidential priority*, meaning that the premises are being used as evidence to support the conclusion in such a way that each premise must be capable of being established without having to depend on the prior establishment of the conclusion, in the supporting line of argumentation backing up the premise. In some contexts of dialogue, evidential priority is not a requirement of the argumentation. For example, in a chain of purely hypothetical reasoning, evidential priority is generally not a requirement.[7]

In a critical discussion, where two participants *White* and *Black* have a conflict of opinions, evidential priority can be an important requirement of their argumentation with each other. Suppose White's thesis to be proved is the proposition W, and Black's thesis to be proved is the proposition B. Suppose that they have a genuine conflict of opinions in the sense that the propositions W and B are *incompatible* (*contraries*), meaning that it is not possible for both W and B to be true. Hence, each has not only the goal of proving his or her own thesis, but also has the objective of casting doubt upon, or critically questioning the thesis of the other party.

In such a context of dialogue, the requirement of evidential priority is generally very significant for the typical sequences of argumentation com-

7. If a chain of reasoning is purely hypothetical, there is no burden of proof.

monly used by both parties in the argumentation stage. Why is this so? It is not too hard to see why it is so, by considering the following type of case.

Suppose White comes up with a sequence of argumentation for her conclusion W, based on premises P, Q, R, S, and T, as outlined in Figure 2. White's compound subargument from S and T to W is linked, meaning that both premises S and T are required to meet the appropriate burden of proof to establish W. White's compound subargument from P and Q to S is convergent, meaning that it is not the case that both premises are required to meet the burden to prove S. White's subargument for T is a *single* argument, with only one premise.[8]

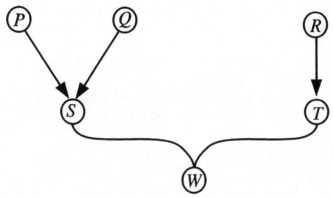

Figure 2

Let's say that all three of White's subarguments in figure 2 are valid, or at least are backed by warrants that Black cannot dispute.

Now in this very common type of case of argumentation, White's goal is to prove W to Black. But Black is inclined, by the nature of his own goals in the dialogue, to doubt, and if possible to question or refute W, as strongly as he can. Therefore, once White's argument as outlined in Figure 2, is presented to him, Black will try to dispute the premises, or at least to question them. The argument from S and T to W is linked. So, to meet the burden of proof required, Black needs only to show that one or the other of these premises is insufficient to stand up as a line of support for W.

Now suppose Black throws doubt on S, and White responds by presenting

8. On the use of argument diagrams to analyze circular argumentation, see Walton and Batten (1984).

a new argument, with premises P and Q (as shown on the left part of Fig. 2). This is a convergent argument. To make it function as convincing, White can choose which premise to use, and Black may therefore have to question or rebut both, to defeat White's argumentation.

But none of White's subarguments will be useful, or any good for the purposes of the dialogue, unless they meet the requirement of evidential priority. In order for White's first subargument, from S and T to W, to be useful and effective, it must meet the requirement of evidential priority. Reason: since Black disputes or doubts the truth of W, he is sure to dispute the truth or acceptability of at least one of S or T. Hence, for White's argument to be of any use to prove her contention, at least one of these premises, S or T, will have to have the potential of being backed up independently of any prior need to presuppose W as part of the chain of argumentation.

Similarly, either P or Q will have to meet the requirement of evidential priority for that part of White's argument to be of any use to fulfill her goals in the dialogue. And R will have to meet the same requirement as a basis for T.

In such a case then, if at any point in the argument diagram, as the sequence of argumentation unfolds, a circular sequence of the pattern P_0, $P_1, \ldots P_n$, P_0, is a danger signal.[9] The circular sequence of reasoning does not necessarily indicate the committing of a fallacy of begging the question.[10] It could be a circle of the form depicted in Figure 3, for example. In this case, the two premises P and Q are part of a convergent argument for the conclusion R. The argument from P to R is circular. But there remains another premise, Q.

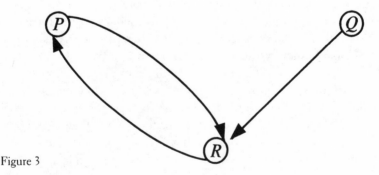

Figure 3

9. Woods and Walton (1982c).
10. Walton (1985a).

The point to be noted in this case is that even though the subargument from P to R has proved useless, because of its failure to meet evidential priority (inevitably so, because of the circle P, R), there is another avenue of support available for the proponent. She can argue that, if the single argument from Q to R has the potential of meeting evidential priority, it can be used to establish R.

Hence it is not hard to see how evidential priority is generally a very significant requirement for many arguments to meet during a critical discussion. Moreover, we can now see why not all circular reasoning (as exhibited by the argument diagram) by itself constitutes a sufficient case of the fallacy of begging the question. To have a case of the committing of this fallacy, two ingredients are necessary. It has to be circular argumentation of a kind that violates the requirement of evidential priority. First, you have to demonstrate that a circular sequence of reasoning exists in a given case, using an argument diagram. Then you have to show that the context of dialogue appropriate for that case is one in which there is a requirement of evidential priority on the argument.

Analysis of Case 1

In case 1, it is easy to see that both ingredients of the fallacy of begging the question are present. The argument takes the form of the dicycle in figure 4, where P is the proposition, "I (the speaker) am the leader." and Q is the proposition, "I have more pearls."

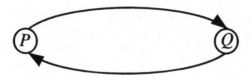

Figure 4

Why does this circular sequence of argumentation violate a requirement of evidential priority that is present in case 1? The reason is that the thieves are engaging in a critical discussion (or perhaps a negotiation) on the subject of how the pearls should be divided. The leader's thesis (point of view) is that he should have more pearls (three, as opposed to two for the others). But his way of proving this conclusion, using the premise "I am the leader." depends on a prior premise that is identical to that very conclusion, to be proved. Such a line of argument is unconvincing, because what is required is some reason that is independent of the conclusion to be proved.

This case fits the kind of framework outlined in connection with the structure diagrammed in figure 2 above. The goal of the leader is to prove his thesis to the two other thieves. They, on the other hand, are inclined to doubt, and if possible to question or refute this thesis.[11] Hence they will (and are obliged, by the nature of their goals in the dialogue) to dispute any premises advanced by the leader, in proving his thesis. But if the leader's argumentation, at any point in its structure, revealed by the diagram, requires relevance on that very initial thesis to be proved, it will be no good. It could never satisfy the (reasonable) requirements of the other two thieves.

Evidential priority is a reasonable and necessary requirement here for any argument to be useful or successful in contributing to the goals of the dialogue. To achieve success, an arguer must convince his opponents of his thesis T using premises that his opponents can, in principle be reasonably persuaded to accept. By the nature of the original conflict of opinions that sets the goals of the dialogue for both sides,[12] the speaker's own thesis T cannot be included in this premise-set. The reason is that T is inherently subject to the hearer's doubt, as part of the structure or purpose of the dialogue as a whole. Failure of evidential priority makes an argument useless for the purpose of rational persuasion required by successful argumentation in such a dialogue.

The reason that the circular argument in case 1 is so transparently fallacious is that it is so clear from the context of dialogue that evidential priority is a requirement of a successful proof.

The analyses of these relatively simple cases shows how the same techniques can be applied to more subtle, problematic, and lengthy cases with good results. The first job is to construct an argument diagram that shows whether the line of reasoning is circular or not, and reveals the circles (if there are any). The second job is to identify the context of dialogue for the given case,

11. In general outline, the type of dialogue in this case could be that of a critical discussion; see van Eemeren and Grootendorst (1984).

12. Ibid.

in order to judge whether evidential priority is an appropriate requirement for the argumentation. The third job is to judge, on the evidence provided by the first two findings, whether they fit together into the pattern of the fallacy of begging the question. Is the circle of a sort that violates a reasonable require-ment of evidential priority for the given case? That is the question to be answered.

As noted, such an evaluation has formal elements. But it is also very much a matter of pragmatic analysis of the context of dialogue in a given case. [13]

13. The author would like to acknowledge the support of the work in this paper by a research grant from the Social Sciences and Humanities Research Council of Canada. Thanks are also due to Bob Pinto and Hans Hansen for critical comments that helped to improve the arguments of the paper.

17

Appeal to Force

John Woods

Ad baculum arguments are those that pivot on appeals to threat or dire consequence ("baculum" is Latin for "stick"). Though not called such, *ad baculum* arguments seem to have been first recognized by the Port-Royal logicians, as witness Arnauld.[1] Modern writers have not done very well with the *ad baculum*. Carney and Scheer characterize it as the error—a special case of the *ad populum* fallacy—of inferring or concluding the truth of a claim on the basis of an appeal to force, for it is the "fear of force [which] cause[s] acceptance of a conclusion."[2] The same words are found in Copi and Cohen (1990, 105): "The argument *ad baculum* [is] the appeal to force to cause the acceptance of a conclusion." Here too the fallacy is thought to be the mistake of concluding the truth of some claim on the basis of a threat. Most authors regret *ad baculum* fallacies as "the abandonment of reason" (Copi and Cohen 1990, 105).

In these writings, and elsewhere, it is plain that *ad baculum* fallacies are thought to be fallacies twice over. For the arguer who knowingly promotes his addressee's fear of force, the fallacy can be seen as a case of trickery or deception, an attempt to dupe the other party into reasoning erroneously. For the addressee, who succumbs to the arguer's trick, the fallacy is delusional in character; the addressee is tripped by his anxiety into thinking that his accep-

---

1. Antoine Arnauld, *The Art of Thinking* [=*La Logique, ou L'Art de Penser* (1662)] (Indianapolis: Bobbs-Merrill, 1964), 289.
2. James D. Carney and Richard K. Scheer, *Fundamentals of Logic*, 3d ed. (New York: Macmillan, 1980), 390.

tance of the truth of the claim in question is justified. In each case the fallacy is thought to be dialectical.

Though they are right to notice dialectical aspects, such accounts are troublesome. They seem not to be believed by their own sponsors. How can "so obvious a fallacy" (Copi and Cohen 1990, 105) trick anybody? It is also doubtful that anything answering to the present notion would qualify as an argument (Woods and Walton 1976a).

Solider analyses of the *ad baculum* are possible, and they require that six types of case be attended to.

CASE 1:

   (1)   (Proposition) P or I'll punch your nose.
   (2)   ∴ P is true.

Case 1 puts considerable pressure on the idea that the *ad baculum* fallacy is a deceptive argument since, for one thing, (1) is transparently irrelevant to the truth of (2). Also strained is the suggestion that case 1 presents an argument at all. Suffice it to say that if we did allow that case 1 did present an argument, the *ad baculum* fallacy would be a fallacy of relevance. A more straightforward judgment is that the idea of the *argumentum ad baculum* is undefined for instances of case 1.

CASE 2:

   (1)   Believe P or I'll punch your nose.
   (2)   ∴ Believe P.

Here we meet with a significant departure. The *ad baculum* is now seen as a prudential argument, an argument not to the effect that a certain fact obtains or that a certain state of affairs is so, but to the effect rather that a certain course of action would be prudent to pursue. The essentially dialectical character of the *ad baculum* is also discernible in case 2 for we imagine that the maker of the argument directs it to an interlocutor who is counseled to do something the prudence of which consists in averting the damage of the arguer's threat. Still, case 2 involves a serious error. Since belief is not a creature of the will, it cannot be summoned up voluntarily. The arguer of case 2 makes the mistake of bidding the addressee to do the impossible.

CASE 3:

(1)   Accept P or I'll punch your nose.
(2)   ∴ Accept P.

Actually, a better formulation of case 3 is one that makes more explicit its dialectical character. Imagine, then, that X and Y are arguer and addressee; then case 3 can be represented as the following dialectical exchange.

X: Accept P or I'll punch your nose.
Y: OK, I accept P.

Case 3 is less dismissible than the previous two. Acceptance, unlike belief, is a creature of the will; so X is not counseling Y to do the impossible. Even so, there is something wrong with X's argument. It bids Y to violate a sincerity condition. The condition in question is that acceptance should be sincere and, in particular, that a rational agent ought not accept claims for which he has contrary evidence or insufficient positive evidence. So X's error is that of suborning dialectical insincerity in Y.

CASE 4: Risk Aversion Strategies·

As before, X and Y are arguer and addressee. X puts to Y the following case.

1. You (Y) agree that P is a real possibility.
2. If P is true, and yet you do not believe that P, then by P's very truth you will suffer momentous disadvantage.
3. On the other hand, If P is false and yet you believe that P, you will be inconvenienced, but well below the level of momentous disadvantage.
4. Given these risks, it would be better if you believe P rather than not.
5. Therefore you should try to acquire the belief that P.

Case 4 is essentially Pascal's Wager to the Christian agnostic (Woods 1987). P here is Christian doctrine. The momentous disadvantage of disbelieving P, in case P should be true, is eternal damnation, for that is what Christian teaching teaches. The inconvenience of believing P, should P be false, is a life constrained by Christian strictures. Given that Y acknowledges that P is a real possibility (never mind that he does not now believe P) the prudent course is a risk aversion or a minimax strategy designed to minimize the worst that could happen to Y in case Y's belief in regard to P turns out to be mistaken.

Case 4 throws up a number of interesting issues. It is worth noting, for one thing, that the threat on which X's argument pivots is not made by X himself. Rather it inheres in the truth of Christian dogma should Christian dogma be true. It is God's threat. Moreover, X does not make the mistake of advising that Y do what he cannot do, namely, to summon up a belief in Christianity by an act of will. Instead he counsels Y to try to get himself to believe, that is, to employ techniques of attitude-modification, such as returning to a life of Christian practice and hoping for the best. A third point is that there is nothing at all fallacious or untoward as such about X's argument. This is not to say that such an argument cannot go wrong. It would go wrong if, for example, X was mistaken in attributing to Y the belief that P is a real possibility. The concept of a real possibility is central to the present analysis and should be explained.

Intuitively Y's situation with regard to P might be thought of as follows. Y used to be an informed, practicing Christian, but now his faith has lapsed. It has not lapsed into total atheistic certitude, however. So his rejection of Christianity could be contrasted with his refusal of, say, Druidism. Though Y could acknowledge the possibility that either is true, the possibility of Druidism is for him wholly empty, and of Christianity less so. Borrowing William James's metaphor, Druidism is a dead option for Y, whereas Christianity is, to some extent at least, a live option. So real possibilities can be equated with live options. Or, more formally, let us define *not* being a real possibility for Y, as follows.

Definition: P is *not a real possibility* for Y if and only if

(i) Y disbelieves P
(ii) Y believes that he knows not-P
(iii) Y acknowledges the possibility that P is true
(iv) Y disbelieves that the truth of (iii) provides any reason, however slight, for believing P.

And so,

Definition: P is a real possibility for Y if and only if it is not the case that it isn't a real possibility for Y.

CASE 5: The Stick-Up

The mugger approaches the visitor to New York, points his Magnum 44 and says, "Your money or your life." Although the threat is the mugger's own, the present case bears a striking resemblance to the previous one. The mugger invites his victim to do some quick cost-benefit calculations to facilitate the appropriate risk-aversion behavior. What the gunman proposes is a certain minimax strategy. There can be little doubt that in the general case the mugger's intervention, though a crime, makes a perfectly rational claim on his victim's compliance. The gunman presses his case competently to the extent that he specifies alternative options for his addressee, to each of which he assigns the costs and benefits attaching to the exercise or not of those options, and this he does in the light of what he takes his addressee's interests to be. The costs and benefits turn directly on the credibility and performability of the arguer's threat. The addressee's options are to hand over his wallet or to refuse. The cost of refusal is death, provided that the victim finds the threat credible and performable; and the benefit of refusal is perhaps his hanging on to his money for a bit longer than had he handed it over in a timely way. The cost of compliance is some degree of impoverishment, and the benefit is that the victim, though poorer, stays alive.

There is plenty of room in these cost-benefit prudential arguments for mistake and for fallacy too. But no fallacy is committed just because the argument pivots on a threat. Besides, it is not by any means the case that just any mistake made in the forwarding of an *ad baculum* argument qualifies as a fallacy. It is certainly a mistake to try to mug a visitor to New York with a banana rather than a Magnum 44, and likewise a blunder to threaten the would-be victim not with death but with the gunman's mild disapproval for the next two minutes. Fanatical traffickers after fallacy might feel that the gunman's mild disapproval is not a relevant consideration in the context of a stick-up. Thus they might plump for attribution of a relevance fallacy. There is perhaps no great harm in speaking this way, but deeper descriptions are available. If I attempt to underwrite a stick-up with a banana, I fail to produce a credible threat. If I offer him my brief and modest scorn, I fail the credible-cost condition. If we are to yield to the suggestion of a relevance fallacy, it is necessary to keep in mind that irrelevance here is the failure of that particular condition. It is also prudent to note that, in other contexts, irrelevance is very much something else. In any event, Carney and Scheer say of gunman-like examples that they "are not or do not involve fallacies."[3] Talleyrand, in one of history's more celebrated wisecracks, said of the execution of the duc d'Enghien, "It's worse than a crime, it's a mistake." This touches our analysis at two places. The gunman case shows that a crime need not be a fallacy and also that a mistake need not be a fallacy. One has to fight hard to convict the *ad baculum* of fallaciousness, and it is worth repeating that whenever an *ad baculum* argument is fallacious it is never so simply on account of its being *ad baculum*.

Prudential arguments abound in everyday life. Who can think of the upbringing of children without resort to threats or bribes? Bribes are close kin of *ad baculum* arguments, except that they substitute rewards for threats. In all other respects they are the same: cost-benefit prudential arguments in promotion of risk aversion—for the risk with promised rewards if failing to qualify for the thing promised. If *ad baculum* arguments are arguments from the "stick," we might well speak of bribes as *ad carotam*—from the "carrot."[4]

Standard arguments against smoking are *ad baculum* and standard arguments for the purchase of this washing powder rather than that are *ad carotam*. Either way, fallacy does not inhere in their basic structures. They are fallacious, if at all, only in details of their particular formulations.

The gunman case affords the opportunity to resist a common misconception. Even among those who acknowledge that the mugger's argument is fallacy-free and that it makes a perfectly rational claim upon compliance, there is nevertheless something very seriously wrong with it, dialectically speaking. It, and all other arguments from the stick, are grave defections from cooperation, what with the routines of rational consensus-building displaced by strategies of intimidation. It is worth emphasizing that the intended contrast has not quite been found in the wording of the preceding sentence. For what better way to build a consensus than force it and what more rational way to maintain it than by attaching sanctions? Of course one knows the contrast that is wanted, but care must be taken against drawing it vacuously. It might be proposed, for example, that consensus building is cooperative just in case it is done freely, that is, in ways untainted by factors *ad baculum*. But now the

3. Carney and Scheer, *Fundamentals of Logic*, 39.

4. *Carotas* has not had a flourishing lexical career. It seems to have first cropped up in the Roman cookbook *Apicius* (after the gourmet Marcus Gabrius Apicius) and published in the century following his death in the first century. *Carotas* has occurred since, but with notable infrequency. Perhaps this is explained by the fact—or what appears to be a fact—that the carrot of contemporary celebrity seems not to have won its place in Rome's descendent culture until the second decade of the present century. It may have had something to do with the introduction of night flying.

claim that the *ad baculum* is a defection from cooperation is true by the prior stipulation.

If it is a misconception to think that threats are always dialectical defections from cooperation, it is perhaps best to reveal the misconception head-on, and without the need to find characterization of the contrast between cooperative and uncooperative consensus formation. This is easily enough done by considering

CASE 6: Negotiations

Negotiations have the following features:

(a) They are reciprocal minimax strategies in which each side attempts to secure an outcome that minimizes the worst disadvantage that it is in the power and intent of the other party to exact. With collective bargaining in industrial settings, for example, it is routinely the case that the maximum disadvantage within the (lawful) power of management to exact is the lockout, and of labor, the strike.

(b) They are discussions held to conventions of rational case-making. Although the threat of disadvantage is at the heart of this form of discussion (and intended to be decisive), it is nevertheless expected that each side will give reasons for its position apart from the prudential factors rooted in their reciprocated threats. That is, each side is required to "explain itself." This we might call the Explanation Condition on negotiation.

(c) There is also involved a further requirement of cooperation, enshrined in the fundamental law on collective bargaining. It provides that settlement should carry a cost for both parties, these costs being in turn reciprocal benefits. It follows, then, that a negotiator's opening position cannot be his closing position. In many jurisdictions this is a requirement of civil law and is called the Good Faith Condition.

It is interesting that the fact that negotiators are rational minimaxers, when taken in conjunction with the Explanation Condition and the Good Faith Condition, suffices to commit the cooperative negotiator to ritual lying or at least to the systematic misrepresentation of his real position, as reflected in diminishingly inaccurate representations of it in a series of on-the-table offers.

Negotiations may nevertheless seem to stand out as paradigms of irrationality and uncooperation in two significant ways. They are *ad baculum* by virtue of the fact that the costs which both parties seek to avoid are threatened by each and allegedly within the power of each to exact. And conformity with the procedural rules entails the systematic use of misrepresentation. In fact, however, it seems extremely implausible that negotiators stand convicted of either irrationality or uncooperation. There is a reason for this. Negotiations have their conventions and conventions are solutions of coordination problems.[5] Whether expressly acknowledged or not, negotiators are pledged to the fulfilment of those conventions, the whole point of which is to coordinate opposing costs and benefits in such a way that agreement can be a rational outcome, never mind that doing so involves ritual uncooperation, an admittedly paradoxical-seeming situation. The air of paradox vanishes, however, to the extent that negotiations are held to the fundamental law on collective bargaining. For if it is an essential requirement that negotiators split their differences, they must have differences to split. Where such differences do not inhere in their respective closing positions, that is to say, at the point of settlement, they will have to be fabricated in order to avoid violating the fundamental law.

It can now be seen that, though a good prudential argument, a mugging is at best a limiting case of a negotiation. An efficiently transacted mugging always violates the Good Faith Condition.

At this juncture, the analysis of the *ad baculum* intersects in an interesting way with the pragma-dialectical account of fallacies (van Eemeren and Grootendorst, 1984, chap. 8: and 1987). The primary insight of the pragma-dialectician is that any violation of the rules of rational conflict resolution counts as a fallacy. So, for example, one way in which a discussant can commit the *ad baculum* fallacy is to break the dialectical rule that bids discussants not to prevent the advancing or criticizing of a thesis. This carries the consequence that if a discussant sought to discourage an opponent's pressing his case by singing "I've got you, Babe" at the top of his lungs, this would count as a fallacious *ad baculum* under pragma-dialectical construal.

Whether readers will be convinced that such is a particularly rich analysis of this fallacy (Woods 1991), it does seem quite clear that "fallacies of negotiation" could be specified pragma-dialectically. In particular, one could plead that violations of either or both the Explanation Condition and the Good Faith Condition deserve the name of (cooperation) fallacies. The pragma-dialectician gives our discussions an interesting additional turn. Collective bargaining, for example, will turn out to be infested by what he calls coopera-

5. David Lewis, *Convention: A Philosophical Study* (Cambridge: Harvard University Press, 1969), 5–51.

tion fallacies, and in so saying he will be seen as calling down a nontraditional concept of fallacy. However, it will also be apparent that the pragma-dialectical account restores a feature of the traditional understanding of the *ad baculum* which our own analysis contradicts. For, in the case of a mugging, the role of the threat is precisely to discourage the victim's making a case for the mugger to desist, and in the case of collective bargaining reciprocal threats make the respective opening positions entirely useless to persist with. Thus although the concept of fallacy is very different from the traditional one, the pragma-dialectical account reimports into the *analysis* of the *ad baculum* a traditional feature, the idea, namely, that threats in rational argumentation are always the occasion of fallacy. An interesting and ironical twist, to be sure.

CASE 7: Veiled Threats

The *ad baculum* is perhaps at its most insidious in the context of veiled intimidation. A good account of Hitler's use of intimidation is given in Zbynek.[6] It will aid exposition to press a distinction between two different types of argument. Roughly speaking an *alethic* argument is an argument about what is the case; a *prudential* argument is, as we have seen, an argument about what should be done. In fact, however, conclusions stating what should be done can always be represented in the form "It is true that such and such should be done" and, by our rough distinction, prudential arguments collapse into alethic ones. Such collapse is averted by introduction of the notion of "deontic formulation." A conclusion about what is the case is given a deontic formulation just in case it asserts or enjoins that a given action should, must, or ought be done or not. An argument whose conclusion is, for example, that it is the case that 2 is a prime number will count as alethic, whereas an argument whose conclusion is that it is the case that you ought to give me your wallet will count as prudential or, as we can now say, as deontic.

Equipped with this distinction we can consider an example of case 7 from Carney and Scheer:

> In 1961 the Western Powers held that they had certain rights in West Berlin, while the Soviet Union denied that they had such rights. Other nations were placed by both powers in the position of having to

6. Zeman Zbynek, *Nazi Propaganda* (New York: Oxford University Press, 1973).

take sides. At that time the Soviet Union announced and tested a nuclear bomb that was about a hundred times more powerful than any United States bomb.[7]

On the stated facts, it is possible to reconstruct two arguments, one alethic and one prudential (or deontic). In the alethic argument the conclusion is that the Soviet Union is objectively correct in saying that the Western Powers lack rights in West Berlin. In the deontic version, the conclusion is that the Western Powers should abandon any claim to rights in West Berlin. It is clear that the alethic argument is not much good, whereas the deontic argument fares much better. That said, it is now possible to characterize the veiled-threat *ad baculum* as an argument forwarded as an alethic argument but whose unexpressed premises or content also present a prudential argument. The veiled-threat *ad baculum* can therefore be regretted on three counts:

(i) In representing itself as a purely alethic argument, it suppresses significant portions of the actual argument by leaving the deontic portion unexpressed. This violates Grice's Quantity Maxim, which bids arguers not to say less than is appropriate for the adjudication of the issue at hand.

(ii) It encourages the suggestion that the alethic argument is correct by virtue of the suppressed truth that the unexpressed deontic argument is or may be correct. Thus it equivocates on the notion of correct argument.

(iii) It misrepresents the significance of Soviet nuclear superiority. Offered as objectively extinguishing the West's claim to rights in Berlin, in fact, it makes of such superiority a disguised threat in the form "If such rights are not abandoned, we the Soviets will or may resort to such superiority." We see, then, that in each of the three cases, the veiled-threat *ad baculum* can be characterized as a fallacy of misrepresentation.

Summary

Thesis 1: The *ad baculum* fallacy is undefined for purely alethic arguments, as with case 1.

7. Zbynek, *Nazi Propaganda*, 39.

Thesis 2: Prudential (or deontic) *ad baculum* arguments are good when compliance with their conclusions is the best cost-benefit or risk aversion outcome.

Thesis 3: Negotiation, especially collective bargaining, is inescapably *ad baculum* (and should be).

Thesis 4: *Ad Baculum* interventions draw differential assessments in shifting dialectical circumstances. A good deontic argument (the gunman's) is a bad piece of negotiation.

Thesis 5: When they occur, *ad baculum* errors are mainly strategic rather than cognitive. For example, trying to negotiate with a mugger is clearly a strategic error. The one type of exception crops up in veiled-threat cases in which the correctness of a suppressed deontic argument leads or is intended to lead a reasoner to accept the conclusion as alethically correct, and this would be a cognitive error plain and simple.

18

Appeal to Ignorance*
Erik C.W. Krabbe

The *argumentum ad ignorantiam*, or appeal to ignorance, is commonly described as a fallacious inference of a statement *p* (or *not-p*) from a premise stating that it is not known, or has not been proven, that *not-p* (or that *p*). As long as the double negation of *p* is considered to be equivalent to *p* (not only with respect to truth value, but also with respect to its epistemic status of being proven, known, or accepted), there is no need to discriminate between these two forms of *ad ignorantiam*, so we may as well concentrate on one of them, say:

(1) *It is not known/proven that not-p. Therefore p.*

The argument is, of course, invalid, but this does not suffice to list it as a particular type of fallacy that deserves a separate analysis. We have to see how this argument is connected with, or functions within, contexts of dialogue (and argumentative texts), and how it can be a real hindrance in reaching the objects of these dialogues.

The roots of the *argumentum ad ignorantiam* are indeed dialectical. It is commonly accepted that the term was introduced by John Locke in his *Essay Concerning Human Understanding* (1690). Locke discusses four sorts of argument "that Men in their Reasoning with others do ordinarily make use of, to prevail on their Assent; or at least so to awe them, as to silence their

*I would like to thank Hans Hansen for his thorough comments on an earlier version of this paper.

Opposition."[1] These are the *argumentum ad verecundiam*, the *argumentum ad ignorantiam*, the *argumentum ad hominem* and the *argumentum ad judicium*, of which the last "alone of all the four, brings true Instruction with it, and advances us in our way to Knowledge."[2] The *ad ignorantiam* is characterized as follows: "Another way that Men ordinarily use to drive others, and force them to submit their Judgments, and receive the Opinion in debate, is to require the Adversary to admit what they alledge [*sic*] as a Proof, or assign a better. And this I call *Argumentum ad Ignorantiam*."[3] According to Hamblin (1970, 161), "Locke does not clearly condemn any of the argument-types, but stands poised between acceptance and disapproval." However, the first three types of argument are clearly stigmatized by him as noninstructive and not leading to knowledge. With respect to the *ad ignorantiam* Locke says: "It proves not another Man to be in the right way, nor that I ought to take the same with him, because I know not a better."[4] Such an argument "may dispose me, perhaps, for the reception of Truth, but helps me not to it."[5] This is all very critical, but since it may "dispose me for the reception of truth," the *argumentum ad ignorantiam* would nevertheless appear to have at least some positive values. Further, we must not overlook the circumstance that the type of dialogue to which Locke refers is one in which knowledge is a primary objective, i.e., inquiry. Even if the *argumentum ad ignorantiam* has no value within a context of inquiry, it still might have one in another context such as a critical discussion held in order to resolve a conflict of opinion (a persuasion dialogue). In that context, it could, perhaps, be said to legitimately lead one to consent to the arguer's conclusion.[6]

In the next section, I shall further investigate the (non)fallaciousness of Locke's *ad ignorantiam* and related dialectical moves. As Hamblin remarked (1970, 162), the problem with *ad ignorantiam*—if there is a problem—has

---

1. John Locke, *An Essay Concerning Human Understanding* [1690], edited by P. H. Nidditch (Oxford: Clarendon Press, 1975), 685–86; IV.17.19. (See this volume, 55.)

2. Ibid., 686, IV.17.22. (See this volume, 56.)

3. Ibid., IV. 17.20. (See this volume, 56.)

4. Ibid., 686–87; IV.17.22. (See this volume, 56.)

5. Ibid.

6. For an assessment of Locke's position, see Hitchcock (1992, 261–63). In Walton (1989b, 259) one finds an interpretation of Locke's type of *ad ignorantiam* that makes it appear to be wholly legitimate. For a survey of types of dialogue see Douglas N. Walton, "What is Reasoning? What is Argument?" *Journal of Philosophy* 87 (1990): 399–419, p. 413; Douglas N. Walton (1992f); and Douglas N. Walton and Erik C. W. Krabbe, *Commitment in Dialogue: Basic Concepts of Interpersonal Reasoning* (Albany: State University of New York Press, forthcoming), sec. 3.1.

to do with "the question of burden of proof." We shall see that a dialectical shift is involved as well.

It is not at all evident what the invalid inference (1), that we are familiar with from the textbook tradition, and Locke's original type of *ad ignorantiam* have in common.[7] Van Eemeren and Grootendorst (1987), feeling that they had to make a choice between two traditions, did not classify *ad ignorantiam* as a violation of their Rule II, which may be called the *Principle of Burden of Proof* (1987, 285), but as a violation of Rule IX (291, 292), a rule pertaining to the evaluation of the discussion in the so-called concluding stage. Thus they were able to present their account of the *ad ignorantiam* as a dialectification of the textbook type. In the section entitled "The *Ad Ignorantiam* as a Fallacy of Dialectical Evaluation*," I shall discuss the "evaluative *ad ignorantiam*" and show how it is related to the "burden of proof" type.

In the section, "Reasoning from a Premise of Ignorance," I concentrate on the logical form of the premise of arguments of type (1). I shall propose a generalized notion of such "ignorance premises" and hence a generalized notion of reasoning from ignorance. It will be seen how reasoning from ignorance leads to the dialectical fallacies that were discussed in the preceding section. The question of the fallaciousness of these explicit appeals to ignorance, both in dialogue and in argumentative texts, will be taken up after that.

Finally, in the section, "Varieties of Reasoning from Ignorance," I shall discuss a variety of ignorance premises and a systematic technique for the description of more complicated forms of *ad ignorantiam*. One registered discussion of such an argument precedes Locke's introduction of the term *argumentum ad ignorantiam*, since it is found in Spinoza's *Ethics* (published in 1677). Spinoza discusses, and rejects, a way of arguing he characterizes as a reduction, not to the impossible (*ad impossibile*), but to ignorance (*ad ignorantiam*):

> For example, if a stone has fallen from a roof onto someone's head and killed him, they will show, in the following way, that the stone

---

7. Either historically or systematically. Woods and Walton 1978b offer a three-part analysis: (i) Suppression of the possibility that a hypothesis could be merely unconfirmed, but not disconfirmed; (ii) a fallacious negation shift as the source of the fallacious inference (1) above; and (iii) a dialectical fallacy of burden of proof. In all three parts the paper is illuminating, but there is little in the way of establishing connections between those parts. Frans H. van Eemeren, Rob Grootendorst, and Tjark Kruiger, *Argumentatieleer 2: Drogredenen* [The discipline of Argument 2: Fallacies], (Groningen: Wolters-Noordhoff, 1986), explicitly claim that there are two disparate senses of *ad ignorantiam* (45, 46).

fell in order to kill the man. For if it did not fall to that end, God willing it, how could so many circumstances have concurred by chance (for often many circumstances do concur at once)? Perhaps you will answer that it happened because the wind was blowing hard and the man was walking that way. But they will persist: why was the wind blowing hard at that time? why was the man walking that way at that same time? If you answer again that the wind arose then because on the preceding day, while the weather was still calm, the sea began to toss, and that the man had been invited by a friend, they will press on—for there is no end to the question which can be asked [*nullus rogandi finis*]: but why was the sea tossing? why was the man invited at just that time? And so they will not stop asking for the causes of causes until you take refuge in the will of God, i.e., the sanctuary of ignorance [*ignorantiae asylum*].[8]

The *Ad Ignorantiam* as a Dialectical Shift

In the following, suppose that *p* stands for a proposition that can typically be decided—if at all—only on a balance of considerations (arguments pro and contra). Suppose further, that the context of dialogue is a persuasion dialogue; that is, a dialogue directed toward the resolution of a conflict of opinion, in which one party, which we shall call the Proponent (P) of *p*, tries to convince the other party (the Opponent, O) that *p* should be accepted. Suppose that O has challenged *p* and that P has offered an argument to support *p*. In a well-regulated system of dialogue, what options should be available to O?

It seems that O should first of all have an opportunity to criticize the argument (the tenability of its premises and the solidity of the connection between premises and conclusion). Furthermore, since an argument may

---

8. Spinoza, *Ethics I, Appendix*; English translation quoted from Benedict de Spinoza, *The Collected Works of Spinoza*, edited by E. Curley, vol. 1 (Princeton N.J.: Princeton University Press, 1985), 443; the Latin words in brackets are quoted from Spinoza, *Ethica ordine geometrico demonstrata* [1677], in Benedictus de Spinoza, *Opera quotquot reperta sunt*, edited by J. van Vloten and J. P. N. Land, vol. 1 (The Hague: Martinus Nijhoff, 1882), 72. This argument occurs among the many examples of complicated appeals to ignorance furnished by Richard Robinson. See Robinson (1971a, 102; case 16v, 108).

well be admitted, yet not be admitted as conclusive, O should have an opportunity to present a counterargument, i.e., an argument for *not-p*. A third option, that I shall not take into account right now, would be to enter into a metadialogue, a dialogue about the procedures or rules of the original dialogue. For instance, O could accuse P of having committed a fallacy. Such an accusation may, of course, coincide with a criticism of the argument, and hence be covered by the first option.[9] If O chooses not to avail herself of any of these options, it would be reasonable to demand that O (at least provisionally) concede *p*.

It is not necessary, for our present purpose, to specify any system of rules for persuasion dialogue. It suffices if we agree that the restriction of options for O, as sketched above, would be a desirable ingredient of a well-structured system of persuasion dialogue, either as a postulated rule or as a consequence of other rules.

Given that the dialectical situation has the features we already suppose it to have, and supposing that we do not take metadialogues into account, what else must we assume for the range of O's options to narrow them down to the two mentioned by Locke? Clearly, it is necessary and sufficient to assume that the opportunity to criticize P's argument has lapsed, i.e., that O's rights in this respect are exhausted. If these are not exhausted, Locke's type of *ad ignorantiam*, reasonable though it may seem, is really fallacious, since it overlooks these (very fundamental) rights of a critical opponent, whereas these rights are crucial for conflict resolution. Did Locke presuppose this last assumption to hold, i.e., did he take it for granted that the discussion about P's argument had been closed? On that interpretation, Locke's type of *ad ignorantiam* would not be fallacious. Unfortunately, Locke's comments are too brief for us to tell.

Of course, if P has not yet presented at least one argument in favor of *p*, an *ad ignorantiam* injunction directed to O—either to present a better (?) argument for *not-p* or concede *p*—would certainly seem to be fallacious. It would overlook P's obligation to defend *p*, and thus enjoin O to cooperate in a violation of the *Principle of Burden of Proof*:

> Whoever advances a standpoint is obliged to defend it if asked to do so.[10]

9. In Krabbe (1992, 275, 276) I argue that narrow-type relevance criticism amounts to a fallacy charge. See also the section, "Reasoning from a Premise of Ignorance," below.
10. Van Eemeren and Grootendorst (1987, 285), Rule II.

But perhaps P is not really violating this principle, since he might be willing to discharge his burden of proof at some later time, and in some systems of dialogue this could be a permissible option. Even so, if the *ad ignorantiam* injunction is understood as a *reaction* to O's challenge of p, it is fallacious. That O challenges p, shows that O is committed to an attitude of critical doubt with respect to p, but it does not show that O is committed to *not-p*. (Of course, O could have her doubts about *not-p* as well.) Hence, O's challenge of p does not involve the assertion *not-p*, which could in turn be challenged by P. To pretend that it does amounts to committing the *straw man fallacy*, i.e., the fallacy of distorting the views of one's adversary, as in the following dialogue fragment:

P: p
O: *Why p?*
P: *Why not-p?*

P's second move could be labeled either *ad ignorantiam* or *straw man*. Whichever label is preferred, what makes the move fallacious is that P, instead of presenting an argument, illicitly tries to shift the burden of proof onto O. If he succeeds he has forced O into a dialectical shift. Not a shift to a completely different type of dialogue (such as a quarrel or a negotiation), but a so-called *internal shift*. Before the shift, there was only one party that had a proposition to defend; after the (illicit) shift, both parties have one. O has been led on to change her attitude toward p from one of critical doubt to a completely negative attitude. This particular type of internal shift is, therefore, more accurately characterized as a *shift of attitude*.[11] In this case the shift is forced and illicit, but, of course, O could also volunteer such a shift of attitude.

If the rules of dialogue would permit answering a challenge by a challenge in this way, O could again retort with *Why not-not-p?* But just shifting the burden of proof back and forth doesn't get one anywhere. Certainly, it will not lead to a resolution of a conflict of opinion. That is the underlying reason why this crude type of *ad ignorantiam* is a fallacy; that it is "wrong in the sense that it frustrates efforts to arrive at the resolution of a dispute [= conflict]" (van Eemeren and Grootendorst 1987, 284).

11. The originally pure conflict of opinion has become mixed. Cf. Else M. Barth and Erik C. W. Krabbe, *From Axiom to Dialogue: A Philosophical Study of Logics and Argumentation* (Berlin and New York: Walter de Gruyter, 1982), 56, 74–75. On dialectical shifts, see Walton (1992f) and Walton and Krabbe, *Commitment in Dialogue*.

But what if there is a strong presumption in favor of *p?* In that case, would it not be *O* rather than *P* who has the burden of proof? Wouldn't it be proper for *P* to answer a challenge by a challenge? A presumption, in dialogue, holds only if both parties agree upon it. So in that case *p* could not be the question at issue of the dialogue, but it could of course be a reason advanced by *P* in order to argue for something else. If *O* challenges a presumption this means that she retracts a concession, but perhaps it means more. Presumptions can plausibly be understood, not as ordinary, retractable concessions, but as constraints on dialogues. When *P* agreed to enter the dialogue, that agreement could have been contingent upon a certain presumption's being in force. *O*'s retraction of commitment to this presumption obviously unsettles *P*'s previous agreement to enter the dialogue. So, wouldn't *P* be justified in withdrawing from the dialogue without suffering defeat? *P* would seem at least to be entitled to challenge a retraction of commitment to a presumption; for instance, *P* might justifiably utter: *Why is there no longer a presumption that p?* Even so, this is not the same as challenging a supposed commitment to an assertion of *not-p.*

Suppose a company of discussants accepts the straw man variety of *ad ignorantiam;* i.e., it accepts *P*'s counterchallenge *Why not-p?* as a full and adequate response to *O*'s challenge *Why p?* What rule of dialogue has implicitly been adopted by this company? Clearly they hold that if *O* appears to be unable to win the (part of the) dialogue concerned with *P*'s challenge, *P* has already won the (part of the) dialogue concerned with *O*'s challenge, i.e., the dialogue about *p.* This idea about who has lost and who has won some part of the dialogue can be formulated as an (unadvisable) rule of dialectic:

Rule 1:   *Ad Ignorantiam Rule:* If X did not successfully defend *not-p,* then Y's defense of *p* has succeeded.

This rule, as we shall see, provides a foundation for the next type of *ad ignorantiam* as well.

The *Ad Ignorantiam* as a Fallacy of Dialectical Evaluation

According to Van Eemeren and Grootendorst (1984, 174), the discussants "terminate the discussion jointly by establishing the final result." Thus, in the *concluding stage* of a critical discussion, both parties try to determine whether the original question in dispute was resolved in one way or another and then adjust their attitudes accordingly. One plausible rule of evaluation would be:

Rule 2:   Suppose that (i) X did not successfully defend *not-p*; but (ii) Y successfully defended *p*. Then X should (provisionally, until further notice) accept *p*.

But if one accepted the *Ad Ignorantiam Rule* (Rule 1), (ii) would follow from (i), and therefore be redundant. This gives us a much simpler rule of evaluation:

Rule 3:   Suppose that X did not successfully defend *not-p*. Then X should (provisionally, until further notice) accept *p*.

But this is too simple. For to follow this rule, generally, is to commit a fallacy of *ad ignorantiam* in the concluding stage of a critical discussion. It exemplifies what van Eemeren and Grootendorst (1987, 292) call *absolutizing the failure of a defense*.

It is a fallacy, because it is rash: given that X's defense of *not-p* was not successful, this does not exclude the possibility that Y's defense of *p* was even less successful, so that one should accept *not-p* rather than *p*, if a choice has to be made. Notice that the reason it is a fallacy is not that X's failure to defend *not-p* successfully would be irrelevant for the question whether or not X should accept *p*. That *is* relevant. Indeed, from the mere fact that Y successfully defended *p* it would be equally rash to conclude that *p* should be accepted, since this does not exclude that there could be a successful defense of *not-p* as well, especially if *p* is the type of proposition that has to be decided on the balance of considerations. But, of course, a successful defense would be relevant.[12]

We have now seen how two types of *ad ignorantiam* as a dialectical fallacy (*shifting the burden of proof* and *absolutizing the failure of a defense*) are related: both are generated by the acceptance of the same rule, namely the *Ad*

---

12. This would exemplify the converse fallacy of *absolutizing the success of a defense* (Van Eemeren and Grootendorst 1987, 291). There are many other ways to commit this latter fallacy, which are versions of the *argumentum ad hominem*. See Barth and Martens (1977, 84). Walton (1989b, 153) notices a close connection between *ad ignorantiam* and the basic *ad hominem* fallacy.

Ignorantiam Rule (Rule 1). It is time to return to the invalid *ad ignorantiam* reasoning of type (1).

Reasoning from a Premise of Ignorance

A premise of ignorance is a premise of the form *not-E-not-p*. Here *E* stands for some "positive" epistemic (i.e., knowledge-related) operator. For instance, *Ep* can be read as short for either of these: X successfully defended *p*; *p* can be successfully defended; *p* has been proven; *p* is provable; it is known (by X) that *p*; *p* is knowable; good arguments for *p* are available; good arguments for *p* can be produced; there is something to say for *p*; something could be said in favor of *p*.

The (or a) general form of argument from ignorance is given by:

(2) *Not-E-not-p. Therefore p.*

You can see that (1) is of this form, if you take *Ep* to stand for *it is known that p* or for *p has been proven*. But this argument form is also closely connected to the fallacious evaluation rule (Rule 3): if you take *Ep* to stand for X *successfully defended p*, you generate a more specific argument form that, if acceptable, would provide a justification for the use of this rule in the concluding stage of a critical dialogue. One may also "justify" the *Ad Ignorantiam Rule* (Rule 1) in this way (if from the premise that X did not successfully defend *not-p* it would follow, at least as a generally acceptable conclusion, that *p*, then the *Ad Ignorantiam Rule* would not be all that bad as a rule of dialogue). Thus it appears that all types of *ad ignorantiam* are related in that they obtain a (spurious) justification once special cases of the (invalid) argument form (2) are taken for granted.

The next question is whether an ignorance premise presented as a reason in argument to defend a point of view, *p*, would in itself constitute a fallacy. Consider the following dialogue fragment:

P: *p*
O: *Why p?*
P: *Not-E-not-p*

The argument P presents in defense of his assertion that p has precisely the form (2). It is invalid, but that, by itself, is no reason to speak of a fallacy. It is now up to O to criticize the argument. She may either criticize the premise, or the premise-conclusion connection. Next it is up to P to meet the criticism. O may, indeed, also claim that the argument is a fallacy. For instance, she might claim that the gap between premise and conclusion cannot possibly be bridged, since the premise is entirely irrelevant to the conclusion. But then the burden of proof is upon O to show this. Why?

First, in reasonable dialogue one has to presume that one's adversary is a serious partner in the dialogue, otherwise conflict resolution would not be possible. Therefore, there is a presumption in favor of P's willingness to at least try to fill the gap. Presumably, he intends the ignorance premise as a good reason for the acceptance of p. So O should at least give him a hearing, or else she should explain why she does not think this is worthwhile (and thus enter upon a metadialogue).

Second, there are plenty of examples that illustrate how an argument with the form (2) could be completed so as to give us a valid or at least a very plausible argument. The examples of a search and of a criminal trial occur in nearly all textbook expositions. In the search case, there has been a thorough inquiry whether p; thorough enough to warrant the conclusion that *if p were not the case then evidence for not-p would have been found* (or, *not-p would have been proven, would be known to hold*, etc.). Together with the appropriate ignorance premise *no evidence for not-p has been found / not-p has not been proven / not-p is not known to hold*, etc., it follows that p. In the criminal trial case, p stands for the proposition that the accused is innocent; the ignorance premise tells us that it has not been proven that the accused is guilty (not innocent); the bridge is provided by a legal presumption of innocence.

As Douglas Walton has pointed out, this type of case is not restricted to legal contexts. For instance, if it is not known whether a certain gun is loaded it may in some contexts be safer to presume that it is loaded (unless there is proof for the opposite). Thus the ignorance premise: *it has not been proven that this gun is unloaded* is, within such contexts, a good reason to accept the proposition that *the gun is loaded*.[13]

Some have objected that these cases are not really arguments from igno-

---

13. Walton (1984, 23; 1989b, 253, 263–64). Reasoning from ignorance in a practical situation is closely related to what in Artificial Intelligence is called "negation as failure," and hence to default reasoning and nonmonotonic reasoning; see D. N. Walton, *Practical Reasoning: Goal-Driven, Knowledge-Based, Action-Guiding Argumentation* (Savage, Md.: Rowman and Littlefield, 1990), 77–79.

rance, since the conclusion p (that *the accused is innocent*, or that *the gun is loaded*) is not really claimed to be true.[14] The conclusion would not be p, but that *one should act as if it were the case that p*. However, what matters in argument is that good reasons are provided for one's adversary to accept a proposition. What the precise meaning of acceptance is, whether it involves belief in the truth of p, or is better described as willingness to act upon p, may depend on the further context of dialogue. Thus in some contexts of dialogue acceptance of p just amounts to the willingness to act in certain ways that, from a quite different and more theoretical perspective, could be described as ways of acting as if p were true. Within a context like the criminal trial or the gun case the distinction is spurious: an argument that goes to show that one should act as if it were the case that p is the same as an argument for p. Thus we do have an *argumentum ad ignorantiam* here, but it is not a fallacy.

We may conclude that an appeal to ignorance in dialogue in itself does not constitute a fallacy. The matter is quite different if the appeal to ignorance occurs, not in explicit dialogue, but in an argumentative text, i.e., implicit dialogue. The author of the text, arguing for a conclusion p, tries to perform the tasks of a Proponent of p, but he has to 'stand in for the Opponent as well. Ideally, the author presents and answers all criticisms and objections that his intended audience, presumably, would have brought forward, if the dialogue had been explicit. Therefore, if we evaluate an argumentative text, we must look for any gaps in the argument, spots at which the intended audience would, plausibly, have asked for additional argument, whereas no such argument is provided by the text. If there are serious gaps of this kind, we charge the author with the fallacy of *insufficient evidence* (or *hasty conclusion*).[15] Clearly, appeals to ignorance often present us with a case where it is by no means evident how the gap is to be filled. Therefore, such appeals are often indicative of a fallacy of insufficient evidence in argument.

Varieties of Reasoning from Ignorance

The verdicts given above on the (non)fallaciousness of appeals to ignorance do not complete the study of *ad ignorantiam*. Rather this study has just begun. First, the types of dialectical move discussed in the sections, "The *Ad*

14. Cf. Robinson (1971a, 105, 106); Maarten Henket, "Het argumentum ad ignorantiam in het recht" [The *argumentum ad ignorantiam* in law]. *Tijdschrift voor taalbeheersing* 6 (1984): 87–92.
    15. See Johnson and Blair (1993, 56–61).

Ignorantiam as a Dialectical Shift" and "The *Ad Ignorantiam* as a Fallacy of Dialectical Evaluation" await further investigation from the perspective of variously specified contexts of dialogue. Second, in order to provide a closer analysis of reasoning from premises of ignorance, we need to have a survey of those premises and of their strengths and weaknesses. This, again, may be achieved by relating the different possible values of *E* in these premises to the various possible gaps in arguments that start from the corresponding premises of ignorance and to types of additional evidence that could obviously bridge these gaps. Here we can do no more than give some indication of what is involved in this second enterprise.

Ignorance premises are unequal in strength: *nothing whatsoever was said in favor of not-p* implies *no good arguments were presented for not-p*. This again (normally) implies that *it is not known that not-p*, and this in turn implies that *not-p has not been proven*. The implications do not hold in the other direction. Each of these ignorance premises can be strengthened by insertion of a possibility operator after the first negation; for instance, *it is not possibly known that not-p* (i.e., *not-p is unknowable*) implies *it is not known that not-p*, and *it has not possibly been proven that not-p* (i.e., *not-p is unprovable*) implies *not-p has not been proven*.

The weaker the ignorance premise the harder it is to bridge the gap in the reasoning. For instance, *not-p has not been proven* is a notoriously weak premise. But even here the gap could be bridged, if *p* belongs to a class of decidable propositions, for one might add the premise that a decision procedure was applied to *p* with some result or other. If the result was not a proof of *not-p* it must have been a proof of *p*.

A premise like *no good arguments were presented for not-p* is much stronger. This premise, and stronger premises, if accepted by an addressee (*X*) would, in a context of persuasion dialogue, warrant the conclusion that *it is not the case that X should accept not-p*. Even stronger claims may sometimes be justified, although they are not implied by the last sentence. For instance, in suitable circumstances, one could justify a negation shift and establish: *X should not accept not-p* (i.e., *it is not the case that it is permissible for X to accept not-p*). But it will be harder to warrant a further negation shift to *X should accept p*. Sometimes, however, additional premises are available that permit an arguer to fill just this gap, for instance: *it is permissible for X to accept p* and *X should, preferably, accept at least one of p and not-p*. If these two premises are joined to the conclusion we assumed to have been reached, namely that *it is not the case that it is permissible for X to accept not-p*, we may get as a final conclusion that *X should accept p*.

Attention should also be given to more complex types of the *ad ignorantiam*, such as the one found in the quotation from Spinoza. Many of these complex types were presented by Richard Robinson (1971a). Most of them can be generated from (2) by further specifications of *E*. In this context, it is convenient to avail oneself of a variable for *binary epistemic predicates*. We shall use the infix notation *qRp*, to be read as short for: *q is a proof of p*, *q accounts for/explains p*, *q accounts for the possibility that p*, *q is a reason for p*, and the like. The symbol ':=' will be used to mean 'becomes' or 'becoming'. We can now easily describe some complex specifications of *E*. For instance *Ep* := *there is a (possible) q such that qRp*. With *qRp* := *q is a proof of p*, we generate the ignorance premise (*not-E-not-p*): *not-p is unprovable*, which we met before.

A much more complicated example would be: *Ep* := *there is a q such that it is known that q is true and that qR(it is known that p)*. With *qRp* := *q would account for p, if p were true* we generate the ignorance premise *not-E-not-p* := *it is not the case that there is a q such that it is known that q is true and that qR(it is known that not-p)*. Replacing the R by its present definiens one gets: *not-E-not-p* := *it is not the case that there is a q such that it is known that q is true and that q would account for the fact that it is known that not-p (if it were known that not-p)*. Or, to put it more simply: *not-E-not-p* := *there is no way known to account for (supposed) knowledge of not-p*. According to Robinson (1971a, 100, case 11), the reasoning implied by the question *How do you know (that not-p)?* employs this premise.

Yet another example is contained in the argument, quoted above, that was condemned by Spinoza. The ignorance premise employed in this piece of reasoning could be formulated as follows: *there is no way that in conjunction with the supposition that this stone did not fall in order to kill this man (God willing it) would account for the fact that this stone fell and killed this man*. It is left as an exercise for the reader to generate the form of this ignorance premise, letting *Ep* := *there is a q such that it is known that q is true and that (q and p)Rr; qRp* := *q (if true) would account for p; r* := *this stone fell and killed this man*. (In addition the argument employs the premises *this stone fell and killed this man* and *God wanted this stone to fall in order to kill this man would (if true) account for the fact that this stone fell and killed this man*.) If you agree with Spinoza, and do not accept this argument, you are faced with the problem of how to draw a line between this argument and more acceptable instances of abduction (arguments to the best explanation), such as: there are bear tracks around, we can explain them if we assume a bear to have walked past, but there is no known way to explain the occurrence of these tracks if we assume that no bear walked past; hence it is reasonable to assume that a bear walked past (see Robinson 1971a, 107v).

As may be clear from these examples, a formal analysis of ignorance premises is potentially a very powerful technique that can be used in further studies of the *ad ignorantiam*. By no other means can we systematically investigate the full wealth of complicated real-life arguing from ignorance that was explored by Richard Robinson (1971a). The next step, however, will be to make the return to dialogue theory in order to find out which dialectical rules might be adopted to handle various appeals to ignorance. Finally, these efforts may lead to practical insights that can be used by arguers that are confronted with such appeals or, perhaps, want to make such appeals themselves.

19

The Appeal to Popularity and Presumption by Common Knowledge

James B. Freeman

Suppose I argued that a particular belief should be accepted because it is a popular, widely held belief. Suppose you argued that a belief was acceptable because that belief is a matter of common knowledge. More specifically, suppose you argued that the belief's being a matter of common knowledge created a presumption in its favor, that barring counterevidence it is rational to accept it, and in this case there is no counterevidence. Are we giving the same justification for our claims? I maintain that we are not and shall endeavor to explain why in this paper. This is crucial, since I want to maintain that appeals to popularity are fallacious while appeals to common knowledge are not. You are not justified in accepting a statement merely because it is popular. All things being equal, you *are* justified in accepting a statement if you recognize it as part of or vouched for by common knowledge. Without explaining the difference between appealing to popularity and appealing to common knowledge, there would seem to be a distinct tension between these two claims. How are these appeals distinct? Let's begin by defining the appeal to popularity and then state why we think such appeals fallacious.

In *Thinking Logically*, we defined the appeal to popularity, which we there called the *bandwagon appeal*, as an argument which claims that because many, most, or all people accept a certain belief or approve a certain course of action, that belief must be true or that course of action must be right.[1] Our calling this the *bandwagon appeal* is intended to dispel confusion. The appeal to popularity is not the same as the *argumentum ad populum*, characterized in a number of logic texts, most notably Copi's classic *Introduction to Logic*, and literally translated as *appeal to the people*. Copi defines the *ad populum* "as the attempt to win popular assent to a conclusion by arousing the emotions and enthusiasms of the multitude rather than by appeal to the relevant facts."[2] Such an attempt is grandstanding. It should be obvious that there are many ways to arouse the emotions and enthusiasms of the multitude besides asserting that many, most, or all people accept some claim. If human beings have a herd instinct, this appeal to popularity may be *a* way of tapping into the enthusiasms or gut emotions of the multitude, but it is not the *only* way. Appeals to anger, hate, or pride may also be quite persuasive, yet here we make no claim, either explicitly or implicitly, that many, most, all people accept some belief or endorse some course of action.

As Copi points out, what we are here calling the appeal to popularity or the bandwagon appeal is a subspecies of the *argumentum ad populum*. In this paper, we shall continue to refer to the bandwagon appeal as the appeal to popularity. These remarks should be sufficient to indicate that we are discussing the subspecies, not the wider *argumentum ad populum*. In defining the appeal to popularity as we do, we follow Johnson and Blair in *Logical Self-Defense*.[3]

Why is the appeal to popularity fallacious? Why should instances of this appeal be numbered among the fallacies? In *Thinking Logically*, we characterized the mistake as an inflation of the weight of popularity as evidence for the correctness of some belief or the appropriateness of some course of action. That many, most, all people accept some belief or endorse some action *prima facie* constitutes some evidence that the belief is true or the action right. If many people are buying a product, isn't the manufacturer doing something right? Isn't the fact that everyone agrees on something a mark that it is true or correct? But, as we have defined it, the appeal to popularity is not so modest. It does not regard popularity as simply a mark, as *some* evidence. It claims that because a belief or action is popular, it *must* be true or right. What is properly some evidence is presented as

1. See James B. Freeman, *Thinking Logically: Basic Concepts for Reasoning*, 2d ed. (Englewood Cliffs, N.J.: Prentice-Hall, 1993), 57. Our entire discussion of this appeal appears on 56–57.

2. Irving M. Copi, *Introduction to Logic*, 7th ed. (New York: Macmillan, 1986), 96.

3. See Ralph H. Johnson and J. Anthony Blair, *Logical Self-Defense* (Toronto: McGraw-Hill Ryerson, 1977), 158–63.

conclusive evidence. The modality "must" is not justified. What are basically some reasons, even weak reasons, are alleged to be conclusive reasons. We see the fallacy lying precisely here.

This was our analysis in *Thinking Logically*.[4] This analysis raises an interesting question. It apparently presupposes that appeals to popularity *by definition* always inflate the value of popularity as evidence to that of being (virtually) conclusive. Couldn't we have a fallacious appeal to popularity when an argument makes the more modest claim that popularity is a sufficient but not necessarily conclusive reason for accepting some claim? Must the inflation always be so rampant? Must weak evidence be touted as conclusive evidence to have this fallacy? Surely inflating the weight of evidence to any degree would be a logical error. But inflating it to the level of sufficiency, we should still have a fallacious argument, a case of hasty conclusion where the premises are too weak to properly support the conclusion. Why not require appeals to popularity to inflate popularity only to the level of sufficiency?

Two important texts define the appeal to popularity just with respect to sufficiency. In *Logical Self-Defense*, Johnson and Blair define the appeal this way:

1. M claims or implies that Q is true (false) and offers as warrant that Q is widely accepted (not widely accepted).
2. The popularity of Q (or lack of it) is not an adequate reason for accepting Q.[5]

For Johnson and Blair, the fallaciousness of this appeal still lies in inflating the value or weight of popularity as evidence. But such inflation need not be to the level of claiming that popularity necessitates or virtually necessitates accepting the conclusion. We may note that inflation to the level of sufficiency is also how Kahane understands this fallacy: "For many people, the crowd is the authority. For them, the fact that a view is generally accepted is sufficient to make that view respectable; the fact that a view is *not* generally accepted is sufficient to make it suspect."[6]

So we shall broaden our definition of the appeal to popularity. We now characterize it as an argument which claims that because many, most, all

---

4. Freeman, *Thinking Logically*, 57.
5. Johnson and Blair, *Logical Self-Defense*, 161.
6. Howard Kahane, *Logic and Contemporary Rhetoric: The Uses of Logic in Everyday Life*, 3d ed. (Belmont, Calif.: Wadsworth, 1980), 37.

people accept a certain belief or approve a certain course of action, we have sufficient reason to accept that belief as true or that course of action as right. But if we accept this broader characterization of the appeal to popularity, are we committed to saying that popularity is never a sufficient reason to accept some belief? But then what of common knowledge as a presumption creating source that may vouch for certain claims?

What does this mean? To say that there is a presumption in favor of a statement means that in the absence of counterevidence or counter-indications, we may accept that statement.[7] The burden of proof lies with those seeking to question or reject the statement to show why their challenge has merit.[8] As Rescher points out in *Dialectics*, presumptions are not indefeasible—they are not statements which are certain or above challenge. Rather they are defeasible. They are statements which we may accept and from which we may reason, which may serve as basic or unargued premises in our arguments, until some challenger presents sufficient evidence to call them into question.[9] To say that common knowledge is a presumption creating source means that if common knowledge vouches for a claim, if that statement is a matter of common knowledge, then we are justified in accepting that claim until and unless we have sufficient evidence against it. Again as Rescher points out in *Dialectics*, at least in disputational debate, there is a presumption in favor of common knowledge as a species of evidence. Common knowledge, for Rescher then, is a standard presumption or acceptability creating source of evidence.

In her text, *A Practical Study of Argument*, Trudy Govier cites common knowledge as a source of premise acceptability: "A premise in an argument is acceptable if it is a matter of common knowledge. That is, if the premise merely states something that is known to virtually everyone, it should be allowed as an acceptable premise. Or, if a premise is very widely believed, and there is no widely known evidence against it, it is often appropriate to allow it as acceptable."[10] As examples of common knowledge, Govier cites "Human beings have hearts" and "There are many trees in Canada."[11] Statements that are matters of common knowledge are acceptable precisely because they are matters of common knowledge.

---

7. Compare Freeman, *Thinking Logically*, 154.

8. Compare Nicholas Rescher, *Dialectics: A Controversy-Oriented Approach to the Theory of Knowledge* (Albany: State University of New York Press, 1977), 30.

9. Rescher, *Dialectics*, 33.

10. Trudy Govier, *A Practical Study of Argument*, 1st ed. (Belmont, Calif.: Wadsworth, 1985), 80.

11. Govier, *Practical Study*, 80–81.

But what does it mean to say that a claim is a matter of common knowledge or that common knowledge vouches for a claim? More trenchantly, what more does this mean beyond saying that many, most, all people accept that claim? If it does not mean more than that, and popularity is never sufficient to warrant acceptance, then it would seem that common knowledge is not a proper source of presumption. If not, then there is something seriously wrong with our understanding of presumption. Are appeals to common knowledge, then, appeals to popularity? Is saying that there is a presumption in favor of a statement, that it is therefore acceptable, because it is a matter of common knowledge, a fallacy?

To resolve this conundrum, we must probe our notion of presumption more deeply. We must first note that, as Trudy Govier points out, common knowledge is a relational concept. What was common knowledge at one time may for various reasons no longer be common knowledge at a later time. A statement is common knowledge in or for a certain cultural-historical context. For those within that context, certain statements are common knowledge and recognizing them as common knowledge renders them acceptable.

Presumption on our view is also a relational notion. Instead of a cultural-historical context being one of the relata, we speak of points in a dialectical exchange. A dialectical exchange is a dialogue between exactly two people discussing some issue in order to reach some rationally justified position concerning its truth or acceptability. One participant is the proponent; the other, the challenger. The proponent puts forward a thesis and defends it by responding to the questions of the challenger. These questions express her perception of the logical weaknesses of the proponent's case.

Each contribution of proponent and challenger determines a point in the dialectical exchange. Each of the proponent's contributions, after his statement of the initial thesis, is intended to foster a presumption for some previously enunciated thesis by giving evidence for it, and to be presumptively true in its own right. At each point in the dialectical exchange, the challenger may be prepared to question or object to at least some of the theses the proponent has advanced up to that point. The proponent may be able to anticipate these challenges and foresee that he could meet them satisfactorily. From his perspective, there is a presumption in favor of his theses at this point, since once he has answered these questions, the challenger should be obliged to concede these theses. From the challenger's perspective, there would not be a presumption for these theses until the proponent met her challenges to her satisfaction. Hence proponent and challenger may differ on just what theses should be conceded at a given point in an exchange. On the other hand, the challenger may have no objections or counterconsiderations to bring against other theses the proponent has advanced and may recognize that simply asking for justification, evidence for these theses would be frivolous. Under these circumstances, the challenger would be obliged to concede these theses. We say that there is a presumption in favor of a statement S at a point p in a dialectical exchange for the challenger C of that exchange if and only if C is obliged to concede S at p.[12] Presumption then is a ternary relation between a statement, a point in a dialectical exchange, and a participant of that exchange.

Acceptability should be understood in terms of challenger presumption. Challengers stand as representatives of the community of rational inquirers. Hence they are committed to continue probing the proponent's case for genuine logical weaknesses either until all their questions have been answered or the proponent resigns the attempt to establish his thesis through argumentation. Hence challengers are bound to bring questions and objections against theses they recognize as genuinely questionable or objectionable. By the same token, should a challenger have no questions or objections to raise against some thesis S, i.e. should there be a presumption in favor of S at this point in the dialectical exchange for this challenger, then that statement should be rationally acceptable from her perspective.[13]

When a challenger recognizes that there is a presumption in favor of a statement from her perspective in a dialectical exchange, she takes into account not just which of the proponent's theses have been established at that point in the exchange, but also her background knowledge of the situation. This background knowledge will include presumption-making principles and whether these principles apply in this case. This applies to common knowledge. It is the *challenger's* role to recognize that being a matter of common knowledge creates a presumption for a claim and that a particular claim is a matter of common knowledge. Hence whether a statement is a matter of common knowledge is a question for the challenger to decide from her perspective.

How then does a claim gain the status of common knowledge for a challenger? In *Thinking Logically*, we pointed out that individuals inherit common knowledge from their societies, although different societies bequeath

---

12. Compare James B. Freeman, "A Dialectical Approach to Statement Acceptability," in Frans H. van Eemeren and Rob Grootendorst et al., eds. (1991a), 341.

13. This indicates that statement acceptability is also a relational notion.

different bodies of common knowledge to their members. How is this transmission effected? How do such claims as Govier's

(1) Human beings have hearts
(2) There are many trees in Canada

or such claims as

(3) George Washington was the first president of the United States
(4) Stealing, except possibly under very unusual circumstances, is wrong

come to be common knowledge for most North Americans with at least a grade school education? At least two sources contribute to our common knowledge. How do we come to know statements such as (1), (3), or (4)? Surely it is because they have been vouched for by "authoritative" sources, by parents and teachers, giving us instruction intended not only for our own interest (as the testimony of expert witnesses might be of interest only to participants in some trial or hearing), but for the common benefit. These are sources for whom there is a presumption of trust, and later experience has given no cause to undermine this trust, at least for the statements counted as common knowledge. Consider (2). Certainly our experience tells us that there are a lot of trees in our immediate vicinity. This is normal. There are few who would be prepared to contradict it. It is part of common knowledge that most areas, even relatively small areas, have a lot of trees. But "authorities" may tell us that Canada comprises a large geographical area. So it is part of common knowledge that (2) there are many trees in Canada.

Suppose a challenger does not recognize a claim as a matter of common knowledge. As I see it, this could happen for one of three reasons:

(1) She has temporarily forgotten that it is a matter of common knowledge.
(2) The cultural transmission mechanisms failed in her case to transmit this item of common knowledge to her.
(3) It simply is not a matter of common knowledge.

Could the proponent's telling her that it was a matter of common knowledge make it common knowledge or create the conditions whereby she could recognize it as common knowledge? Let us consider each case in turn.

Should she have forgotten that the claim was a matter of common knowledge, reminding her that it was would not *make* it common knowledge or constitute a reason for her saying it was a matter of common knowledge. It might jog her memory that authoritative sources had vouched for the claim. But that is what made the claim common knowledge or what gave her reason to recognize the claim as common knowledge. If the cultural authorities had failed to transmit that something was common knowledge, telling the challenger that it was would not make it common knowledge or give her reason to regard it as common knowledge. For that, she would have to be introduced to the relevant "authorities." Finally, if something is not a matter of common knowledge, saying that it is constitutes a statement which is just plain false. It obviously will not make it a matter of common knowledge or constitute proper evidence for saying that it is.

The point is this: Recognizing a statement as a matter of common knowledge is a result of our "lived experience." That S is a matter of common knowledge cannot become a part of *our* knowledge simply by our being told that S has common knowledge status. Our experience must indicate that proper sources vouch for S. Hence, in judging that a statement is acceptable because it is a matter of common knowledge, a challenger must recognize that the statement has common knowledge status out of *her* experience which she brings to the dialectical situation. When it comes to judging that there is a presumption in favor of a statement on the basis of common knowledge, that judgment is reserved for the challenger to make on the basis of her experience. It is not a judgment for the proponent to offer as a premise to support or justify the statement. Such a premise, that S is a matter of common knowledge, is either questionable or false. There is no presumption for the statement "S is a matter of common knowledge" from the point of view of a challenger who does not recognize S as a matter of common knowledge.

Hence, appeals to common knowledge, at least appeals by challengers to the common knowledge included in their own background knowledge, are not appeals to popularity. They are certainly not appeals by proponents that everybody accepts some claim. This means that we may maintain that appeals to popularity are improper or fallacious without renouncing common knowledge as a proper source of presumption. Appeals to popularity are basically hasty conclusion fallacies. The data concerning the popularity of the belief are simply not sufficient to warrant accepting the belief. The logical error in an appeal to popularity lies in its inflating the value of popularity as evidence. The claim that a belief is commonly held does not constitute proper grounds for recognizing it as common *knowledge* by some challenger. For that, the challenger must recognize that the belief is properly vouched for by sources for which there is a standing presumption of trustworthiness. It is legitimate for the challenger to recognize these presumptions out of her background knowledge of the situation. The very need to justify a belief shows it is not common knowledge in the dialectical situation where the proponent is arguing. His claim that it is amounts to claiming that the belief should be accepted because it is popularly accepted. That is the fallacious appeal to popularity.

20

Appeal to Authority

James Bachman

All the best authorities agree: *ad verecundiam*, the appeal to authority, is no fallacy. But we need not modestly defer to the experts; an examination of this reasoning strategy will enable us to see for ourselves the fallacy of calling the appeal to authority a fallacy. *Ad verecundiam* concerns strategies for effective reasoning, and strategies may be more or less wisely employed.

One way to capture the issues raised by the appeal to authority is to situate the appeal to authority in a model of reasoning that distinguishes between *rules for correctness* and *strategies for effectiveness*. We begin with a brief description of such a model and then apply it to the appeal to authority.

The Interrogative Model of Reasoning

Jaakko Hintikka has collaborated with several colleagues over the past decade to develop an interrogative model of reasoning.[1] The model identifies two different kinds of steps or moves as the fundamental ingredients of rational inquiry: *interrogative steps* and *logical inference steps*. *Interrogative steps* are

1. For a more detailed study of this model, see J. Hintikka (1987); J. Hintikka, "The Role of Logic in Argumentation," *Monist* 72 (1989): 3–24; J. Hintikka and J. Bachman, *What If? . . . Toward Excellence in Reasoning* (Mountain View, Calif.: Mayfield, 1991); and J. Hintikka and M. B. Hintikka, "Sherlock Holmes Confronts Modern Logic: Toward a Theory of Information Seeking Through Questioning," in *Argumentation: Approaches to Theory Formation*, edited by E. M. Barth and J. L. Martens (Amsterdam: John Benjamins, 1982), 55–76.

those steps that seek or gather information for an inquiry or argument. Information-seeking is modeled as an activity of addressing questions to sources. The model speaks of these sources as "oracles." *Logical inference steps* are those steps in reasoning that deductively draw out what is contained in the information made available by interrogative steps. All inference steps are required to be deductive and therefore truth preserving. Problems of uncertainty in reasoning are thus focused in the other key aspect of reasoning, the gathering of information through interrogative steps. The model mandates no set order of steps for the development of an argument. Interrogative and logical inference steps are employed as needed, just as in everyday reasoning.

The interrogative model treats ordinary oral and written expressions of inquiries as incomplete sketches of what are usually indefinitely complex arguments. The model distinguishes between *analyzing* a sketch, *evaluating* a sketch, and *constructing* a new or enhanced inquiry based on or in reaction to a sketch. *Analysis* is the foundation for *evaluation* and *construction*. Analysis of an oral or written sketch involves the following activities:

1. Interrogative steps are distinguished and disentangled from inference steps. Information in use in the inquiry is treated as information gained by receiving answers to questions. Interrogative analysis requires noting what kinds of questions are being asked and what the sources are to which the inquiry looks for answers. Analysis does not include the evaluative task of assessing the reliability of answers in use in the inquiry.
2. The interrogative model requires all inferences to be valid deductive inferences. The reported sketch must usually be enriched by importing background information that is required and was perhaps intended if the inquiry is to have any possibility of leading deductively to its proposed conclusion. Analysis imports this additional information as answers to tacit questions presumed to be involved in the inquiry. The model requires the analyst to enrich the sketch in this way for three reasons:
   a. The effort to enrich the sketch may help one discover hidden strengths or weaknesses in the argument that may be relevant to evaluation and/ or construction of related inquiries.
   b. The model is exploiting the insight that the most interesting and creative work undertaken in a typical everyday inquiry involves information-seeking by questioning rather than logical inference. The effort of making all the inference steps valid deductive inferences through interrogative importation of sufficiently strong intermediate premises both

eliminates pedestrian errors in deduction and focuses the analyst's attention on the interrogative process. The analyst must imagine the kinds of questions that need answering in order for the inferences to go through to the ultimate conclusion.

c. Weaknesses, implausibilities, uncertainties, and errors in the original sketch come to be analyzed as problems with the seeking and gathering of information through questions. The model shows the art of everyday reasoning to be in large measure the art of imagining, posing, and successfully obtaining answers to salient questions.

Definitory Rules and Strategies

The interrogative model of reasoning highlights a distinction between *definitory rules for correctness* and *strategies for effectiveness*. The former define the steps admissible in correct reasoning, while the latter suggest ways to make creative use of the steps allowed by the definitory rules. The model draws an analogy between rules and strategies in games and rules and strategies in reasoning. For example, the game of chess has rules that define how to play (the bishop moves diagonally) and then strategies for more effective play (trading your bishop for the opponent's queen will usually strengthen your position). Similarly, reasoning has definitory rules that define how rational inquiry proceeds (*affirming the consequent* is an incorrect inference move) as well as strategic principles for more effective pursuit of rational inquiry (in a truth-seeking inquiry try to use independent sources of information that can be checked against each other).

In the model *logical inference steps* are governed by the usual definitory rules that characterize valid deductive inference. Logical inference steps also can be guided by strategic considerations, such as, for example, rules of thumb concerning which formulas to instantiate and when to instantiate them in a complex line of reasoning. Typically, however, everyday reasoning employs inferences in relatively simple ways so that knowledge of sophisticated deductive strategies is not required. Undergraduate introductions to rational inquiry rightly devote much attention to enabling students to observe and follow the definitory rules that govern elementary deductive inference. The interrogative model suggests, however, that attention should also be paid to strategic rules governing information seeking by questioning.

The interrogative model identifies a few definitory rules that govern the information-seeking *interrogative steps*. These include rules that require the presupposition of a question to be established in order for a question to be asked. People do not, however, usually break definitory rules in their search for information. Progress in the art of interrogation mostly depends upon paying careful attention to strategic principles governing effective questioning rather than upon mastery of definitory rules.

Thus, the interrogative model suggests that excellence in everyday reasoning will require faithful observance of definitory rules for deductive inference combined with an appreciation of strategic principles for posing questions and examining answers. The "science" in everyday reasoning lies mostly in deduction; skill in deductive inference is a necessary but not sufficient condition for success in reasoning. The art and excellence in reasoning lies in interrogation. The interrogative model of reasoning focuses attention not simply on valid inference but also especially on excellence in the art of questioning.

Classification of Fallacies

The interrogative model of reasoning diagnoses errors in reasoning according to whether they involve *definitory* or *strategic* errors in *logical inference steps* or in *interrogative steps*.

Errors in Logical Inference Steps

The model identifies most of the so-called formal fallacies as violations of the *definitory* rules for logical (deductive) inference. *Denying the antecedent*, for example, is a violation of the definitory rules of logical inference. Interrogative analysis of an argument sketch usually eliminates definitory errors in the logical inference steps, because the model requires inference steps to be transformed into valid deductive inferences. If, however, an oral or written sketch of an inquiry is riddled with fatal and irreparable definitory errors in inference that resist elimination, the analyst may simply *evaluate* the sketch to be hopelessly flawed.

Strategic errors in elementary logical inference are less often seen. One simple example of a strategic error in inference would be to take a permitted step of conjunctive simplification or of disjunctive syllogism that is irrelevant to establishing the ultimate conclusion of the argument. Taking an unnecessary or irrelevant inference step involves no definitory error, but the unnecessary step would be perhaps confusing or misleading and might prevent the reasoner from completing the line of reasoning. Even if the irrelevant step does not prove fatal to the argument, such a move would be inefficient and in that sense make the reasoning less effective. Interrogative analysis of an argument sketch usually cleans up strategic errors in inference, but if these errors have prevented the argument from reaching its ultimate conclusion, they may lead to a negative evaluation or to an attempt to sketch a new and improved line of inquiry.

Errors in Interrogative Steps

Definitory rules for interrogative steps are few and simple, and definitory interrogative errors are not often found. The traditional fallacy of *many questions* indicates one way in which *definitory* errors may arise in an interrogative step. The definitory rules for interrogative steps require that the presupposition of a question be established before a question may be asked. Questions often have such obvious and unproblematic presuppositions that they need no explicit statement in an argument sketch. But a question like "Have you stopped cheating on your homework?" has a presupposition that may not have been established, namely, that the person has at some time cheated. To ask a question whose presupposition is not established is to violate a definitory rule of the game of questioning. Occasionally a missing presupposition is seen to be so preposterous as to lead to a negative evaluation of the argument.

The interrogative model diagnoses many of the errors that are typically treated under the heading of "informal fallacy" as involving *strategic* considerations in interrogative steps. Discussion of the *appeal to authority* provides an opportunity to consider strategic principles for interrogative steps in reasoning.

The Appeal to Authority and Strategies for Interrogative Steps

The interrogative model treats the issues involved in the *appeal to authority* as concerned with strategies for effective questioning. People do not typically appeal to authorities either to validate steps of logical inference or to vindicate a proposed strategy for disentangling a difficult deductive demarche. (I leave aside the problem by what authority Descartes managed to regain confidence in mathematical deductive reasoning after Meditation One.)

Authorities are typically invoked to serve as sources of information. The appeal to authority thus usually concerns interrogative steps in reasoning. No definitory rule for interrogative steps forbids an inquirer from invoking an authority. Errors in the appeal to an authority must therefore involve strategic considerations in the art of asking and answering questions.

According to the interrogative model of reasoning, worries about the appeal to authority are reminders that many of our inquiries and arguments employ oracles whose answers to our questions are not infallible. If we are to be successful in reasoning, we need strategies for evaluating the reliability of the answers we receive to our questions and for determining whether and how to admit those answers into our arguments. Errors involving the appeal to authority will thus be strategic errors concerning failure to employ strategies of answer and oracle evaluation that would have made our reasoning more effective.

Evaluating Answers and Oracles

The interrogative model makes evaluation of answers and oracles a central task for evaluating inquiries and for guiding revision and improvement of a line of reasoning. Interrogative analysis of an oral or written sketch of an inquiry puts the inquiry into a form that facilitates isolating and evaluating interrogative steps that may be problematic. Thorough analysis of a sketch shows how information comes into the inquiry through answers to questions, what the oracles are that are being addressed, and what role the information gained plays in the deductive inferences that lead to the ultimate conclusion of the inquiry.

A critic can always ask, Why did you accept that information from that source? The interrogative model advises inquirers to fasten on the interrogative steps that are most vulnerable to such a question to consider whether strategies available for strengthening a vulnerable step have been adequately exploited. A search for a strategy to strengthen a vulnerable interrogative step can often be thought of as a search for a subordinate line of inquiry that would strengthen confidence in the step.

A Textbook Analysis in Light of the Interrogative Model

The interrogative model predicts that any useful discussion of the appeal to authority will formulate strategies for evaluating problematic oracles and answers. Consider Govier's approach in the second edition of A *Practical Study of Argument*.[2]

Govier discusses appeal to authority under the heading "Proper Authority."[3] She advises that "when people are experts or authorities in some area of knowledge . . . it may be reasonable for us to accept what they say simply because they have said it."[4] This advice is clearly not a definitory rule for reasoning. As the interrogative model suggests, principles for interrogative moves usually involve strategic considerations.

Govier proceeds to offer further advice concerning when the strategy of accepting information from "proper" authorities might be ill-advised. If one suspects "dishonesty, vested interest, . . . joking, and so on," then the original strategy may be "undermined." She sums up her advice in a series of conditions that should be met for accepting a premise P from an authority:

1. P falls within K, where K is a recognized body of knowledge.
2. The person whose authority is cited is an expert on K.
3. The experts on K agree about P.
4. The person whose authority is cited does not have a vested interest in P's being true, nor has he been dishonest about matters related to P in the past.[5]

The interrogative model suggests that strategies for checking authorities often involve constructing subordinate lines of inquiry that would strengthen confidence in an oracle's answer. Govier says that in checking the various conditions, "we have, in effect, constructed our own subargument on behalf of a premise."

Govier's account of the issues that require attention in the use of authorities is competent and helpful. The account can be located in a larger theoretical framework by reference to insights from the interrogative model. According to the model, in any discussion of the appeal to authority we are examining strategic considerations concerning evaluation of answers and oracles in inquiry.

2. Trudy Govier, A *Practical Study of Argument*, 2d ed. (Belmont, Calif.: Wadsworth, 1988).
3. Ibid., 82–84.
4. Ibid., 82.
5. Ibid., 83.

Illegitimate Authorities

Textbook examples of errors involving the appeal to authority typically use oracles that are human beings whose credibility as an oracle for the inquiry in question is easily challenged. The examples are structured so that no effective strategy can avail against the critic's question: Why did you accept that answer from that source?

> "What car should I buy? Michael Jordan says, 'a Chevy Blazer.' "

Why would you accept advice on automobiles from that man? A subordinate inquiry reveals that he is perhaps the greatest basketball player ever, but connecting that information with the desired conclusion that he be an expert on automobiles proves impossible.

No one doubts that an error in reasoning occurs in these cases. But the interrogative model of reasoning argues that, even in the most obvious examples, the error should be seen to be the failure to employ strategies that would strengthen the line of inquiry. Students are not helped if they are given the impression that some fixed, definitory rule of reasoning forbids seeking information from celebrities and the other characters who populate textbook examples. They should be disabused of the analogy to definitory rules that so often infects instruction in the informal fallacies. Instead they should be pointed to and exercised in strategies for evaluating answers and oracles in use in an inquiry.

Strategies for Testing Legitimate Authorities

More interesting and instructive examples involve oracles that are *prima facie* legitimate. If I am inquiring about a health problem, why not consult a physician? Indeed, consult a physician, but the inquiry may be more successful if I deploy strategies that double-check the credibility of the oracle. What experience have I or others had in the past with this physician? Should I seek a second opinion and examine how the first physician's answers to my questions compare with the second's?

Perhaps an attorney is helping me with a complex legal problem. No other counsel is available to me, and I lack independent knowledge by which I might check the attorney's competence on the problem at hand. I commit no crime against the definitory rules of reason by relying on this oracle, but I may employ more or less effective strategies for assessing my oracle's competence. I can perhaps probe this oracle by coming at the problem from a variety of angles and examining whether the attorney's answers hang together with a consistency that suggests that they arise from a sure-handed grasp of the issues. Or, I may have reliable knowledge about other legal matters in which I have been involved and can test the attorney's competence on those matters. An estimate of the attorney's competence in other legal matters may provide an oblique measure of how much I should trust him or her in this case.

Authorities Stipulated to Be Infallible

Questions about the reliability of sources play different roles in different kinds of inquiry. For example, the purpose of a legal argument might be simply to show what follows from statutes and precedents. In such an inquiry the statutes and precedents function as unimpeachable oracles, and the answers obtained from them will not be called into question. No strategy for assessing these oracles will be needed.

Similarly, in certain types of moral inquiry, the goal might be to determine what conclusion follows from a theory upon which the inquirers are agreed. In such a case, the inquirers will not likely employ strategies designed to test the adequacy of interrogative steps for which the theory serves as the oracle.

An inquirer seeking to refute an opponent may also be willing to stipulate the opponent's answers to questions. The strategy for refutation may be to entangle the opponent in the "Consequences drawn from his own Principles, or Concessions." This strategy seems to be part of what John Locke had in mind when he briefly introduced and characterized what he called the *Argumentum ad Hominem*.[6]

What Was Locke Troubled About?

John Locke seems to have been the first to discuss problems with appeals to authority under the heading of *Argumentum ad Verecundiam* (IV.17.19).[7] Hamblin (1970, 41) notes that Locke "does not clearly say" that he considers the *argumentum ad verecundiam* to be a fallacy. In his nineteenth-century edition of Locke's *Essay*, Alexander Fraser appends an instructive footnote to

6. John Locke, *An Essay Concerning Human Understanding* [1690], edited by A. C. Fraser (New York: Dover, 1959), IV.17.21. (See this volume, 56.)
7. Ibid., IV.17.19. (See this volume, 55.)

Locke's discussion: "Locke is always chary of appeals to human authority, which in medieval reasonings had so much taken the place of a purely intellectual appeal. Yet, in many cases, one's judgment of the trustworthiness of the judgment of another person is the only available foundation in reason for an opinion of one's own."[8]

Locke recommends a strategy of avoiding as much as possible reliance upon human authority. His strategy would have seemed especially attractive in an age when exaggerated confidence in the powers of the individual rational inquirer was becoming the rule. If the individual inquirer is believed to be more likely to seek and gather valuable information in independence from community or tradition, then the appeal to traditional and communal authorities will not appear to be an effective strategy for inquiry.

Locke's strategy of avoiding reliance upon human authority does not recommend itself so strongly in a time when inquirers are more alert to how tradition and community inevitably contribute to the ways in which we formulate questions and discover answers. Fraser is right that we must often incorporate the judgments of others into our own reasoning.

When this is recognized, the strategy will be not to eschew all appeals to authority but to seek ways of testing the authorities upon which we must inevitably rely. Aristotle's use of "endoxa" may not have involved such a bad strategy after all (Hintikka, 1987, 232–34). The interrogative model advises not that we should eschew all human authority, but that we deploy strategies of oracle and answer evaluation that strengthen the elements of criticism and self-correction in the taking of interrogative steps.

Other Factors Governing Choices of Strategy

Definitory rules for reasoning are simply to be obeyed, but the interrogative model shows that strategies for sharpening our reasoning are chosen in the light of purposes, goals, and available resources. For example, a scientist might wish that an important result upon which he or she must rely could be more thoroughly tested in his or her own laboratory. But limitations of time and other resources may dictate that the result be admitted into the current inquiry without further investigation.

The appeal to authority resists categorization as a simple crime against reason, because the mistakes have more to do with poor choices of strategy than with the breaking of a definitory rule. The interrogative model shows

8. Ibid., 410 n.2. (See this volume, 55.)

that the problems in appeals to authority are not usually susceptible to solution by prescribing a "law of reason."

The Appeal to Authority in Relation to Other Fallacies

The interrogative model sheds light on why categorizing and analyzing the traditional fallacies has been so difficult. Many traditional fallacies do not so much indicate crimes against the definitory rules of reasoning as problems that arise in choosing and deploying strategies for successfully seeking and gathering information through questioning. Because many of the root problems involving strategies for interrogative steps are closely related, difficulties arise in making strict distinctions among the fallacies that concern strategies for questioning.

Abusive Ad Hominem

Locke's original characterization of the *argumentum ad hominem* was briefly mentioned above in connection with issues involving the appeal to authority. Modern characterizations of *abusive ad hominem* also concern themselves with strategies for assessing sources of information, and these concerns once again overlap those raised in the discussion of the appeal to authority.

Traditional worries about the appeal to authority remind inquirers that in many circumstances effective inquiry requires strategies for testing the reliability of an oracle. Traditional worries about abusive *ad hominem* remind inquirers that some misguided strategies for testing an oracle yield little insight into the oracle's reliability. An oracle may, for example, have unusual and offending political or religious views, but that fact may have little to do with the reliability of his or her answers to questions pertinent to the current inquiry.

Sometimes traditional worries about the appeal to authority and about abusive *ad hominem* are also used to remind inquirers that evaluation of *logical inference steps* in an argument does not require strategies that focus on the character or motives of the individual who proposed the inferences. Logical inference steps can be assessed by reference to the definitory rules of deductive inference, and little attention need be paid to the character or motives of the original source of the inferences. Misguided attempts either to certify or to defeat deductive inferences by lauding or impugning the character of the reasoner derive their deceptive strength from the fact that a reasoner who proposes a line of inferences is often also a source of the information upon which the inferences are operating. Examination of the reasoner's character or motives *is* often relevant to assessing the reasoner's reliability as an oracle.

Begging the Question

The interrogative model locates traditional concerns about *ad verecundiam* and *ad hominem* primarily in the discussion of strategies for interrogative steps rather than in examination of definitory or strategic rules for logical inference. The model also locates the problems concerned with the traditional fallacy of *begging the question* in this same neighborhood. Confusions about the precise problem in question begging repeatedly arise from the mistaken attempt to treat question begging as an error in logical inference.

According to the interrogative model, significant inquiry usually involves a series of interrogative steps interspersed with logical inference steps. Important and complex problems are rarely solved in one or two big reasoning steps. But human inquirers like to take short cuts whenever possible, and sometimes a short cut on the way to a proposed conclusion is justified. For example, if I am curious about when the phrase *ad verecundiam* first appeared in the literature on fallacies, recourse to Hamblin (1970) may conclude my inquiry rapidly and satisfactorily for my purposes; on page 41 he points to Locke.

If, however, a colleague familiar with medieval literature thinks he or she recalls some evidence that Hamblin may have overlooked, I am challenged no longer to rely on Hamblin's authority but to incorporate more interrogative research steps into my inquiry. The point is that I can approach the main question about which I am inquiring through a more or less complicated series of interrogative and logical inference steps. If an oracle like Hamblin will directly answer my principal question, no other steps may be needed. In accepting Hamblin as an authority I break no definitory rule of inference or interrogation, but my strategy of relying on his work may be open to criticism.

Traditional worries about begging the question serve to remind us that a particular inquiry rests upon an indefinitely complex set of interrogative possibilities. The decision to lengthen or shorten the path of inquiry by accepting or testing or rejecting particular sources of information is a strategic decision that is affected by available time and resources and by the inquirer's or the critic's motives and interests. Discussion of begging the question turns out to be another way of highlighting issues concerning strategies for assessing when an inquirer should rest content with the answers and oracles currently in play in the inquiry.

Conclusion

The interrogative model is a comprehensive theory of reasoning that enables us to probe beneath the specific warnings formulated in the traditional fallacies. The model suggests that many of the traditional fallacies do not entangle us in crimes against the definitory rules of reason but in complex considerations concerning strategies for improving lines of inquiry.

The appeal to authority, as we have seen, resists categorization as a simple crime against the laws of reason. The formulation of fixed rules concerning when the appeal to an authority is legitimate or fallacious is misleading, because strategies for assessing answers and oracles are dependent in part upon the inquirer's specific situation and purposes. Discussions of the appeal to authority and of most of the other "informal fallacies" should concentrate not on stigmatizing fixed errors but on enabling reasoners to see the strategic problems they face as they pursue excellence in rational inquiry.

21

Equivocation
Lawrence H. Powers

The One Fallacy Theory

The fallacy of equivocation in the broadest sense is the fallacy of trading on an ambiguity.

I hold a controversial theory I call the One Fallacy Theory. According to this theory, there is only one fallacy, the fallacy of trading on an ambiguity. So equivocation is not only an important fallacy; it is the only fallacy.

My expounding my theory here will serve to focus the reader's attention on the fallacy of equivocation. The reader should, however, keep in mind that my theory is not a widely accepted and well-established viewpoint, but a highly controversial one. The reader should therefore regard it as a hypothesis.

A *fallacy* is committed when an argument that is not good nonetheless *appears* to be good. The "goodness" in question may vary from case to case. A deductively invalid argument may appear deductively valid. An inductively weak argument may appear inductively strong. A dialectically inappropriate argument may appear dialectically appropriate. But the One Fallacy Theory insists that there is no fallacy if there is no clearly specifiable *appearance* of goodness. An invalid argument should not be called a fallacy unless it clearly *appears* to be valid.

Consider the so-called Fallacy of Affirming the Consequent. Suppose Dobbin is a horse. We argue

If Dobbin is a man, Dobbin is an animal.
Dobbin is an animal.

Therefore Dobbin is a man.

The argument is invalid. It has the invalid form

$$p \supset q$$
$$q$$
$$p.$$

The argument does not as stated appear to have any form except this invalid one. It does not appear to be any more valid than it is. My theory concludes that it is *not* a fallacy, but just an invalid argument. More generally, since there are no ambiguities in formal languages, there are no fallacies committed in such languages.

On the other hand, Aristotle suggests the following argument:[1]

Man is animal.
Dobbin is animal.
Therefore Dobbin is man.

Here the first premise is "man is animal." In English this would be stated "A man is an animal," but in Greek there were no indefinite articles. But "man is animal" *looks* like "Cicero is Tully." So our argument looks like the *valid* argument:

Cicero is Tully.
This is Tully.
Therefore this is Cicero.

So our argument *is* a fallacy. It equivocally reads "man is animal" as "man is one and the same thing as animal."

Consider the so-called Fallacy of *Ad Baculum*, or Appeal to Force. We argue:

If you don't agree that Nixon was a great president,
I will beat your head with an ax-handle and twist off all your fingers!
Therefore Nixon was a great president! Right!?

---

1. See Hamblin's analysis (1970, 85–86).

Now this argument is not only deductively invalid; it also gives no evidence at all for the truth of its conclusion. But does it *appear* to give any such evidence? No. It is bad and nakedly bad. It is therefore no fallacy.

But call the above argument A. Here is another argument, *B*, which is a meta-argument about A.

> *B*. If the premise of A is true, then, since you don't want your head beat and your fingers twisted off, you have a strong motive for believing A's conclusion. Therefore A gives you a strong reason for believing its conclusion. Therefore A is a good argument.

Argument B equivocates on the term "reason." A *reason* for believing a conclusion may be a *motive* for the *act* of believing that conclusion; or it may be *evidence* for the *truth* of that conclusion. A gives the former rather than the latter, and is therefore a bad argument. But B equivocally argues that A is good. The real fallacy is in B rather than A.

Consider the Fallacy of the Loaded Question. I ask you:

> Is your insanity curable?

I thereby appear to have convicted you of being insane. Is there a real fallacy here?

I believe there is a real fallacy here, but that people often wrongly explain what the fallacy is.

It is often said that the above question presupposes that you are insane. Since no argument has been given for this false assumption, we have an example of the fallacy of begging the question, or making unwarranted and arbitrary assumptions.

The One Fallacy Theory holds that there is no such fallacy as begging the question. Making an unwarranted assumption does not deserve to be called a fallacy, since such an assumption is neither argued for nor even apparently argued for.

Yet in our loaded question, there really is a fallacy. A question presupposes the disjunction of its possible answers. This disjunction is not "you are insane" but rather "either your insanity is curable or your insanity is not curable." And, as Bertrand Russell has pointed out in his theory of definite descriptions,[2] this disjunction is grammatically ambiguous.

2. Bertrand Russell, "On Denoting," *Mind* 14 (1905): 479–93.

"Your insanity is not curable" could be the negation of the first disjunct and say "There is *not* an insanity both possessed by you and also curable." Or it might negate only the curability part: "There is an insanity which you possess but it is *not* curable."

On one reading, the whole disjunction is an unchallengeable instance of the logical law of excluded middle. On the *other* reading, both disjuncts say you are insane. Thus your insanity is derived by a fallacy of grammatical equivocation from a law of logic. Your insanity is *not* unwarrantedly *assumed*, but rather fallaciously *derived*.

The fallacy mediates this derivation:

Either it is true you have a curable insanity or it is not true.

Therefore either you have a curable insanity or you have an incurable insanity.

These examples illustrate how the One Fallacy Theory works. It insists that there is no fallacy unless there is a clearly specifiable *appearance* of validity (or goodness of whatever kind). Since I believe there is no clear way to make an argument *appear* to have a goodness it really lacks except by playing with ambiguities, every real fallacy will turn out to be a fallacy of equivocation.

Types of Equivocation

The One Fallacy Theory allows that the one fallacy can be usefully divided into many. We can separate out different kinds of ambiguity. Indeed Aristotle already did this in a useful way in his *On Sophistical Refutations* in the first part of his list of "sophisms" or fallacies.

The history of fallacy theory is one of going the wrong way.[3] Aristotle started out in *On Sophistical Refutations* quite close to my One Fallacy Theory. The first half of his list is just what my theory approves of: different kinds of ambiguity. The second half turns out to be mostly agreeable also in the sense that, for instance, his way of affirming the consequent turns out to be a real fallacy. My only major disagreement is about begging the question and a variant of it. Further, Aristotle practically asserts the One Fallacy Theory himself at one point in his discussion.[4]

3. For history, see Hamblin's excellent book (1970, chaps. 2–4).
4. See Hamblin (1970, 80), conjoining *Soph. Ref.* 167a85 and 168a19.

But then Aristotle explains his list wrongly in another work (the *Rhetoric*) and departs from One Fallacy orthodoxy. Then in the seventeenth century, a whole bunch of new "fallacies" are recognized, distorting the concept of "fallacy" practically beyond recognition. The One Fallacy Theory takes us back to Aristotle's original conception,[5] and my own list of types of fallacy will roughly follow Aristotle's.

All the fallacies involve playing with ambiguities. So we divide the different types of ambiguity. A sentence is built out of words or word-parts or phrases to which meanings are conventionally assigned. The meanings of the ultimate meaningful parts are said to be *lexically* assigned. Thus in "rented" a meaning is assigned to "rent" and one to the part "ed." The phrase "fell off the wagon" may be understood literally in terms of its parts "fell," "off," "the," and "wagon," or lexically as a whole receive the meaning "went back to drinking." The lexically meaningful parts are then put together grammatically to make up the sentence.

If a lexical part has more than one meaning, we have a *lexical* ambiguity. (Sometimes "equivocation" is used in a narrower sense than mine to cover only lexical equivocations.) If the lexical parts are unambiguous, but it is ambiguous how the parts are grammatically put together, we have a grammatical ambiguity, also called an *amphiboly*.

Accidental Lexical Ambiguity

Often, a lexical ambiguity is an accidental feature of a particular language. It just happens that "bank" refers to a slope ("the bank of the river") and also to a money depository ("First National Bank").

> Rivers don't have any money, so it is silly for them to have banks!

Or the word "runs" refers to continuing along ("the river runs through the valley," "the hallway runs to the back of the house") or to moving oneself by means of one's feet ("the man runs," "the horses run").

> The river runs; whatever runs has feet. Therefore the river has feet.[6]

Or the phrase "turns into" may signify altering direction into something ("the car turns into the street," "the train turns into the station") or it may signify

5. Hamblin's (1970) critique of the history ought to lead *him* to a One Fallacy Theory, but ironically his positive theories wander away into the usual (in my view) unprofitable directions.

6. S. M. Engel (1980), 14.

being transformed into something ("at the princess's kiss, the ugly frog turned into a handsome prince").

> The great magician drove along the street and then turned his car into a garage. Wow! What a great trick! He *turned his car into a garage!*

Fallacy of Mispronunciation

Aristotle notes that sometimes a written word has two different pronunciations and two different meanings. He calls this a fallacy of accent, but "fallacy of accent" has come to have a different meaning. Fallacies of mispronunciation were much more common in ancient Greek than they are in English, but here is an example:

> The workers were unionized, and therefore possessed no extra electrons!

The fallacy depends on the fact that the written word "unionized" can be pronounced so as to be the negation of "ionized." An atom is ionized if it has more or fewer electrons than usual.

Fallacy of Misspelling

Conversely, a spoken word might be ambiguous, though different spellings clear up the ambiguity when it is written down.

> Fluffy is a bear cub. Therefore he has no fur.

Here the fallacy does not really work when written down, but, when spoken, "bear" can be confused with "bare."

Modern fallacy of accent

Misspelling and mispronunciation are subtypes of lexical ambiguity. What is nowadays called a "fallacy of accent" is a much more complicated phenomenon. I say, looking grimly at the other students, "Well, *John* is good at philosophy." I thereby imply, without actually saying so, that the other students are terrible at philosophy. This is not yet a fallacy, but an illustration of how emphasizing a word W can imply that what is being said of W is true of W and only W.[7]

One of the other students now jealously reports the conversation to his friends: "The professor admitted that John is good at *philosophy*. So surely we may conclude that John is lousy at history, math, English, . . ." This is the fallacy of accent. The student correctly reports the literal meaning of what was said (John is good at philosophy), but incorrectly suggests an extra implied meaning (John is good only at philosophy) that was not originally intended.

In the modern fallacy of accent, something is said that is correct as far as its literal meaning is concerned, but the statement is italicized so as to generate an implied meaning that is unwarranted. Unlike most other types of equivocation I discuss here, this fallacy does not involve any ambiguity in the *literal* meaning of a statement, but instead misconstrues an extra implied meaning (Grice's conversational implicature).

Earlier I said that affirming the consequent is an invalid argument rather than a fallacy, but I admitted that it could be a symptom of a fallacy. One could, following Aristotle's idea, translate "Every man is an animal" into "To be a man is to be an animal" and then misread this as saying "Being a man and being an animal are the same thing." However, the fallacy of accent suggests a *different* fallacious way of affirming the consequent. Everyone knows that Dobbin is an animal *if* he is a man. So, by accent, Dobbin is an animal if *and only if* Dobbin is a man.

Grammatical Ambiguity, also Called Amphiboly

In cases of pure amphiboly, the lexical parts are all unambiguous, but it is ambiguous how they are grammatically put together.

> I saw the thief with my binoculars. So he must have stolen my binoculars!

Here it is unclear whether "with my binoculars" modifies "thief" or "saw." My favorite example of amphiboly is the following very complicated one:

---

7. For theoretical insights relevant to this fallacy, see H. P. Grice, "The Causal Theory of Perception," in *Perceiving, Sensing and Knowing*, edited by R. J. Swartz (Garden City, N.Y.: Anchor Books, 1965), 438ff.; and R. Chisholm, "J. L. Austin's Philosophical Papers," *Mind* 73 (1964): 2.

> John saw a picture of the prettiest girl he had ever seen hanging on a
> locker door.[8]

Here it is unclear who or what is hanging on the locker door. The picture?
John? The girl? Students in one of my classes pointed out a further ambiguity.
How pretty is the girl? The prettiest John has ever seen? The prettiest of those
he has seen while he was hanging on a locker door? The prettiest he has seen
who were hanging on locker doors?

Another example comes from Quine.[9]

> This girl's school is little.
> Therefore it's a little girl's school.
> Therefore it's a school for little girls.

Here the essential move is from "little (girl's school)" to "(little girl's) school."

Some examples of the supposed fallacy of composition or division are
amphibolies, depending on unclarity about whether the predicate applies to
each subject or only to all taken together.

> Why do black sheep eat less than white ones? Because there are fewer
> of them![10]

Does *each* black sheep eat less or only the group of all black sheep taken
together?

> The jury are divided.
> John and Joe and Mary are the jury.
> Therefore John is divided.

It is unclear whether the group as such is divided or each member is divided.

I said earlier that no fallacy can be committed in a properly constructed
formal language. Thus the invalid argument

$$\frac{\sim (p\ \&\ q)}{\sim p\ \&\ \sim q}$$

8. Engel (1980), 2.
9. W. V. O. Quine, *Word and Object* (Cambridge: MIT Press, 1960), 137.
10. Engel (1980), 21.

is nakedly invalid and is no fallacy. But such "formal fallacies" are often formal symptoms of real fallacies committed in ordinary language. Thus I look at the premise "$\sim (p \ \& \ q)$" and I say "This premise asserts the falsity of P and Q." My English phraseology is grammatically ambiguous. Am I speaking of the falsity of the conjunction "P and Q" or of the falsity of the conjunct P and of the conjunct Q? Thus equivocating in English, I arrive at the conclusion "$\sim p \ \& \ \sim q$."

Mixed Fallacy

Sometimes lexical and grammatical ambiguity are simultaneous.

> The tree waves its branches and leaves. So the tree must be going away.

Here "leaves" is lexically ambiguous. Is it the present tense of "leaving" or the plural of "leaf"? But in switching the lexical meaning, we also rearrange the grammar. Is "leaves" conjoined with "branches" or with "waves"?

> Good steaks are rare these days. So don't order your steak well done.[11]

Here there is a mixed fallacy. In the premise "rare" may be applied to good steaks as a class (they are rarely found) or to each good steak (it is lightly cooked). As the grammar shifts, so does the lexical meaning of "rare."

Grammatical Misconstruction

This differs from amphiboly proper in that one reading of a sentence is a *misreading* and is not really in accord with correct understanding of English. Aristotle notes[12] that in an example like

Q.   What does John *do* in Denver?
A.   He lives there.

the word "lives," though a verb, does not represent an activity, and so A does not answer Q. Similarly Kant said that "exists," though a verb, does not express a predicate.

11. Ibid., 16.
12. Aristotle, *Soph. Ref.* 166b17.

It has been said[13] that all bad metaphysics rests on grammatical miscon-struction. Thus philosophers[14] have claimed the argument

There is a possibility that John will come.
Therefore there are such things as possibilities.

misunderstands the grammar of the use of "possibility."
These cases are disputable. Clearer cases are:

The average family in Tulsa has 1½ children.
Therefore there is a family in Tulsa with 1½ children.

and, from Lewis Carroll,[15]

I passed nobody on the road (the road was empty).
Therefore nobody is slower than I am.

Some of these examples involve misunderstanding of the grammatical role of a single word: "lives," "exists," "nobody." They are, however, *not* lexical ambiguities; the word is not given some other meaning than usual; rather its role in the sentence is misunderstood.
From my dissertation,[16]

I threw a baseball quickly.
Therefore there was a baseball quickly and I threw it.

Here I treat "quickly" as an adjective rather than an adverb.
Finally,

13. G. Ryle, "Systematically Misleading Expressions," *Proceedings of the Aristotelian Society* 32 (1931–32); reprinted in *The Linguistic Turn*, edited and with an introduction by Richard Rorty, 85ff. (Chicago: University of Chicago Press, 1967).
14. W. Alston, "Ontological Commitments," in *Philosophy of Mathematics*, edited by P. Benacerraf and H. Putnam (Englewood Cliffs, N.J.: Prentice-Hall, 1964), 250.
15. Lewis Carroll, *Through the Looking Glass and What Alice Found There* (London: Mac-millan, 1872), 143–44.
16. "Knowledge and Meaning in Philosophy" (Cornell University, 1977). I first developed the One Fallacy Theory in this dissertation, which presents a theory of philosophical (dialectical) method; afterward I read Hamblin's (1970) account of the history.

John is an alleged murderer.

Therefore John is a murderer.

If someone is a tall murderer, he is a murderer who is tall. But that John is an alleged murderer means it is *alleged that* he is a murderer.

Nonaccidental Lexical Ambiguity

Here the different meanings of a word are logically related to each other. This kind of lexical ambiguity, unlike the accidental kind, tends to be translatable from one language to another.

From Aristotle:[17]

The roasted pig on my plate is very full of vitamins and very healthy.

Therefore the pig is likely to jump up and run around the dining room.

Here, I am "healthy" when I possess health, but my food is "healthy" when it *causes* health in me. The pig is not healthy in the first sense; it is dead. Type-token ambiguities fall into this category.

There are five words in "The cat ate the mouse."

There are four words: "cat," "ate," "mouse," and "the."

Therefore 5 = 4.

The first premise counts word tokens (occurrences); the second, word types.

The two women came to the party in the same dress. (type)

Therefore they must have really squeezed to get into only one dress! (token)

Product-process ambiguities are also of this category. The workers are *building* a *building*. Their efficient *construction* of the complex *construction* is impressive. In halting *speech*, the speaker delivered his *speech*. Pierre's fast *painting* of the large *painting* was amazing.

Fallacies involving vagueness are often called "sorites" or "slippery slope

17. Aristotle, *Metaphysics* 1003a35.

arguments." You can't save someone from baldness by adding a single hair. So, it is argued, you can't save him by adding a single hair a million times, or, in other words, adding a million hairs. Vagueness is best analyzed as a kind of nonaccidental ambiguity in which the various meanings agree in applying to certain "clear cases" and in excluding "clear non-cases" but disagree about "borderline cases."

If there were exactly two senses of "bald" and, in one sense, a bald man had less than 300 hairs and, in the other sense, he had no more than 400, you could not turn a clearly bald man (299 hairs) into a clearly nonbald man (401 hairs) by adding one hair.

Relative Terms

Suppose Mary is five feet tall, John is six feet tall, and Abe is seven feet tall.

Mary is five feet tall.
John is taller.
Abe is seven feet tall.
_____

Therefore, since we said John is taller, he must be almost eight feet tall!

From Plato,[18]

This dog is a father and this dog is mine.
_____

Therefore this dog is my father.

Suggested by Aristotle,[19]

Dumbo is a *small* elephant.
Tutu is a *large* French Poodle.
Therefore Tutu is larger than Dumbo.

In these cases the key words ("taller," "mine," "small," or "large") are not lexically ambiguous, but are understood to apply relative to some further reference (taller than whom? small as a what? my what?)

18. Plato, *Euthydemus* 298ff.
19. *Categories* 6b9.

The following fallacious argument from authority involves a relative term:

Einstein says this ice cream is nutritious.
Einstein is an authority [but about what?].
So this ice cream must be nutritious.

The important Fallacy of Incomplete Evidence may be analyzable as a fallacy of the relative term "probable." A conclusion may be probable on some of our evidence but not probable on all of it. Thus,

Most physicists are men.
Professor Judy Smith is a physicist.
So, probably, Professor Judy is a man.[20]

John examined a million crows and all of them were black.
So, probably, all crows are black.
Look! This crow here is white!
So, probably, this crow here is both black and white.

The fallacy of incomplete evidence provides yet a *third* way—perhaps nowadays the most popular way—of explaining affirming the consequent. Let X be an instance of affirming the consequent

1. X has (a) an if-then premise
        (b) a second premise which is one of the first premise's
              components
        (c) a conclusion which is the other.
2. Usually, when one sees an argument with (a), (b), and (c), it
    is a valid argument [because it is *modus ponens*].
3. Therefore [probably] X is valid.

This argument overlooks invalidating features of X. As an *inductive* fallacy, this argument pretends to show only the *probable* validity of X.

20. Merrilee Salmon, *Introduction to Logic and Critical Thinking* (San Diego, Calif.: Harcourt Brace Jovanovich, 1984), 76.

Other Types of Ambiguity

My list of types of ambiguity does not exhaust the possible types. Generally, different types of ambiguity reflect different ways that meanings attach to language. I have concentrated on types involving literal explicit meanings. But implicature departs from this emphasis and relative terms involve elliptical expressions to be filled out by the reader. Ambiguities can also be generated by figures of speech, such as metaphor, simile, or irony. Examples of the last two:

> It says here that Sir Girwin courageously strode into battle like a lion. So I conclude that he must have been long-overdue at his barber's!

> Fred says that Mrs. Alma's Pie is delicious—like castor oil mixed with sand. I think I'll get myself some of that pie and have it with castor-oil-and-sand sauce!

General Issues

The reader may protest against my examples of fallacies. "A fallacy should *appear* to be valid. These examples don't appear valid *to me!*" My One Fallacy Theory does not insist that fallacies appear valid *to* someone, only that they have an appearance, however quickly seen through, of being valid.

Obviously I would not try to illustrate the concept of *fallacy* by presenting examples that readers would actually take to be *valid arguments!* Readers might think that "fallacy" meant "valid argument"!

Often a fallacy is quickly seen through because the conclusion (rivers have feet, say) is so obviously false and the premise (rivers run) is so obviously true. The similar fallacy might *not* be seen through if committed about abstract and unfamiliar contents.

In philosophy, we spend half our time arguing that our opponent's arguments are fallacious. No philosophers admit to being equivocators, but all philosophers agree that the *other* philosophers are equivocating. Exactly where the equivocations are is part of what everybody argues about.

For instance, opponents of my One Fallacy Theory will say that I use "appearance" in an unusually narrow sense or that my (quite traditional) definition of "fallacy" does not reflect current usage.

Equivocations in philosophy are rarely of the accidental type. They usually involve amphibolies, misconstructions, relative terms, or nonaccidental lexical ambiguities.

Finally, a last word about the One Fallacy Theory. Don't accept that theory on my say-so, but *test* it against other essays in this book—as I shall be doing myself! Are the *examples* given there really fallacies? Are they counterexamples to my theory? Do the essays all use "fallacy" in the same sense? Consider essays earlier in this book. Is my theory relevant to the desiderata for a good theory of fallacy? Assessing my theory in this way, you will be reflecting on the role of equivocation in fallacy theory.

22

Post Hoc Ergo Propter Hoc

Robert C. Pinto

Since the publication of Hamblin's *Fallacies* in 1970, a serious literature on fallacies has begun to emerge outside the textbooks—a literature sampled in Parts II and III of this volume. It is in the context of these developments that I propose to look at what has and can be said about the fallacy known as *post hoc ergo propter hoc*.

My conclusion will, in one respect, be pessimistic, for I will argue that we do not now have, and are not likely to develop, any theory of fallacy or of causal reasoning that will clarify what is puzzling about *post hoc* fallacies. In another respect, my conclusion will be optimistic, for I will suggest that there does exist an entrenched critical practice that anchors our talk about the *post hoc* fallacy and renders it illuminating.

The concept of *post hoc* as a defective sort of reasoning or argument goes back to Aristotle. I quote in its entirety what he says about it in Book II, chapter 24 of the *Rhetoric*: "Another line [of argument that is a spurious enthymeme] consists in representing as causes things which are not causes, on the ground that they happened along with or before the event in question. They assume that, because B happens after A, it happens because of A. Politicians are especially fond of taking this line. Thus Demades said that the policy of Demosthenes was the cause of all the mischief, 'for after it the war occurred.' "[1]

Post hoc has remained in the textbook literature ever since, and modern

---

1. *Rhetoric* 1401b30–33. Hamblin points out that the *non causa pro causa* of this passage should not be confused with that of *Soph. Ref.* 167b21ff. (Hamblin 1970, 79–80).

textbooks typically do not say a great deal more about this fallacy than Aristotle did. In a 1977 article in *The Review of Metaphysics* Woods and Walton attempted a "theoretically unified approach to the *post hoc*" (1977e, 592). They wrote: "Our analysis here is not the final word on the *post hoc*; we hope rather that it provides a systematic groundwork for the further exploration of causal fallacies" (593). Further exploration does not seem to have occurred in the journals, however.

The theoretical account in the 1977 article centered on the claim that "any correct inductive argument from correlation to causation, requires five premise-types" (1977e, 580). Part III of the article presented a schema in which the first of five premise-types asserts the existence of a correlation, and the conclusion asserts the existence of a causal relation.[2] Part IV listed seven "sophisms" that had been distinguished in traditional treatments of informal fallacies, and Part V attempted to illuminate the sophisms by relating them to the schema and its premise types.

But five years later, in their textbook *Argument: The Logic of the Fallacies*, Woods and Walton wrote (1982a, 83): "It is not easy to offer an analysis of the fallacy of *post hoc*, because there is no widespread agreement on how to analyze the concept of causation. Consequently, no established theory of what, precisely, is wrong about *post hoc* reasoning can be offered at present." And though the "seven sophisms" remain in the later book, the requirement of five premise-types has disappeared, and with it the attempt to explicate the fallacies by reference to a theoretical model of good causal reasoning.

In Walton, the core of the seven sophisms remains under the rubric "Six Kinds of *Post Hoc* Errors" (1989a, 215). However, that material is incorporated, not into a theory of causal *fallacies*, but into a theory of critical questions to be raised in the course of inquiry or of critical discussion.[3]

---

2. The schema, presented in part III, is as follows:
(P1) There is a positive correlation between Θ and Φ
(P2) It is not the case that Φ causes Θ.
(P3) It is not the case that there is a third factor Ψ that causes both Θ and Φ where Θ does not cause Ψ.
(P4) There are no relevant instances of Θ-and-not-Φ.
(P5) Θ is pragmatically relevant.
Therefore, Θ causes Φ.

3. Walton deliberately eschews the word "fallacy." He writes (1989a, 225): "Instead of putting down an argument by condescendingly claiming that it commits a *post hoc* fallacy, it is more constructive to raise specific questions about the strength of the argument from the correlation to the causal conclusion. Such a criticism is more constructive because it may suggest specific critical questions. Answering these critical questions could strengthen the causal argument through subsequent critical discussion that introduces new evidence."

As we will see in the next section, Woods and Walton understand the fallacy of *post hoc* to be something different from what Aristotle did; for them, it involves reasoning from correlations to causal generalizations. But apart from the work of Woods and Walton, there has been little attempt at serious or rigorous theorizing about the *post hoc* fallacy.

A brief review of the literature reveals that there are at least three distinguishable kinds of reasoning that have been labeled *post hoc*. Copi and Cohen (1990, 101) describe *post hoc, ergo propter hoc* as "the error of concluding that an event is caused by another simply because it *follows* the other." They say, "We know, of course, that mere temporal succession does not establish a causal connection; but we can be tricked."

Kelley, in *The Art of Reasoning*, says:

> The fallacy has to do with causality, and it has the structure:
>
> A occurred before B
> $\downarrow$
> A caused B
>
> Such reasoning is fallacious because many events that precede a given event have nothing to do with it. . . .[4]

These descriptions, and some of the examples used by these authors, suggest that the fallacy occurs when one reasons from the fact that one *particular* event preceded another *particular* event to the conclusion that the first *particular event* caused the second. Copi and Cohen's examples include concluding that peculiar weather conditions were caused by the underground testing of a nuclear device that preceded them; and concluding that an aggressive move in foreign policy caused an international event for which we had been hoping. Kelley's include "speculation about the causes of historical events such as the Civil War, the causes of economic phenomena such as the Great Depression, or causes of sociological trends such as the increasing divorce rate." Let us call this sort of inference the *causal interpretation of particular events*. It is this sort of reasoning or argument that Aristotle appears to have had in mind in the passage from the *Rhetoric* quoted above.

But other examples used by Copi and Cohen and by Kelley suggest a

---

4. David Kelley, *The Art of Reasoning* (New York: Norton, 1988), 125–26.

pattern of reasoning in which we conclude that one *kind* of event causes another *kind* of event from the fact that events of the first kind preceded events of the second kind. Thus Copi and Cohen (1990, 101–2) write: "In primitive beliefs the error is sometimes blatant; we will all reject as absurd the claim that beating drums is the cause of the sun's reappearance after an eclipse, despite the evidence offered that every time drums have been beaten during an eclipse the sun has reappeared!" And Kelley gives the following as an example: "Stock market advisors sometimes make predictions on the basis of a few indicators which, in the past, happened to precede a rise or fall in prices."[5]

Indeed, the treatments of *post hoc* by Woods and Walton (1977e; 1982a) and Walton (1989a) define the fallacy as an incorrect inductive argument from correlation to cause or, more precisely, "the spurious inflation of the evidential value of the correlation owing to the suppressing or failing to take into account other causally relevant factors of various kinds" (Woods and Walton 1977e, 580). Walton (1989a, 213) characterizes the "traditional conception" as follows: "the *post hoc* is said to occur when it is concluded that A causes B simply because one or more occurrences of A are correlated with one or more occurrences of B." In what I just called the causal interpretation of particular events, the conclusion of *post hoc* reasoning is a proposition to the effect that one particular event caused another particular event. In the conception advanced by Woods and Walton, the conclusion of *post hoc* reasoning is a *causal generalization* (a proposition to the effect that one *kind* of thing or event causes or tends to cause another *kind* of thing or event). Let us call such reasoning *the inference from correlation to causality*.

A third conception of the fallacy of *post hoc ergo propter hoc* emerges from Book V of Mill's *System of Logic*. There Mill treats *post hoc* as a species of faulty generalization and appears to construe it as the attempt to establish a causal law from a single sequence of events. Though his examples (e.g., "that England owes her industrial preeminence to her restrictions on commerce") don't seem to fit this characterization very well, his comment about his examples is as follows:

> In these and similar cases, if it can be rendered probable by other evidence that the supposed causes have some tendency to produce the effect ascribed to them, the fact of its having been produced, though only in one instance, is of some value as a verification by specific

5. Kelley, *Art of Reasoning*, 126.

experience: but in itself it goes scarcely any way at all towards establishing such a tendency, since, admitting the effect, a hundred other antecedents could show an equally strong title of *that* kind to be considered as the cause.[6]

In Mill's diagnosis of *post hoc* reasoning, then, the fact that one is basing a generalization on just one instance appears to be an essential ingredient of the fallacy. (Compare Walton [1989a, 215–16], where one of the six kinds of *post hoc* error is said to occur "when the number of positive correlations between the events in question is too small to rule out coincidence.") Let us call this type of inference *causal generalization from one sequence of events.*

We then have either three conceptions of *post hoc* reasoning, or three species of *post hoc* reasoning:

1. *Causal interpretation of particular events* (concluding that particular event A caused a particular event B from the fact that A preceded B)
2. *Inference from correlation to cause* (concluding that there is a causal relation between two event types from the fact that those event types are positively correlated)
3. *Causal generalization from one sequence of events* (concluding that there is a causal relation between two event types A and B from the fact that a single instance of A was followed by an instance of B).

Now it is an open question whether *all post hoc* reasoning is fallacious, whether every instance of reasoning of these three sorts is an instance of a fallacy. Let us say that the *fallacy* of *post hoc ergo propter hoc* occurs when (a) one of these three kinds of reasoning or inference occurs and (b) its occurrence constitutes an error in reasoning.

It is fairly easy to see that *post hoc* reasoning—at least of the sort that proceeds from genuine correlation to cause—need not be fallacious. Many authors have pointed out that the inference from correlation to cause may lend significant support to a causal hypothesis. Calling the standard treatment of *post hoc* "puzzling," Hamblin (1970, 37) remarks: "If we know that B *always* occurs after A we are well on the way to setting up a causal law, and the

---

6. John Stuart Mill, *A System of Logic* (New York: Harper and Brothers, 1872), Book V, chap. v, 5, p. 490.

precise difference between necessary connection and constant conjunction has been matter for debate among philosophers at least since Hume."

Woods and Walton make a similar point when, as noted above, they explain *post hoc* in terms of "the spurious inflation of the evidential value of the correlation." If the degree of belief—or the kind of doxastic attitude—which we entertain toward a causal conclusion is appropriate to the extent and character of the correlational evidence, then it is hard to see that any fallacy is committed. I have argued elsewhere[7] that we ought to generalize the notion of argument to cover not just the cases in which we come to be *convinced* of a conclusion, but to all those cases where we modify our doxastic attitude toward a proposition on the basis of evidence found or presented. On such a conception, coming to *suspect* that A caused B on the ground that A (saliently) preceded B would count as an inference; and the attempt to persuade someone to suspect A as the cause of B on the ground that A saliently preceded B would count as an argument. Such cases might well count as nonfallacious cases of *post hoc* reasoning or argument, even in situations where the evidence would not warrant being confident that A caused B.

But what about the kind of *post hoc* reasoning that I've called causal interpretation of particular events? Can the mere fact that one event followed another in time make it reasonable even to *suspect* that the first caused the second? And can *post hoc* reasoning ever justify a doxastic attitude toward a causal proposition that is stronger than suspicion?

If *post hoc* reasoning is defined as reasoning in which someone concludes that an event is caused by another simply because it follows the other, then I doubt it is possible for *post hoc* reasoning to occur. Try to imagine someone reasoning, or arguing, for a causal conclusion simply on the basis of a temporal sequence—for example, someone allegedly reasoning that Gorbachev's fall was caused by the fact that Madonna's lover cut himself shaving, simply and solely on the grounds the lover cut himself the day before Gorby's fall began.[8] I maintain that such an incident could not count

---

7. R. C. Pinto, "Generalizing the Notion of Argument." In van Eeemeren, Grootendorst et al. (1991a), 137–46.

8. Notice that one *could* interpolate a narrative in which these events are causally connected: Madonna's lover is a key member of the Central Committee, the combination of his vanity and the scar keep him from an important meeting, as a result of his absence from the meeting a crucial vote is lost, etc. This narrative—though highly unlikely—is not "beyond reason." What would be beyond reason is the inference from "This happened the day before the fall" to "This caused the fall" in the absence of any narrative that would connect the two events.

as an example of human reasoning or anything that could be seriously construed as human argument; the assumption of a certain minimum rationality is required for anything to be interpreted as reasoning, and such minimum rationality would be lacking in the case described. People who reason from a *post hoc* to a *propter hoc* must see in the events temporally related something more than mere temporal succession.

Consider this example concerning a passenger on board the doomed Italian liner, Andrea Doria:

> On the fatal night of the Doria's collision with the Swedish ship Grisholm, off Nantucket, the lady retired to her cabin and flicked the light switch. Suddenly there was a great crash and grinding metal, and passengers and crew ran screaming through the passageways. The lady burst from her cabin and explained to the first person in sight that she must have set the ship's emergency brake.[9]

Two things are interesting about this example. First, the passenger didn't conclude simply that flicking the switch caused the audible crash; she interpolated a narrative that would make such a connection intelligible: the switch she flicked set an emergency brake—she assimilated what happened on the ship to something that might happen on a train. Second, the interpolated narrative is an implausible one: ships don't have brakes, and if they did, it's unlikely that the "brake pedals" would be located in individual cabins and shaped like light switches. (But, then, what would we think of her reasoning if she had reported a sign above the light switch that said "Use only in the event of an emergency"?)

Post hoc reasoning takes place against a backdrop of experience, knowledge, and perceptual expectation that shapes its direction and renders it at least minimally rational. But then *post hoc* reasoning never is concluding that one event is caused by another *simply* because it follows the other.

But if *post hoc* reasoning always involves background knowledge in addition to the knowledge of the temporal sequence of two events, then that background knowledge may well render the causal conclusion a solid one. That, I think, is what actually happens in much of the causal interpretation of particular events we make on the fly in the midst of our practical affairs. I hear the motor start after I see you turn the key in the ignition—and con-

---

9. Quoted in Woods and Walton (1977e, 584). The quote is from David Hacket Fischer, *Historians' Fallacies* (New York: Harper and Row, 1970), 166.

clude that the one event caused the other. (And I will quite reasonably hold you responsible for starting the car—without considering the likelihood of coincidence or any alternate hypotheses about what caused the car to start). I see the window shatter as the ball strikes it, and have no doubt about the cause of the broken window (and on the basis of my *post hoc* conclusion am prepared to demand compensation from the person who threw the ball).

Now someone may object that these aren't cases of *post hoc* reasoning at all, but simply the application of well-established causal generalizations to the case at hand. But why shouldn't the application of causal generalizations to particular temporal sequences count as *post hoc* reasoning? More to the point, there are examples importantly similar to those just cited which do *not* involve the application of well-established causal generalizations to the case at hand. Consider three:

1. Imagine a child bouncing a rubber ball against her bedroom wall, and suppose a vertical hairline crack the length of the wall appears immediately after an impact at the exact spot where the ball struck. To my knowledge, hairline cracks in plaster are normally caused by stress on the butter coat generated as a house settles, and not as a result of impact. In fact, I don't know whether impact from a rubber ball could produce such a crack in plaster. But if I were to witness such an event, I would certainly conclude that the crack was caused by the ball. Would my conclusion be unreasonable?
2. Suppose you have a lipstick stain on your shirt that you want to remove. You have no idea whether cigarette lighter fluid will remove it, but you apply some to the stain and as you rub it with a cloth the stain disappears. Isn't it reasonable to conclude that, on this occasion at least, rubbing a lipstick stain with lighter fluid caused it to disappear?
3. In the movie *Awakenings* we are shown a psychiatrist administering L-dopa in greater and greater dosages to a catatonic patient who has not spoken or responded in normal ways for many years. Eventually, a few hours after one of the doses, the patient's demeanor and behavior change radically and he begins to speak and to respond in relatively normal ways. Anyone watching the movie concludes that the L-dopa has produced this effect. Are we all guilty of the fallacy of *post hoc ergo propter hoc?*

My intuitions are that in each of these cases, it is reasonable to be fairly confident that a causal relation obtains on the basis of essentially *post hoc* evidence. There are no causal generalizations lying in the background that we can apply to the case at hand, but there are *analogies* on which we draw. We are familiar with many sorts of case in which impact produces damage of one kind or another; we take the effect of the ball on the plaster to be analogous to these. We are familiar with many sorts of case in which flammable liquids are able to remove various kinds of stain (from *some* kinds of fabric); we take the effect of the lighter fluid on the lipstick to be analogous to these. Moreover, the events we interpret as cause are *salient* in a way that is difficult to explain but which is, I submit, familiar and readily apparent. The impact of the ball, the rubbing with fluid, the administering of the drugs come to our attention when we think about the crack, the disappearance of stain, the improvement in the patient's condition. In addition, nothing else suggests itself as a possible or plausible explanation of the events we interpret as the effects of these causes.

If *post hoc* reasoning need not be fallacious, what then are we to make of the fallacy of *post hoc ergo propter hoc*. How does defective or fallacious *post hoc* reasoning differ from the nondefective sort? Can we devise a set of rules or guidelines such that, if they are not followed, *post hoc* reasoning is defective? Or such that if they are followed, *post hoc* reasoning is sound? I do not think so.

Look, for example, at the six types of *post hoc* error listed in Walton (1989a, 215–24). Some of them are things that aren't always errors (a small sample or a sample of one); others characterize false conclusions rather than errors in reasoning (getting the causal relationship backward, overlooking a third factor that is the common cause of the correlates, erroneous extrapolation beyond a given range of cases); others are pragmatically undesirable outcomes (overlooking the complex chain of linkages in a causal sequence). These "errors" are worth noting with an eye to formulating "critical questions" about a piece of causal reasoning (which is the role Walton wants for them). But they do not describe faults that a reasoner or arguer can be expected to avoid in every case. No matter how good one's methodology, for example, it won't *guarantee* that common causes of correlates won't be overlooked. Nondeductive inference simply doesn't offer such guarantees.

There is, I think, a reason in principle why there can be no set of stateable rules that pick out the good inferences from the bad ones, the winners from the losers, the proofs from the fallacies—especially when it comes to inferences whose conclusions are causal, and therefore explanatory. Inferences are readjustments in our doxastic commitments or attitudes—precipitated, of course, by observation or by argument—but dependent nonetheless on global factors of overall coherence, simplicity and conservatism. Any strictly "local" rule—anything like an algorithm—will hold only *ceteris paribus*, will always be liable to be overridden by other considerations.

An additional reason is that our reasoning and our arguing takes place under constraints of time and resources and in the service of nontheoretical ends. How good an inference must be to be good enough will therefore be dictated by practical considerations too various for a "logic of the fallacies" to master.

Bereft of theory—at least of the kind of theory that can ground principled judgments as to what is and isn't a fallacy—what becomes of fallacy talk in general and of the concept of *post hoc* fallacies in particular?

We acquire our fallacy concepts—our mastery of fallacy labels such as *post hoc ergo propter hoc*—from sources like Aristotle who provide us basically with examples or exemplars, together (sometimes) with a gloss. The examples are examples of inferences or arguments seen or presumed to be bad, and the gloss (if supplied) calls attention to some of the features of the example that make it an example of bad reasoning or argumentation.

"Politicians are especially fond of taking this line. Thus Demades said that the policy of Demosthenes was the cause of all the mischief, 'for after it the war occurred.'" No gloss is offered in Aristotle's text, but in the Lyceum one could well have been reminded how complex was the series of events that lead up to a war and (perhaps) how tenuous the connection of Demosthenes' policy with such events. Exemplars can anchor our use of fallacy labels, even if they don't provide us with necessary and sufficient conditions for committing the fallacy. Thus, the claim that supply-side economics produced the recession is a lot more like Demades' claim than is the claim that L-dopa produced profound changes in a patient the day after he took it.

Equally important is the context in which fallacy labels are (or should be) used: namely, a context of critical discussion in which there is an onus on one who lays a fallacy charge to motivate it ("But look at all the other possible explanations you're overlooking!") and an opportunity for one so accused to defend herself ("Let me show you why none of those explanations will do").[10]

---

10. Earlier versions of this paper were read at meetings of the Ontario Philosophical Society in London, Ontario (October 1992) and of the Canadian Philosophical Association in Ottawa, Ontario (May 1993).

PART IV

Fallacies and Teaching

Introduction

With the possible exception of Alfred Sidgwick,[1] fallacy theorists have never claimed that a thorough knowledge of the fallacies could serve as a satisfactory substitute for a knowledge of the positive criteria of good arguments. From Aristotle to Mill, we find that the fallacies are of secondary importance to knowledge about what makes arguments good. Even so, a study of the fallacies has been considered desirable not only for students of logic, but for educated people in general. Mill's view was that "the only complete safeguard against reasoning ill, is the habit of reasoning well";[2] however, he also thought that we are prone to commit errors from time to time, and that therefore knowledge of the fallacies serves as a kind of secondary line of defense against being deceived, or committing errors ourselves.

Since the 1960s more and more universities and colleges have introduced courses with names such as "Critical Thinking," "Informal Logic," and "Reasoning Skills." Many of these courses devote some time to the fallacies for the same reason that Arnauld and Nicole thought they were important, namely, that "as examples to be avoided often strike us more than examples to be imitated, it will not be without its use to set forth the principal classes of bad reasoning, . . . since this will enable us yet more readily to avoid them."[3] Some instructors, however, go even further and design their courses around what they take to be the most important fallacies. By teaching the fallacies—that is, by teaching what the fallacies are—and by giving examples of fallacious arguments, they believe themselves to be indirectly teaching critical, logical, or reasoning skills. It is the utility of this approach that the two papers in this section discuss. Hitchcock argues that teaching the fallacies is a poor way to teach critical thinking, whereas Blair defends the legitimacy of the approach, given certain restrictions.

Hitchcock examines the case for using the fallacies as a framework for a critical thinking course. He imagines the argument that would be made to defend such a course: the fallacies are common mistakes; therefore, instruction in how to identify and avoid them is a legitimate purpose for a course in

---

1. Alfred Sidgwick, *Fallacies: A View of Logic from the Practical Side* (New York: Appleton, 1884).

2. *A System of Logic*, this volume, 86.

3. *Port-Royal Logic*, this volume, 39.

critical thinking. This argument, however, is found wanting in several respects. First of all, not every fallacy on the traditional list is a truly *common* mistake. Some of them, still on the list, are peculiar to past historical eras, e.g., many questions seems to have little currency outside the framework of the contentious dialogues Aristotle described. Second, since Aristotle's time the list of fallacies has grown unsystematically and there is not much reason to think that the list we have inherited represents all, or even most, of the important kinds of failures of rationality students should be familiar with. Finally, empirical results to date fail to establish that any of the fallacies are committed with significant frequency, thus casting doubt on the claim that collectively they represent common mistakes. These reasons, taken together, cast considerable doubt on the argument for building a critical thinking course on the fallacies.

Even if we suppose that fallacies do occur with noticeable frequency, thinks Hitchcock, there remain good reasons not to use them as the framework for a course on critical thinking. One reason for this is that it is difficult to determine when a form of argument, e.g., *ad verecundiam*, is legitimate and when it is not. Because of this difficulty, which inheres in most nonformal fallacies, our time is better spent teaching the canons of good reasoning rather than the characteristics of some of the kinds of bad reasoning. Furthermore, a training in critical thinking based primarily on a study of the fallacies is likely to foster a disposition in the student to be overcritical and may even lead her to judge very good arguments as fallacious. Finally, argues Hitchcock, familiarity with the fallacies is of little use in teaching argument construction.

Although Blair and Hitchcock hold similar views about the nature of critical thinking, Blair comes to very opposite conclusions about the value of basing a critical thinking course, or a course in informal logic or argumentation theory, on the fallacies. Given certain qualifications, thinks Blair, a course on the fallacies is an effective way to accomplish the goal of instilling critical thinking skills. Central to his argument is the distinction between inferring and arguing. Because these are different activities there could be critical thinking courses devoted solely to the one rather than the other. However, because examples of actual fallacies are exemplifications of arguments (*arguings*), any course that wants to give a central place to the study of the fallacies should be a course on argumentation rather than on inference.

Blair's most important qualification governing the teaching of the fallacies in critical thinking courses is essentially that it be done with care and in light of the best research on the fallacies. Courses that only give a brief or perfunctory explanation of the fallacies, or that teach superficial analyses of them, will do more harm than good. These pitfalls being avoided, Blair thinks that there are a number of good reasons to base a course on critical thinking around the fallacies. These reasons include the observations that each fallacy provides a "bite-sized learning chunk" easily digested by students, and that—contrary to Hitchcock—the fallacy names *are* used in public discourse. More important, however, is that in a well-designed course on the fallacies students will not only learn what the fallacies are; they will also learn that discrimination and caution must be used in making fallacy judgments. In this way students come to appreciate the difficulty of argument interpretation and they learn something about the standards of good arguments and good argumentation, as well as the most common flaws that one is likely to encounter.

The issue of whether a fallacies approach to teaching critical thinking is useful should be seen in the wider context of the debate about the value of critical thinking courses in general. A good entry into the discussion is John McPeck's *Teaching Critical Thinking: Dialogue and Dialectic*[4] in which McPeck argues his skepticism with regard to the value of critical thinking courses. The same volume contains criticisms of McPeck's position by Harvey Siegel and Stephen Norris, among others.[5]

---

4. New York: Routledge, Chapman and Hall, 1990.

5. See also McPeck's earlier work, *Critical Thinking and Education* (New York: St. Martin's, 1981). Another useful exchange of ideas is McPeck's article, "What Is Learned in Informal Logic?" (*Teaching Philosophy* 14 [1991]: 25–34), and the reply by J. A. Blair and R. H. Johnson, "Misconceptions of Informal Logic: A Reply to McPeck" (same issue, 35–52).

23

Do the Fallacies Have a Place in the Teaching of Reasoning Skills or Critical Thinking?

David Hitchcock

> The fallacies generally turn out not to be fallacies—unless one builds into the identification process, and hence into the labels, all the skills needed for analysis without the taxonomy of fallacies. In that case one has made it a formal approach, and the encoding (i.e. diagnosing) step has become the tricky one.
>
> —Michael Scriven, *Reasoning*

Almost two decades ago, at the end of a course in introductory symbolic logic, I turned to a section of the text that dealt with informal fallacies. The students' interest immediately rose. Here were passages of prose recognizably like the things they were used to hearing and reading, and it was great fun to label the commonly made mistakes. Unlike the meaningless letters and novel symbols of the propositional and first-order predicate calculus, these exercises had obvious application to everyday life.

When it came time to discuss examples and grade exercises, however, the attractiveness of this approach began to fade. For any passage, students produced more than one fallacy label for a single mistake. Worse, I was unable to work out which of the labels was correct; the types of fallacies recognized in our taxonomy were apparently not mutually exclusive. Worse still, when I included on a test some passages that contained no fallacies at all, students unhesitatingly identified the fallacy and were able to argue just as convincingly for its presence as in the case of the truly fallacious passages. Students were apparently able (and willing) to find a fallacy in anything.

In the light of this experience, in my teaching of critical thinking, I have chosen texts[1] that contain almost no mention of fallacies and have avoided explicit teaching of fallacies, though occasionally some appeared as privations of desirable criteria of good arguments.

Having been asked to discuss whether the fallacies have a place in the teaching of reasoning skills/critical thinking, I must now reexamine my skepticism about the value of a fallacies approach. I begin with some remarks about what we are trying to teach when we teach reasoning skills/critical thinking. Since to many people it seems obvious that the fallacies have a place in teaching critical thinking, I begin my consideration of the place of fallacies by articulating the most obvious argument for their inclusion ("The Case for Fallacies," below) and revealing its weaknesses. The weaknesses of the case for including the fallacies lead naturally to some direct arguments against including them ("The Case Against Fallacies"). I conclude ("Open Questions") by indicating open questions that deserve further research.

Critical Thinking as an Educational Goal

In teaching students to think critically, we are trying not only to impart knowledge and improve skills but also to foster a critical spirit, one that examines the credentials of the intellectual products (e.g., arguments, statements, questions, experimental designs, hypotheses) it encounters (including one's own products) rather than accepting them blindly or following preconceived prejudices.[2] People who have learned to think critically tend to apply the standards of reason to all intellectual products they encounter, their own as well as other people's, the conclusions they agree with as well as those they

1. Michael Scriven's *Reasoning* (New York: McGraw-Hill, 1976), my own *Critical Thinking* (Toronto: Methuen, 1983), Alec Fisher's *The Logic of Real Arguments* (Cambridge: Cambridge University Press, 1988), and Govier (1992).

2. Among those who have emphasized the importance of the attitudinal component of the ideal critical thinker are Edward M. Glaser, *An Experiment in the Development of Critical Thinking* (New York: Teachers College Press, 1941); Richard M. Paul, "Teaching Critical Thinking in the Strong Sense: A Focus on Self-deception, World Views and a Dialectical Mode of Analysis," *Informal Logic Newsletter* 4, no. 2 (1982): 2–7; Harvey Siegel, *Educating Reason: Rationality, Critical Thinking and Education* (New York: Routledge, 1988); and Robert H. Ennis, "Critical Thinking: A Streamlined Conception," *Teaching Philosophy* 14 (1991): 5–24.

dissent from or are uncertain about. The disposition of a critical thinker is not merely a disposition to suspend judgment. On the contrary, a critical thinker will make judgments when the evidence and argument warrant making them in a particular pragmatic context; she is in Ennis's words "focused on deciding what to believe or do."[3] When teaching critical thinking, therefore, we do not want to inculcate a disposition to find all arguments and evidence inadequate. Critical thinking need not be negative thinking; it should have an element of appreciation, like art or film or literary criticism, rather than resembling the judging involved in convicting and sentencing criminals.

Thus the following features of critical thinking are relevant to the question of whether there is a place for the fallacies in teaching critical thinking:

1. The goal of teaching critical thinking is to foster a balanced disposition to appraise intellectual products, not a disposition to look for mistakes.
2. Although critical thinking involves appraisal, it includes appraisal of one's own mental products as part of an ongoing process of inquiry, and is in this sense constructive.
3. Whether applied to one's own thinking or others', critical thinking should sometimes result in a judgment that the intellectual product under examination is acceptable.

The Case for Fallacies

At first glance, it seems obvious that there is a place for fallacies in teaching critical thinking. If fallacies are, as is commonly thought, common mistakes in reasoning that often deceive both those who commit them and those to whom arguments are directed, then those who are teaching students to monitor intellectual products for acceptability should transmit humanity's acquired knowledge of what the most common mistakes are and develop the ability and disposition to recognize them and respond appropriately. A student who is taught, for example, the concept of a biased sample and given practice and feedback on recognizing and commenting appropriately on systematic bias in the selection of samples should be more likely to recognize such bias in the future than if she is not taught the concept or given the

3. Robert H. Ennis, "A Logical Basis for Measuring Critical Thinking Skills," *Educational Leadership* 43, no. 2 (1985): 45.

practice. In this respect, then, she will be better at monitoring intellectual products for acceptability—better at critical thinking. If she undertakes some sample-based research of her own, she is likely to be more sensitized than otherwise to the importance of avoiding systematic bias in the sampling procedure. Similarly for other fallacies—straw man, begging the question, missing the point (*ignoratio elenchi*), *post hoc*.

This argument, which I hope is a plausible conjecture about the thinking of those who defend a fallacies approach, is not so compelling as it first seems to be.

To begin with, its appeal to tradition is weak. Many pieces of lore are handed down in a society simply because they got there once in some fortuitous way and have been repeated. Think for example of the belief in medicine of the efficacy of bloodletting, or any number of popular superstitions. The fallacies tradition, as Hamblin (1970) has shown, is an unsystematic accretion developed from Aristotle's listing of the tricks used by quarrelsome debaters in a stylized form of antagonistic question-and-answer discussion known as *elenchus* or refutation. Aristotle's list includes tricks peculiar to this type of discussion (e.g., many questions) or peculiar to the Greek language (e.g., accent), which are of little relevance to the exercise of critical thinking in the late twentieth century. Over the centuries, this or that textbook has introduced this or that innovation without much justifying support. Textbooks repeat what previous textbooks include, and the resulting mishmash is "so incoherent that we have every reason to look for some enlightenment at its historical source" (Hamblin 1970, 50).

Setting aside the appeal to tradition, do fallacies in fact occur? More than one contemporary philosopher has argued that they do not. Massey (1975a, 1981) points out that one cannot condemn an argument on the basis that it commits a formal fallacy such as denying the antecedent or affirming the consequent, because not all arguments which have an invalid form are invalid; in fact, all valid arguments are of the invalid form "$p_1, \ldots, p_n$, therefore q." In the absence of a systematic theory of the grammar of natural languages, we cannot prove that an argument in a natural language is of no valid form; the only way to prove invalidity, according to Massey, is to show that in fact the premises are true and the conclusion is false. George (1983) objects that we can recognize "the form" of natural-language arguments. Govier's remark that "formal proofs of invalidity are sometimes possible, given the correctness of necessary preformal assumptions" (1987, 189) indicates the limits of such proofs of invalidity.

Massey's argument applies only to formal fallacies. Finocchiaro (1981) complements it by appealing to the paucity of real examples in textbook treatments of informal fallacies and the poor interpretation of the few real examples which do occur. He concludes that "there are probably no common errors in reasoning. That is, logically incorrect arguments may be common, but common types of logically incorrect arguments probably are not" (Finocchiaro 1981, 15). Govier (1987, 190–97) rightly criticizes Finocchiaro's conclusion as hasty, pointing out that a competing plausible explanation of the poverty of the textbook treatments is the disinclination of philosophers to do empirical research. In an interesting twist, she also attempts to use Finocchiaro's argument against itself, since (she claims) it implies that logic texts often commit the straw man fallacy—namely, by unjustly or uncharitably interpreting as fallacious the few real-life examples they do discuss. But on Govier's own account (1992, 157) the straw man fallacy consists in claiming to have refuted a position on the basis of a misrepresentation of it; the poor interpretations in the logic texts do not refute the arguments they stigmatize as fallacious, but expose an alleged flaw in them.

Govier's critique, then, does not establish that Finocchiaro is mistaken, only that he has not proved his point. There is considerable psychological research on the kinds of mistakes in reasoning (especially conditional, inductive, and statistical reasoning) that people systematically make.[4] But the inductive "mistakes" identified in such research are according to Cohen (1982) defensible on the Baconian approach to induction for which he argues. Furthermore, since these are mistakes identified in experimental tasks, they may or may not show up in the arguments people deploy in real-life situations.

We are left, it seems, with impressionistic conjecture. Let me report my own conjecture: Most of the fallacies in the traditional list are not very common occurrences. But some are. Thus, in debating contexts, various kinds of questionable diversionary tactics are common: attacking the person, attacking a straw man, arguing for an irrelevant (or at least a different) conclusion, begging the question at issue, using loaded terminology. In monological arguments we often find biased sample, hasty generalization, failure to consider alternative explanations (hasty conclusion), and suppressed evidence. In reasoning by ourselves we are likely to exhibit confirma-

---

4. See, for example, Richard Nisbett and Lee Ross, *Human Inference: Strategies and Shortcomings of Social Judgment* (Englewood Cliffs, N.J.: Prentice-Hall, 1980), and Daniel Kahneman, Paul Slovic, and Amos Tversky, eds., *Judgment under Uncertainty: Heuristics and Biases* (New York: Cambridge University Press, 1982).

tion bias, the Concorde fallacy, the gambler's fallacy, and Monday-morning quarterbacking.[5] Some of these fallacies are peculiar to the contexts in which they usually occur. Confirmation bias, for example, does not show up in arguments produced as a result of it, even in the form of suppressed evidence, since the arguer is not so much suppressing evidence as reporting the outcome of an inquiry strategy which makes it likely that she will not come across any evidence that needs to be suppressed.

The most readily identifiable kinds of deception in everyday discourse, however, are not mistakes in reasoning, but misleading presentations of information. The so-called gee-whiz graph[6] exaggerates the amount of a change, for example in the value of some currency, by putting the x-axis at something other than zero; a minor perturbation can in this way be made to look like a catastrophic fall or a booming surge. What I have called the "dangling relative"[7] occurs in advertisements that trumpet "50% off" without specifying the price from which the 50% has been taken.

Even if we concede that fallacies do occur—that is, that there are recurring types of mistakes in reasoning which tend to deceive the consumers of arguments—it is not obvious that the best way to teach people to avoid committing them and to respond appropriately when others make them is to teach a list of mistakes and provide practice with examples. This is like saying that the best way to teach somebody to play tennis without making the common mistakes (and to recognize these mistakes in others' play) is to demonstrate these faults in action and get him to label and respond to them. Rational inquiry and arguing a case, like playing tennis, are complex skills, where the mistakes are deviations from doing it correctly. What the tennis coach teaches is how to do it correctly. Then the coach watches the learner, and corrects the mistakes peculiar to that learner. In teaching critical thinking, then, one should teach the rules of good reasoning, and draw the learner's attention to those mistakes that she actually commits. Like a good tennis player or a good dancer, a good reasoner can recognize mistakes in performance and characterize them appropriately with-

---

5. Confirmation bias involves looking only for evidence that supports a hypothesis one is investigating, thus ignoring any disconfirming evidence which may exist. The Concorde fallacy is the assumption that the amount of time and money one has already invested in an option gives one some reason to continue pursuing that option. The gambler's fallacy is thinking that past results in a sequence of independent chance events affect the probability of the next event in the sequence. Monday-morning quarterbacking evaluates the merits of a decision under uncertainty or risk on the basis of what the outcome turned out to be rather than on what the decision-maker could reasonably be expected to know at the time of making the decision.

6. Darrell Huff, *How to Lie with Statistics* (New York: Norton, 1954).

7. In my *Critical Thinking*, 163.

out having been taught a list of common mistakes. Knowing how to reason well, a good reasoner will recognize when some requirement of good reasoning is not satisfied.

The Case Against Fallacies

The case for fallacies, obvious as it seems, has turned out to be weak. A sustained critique of this argument has left us with the suggestion that in teaching critical thinking the fallacies are a diagnostic tool for pointing out to learners the mistakes they are habitually committing.

The weaknesses of the case for including the fallacies can be supplemented by a number of reasons for hesitating to include them. These reasons apply particularly to approaches to teaching critical thinking that use the fallacies as a framework (e.g., Kahane 1988; Johnson and Blair 1993).

First, the correct identification of an argumentative move as a fallacy, as Scriven observed in the passage quoted at the beginning of this chapter, requires a complex apparatus of analysis. In some cases, such as the various fallacies of irrelevant appeal (*ad populum, ad hominem, ad verecundiam*), one needs to deploy a fairly sophisticated conception of when the generic move involved is legitimate in order to be able to tell that a particular case is illegitimate; it is only "irrelevant" appeals to popularity, to the person, or to authority that are fallacious, and the criteria for irrelevance are complex and tricky to apply. In other cases, such as begging the question or biased sample, the move is always illegitimate but one needs to deploy a sophisticated conception of when it takes place, a conception that involves implicitly characterizing the contrast concept (justification without assuming the truth of the conclusion, sampling from the target population by one of a number of methods not systematically biased). In either case, it makes more sense to teach the analytical apparatus for correct reasoning (and to let the fallacy fall out as a kind of deviation) than to begin with the fallacies.

Second, fallacy labels are not necessary to the exercise of critical thinking; everything that can be said with the use of these labels can be said without them, and in general said more clearly. The labels have not become part of our everyday vocabulary; they have the flavor of the academic world about them, and must be explained when used outside an academic context. Such an explanation was necessary, for example, when a panelist on a Canadian radio broadcast on 2 October 1992 wondered whether commentators were committing a *post hoc* fallacy in blaming the prime minister's dramatic tearing up of a recently negotiated constitutional accord for a drop in the value of the Canadian dollar and resulting rise in interest rates. The fallacy of begging the question is so far from the consciousness of educated people today that they use the expression "beg the question" most commonly to mean "raise the question." Such people may nevertheless be quite capable of recognizing and dealing with the illegitimate assumption in debate of the point at issue. Perhaps for this reason Robert Ennis in his most recent taxonomy of the abilities of the ideal critical thinker lists employing and reacting to fallacy labels in an appropriate manner as *"auxiliary critical thinking abilities*—having them is not constitutive of being a critical thinker."[8]

Third, a fallacies approach is unduly negative. It fosters an attitude of looking for the mistake, and of stopping once one has found something one can pin a fallacy label on, rather than coming to grips with the substance of what one is discussing. Most arguments are neither ironclad proofs nor a tissue of error; their appraisal requires a careful, just, and even sympathetic working through of the argument. Teaching students to look for mistakes that they can label is not likely to promote that kind of approach. It is likely to promote the attitude of a "hanging judge" who looks for a basis on which to convict and sentence accused persons, rather than the attitude of a film critic who appreciates the merits of the films she watches.

Fourth, learning the fallacies is of no help in learning to construct good arguments of one's own, and of little help in learning to appreciate the merits of good arguments—both of which, I have urged, are components of critical thinking. By contrast, learning to construct good arguments or at least to appreciate the merits of good arguments is of great help in learning to recognize and respond to mistakes in reasoning. Using fallacies as a framework for teaching critical thinking draws upon and encourages our sense that we are besieged by persuasive appeals which are subtly deceptive. It is pleasing, particularly to young people beginning to think for themselves, to have an arsenal of labels with which to reject attempts of their elders to stampede them into a certain way of thinking. Pleasing as it is, however, the "pin the fallacy on the argument" game is a childish sport that does not conduce to an adult appreciation of the strengths and weaknesses of the intellectual products presented to us for our acceptance.

8. Robert Ennis, "Critical Thinking: A Streamlined Conception," 9. The emphasis is Ennis's.

Open Questions

I have articulated my skepticism about giving a large role to the fallacies in teaching critical thinking. I have pointed out weaknesses in the obvious argument for including them. And I have given some reasons for excluding them, or at least for not taking a fallacies approach to teaching critical thinking.

These arguments, however, have suffered from the lack of good relevant empirical research. Here are two questions such research could answer.

First, *What kinds of mistakes in reasoning occur commonly in arguments?* To undertake this research requires at least a preliminary list of purported fallacies, perhaps culled from the literature. This list should be subject to revision in the light of the critical examination of a large selection of argumentative texts culled in some unbiased way from the full range of contexts in which arguments occur. Such a corpus would be a useful object of study for other empirical investigations of argument, and might deserve publication in its own right. Since even the most common fallacies might occur only once in a hundred arguments, the number of passages requiring examination would be very large.

Second, *What effect does teaching the fallacies have on the development of critical thinking dispositions and skills?* The Educational Resources Information Center (ERIC) lists no publications on this topic under the intersection of "fallacies" with "logic" or "informal logic" or "critical thinking." We need a controlled study of the differential effects of various approaches to teaching critical thinking: a fallacies approach that takes the fallacies as the framework (e.g., Kahane 1988; Johnson and Blair 1993), a multifaceted approach in which the fallacies are a section of a course (e.g., Copi and Cohen 1990), an integrated infusion approach in which the fallacies appear as privations of one or another criterion of a good argument (e.g., Govier 1992), a positive approach in which the fallacies are hardly mentioned,[9] and perhaps others. Such a study should compare the outcomes, not on a standard examination that students take for credit (since such an examination would have a strong steering effect which would mask differences in learning) but on a valid measure of critical thinking dispositions and skills.

---

9. Among texts that adopt such an approach are Michael Scriven's *Reasoning*, and my own *Critical Thinking*.

24

The Place of Teaching Informal Fallacies in Teaching Reasoning Skills or Critical Thinking

J. Anthony Blair

Where does teaching the traditional fallacies, such as Woods's gang of eighteen (1992), belong in the teaching of reasoning skills or critical thinking? Is it essential, just useful, or instead, counterproductive or even miseducational? The right answer is, to be sure, "It all depends. . . ." I shall argue that it can be useful, in certain circumstances, when done appropriately. In making my case I shall discuss how "reasoning skills" and "critical thinking" are understood, explain what teaching fallacies entails, and consider some classroom do's and don'ts.

Reasoning Skills and Critical Thinking

Although there is a reason for teaching the fallacies in their own right, as part of the Western European intellectual tradition, my concern here is with their inclusion in reasoning skills or critical thinking courses, whose goals tend to be fairly directly practical. Such goals do not preclude teaching fallacies in teaching reasoning skills or critical thinking. To see why not, we must have a precise idea of the objectives of such courses.

After considerable controversy, a consensus about the general outlines of a reasoning or critical thinking course is emerging in the literature.[1] The minimal aim of such courses is to improve students' reasoning practices, including: skills in drawing warranted inferences and avoiding unwarranted ones; sensitivity to problematic claims and assumptions, and to inadequate bases for inferences; the ability to evaluate claims, assumptions, and inferences with good judgment; the disposition to exercise these skills and abilities as a matter of habit—and consistently, that is, in and directed upon one's own thinking as well as in evaluating that of others.

When designed by philosophers, such courses have tended to focus on argument analysis: the interpretation and assessment of arguments. Why? It is thought that a responsible epistemic or moral agent must be vigilant against problematic claims or conduct and so be able to assess the grounds offered, or available, to support them. And it is held that assessing grounds and separating cogent from noncogent justifications consists centrally of interpreting and assessing arguments. The analysis of arguments has seemed to philosophers to be either identical with (e.g., Hoaglund)[2] or necessary for (Johnson and Blair 1993) critical thinking.

Yet argument analysis is not identical to reasoning understood, narrowly, as inferring. One can infer without arguing (as Harman has shown)[3] and one can argue without inferring (witness the arguer who does not make the inferences he invites from his interlocutor). Thus the interpretation and critique of inference is distinct from the critique and interpretation of argument. Furthermore, an argument, except in the logician's technical narrow sense, includes more than the "semantic" (Walton 1989a, 114) or illative core that constitutes each of its component invited inferences—the "set of propositions one of which allegedly follows from the others."[4] It follows that teaching good argumentation practices will not be the same as teaching either

1. See, for example, Michael Scriven, "Defining Critical Thinking" (unpublished manuscript, 1992), 1; Robert H. Ennis and Stephen P. Norris, *Evaluating Critical Thinking* (Pacific Grove, Calif.: MidWest Publications, 1989), 3; Jerry Cederblom and David W. Paulsen, *Critical Reasoning*, 3d ed. (Belmont, Calif.: Wadsworth, 1991), 8; and Harvey Siegel, *Educating Reason* (New York: Routledge, 1988), 34 and 39.

2. John Hoaglund, *Critical Thinking: An Introduction to Informal Logic* (Newport News, Va.: Vale, 1984).

3. Gilbert Harman, *Change in View* (Cambridge: MIT Press, 1986).

4. Argument is a complex act relying on linguistic and other conventions, with social, pragmatic, and dialectical, as well as epistemic components or aspects (see van Eemeren and Grootendorst 1984). Moreover, most arguments have a far more complex structure than any semantic/illative core displays, with combinations of multiple parallel arguments with a single conclusion and multiple layers of premise-supporting arguments (see Johnson and Blair 1993). The structure of an inference is simple in comparison.

good reasoning practices or the logic of valid inferences. The place of informal fallacies in the critical thinking curriculum must take the distinctions among argument, inference, and logic into account.

Conceptions of Fallacy

Most conceptions of informal fallacy associate fallacies in some essential respect with arguments or argumentation. If these conceptions are right, then informal fallacies should be taught only in critical thinking courses insofar as they deal with argumentation, and courses on inference or other forms of reasoning that do not touch on argumentation should not make reference to fallacies.

The concept of fallacy was first made the object of study, by Aristotle, in the context of argumentation, and argumentation remains the *locus classicus* of fallacies. But the concept of fallacy is not analytically tied to that of argument or argumentation.[5] Inferences can be as guilty of such fallacies as *post hoc* reasoning and hasty generalization as can arguments. Even fallacies paradigmatically associated with argumentation, such as straw person, *ad hominem*, guilt by association, and two wrongs make a right, can be committed by the nonarguing inferrer. If faulty inferences in their own right may be termed fallacious, then the path is conceptually clear to teach fallacies in critical thinking courses that deal with reasoning construed as inferring, but not with arguments.

What, then, is a fallacy? For present purposes I am satisfied to follow Woods's (1992) plausible account. According to Woods, the traditional fallacies are of two types: first, those errors that are delusions—malfunctions which are natural to commit and committed confidently (everybody makes them and they are hard to correct); second, those that are snares—cognitive turns which entrap the theorist in difficult and intractable philosophical questions. Fallacies so conceived can occur in reasoning that does not occur or issue in arguments, as well as in reasoning that does. This conception picks out the "traditional eighteen" or so fallacies that Woods's account serves (or tries) to legitimize. I here list many of the labels for fallacies included on such lists, along with some relatives and subspecies: ambiguity (also equivoca-

---

5. I here part company with van Eemeren and Grootendorst (1992a). I would argue that theirs is a theory of the fallacies associated with arguments, not "the" theory of fallacies.

tion); versions of *ad hominem* (the abusive, and the variants of the circumstantial); guilt by association; *ad ignorantiam*; *ad populum* (appeal to popularity and appeal to emotions versions); *ad verecundiam*; part-whole fallacies (composition, division); faulty analogy (inductive, a priori), two wrongs make a right; false dilemma; *ignoratio elenchi*, straw person, red herring; many questions (including loaded question); *petitio principii* (epistemic, dialectic); *post hoc ergo propter hoc*, correlation-cause conflation; *secundum quid* (hasty conclusion and hasty generalization); slippery slope (causal or from precedent or mixed).

Teaching Fallacies

Having described in general terms the subject-matter of a course in critical thinking or reasoning skills, and having explained what I mean by a fallacy, I can turn to the third task of this article: explaining how fallacies should be taught. In what follows I first discuss teaching fallacies when teaching argument analysis, and then teaching fallacies when argument is not a central focus.

Teaching Argument Using Fallacies

Teaching the fallacies can serve as a gateway to argument interpretation. No assessment of the cogency of the semantic/illative core of a working argument (or nest of arguments) can fairly begin until the contours and details of the argumentation have been identified.[6] Students find the interpretation of working arguments extremely difficult, which is unsurprising when the hermeneutic complexity of the task is appreciated. The text as a whole needs to be situated in several dimensions: What is the issue? Who is discussing it? Why is it controversial for them in the circumstances? What contending positions are known to have been taken? What interests are at stake? Who is the intended audience? What are the interlocutors' goals on this occasion? What are the time and space constraints? Answers to these and other questions must be found or assumed. Underlying meanings must

6. By a "working" argument, I mean one that has been made by someone to try to persuade or convince someone, or for some other purpose than to provide an example or illustration of an argument for interpretation, analysis, or critique.

be brought to the surface (for example, irony made literal). The propositions making up the arguments must be distinguished, disentangled from their textual scaffolding, and placed in the appropriate relationships of support, a job requiring linguistic expertise and presupposing familiarity with conceptions of numerous argument schemes. Vagueness and ambiguity must be noted for future reference. These tasks interrelate and must be carried out more or less simultaneously. It is a daunting prospect, yet it has to be made manageable for beginners.

One approach is to teach separately each set of the theoretical fundamentals, giving the student the keys that unlock each different hermeneutical problem. Although attractive, that approach is impossible in a one-semester or even a two-semester undergraduate course. It best fits programs in which students can be required to take several courses that prepare the ground for high-level textual interpretation.

Another approach is to rely on students' linguistic intuitions, combined with a much simplified model of argument. The instructor starts from artificial examples, moves to very simple working arguments, and then gradually introduces more and more complex and subtle working arguments, modeling good interpretation and coaching the students. Such an approach can work well in small groups, though it has the drawback of giving students limited theoretical understanding of what they are learning.

A third approach is to introduce students to some of the fallacies, both by supplying paradigm examples and by identifying the typical conditions constitutive of the fallacies in question. The cogent arguments that the fallacious ones approximate or counterfeit, and the principles of their cogency, are introduced at the same time. The cogent argument patterns and their corresponding fallacious versions are abstractions from real arguments. They serve as exemplars to use when deciphering the working arguments in which the fallacies are committed. The student is thus armed with (a) patterns that help guide the extraction of arguments from texts, (b) an account of why the patterns are cogent, and (c) an account of why their fallacious counterparts are not cogent. The defining conditions of each fallacy also refer to the features of the contexts which are germane to the analysis (for example, that the arguer is responding to a criticism). Texts exhibiting the associated nonfallacious argument scheme can then be introduced, so the student can learn to distinguish the two. Later, borderline or controversial arguments can be provided, so the student can appreciate how the fallacious argument scheme and its corresponding cogent argument scheme are both idealizations.

This third approach combines nicely with teaching argument assessment, since a fallacy critique is essentially evaluative, a fallacious argument being a defective argument. Learning to understand various fallacies, and acquiring the skill of recognizing fallacious arguments, are obviously parts of learning how to evaluate arguments.

The precise role the concept of fallacy will play in argument critique will depend on whether one takes a "fatality" or an "injury" view of what constitutes a fallacy. Some theorists (e.g., Walton 1989a) reserve the term "fallacy" for a grievous flaw in reasoning or argument: "To claim that an argument contains a fallacy is a strong form of criticism implying that the argument contains a serious logical error and even more strongly implying that the argument is based on an underlying flaw or misconception of reasoning and can therefore be refuted" (16). Others (e.g., Johnson and Blair 1993) mean by "fallacy" any shortfall from cogency:

> By a fallacy, we mean a pattern of argument that violates one of the criteria (relevance, sufficiency, acceptability) which good arguments must satisfy. (48)
>   . . . [T]he charge of fallacy is nothing more than an initial probe of the argument. It is an attempt to locate a potential weakness, not the bold . . . assertion that because of this flaw the argument goes by the board. Even if the charge of fallacy is justified in a given instance, that does not mean the argument cannot be repaired over the flaw (51).[7]

In either view, fallacies can be taught as a tool for argument evaluation. The "fatality" view has to allow that there can be arguments with flaws akin to fallacies, but that are not fallacious because the flaws are not "serious logical errors" and the arguments cannot be "refuted," even though they may require repair (such as the addition of qualifications or provisos, or of more evidence). The "injury" view has to grant that fallaciousness comes in degrees, and hence (perhaps counterintuitively) that fallacious arguments can provide relatively strong support for their conclusions. The way the fallacies will be presented in using them to teach argument assessment will have to vary accordingly, but in either view these facts have to be accommodated: working arguments come in degrees of strength; some can be improved; some are flawed beyond repair.

I have been suggesting that fallacies can be introduced in ways compatible

---

7. Notice that both accounts identify fallaciousness with arguments.

with and illuminating for argument analysis, deepening students' appreciation of arguments. Teaching the fallacies has other benefits: (1) Learners find any labels helpful, and the fallacies provide a manageable set. (2) The fallacy names serve as handy mnemonic devices since they are striking, often descriptive of the argument patterns involved. (3) Learners master material best in medium-sized chunks, big enough for ready identification and retrieval, small enough to be digested in a lesson or two. The fallacies provide bite-sized learning chunks. (4) Such chunks also enable students to experience success in reasonable increments, which is important in encouraging perseverence in the hard work of mastering difficult material and skills. (5) Argument analysis skills are mastered only through extensive practice, and learning each new fallacy one after another entails a repeated analysis of arguments, hence practice in just-learned analytic skills. (6) As their repertoire of fallacies accumulates, students gradually enrich their critical abilities. (7) Fallacies learned earlier recur, so students get constant review of the earlier fallacies along with the later. (8) As more fallacies are added, the subject gets increasingly complex, since more and more distinctions are required, but this accumulation of complexity happens, again, in manageable increments. (9) Many fallacy labels have currency in public discourse, so students become increasingly aware, as they learn, that critical discussion is a public activity of discourse communities, not solitary and private. (10) The currency of the fallacy labels matches the ubiquity in public discourse of the mistakes they denote, so students appreciate that their critical skills have immediate, practical applicability. (11) Finally, it becomes apparent to students how they themselves have tended to commit various fallacies, and thus that these critical tools are applicable to their own thinking as well.

Reasons for Not Teaching Fallacies

Reasons against teaching fallacies when teaching argument analysis, misconceptions of fallacies aside, seem to boil down to (a) alternative approaches that accomplish other desirable goals, (b) lack of time, and (c) reasons for not teaching poor conceptions of fallacies or for not teaching fallacies badly.

(a) There are undoubtedly good ways to teach argument analysis without using fallacies as the vehicle. I am not arguing that fallacies *must* be taught, or that the *best* way to teach the knowledge and skills involved here is by teaching fallacies. My position can be refuted only by showing that the other ways are consistently *better*.

(b) Teaching a significant group (say ten or more) of the fallacies appropriately means making them the centerpiece of a one-semester course. They are so complex, and so many qualifications, and so much practice and coaching, are needed to teach them in a way that does not distort or trivialize them or their use, that it is a mistake to try to teach fallacies as a minor part of a course focused elsewhere. A two- or three-lecture packet risks educational irresponsibility. No two- or three-week unit can do them all justice. Almost certainly more harm than good is done in briefly sketching a distortingly oversimplified conception of fallacy, in ignoring or underemphasizing the difficulties of interpreting working arguments, and in rushing over the careful discriminations and qualifications that are part of appropriate argument evaluation using the fallacies. If anyone has devised a way to avoid these dangers, I am not aware of it.

On the other hand, introducing one or another of the fallacies when it comes up naturally in the context of a course on argumentation not designed around the fallacies is unobjectionable, as long as the complexity and subtlety of each fallacy are taught as well. For example, a discussion of *post hoc* can be inserted in a unit on causal argumentation, and a version of hasty conclusion fits naturally in a unit on arguments from statistical evidence. A course focused on political debate might well deal with *ad hominem*, straw person, guilt by association, and two wrongs make a right. But, to repeat, the fallacies should be introduced in such settings only if they are not oversimplified or distorted.

(c) Other objections to teaching fallacies in a course on argumentation turn out to be nothing but remonstrations against doing a bad job of it. Some objections cite conceptions of fallacy that are outdated or that never were supported by careful scholars.[8] For instance, it has been said that it is wrong to teach a fallacy like the abusive *ad hominem* because there are valid or cogent *ad hominem* arguments. But the *fallacy* of abusive *ad hominem* is not a justified challenge to a person's credibility or character; it is an illegitimate attack on the person to discredit the person's position. General conditions for such illegitimacy can be listed. So the objection boils down to opposition to teaching a mistaken conception of the abusive *ad hominem* fallacy, a view any defender of teaching fallacies can heartily endorse.

Other cases are perhaps not so clear-cut. Some traditional fallacies, such

8. Many critics could benefit from reading Woods and Walton (1982a; 1989), as well as their more recent work (e.g., Walton 1987a; 1989a; 1991a; 1992c; 1992d; and Woods 1992); and they should know the Amsterdam School's pragma-dialectical theory (van Eemeren and Grootendorst 1984, 1992a). There is a growing important literature on fallacies to be found in the journals, especially in *Informal Logic* and *Argumentation*.

as appeals to force or pity, are alleged either not to be fallacious or not to occur in arguments. But both challenges are controversial in the journal literature. In any case, it would be a hasty generalization or guilt by association to ban all traditional fallacies because of problems with one or two.

The case against teaching fallacies that relies on the premise that the so-called fallacies can be readily discredited tends also to rely on straw person arguments: attacks on long-abandoned (or never held) analyses or the misclassification of a few controversial borderline cases treated as typical.[9] Only if the anti-fallacy case were made using as its targets the careful analyses of theorists such as Woods and Walton (1982a; 1989), Walton (1987b; 1989a) or van Eemeren and Grootendorst (1992a), would it deserve careful scrutiny. I know of no such a case.

Teaching fallacies has also been challenged by objecting to what amounts to poor teaching as if it were typical or inevitable. There are admittedly dangers in spending just a short time on fallacies, and these dangers can befall even a longer course focused on fallacies. Careless or inexperienced instructors can underplay the difficulties of argument interpretation, can present indefensible conceptions of fallacies, and can leave students with the false impression that evaluation using the "injury" conception of fallacy always refutes the argument or that a spray of fallacy allegations constitutes responsible logical criticism. So yes, assuredly there are dangers, and bad instructors will fall prey to them. However, I would worry equally about the job weak instructors will do with any tool of argument criticism.

Admittedly, there are risks to teaching the fallacies even for the knowledgeable and careful instructor. I shall mention three: (1) The focus on fallacies can lead students to be preoccupied with the negative (the weaknesses, the flaws) and to overlook the positive (merits or strengths). Special attention has to be devoted to teaching students to provide an overall assessment of an argument's strengths and weaknesses. (2) Students first learning to use fallacies to critique arguments tend to be on the lookout for every little flaw they can find, and so to rank minor slips on a par with major blunders. A deliberate effort to foster discrimination is needed, so students will distinguish major or fatal flaws from problematic components that can be easily repaired or simply jettisoned without loss. (3) The attention to argument analysis required by teaching the fallacies can divert time and attention from teaching how to construct strong or cogent arguments, since the two employ distinct

9. See Trudy Govier, "Who Says There Are No Fallacies?" *Informal Logic Newsletter* 5, no. 1 (1982): 2–10; and R. H. Johnson (1987; 1989).

sets of skills. A distinct instructional component on argument construction should be added. These three are very real dangers, and they represent challenges for even the best teachers.

Do these or other risks mean that any fallacy approach is fated to founder? If not, then the critic must show that it is more difficult to surmount them when teaching fallacies than it is to overcome the dangers of alternative courses of instruction. Every approach will have its attendant risks of misunderstanding or misuse, so the case against teaching the fallacies has to show that its particular dangers are greater, or harder to surmount, than those of available alternatives.

Using the Fallacies to Teach Reasoning

So far the discussion has been restricted to the teaching of argument analysis using fallacies. To the extent that argumentation plays a central role in critical thinking, these remarks apply equally to teaching fallacies as a part of a critical thinking course that uses argumentation as the entry vehicle. But what of the course in which the focus is on teaching reasoning or critical thinking without (much) reference to argumentation? If a fallacy can be a mistake in extra-argumentative reasoning, then could not the fallacies equally well be taught as elements of a course in such reasoning?

There is a close parallel between teaching a few fallacies in passing in a course in argumentation, and teaching a few fallacies in passing in a non–argumentation-centered course in reasoning. There will be, in both courses, opportunities to introduce one or another fallacy as a recurring mistake—whether in argumentation or in reasoning. It can be beneficial to do so, as long as the treatments of the fallacies included are thorough and scholarly.

No such parallel exists, however, between an argumentation course organized around the fallacies and a possible reasoning course organized around the fallacies. The gang of eighteen are as a group too closely associated with arguments and argumentation. The fallacies are most readily available for study in texts of public discourse, and in such texts the discourse type most commonly and strikingly displaying fallacies is argumentation. People probably commit fallacies in their nonargumentative reasoning with no less frequency than they do in their argumentation, but it tends to be the argumentation that gets expressed in texts and is thus readily available for public scrutiny. These texts are the most accessible raw material for a course in fallacies. In sum, it will be hard for a course focused on the fallacies to avoid a concomitant focus on argumentation, even if there is no necessary connection between argumentation and (most of) the fallacies.

From all these considerations, I conclude that the place for an extensive treatment of the fallacies is in a course on argument analysis designed specifically to incorporate them. Otherwise, the teaching of fallacies should be restricted to introducing a few of them, as appropriate, in a course in argumentation or reasoning that is otherwise focused. Fallacies should not be taught as a separate short unit in a course either in argumentation or in reasoning. And a course in extra-argumentation reasoning organized around the fallacies seems a dubious venture. In any case, the teaching of fallacies requires attention to the most up-to-date scholarly analyses, and taking pains to counter various dangers. Any such instruction, even if successful, will not teach all the skills of critical thinking, but it can teach some of the important ones. [10]

10. My thanks to the editors of this volume, Hans V. Hansen and Robert C. Pinto, for their extensive, meticulous, and enormously helpful suggestions for improving the original version of this chapter, almost all of which I have had the good sense to follow.

Select Bibliography of Recent Work on the Fallacies

Hans V. Hansen

This bibliography gathers the most important research of the last twenty-five years on individual fallacies and fallacy theory, but also includes some entries from earlier in the century. Hamblin's bibliography, in *Fallacies* (1970, 304–16) is an excellent guide to the historical sources.

For those entries below whose titles do not make clear what the subject of the entry is, we have added a short note. The criteria of inclusion are as follows: (1) articles on individual fallacies or fallacy theory that have appeared in refereed journals; (2) textbooks that have made a significant practical or theoretical contribution to the study of fallacies, or whose treatment of fallacies has been widely discussed, or that take a fallacies approach to informal logic or critical thinking; and (3) conference proceedings and other collections that contain a significant number of papers of interest. Additional references to published work on the fallacies, as well as informal logic and argumentation theory in general, may be found in H. V. Hansen, "An informal logic bibliography," *Informal Logic* 12 (1990): 155–84.

I would like to acknowledge the invaluable assistance of Peter Houtlosser (University of Amsterdam) and Mark Letteri (University of Windsor) in preparing this bibliography.

Abate, Charles J. 1979. Fallaciousness and invalidity. *Philosophy and Rhetoric* 12:262–66.

Adler, Jonathan E. 1993. Critique of an epistemic account of fallacies. *Argumentation* 7:263–72. [Criticism of Fogelin and Duggan 1987].

———. 1994. Fallacies and alternative interpretations. *Australasian Journal of Philosophy* 72:271–82.

Bäck, Allan. 1987. Philoponus on the fallacy of accident. *Ancient Philosophy* 7:131–46.

Bar-Hillel, Yehoshua. 1964. More on the fallacy of composition. *Mind* 73:125–26. [Reply to Rowe 1962].

Barker, John A. 1976. The fallacy of begging the question. *Dialogue* 15:241–55.

———. 1978. The nature of question-begging arguments. *Dialogue* 17:490–98.

Barth, E. M., and J. L. Martens. 1977. *Argumentum ad hominem*: From chaos to formal dialectic. *Logique et Analyse* 20:76–96.

Basu, Dilip K. 1986. A question of begging. *Informal Logic* 8:19–26. [Reply to Woods and Walton 1982b].

———. 1994. Begging the question, circularity and epistemic propriety. *Argumentation* 8:217–26.

Behling, Richard W. 1987. On the naming of formal fallacies. *International Logic Review* 18:69–70. [Reply to Wertz 1985].

Bencivenga, Ermanno. 1979. On good and bad arguments. *Journal of Philosophical Logic*, 8:247–59. [Reply to Massey's 1975 papers].

Biro, J. I. 1977. Rescuing "begging the question." *Metaphilosophy* 8:257–71.

———. 1984. Knowability, believability and begging the question: A reply to Sanford. *Metaphilosophy* 15:239–47.

———. 1987. A sketch of an epistemic theory of fallacies. In Van Eemeren, Grootendorst, et al. 1987b, 65–73.

Biro, John, and Harvey Siegel. 1992. Normativity, argumentation and an epistemic theory of fallacies. In Van Eemeren, Grootendorst, et al. 1992, 85–103.

Blair, J. Anthony, and Ralph H. Johnson, eds. 1980. *Informal Logic: The First International Symposium*. Inverness, Calif.: Edgepress. [Selected papers from the First International Symposium on Informal Logic].

———. 1987. The current state of informal logic and critical thinking. *Informal Logic* 9:147–51.

———. 1991. Misconceptions of informal logic: A reply to McPeck. *Teaching Philosophy* 14:35–52. (Reply to McPeck 1991).

Brinton, Alan. 1985. A rhetorical view of the *ad hominem*. *Australasian Journal of Philosophy* 63:50–63.

———. 1986. Ethotic argument. *History of Philosophy Quarterly* 3:245–58.

———. 1987. Ethotetic argument: Some uses. In Van Eemeren, Grootendorst, et al. 1987c, 246–54.

———. 1988a. Appeal to the angry emotions. *Informal Logic* 10:77–87.

———. 1988b. Pathos and the "appeal to emotion": An Aristotelian analysis. *History of Philosophy Quarterly* 5:207–19.

———. 1992. The *ad baculum* re-clothed. *Informal Logic* 14:85–92. [Disagrees with some conclusions in Wreen 1987b, 1988a, 1988b, 1989].

———. 1994. A plea for *argumentum ad misericordiam*. *Philosophia* 23:25–44.

Broad, C. D. 1950. Some common fallacies in political thinking. *Philosophy* 25:99–113.

Broyles, James E. 1975. The fallacies of composition and division. *Philosophy and Rhetoric* 8:108–13.

Bueno, Anibel A. 1988. Aristotle, the fallacy of accident, and the nature of predication: A historical inquiry. *Journal of the History of Philosophy* 26:5–24.

Burke, Michael. 1994. Denying the antecedent. *Informal Logic* 16:23–30.

Capaldi, Nicholas. 1973. *The Art of Deception*. Buffalo, N.Y.: Prometheus Books.

Cohen, L. Jonathan. 1979. On the psychology of prediction: Whose is the fallacy? *Cognition* 7:385–407.

————. 1980. Whose is the fallacy: A rejoinder to Daniel Kahneman and Amos Tversky. *Cognition* 8:89–92.

————. 1982. Are people programmed to commit fallacies? *Journal for the Theory of Social Behaviour* 12:251–74.

Cole, Richard. 1965. A note on informal fallacies. *Mind* 74:432–33.

Colwell, Gary. 1989. God, the Bible and circularity. *Informal Logic* 11:61–73.

Copi, Irving M., and Carl Cohen. 1990. *Introduction to Logic.* 8th ed. New York: Macmillan. [Earlier editions, beginning with the first in 1953, were authored by Copi alone].

Cowan, Joseph L. 1969. The gambler's fallacy. *Philosophy and Phenomenological Research* 30:238–51.

Crouch, Margaret A. 1991. Feminist philosophy and the genetic fallacy. *Hypatia* 6:104–17.

————. 1993. A "limited" defense of the genetic fallacy. *Metaphilosophy* 24:227–40.

Eemeren, Frans H. van, and Rob Grootendorst. 1984. *Speech Acts in Argumentative Discussions.* Dordrecht: Foris. [chap. 8 considers a code for rational discussants and its relation to the fallacies].

————. 1987. Fallacies in pragma-dialectical perspective. *Argumentation* 1:283–301.

————. 1989. A transition stage in the theory of fallacies. *Journal of Pragmatics* 13:99–109.

————. 1992a. *Argumentation, Communication, and Fallacies.* Hillsdale, N.J.: Erlbaum.

————. 1992b. Relevance reviewed: The case of *argumentum ad hominem. Argumentation* 6:141–59.

————. 1993. The history of the *argumentum ad hominem* since the seventeenth century. In Krabbe et al. 1993:49–68.

Eemeren, Frans H. van, Rob Grootendorst, J. Anthony Blair, and Charles Willard, eds. 1987a. *Argumentation: Across the Lines of Discipline.* Dordrecht: Foris. [Proceedings of the First International Society for Study of Argumentation Conference, 1986. Vol. 1].

————. 1987b. *Argumentation: Analysis and Practices.* Dordrecht: Foris. [Proceedings of the First International Society for Study of Argumentation Conference, 1986. Vol. 3].

————. 1987c. *Argumentation: Perspectives and Approaches.* Dordrecht: Foris. [Proceedings of the First International Society for Study of Argumentation Conference, 1986. Vol. 2].

————. 1991a. *Proceedings of the Second International Conference on Argumentation, Volume 1A.* Amsterdam: Sicsat. [Proceedings of the Second International Society for the Study of Argumentation Conference, 1990. Vol. 2].

————. 1991b. *Proceedings of the Second International Conference on Argumentation, Volume 1B.* Amsterdam: Sicsat. [Proceedings of the Second International Society for the Study of Argumentation Conference, 1990. Vol. 3].

————. 1992. *Argumentation Illuminated.* Amsterdam: Sicsat. [Proceedings of the Second International Society for the Study of Argumentation Conference, 1990. Vol. 1].

Engel, S. Morris. 1961. Hobbes's "table of absurdity." *Philosophical Review* 60:533–43.

————. 1980. *Analyzing Informal Fallacies.* Englewood Cliffs, N.J.: Prentice-Hall.

————. 1986a. Explaining equivocation. *Metaphilosophy* 17:192–99.

————. 1986b. Fallacy, wit, and madness. *Philosophy and Rhetoric* 19:224–41.

————. 1986c. Wittgenstein's theory of fallacy. *Informal Logic* 8:67–80.

————. 1989. The many faces of amphiboly. *Metaphilosophy* 20:347–55.

————. 1991. Understanding, finally, what it is to "Beg the Question." *Metaphilosophy* 22:251–64.

————. 1994. *With Good Reason: An Introduction to Informal Fallacies.* 5th ed. New York: St. Martin's. [1st ed. 1976].

Facione, Peter. 1987. Teaching about fallacies. *Teaching Philosophy* 10:211–17.

Fair, Frank. 1973. The fallacy of many questions: Or how to stop beating your wife. *Southwestern Journal of Philosophy* 4:89–92.

Fearnside, W. Ward, and William B. Holther. 1959. *Fallacy: The Counterfeit of Argument.* Englewood Cliffs, N.J.: Prentice-Hall.

Feuer, Lewis S. 1983. The genetic fallacy re-examined. In *Sidney Hook: Philosopher of Democracy and Humanism,* edited by Paul Kurtz, 227–46. Buffalo, N.Y.: Prometheus Books.

Finocchiaro, Maurice. 1974. The concept of *ad hominem* argument in Galileo and Locke. *Philosophical Forum* 5:394–404.

————. 1981. Fallacies and the evaluation of reasoning. *American Philosophical Quarterly* 18:13–22.

————. 1987. Six types of fallaciousness: Toward a realistic theory of logical criticism. *Argumentation* 1:263–82.

Fischer, David H. 1978. *Historians' Fallacies: Toward a Logic of Historical Thought.* New York: Harper and Row.

Fogelin, Robert J., and Timothy J. Duggan. 1987. Fallacies. *Argumentation* 1:255–62.

Gelber, Hester Goodenough. 1987. The fallacy of accident and the *dictum de omni. Vivarium* 25:110–45.

George, Rolf. 1983. A postscript on fallacies. *Journal of Philosophical Logic* 12:319–25.

Gerber, D. 1974. On *argumentum ad hominem. The Personalist* 55:23–29.

————. 1977. Reply to Woods and Walton's "*Ad hominem, contra* Gerber." *The Personalist* 58:145–46. [Reply to Woods and Walton 1977b].

Good, I. J. 1959. A classification of fallacious arguments and interpretations. *Methodos* 11:147–59.

Goodwin, David. 1992. The dialectic of second-order distinctions: The structure of arguments about fallacies. *Informal Logic* 14:11–22.

Goudge, T. A. 1961. The genetic fallacy. *Synthèse* 13:41–48.

Govier, Trudy. 1982. What's wrong with slippery slope arguments? *Canadian Journal of Philosophy* 12:303–16.

————. 1983. *Ad hominem:* Revising the textbooks. *Teaching Philosophy* 6:13–24.

————. 1987. *Problems in Argument Analysis and Evaluation.* Dordrecht: Foris.

————. 1992. *A Practical Study of Argument.* 3d ed. Belmont, Calif.: Wadsworth. [1st ed. 1985].

Groarke, Leo. 1991. Critical study of Woods and Walton's *Fallacies: Selected Papers, 1972–1982. Informal Logic* 13:99–112.

Grootendorst, Rob. 1987. Some fallacies about fallacies. In van Eemeren, Grootendorst, et al. 1987a, 331–42.

Hamblin, Charles L. 1970. *Fallacies.* London: Methuen. [Available from Newport News: Vale Press].

Hample, Dale. 1982. Dual coding, reasoning and fallacies. *Journal of the American Forensic Association* 19:59–78.

Hanson, Norwood R. 1967. The genetic fallacy revisited. *American Philosophical Quarterly* 4:101–13.

Hinman, Lawrence. 1982. The case for *ad hominem* arguments. *Australasian Journal of Philosophy* 60:338–45.

Hintikka, Jaakko. 1987. The fallacy of fallacies. *Argumentation* 1:211–38.

Hitchcock, David. 1992. Relevance. *Argumentation* 6:251–70. [Includes section devoted to the relevance of "ad" appeals].

Hoffman, Robert. 1971. On begging the questions at any time. *Analysis* 32:51.

Hohmann, Hanns. 1991. Fallacies and legal argumentation. In Van Eemeren, Grooten-dorst et al. 1991b, 776–81.

Hon, Giora. 1991. A critical note on J. S. Mill's classification of fallacies. *British Journal for the Philosophy of Science* 42:263–68.

Hooke, A. E. 1991. Tortuous logic and tortured bodies. Why is the *ad baculum* a fallacy? In Van Eemeren and Grootendorst, et al. 1991a, 391–96.

Iseminger, Gary. 1989. The asymmetry thesis. *The Monist* 72:25–39. [Discussion of Massey 1975a, 1975b, 1981].

Jackson, Frank. 1984. *Petitio* and the purpose of arguing. *Pacific Philosophical Quarterly* 65:26–36.

Jacquette, Dale. 1989. The hidden logic of slippery slope arguments. *Philosophy and Rhetoric* 22:59–70.

———. 1994. Many questions begs the question (but questions do not beg the question). *Argumentation* 8:283–89.

Jason, Gary. 1984. Is there a case for *ad hominem? Australasian Journal of Philosophy* 62:182–85.

———. 1986. Are fallacies common? A look at two debates. *Informal Logic* 8:81–92.

———. 1987. The nature of the *argumentum ad baculum. Philosophia* 17:491–99.

———. 1988. Hedging as a fallacy of language. *Informal Logic* 10:169–75.

———. 1989. Fallacies are common. *Informal Logic* 11:101–6.

Johnson, Oliver A. 1967–68. Begging the question. *Dialogue* 6:135–50.

Johnson, Ralph H. 1987. The blaze of her splendours: Suggestions about revitalizing fallacy theory. *Argumentation* 1:239–53.

———. 1989. Massey on fallacy and informal logic: A reply. *Synthèse* 80:407–26. [Reply to Massey 1981].

———. 1990. Hamblin on the standard treatment. *Philosophy and Rhetoric* 23:153–67.

———. 1991. In response to Walton. *Philosophy and Rhetoric* 24:362–66. [Reply to Walton 1991d].

Johnson, Ralph H., and J. Anthony Blair. 1985. Informal logic: The past five years, 1978–83. *American Philosophical Quarterly* 22:181–96.

———. 1993. *Logical Self-Defense*. 3d ed. Toronto: McGraw-Hill Ryerson. [1st ed. 1977].

———. 1994. *New Essays in Informal Logic*. Windsor: Informal Logic.

Kahane, Howard. 1980. The nature and classification of fallacies. In Blair and Johnson 1980, 31–39.

———. 1992. *Logic and Contemporary Rhetoric, The Use of Reasoning in Everyday Life*. 6th ed. Belmont, Calif.: Wadsworth [1st ed. 1971].

Kirwan, Christopher. 1979. Aristotle and the so-called fallacy of equivocation. *Philosophical Quarterly* 29:35–46.

Kleiman, Lowell. 1970. Pashman on Freud and the genetic fallacy. *Southern Journal of Philosophy* 8:63–65. [Reply to Pashman 1970].

Klosko, George. 1983. Criteria of fallacy and sophistry for use in the analysis of Platonic dialogues. *Classical Quarterly*, n.s., 33:363–74.

———. 1987. Plato and the morality of fallacy. *American Journal of Philology* 108:612–26.

Krabbe, Erik C. W. 1992. So what? Profiles for relevance criticism in persuasion dialogues. *Argumentation* 6:271–83. [Includes discussion of some of the fallacies of relevance.]

Krabbe, Erik C. W., and Douglas N. Walton. 1993. It's all very well for you to talk! Situationally disqualifying *ad hominem* attacks. *Informal Logic* 15:79–91.

Krabbe, Erik C.W., R. J. Dalitz, and P. A. Smit, eds. 1993. *Empirical Logic and Public Debate*. Amsterdam: Rodopi.

Lavine, T. Z. 1962. Reflections on the genetic fallacy. *Social Research* 29:321–36.

Leddy, Thomas. 1986. Is there a fallacy of small sample? *Informal Logic* 8:53–56.

Levi, Don S. 1994. Begging what is at issue in the argument. *Argumentation* 8:265–82.

MacIntosh, J. J. 1991. Theological question-begging. *Dialogue* 30:531–47.

Mackenzie, Jim. 1979. Question begging in non-cumulative systems. *Journal of Philosophical Logic* 8:117–33.

———. 1984a. Begging the question in dialogue. *Australasian Journal of Philosophy* 62:174–81.

———. 1984b. Confirmation of a conjecture of Peter of Spain concerning begging the question. *Journal of Philosophical Logic* 8:117–33.

———. 1988. Distinguo: The response to equivocation. *Argumentation* 2:465–82.

———. 1994. Contexts of begging the question. *Argumentation* 8:227–40.

Mackie, John L. 1967. Fallacies. In *Encyclopedia of Philosophy*, edited by Paul Edwards, 3:169–79.

Maier, Robert. 1987. Cognitive development and fallacies. In Van Eemeren, Grootendorst, et al. 1987b, 75–82.

Marks, Joel. 1988. When is a fallacy not a fallacy? *Metaphilosophy* 19:307–12.

Marshall, Ernest. 1987. Formalism, fallacies, and the teaching of informal logic. In Van Eemeren, Grootendorst, et al. 1987b, 386–93.

Massey, Gerald. 1975a. Are there any good arguments that bad arguments are bad? *Philosophy in Context* 4:61–77.

———. 1975b. In defense of the asymmetry. *Philosophy in Context (Supplementary)* 4:44–55.

———. 1981. The fallacy behind fallacies. *Midwest Studies in Philosophy* 6:489–500.

McMurtry, John. 1986. The *argumentum ad adversarium*. *Informal Logic* 8:27–36.

McPeck, John. 1991. What is learned in informal logic courses? *Teaching Philosophy* 14:25–34. [Criticism of the purported value of teaching the fallacies as part of critical thinking].

Michalos, Alex C. 1976. *Improving Your Reasoning* (2d ed.). Englewood Cliffs, N.J.: Prentice-Hall. [1st ed. 1970].

Minot, Walter S. 1981. A rhetorical view of fallacies: Ad *hominem* and ad *populum*. *Rhetorical Society Quarterly* 11:222–35.

Nuchelmans, Gabriel. 1993. On the fourfold root of *argumentum ad hominem*. In Krabbe et al. 1993, 37–47.

Oliver, James Willard. 1967. Formal fallacies and other invalid arguments. *Mind* 76:463–78. [Anticipates Massey's papers on the asymmetry thesis].

Palmer, Humphrey. 1981. Do circular arguments beg the question? *Philosophy* 56:387–94.

Parker, Richard A. 1984. *Tu quoque* arguments: A rhetorical perspective. *Journal of the American Forensic Association* 20:123–32.

Pashman, Jon. 1970. Is the genetic fallacy a fallacy? *Southern Journal of Philosophy* 8:57–62.

———. 1971. Reply to Mr. Kleiman. *Southern Journal of Philosophy* 9:93–94. [Reply to Kleiman 1970].

Pirie, Madsen. 1965. *The Book of Fallacy: A Training Manual for Intellectual Subversives*. London: Routledge and Kegan Paul.

Prasad, Rajendra. 1950. The Jaina conception of fallacies. *Philosophical Quarterly* [India] 23:69–74.

Remland, Martin. 1982. The implicit *ad hominem* fallacy: Nonverbal displays of status in argumentative discourse. *Journal of the American Forensic Association* 19:79–86.

Rescher, Nicholas. 1987. How serious a fallacy is inconsistency? *Argumentation* 1:303–16.

Riepe, Dale. 1966. Some reconsiderations of the *argumentum ad hominem*. *Darshana International* 6:44–47.

Robinson, Richard. 1941. Ambiguity. *Mind* 50:140–55.

———. 1942. Plato's consciousness of fallacy. *Mind* 51:94–114.

———. 1971a. Arguing from ignorance. *Philosophical Quarterly* 21:97–108.

———. 1971b. Begging the question, 1971. *Analysis* 31:113–17.

———. 1981. Begging the question, 1981. *Analysis* 41:65.

Rohatyn, Dennis. 1987. When is a fallacy a fallacy? In van Eemeren, Grootendorst, et al. 1987b, 45–55.

Rowe, William L. 1962. The fallacy of composition. *Mind* 71:87–92.

Salmon, Wesley. 1984. *Logic*. 3d ed. Englewood Cliffs, N.J.: Prentice-Hall. [1st ed. 1963].

Sanford, David. 1972. Begging the question. *Analysis* 32:197–99.

———. 1977. The fallacy of begging the question: A reply to Barker. *Dialogue* 16:485–98. [Reply to Barker 1976].

———. 1981. Superfluous information, epistemic conditions of inference, and begging the question. *Metaphilosophy* 12:145–58.

Schedler, George. 1988. The argument from ignorance. *International Logic Review* 11:66–71.

Schellens, P. J. 1991. *Ad verecundiam* and *ad hominem* arguments as acceptable fallacies. In Van Eemeren and Grootendorst, et al. 1991a, 384–90.

Schlecht, Ludwig F. 1991. Classifying fallacies logically. *Teaching Philosophy* 14:53–64.

Schmidt, Michael F. 1986. On classification of fallacies. *Informal Logic* 8:57–66.

———. 1991. Inconsistency, falsity, incompleteness, begging the question and missing the point. In Van Eemeren and Grootendorst, et al. 1991a, 403–10.

Scriven, Michael. 1987. Fallacies of statistical substitution. *Argumentation* 1:333–49.

Secor, Marie 1987. How common are fallacies? *Informal Logic* 9:41–48. [Response to Jason 1986].

———. 1989. Bentham's *Book of Fallacies*: Rhetorician in spite of himself. *Philosophy and Rhetoric* 22:83–93.

Sorensen, Roy A. 1989a. Slipping off the slippery slope: A reply to Professor Jacquette. *Philosophy and Rhetoric* 22:195–202.

———. 1989b. P, therefore P, without circularity. *Journal of Philosophy* 88:245–66.

Sparkes, A. W. 1966. Begging the question. *Journal of the History of Ideas* 27:462–63.

Sprague, Rosamund Kent. 1962. *Plato's use of fallacy: A study of the* Euthydemus *and some other dialogues*. London: Routledge and Kegan Paul.

Suber, Peter. 1994. Question-begging under a non-foundational model of argument. *Argumentation* 8:241–50.

Vate, Dwight van de, Jr. 1975a. The appeal to force. *Philosophy and Rhetoric* 8:43–60.

———. 1975b. Reasoning and threatening: A reply to Yoos. *Philosophy and Rhetoric* 8:177–79.

Walton, Douglas N. 1977. Mill and De Morgan on whether the syllogism is a *petitio*. *International Logic Review* 8:57–68.

———. 1980a. *Petitio principii* and argument analysis. In Blair and Johnson 1980, 41–54.

———. 1980b. Why is the *ad populum* a fallacy? *Philosophy and Rhetoric* 13:264–78. Also in Woods and Walton 1989, 209–20.

————. 1981. The fallacy of many questions. *Logique et Analyse* 95–96:291–313. Also in Woods and Walton 1989, 233–51.

————. 1982. *Topical Relevance in Argumentation*. Amsterdam: John Benjamins.

————. 1984. *Logical Dialogue-Games and Fallacies*. Lanham, Md.: University Press of America.

————. 1985a. Are circular arguments necessarily vicious? *American Philosophical Quarterly* 22:263–74.

————. 1985b. *Arguer's Position: A Pragmatic Study of 'Ad Hominem' Attack, Criticism, Refutation and Fallacy*. Westport, Conn.: Greenwood.

————. 1987a. The *ad hominem* argument as an informal fallacy. *Argumentation* 1:317–31.

————. 1987b. *Informal Fallacies: Towards a Theory of Argument Criticisms*. Amsterdam: John Benjamins.

————. 1987c. What is a fallacy? In Van Eemeren, Grootendorst, et al. 1987a, 323–30.

————. 1988. Question-asking fallacies. In *Questions and Questioning*, edited by M. Meyer, 195–221. Berlin: De Gruyter.

————. 1989a. *Informal Logic: A Handbook for Critical Argumentation*. Cambridge: Cambridge University Press.

————. 1989b. *Question-Reply Argumentation*. New York: Greenwood.

————. 1990. Ignoring qualifications (*secundum quid*) as a subfallacy of hasty generalization. *Logique et Analyse* 33:113–54.

————. 1991a. *Begging the Question: Circular Reasoning as a Tactic of Argumentation*. New York: Greenwood.

————. 1991b. Bias, critical doubt, and fallacies. *Argumentation and Advocacy* 28:1–22.

————. 1991c. Critical faults and fallacies of questioning. *Journal of Pragmatics* 15:337–66.

————. 1991d. Hamblin on the standard treatment of fallacies. *Philosophy and Rhetoric* 24:353–61. [Reply to R. H. Johnson, 1990].

————. 1992a. Commitment, types of dialogue, and fallacies. *Informal Logic* 14:93–103.

————. 1992b. Nonfallacious arguments from ignorance. *American Philosophical Quarterly* 29:381–87.

————. 1992c. *The Place of Emotion in Argument*. University Park: Pennsylvania State University Press.

————. 1992d. *Plausible Argument in Everyday Conversation*. Albany: State University of New York Press.

————. 1992e. *Slippery Slope Arguments*. Oxford: Oxford University Press.

————. 1992f. Types of dialogue, dialectical shifts and fallacies. In Van Eemeren, Grootendorst et al., 1992, 133–47.

————. 1992g. Which of the fallacies are fallacies of relevance? *Argumentation* 6:237–50.

————. 1993. The speech act of presumption. *Pragmatics and Cognition* 1:125–48.

————. 1995. *A Pragmatic Theory of Fallacy*. Tuscaloosa: University of Alabama Press.

————, and L. M. Batten. 1984. Games, graphs, and circular arguments. *Logique et Analyse* 27:133–64.

Weiss, Stephen E. 1976. The sorites fallacy: What difference does a peanut make? *Synthèse* 33:253–72.

Wertz, S. K. 1985. When affirming the consequent is valid. *International Logic Review* 16:17–18.

White, David. 1985. Slippery slope arguments. *Metaphilosophy* 16:206–13.

Williams, M. E. 1967–68. Begging the question? *Dialogue* 6:567–70.

Wilson, Kent. 1988. Circular Arguments. *Metaphilosophy* 19:38–52.

———. 1993. Comment on Peter of Spain, Jim Mackenzie, and begging the question. *Journal of Philosophical Logic* 22:323–31.

Wohlrapp, Harald. 1991. *Argumentum ad baculum* and ideal speech situation. In Van Eemeren, Grootendorst et al. 1991a, 397–402.

Wolfe, Julian. 1986. Inconsistency: A fallacy? *Informal Logic* 8:151–52.

Woods, John. 1980. What is informal logic? In Blair and Johnson 1980, 57–68. Also in Woods and Walton 1989, 221–32. [Investigates the formal approach to some fallacies, especially composition and division].

———. 1987. *Ad baculum*, self-interest and Pascal's wager. In Van Eemeren, Grootendorst, et al. 1987a, 343–49.

———. 1988. Buttercups, GNP's and quarks: Are fallacies theoretical entities? *Informal Logic* 10:67–76.

———. 1991. Pragma-dialectics: A radical departure in fallacy theory. *Communication and Cognition* 24:43–54.

———. 1992. Who cares about the fallacies? In Van Eemeren, Grootendorst et al. 1992, 23–48.

———. 1993. *Secundum quid* as a research programme. In Krabbe et al. 1993, 27–36.

Woods, John, and Douglas N. Walton. 1972. On fallacies. *Journal of Critical Analysis* 4:103–11. Also in Woods and Walton 1989, 1–10.

———. 1974. *Argumentum ad verecundiam*. *Philosophy and Rhetoric* 7:135–53. Also in Woods and Walton 1989, 11–28.

———. 1975. *Petitio principii*. *Synthèse* 31:107–27. Also in Woods and Walton 1989, 29–45.

———. 1976a. *Ad baculum*. *Grazer Philosophische Studien* 2:133–40. Also in Woods and Walton 1989, 47–53.

———. 1976b. Fallaciousness without invalidity? *Philosophy and Rhetoric* 9:52–54.

———. 1977a. *Ad hominem*. *Philosophical Forum* 8:1–20. Also in Woods and Walton 1989, 55–73.

———. 1977b. *Ad hominem, contra* Gerber. *The Personalist* 58:141–44. Also in Woods and Walton 1989, 87–91.

———. 1977c. Composition and division. *Studia Logica* 36:381–406. Also in Woods and Walton 1989, 93–119.

———. 1977d. *Petitio* and relevant many-premissed arguments. *Logique et Analyse* 20:97–110. Also in Woods and Walton 1989, 75–85.

———. 1977e. *Post hoc, ergo propter hoc*. *Review of Metaphysics* 30:569–93. Also in Woods and Walton 1989, 121–41.

———. 1978a. Arresting circles in formal dialogues. *Journal of Philosophical Logic* 7:73–90. Also in Woods and Walton 1989, 143–59.

———. 1978b. The fallacy of *ad ignorantiam*. *Dialectica* 32:87–99. Also in Woods and Walton 1989, 161–73.

———. 1979. Equivocation and practical logic. *Ratio* 21:31–43. Also in Woods and Walton 1989, 195–207.

———. 1981. More on fallaciousness and invalidity. *Philosophy and Rhetoric* 14:168–72.

———. 1982a. *Argument: The Logic of the Fallacies*. Toronto: McGraw-Hill Ryerson.

———. 1982b. The Petitio: Aristotle's five ways. *Canadian Journal of Philosophy* 12:77–100.

———. 1982c. Question-begging and cumulativeness in dialectical games. *Nous* 16:585–605.

————. 1989. *Fallacies: Selected Papers, 1972–82.* Dordrecht: Foris.

————. 1992. *Critique de l'Argumentation: Logiques des sophismes ordinaires.* Paris: Éditions Kimé. [Translations of most of the papers in Woods and Walton 1989, with a new introduction].

Wreen, Michael J. 1987a. When no reason is good reason. In Van Eemeren, Grootendorst, et al. 1987b, 56–64. [On the *ad ignorantiam*].

————. 1987b. Yes, Virginia, there is a Santa Claus. *Informal Logic* 9:31–39. [On the *ad baculum*].

————. 1988a. Admit no force but argument. *Informal Logic* 10:89–95. [Criticizes the standard treatment of the *ad baculum* fallacy].

————. 1988b. May the force be with you. *Argumentation* 2:425–40. [On the *ad baculum*].

————. 1989a. A bolt of fear. *Philosophy and Rhetoric* 22:131–40. [On the *ad baculum*].

————. 1989b. Light from darkness, from ignorance knowledge. *Dialectica* 43:289–314. [On the *ad ignorantiam*].

————. 1993. Jump with common spirits. *Metaphilosophy* 24:61–75. [On the *ad populum*].

————. 1994a. What is a faliacy? In Johnson and Blair 1994, 93–102.

————. 1994b. Look Ma! No Frans. *Pragmatics and Cognition* 2:285–306. [Critical assessment of the Pragma-Dialectical conception of fallacies].

Yackulic, R. A., and I. W. Kelly. 1984. The psychology of the 'Gambler's Fallacy' in probabilistic reasoning. *Psychology, A Quarterly Journal of Human Behaviour.* 21:55–58.

Yoos, George. 1975. A critique of van de Vate's "The appeal to force." *Philosophy and Rhetoric* 8:172–76.

Contributors

JAMES V. BACHMAN received his M.A. in theology from Cambridge University and his Ph.D. in philosophy from Florida State University. He is coauthor, with Jaakko Hintikka, of *What If . . . ? Toward Excellence in Reasoning* (Mayfield, 1991). Since 1989, he has held the John R. Eckrich Chair in Religion and the Healing Arts at Valparaiso University in Indiana, and he serves on the board of directors of the Chicago Clinical Ethics Programs.

J. ANTHONY BLAIR, educated at McGill University and the University of Michigan, is professor and chair of the Philosophy Department at the University of Windsor, coeditor of the journal *Informal Logic*, and coauthor with R. H. Johnson of the texts *Logical Self-Defence* (3d ed., McGraw-Hill, 1994), and with R. C. Pinto, *Reasoning: A Practical Guide* (Prentice-Hall, 1993). He has cochaired conferences on informal logic and argumentation at Windsor and the University of Amsterdam, and has lectured and published widely on informal logic, fallacies and fallacy theory, argumentation, and critical thinking.

ALAN BRINTON received his Ph.D. from the University of Minnesota in 1974 and has taught philosophy at Boise State University since 1975. His recent work has been mainly concerned with the history of rhetoric and the significance of rhetorical conceptions for informal logic and moral philosophy, and has appeared in journals such as *Rhetorica, Philosophical Quarterly, Informal Logic, Philosophia*, and the *British Journal for the History of Philosophy*. He is on the editorial board of *Philosophy and Rhetoric*.

FRANS H. VAN EEMEREN and ROB GROOTENDORST are professors of discourse and argumentation studies in the Department of Speech Communication at the University of Amsterdam, the Netherlands. They are coeditors of the international journal *Argumentation*. Together with J. Anthony Blair and Charles A. Willard, they founded the International Society for the Study of Argumentation (ISSA). Van Eemeren and Grootendorst have published a great number of books and articles; their main books in English are: *Speech Acts in Argumentative Discourse* (Foris, 1984); *Argumentation, Communication, and Fallacies* (Erlbaum, 1992); with Tjark Kruiger, *Handbook of Argumentation Theory* (Foris, 1987); and with Sally Jackson and Scott Jacobs, *Reconstructing Argumentative Discourse* (University of Alabama Press, 1993). Several of their publications have been translated into French, German, Russian, and Chinese.

MAURICE A. FINOCCHIARO received his B.S. degree from the Massachusetts Institute of Technology in 1964 and his Ph.D. from the University of California–Berkeley in 1969. He is the author of *Galileo and the Art of Reasoning* (Reidel, 1980) and of *Gramsci and the History of Dialectical Thought* (Cambridge University Press, 1988). He is a former fellow of the National Endowment for the Humanities and of the American Council of Learned Societies, and Distinguished Professor of Philosophy and department chair at the University of Nevada–Las Vegas.

JAMES B. FREEMAN received his Ph.D. from Indiana University in 1973. He has authored *Thinking Logically* (Prentice-Hall, 2d ed., 1993) and *Dialectics and the Macrostructure of Arguments* (de Gruyter, 1991). He has taught in the Department of Philosophy at Hunter College, City University of New York, since 1978, where he is currently professor and chair of the department.

TRUDY GOVIER received her Ph.D. from the University of Waterloo in 1971. She is author of four books, including *A Practical Study of Argument* (Wadsworth, 1985, 1988, 1992) and *Problems in Argument Analysis and Evaluation* (Foris, 1987), and numerous essays and papers. Formerly associate professor of philosophy at Trent University in Peterborough, Ontario, Govier has also taught at the University of Calgary.

HANS V. HANSEN received his Ph.D. from Wayne State University and has taught at McMaster University and the Universities of Windsor and Amsterdam. He now teaches at Brock University in St. Catharines, Ontario. His research interests are in ethics and the history of logic. He is consulting editor to *Informal Logic* and coeditor of this volume.

DAVID HITCHCOCK is the author of *Critical Thinking* (Methuen, 1983) and of articles on Plato and on various topics in the theory of argument. He is associate professor of philosophy at McMaster University in Hamilton, Ontario.

RALPH H. JOHNSON received his Ph.D. from the University of Notre Dame. He is University Professor and professor of philosophy at the University of Windsor, where he has taught since 1966. He is coeditor of the journal *Informal Logic*, coauthor of *Logical Self-Defence* (3d ed., McGraw-Hill, 1994) and is the author of numerous papers and articles on fallacies, informal logic, and argumentation theory.

ERIK C. W. KRABBE studied philosophy and mathematics at the University of Amsterdam. In 1982 he received his Ph.D. from Groningen University. He is coauthor, with E. M. Barth, of *From Axiom to Dialogue: A Philosophical Study of Logics of Argumentation* (de Gruyter, 1982). He is an alumnus of the Netherlands Institute for Advanced Study in the Humanities and Social Sciences and a member of the editorial board of *Argumentation*. He has taught since 1969 and at Groningen University since 1988.

GERALD J. MASSEY is Distinguished Service Professor of Philosophy and professor of history and philosophy of science at the University of Pittsburgh. He took his Ph.D. at Princeton University in 1964 under the direction of Carl G. Hempel. He is the author of *Understanding Symbolic Logic* (Harper and Row, 1970) and coeditor of *Thought Experiments in Science and Philosophy* (Rowman and Littlefield, 1991) and of *Problems of the Internal and External Worlds* (University of Pittsburgh Press, 1993).

ROBERT C. PINTO received his Ph.D. from the University of Toronto in 1973. He is coauthor, with J. A. Blair, of *Reasoning: A Practical Guide* (Prentice-Hall, 1993). He is associate editor and member of the editorial board of *Informal Logic*, and a member of the editorial board of *Argumentation*. Since 1963, he has taught in the department of philosophy at the University of Windsor.

LAWRENCE H. POWERS received his Ph.D. from Cornell University in 1976. He is the author of papers on metaphilosophy, various aspects of logic (deontic, syllogistic, relevance), and epistemology. Since 1965 he has taught at Wayne State University in Detroit.

DOUGLAS WALTON received his Ph.D. from the University of Toronto in 1972. He is a former Killam Research Fellow and fellow at the Netherlands

Institute for Advanced Study in the Humanities and Social Sciences. A winner of the ISSA Prize, and the Erica and Arnold Rogers award, for his research contributions in the field of argumentation, he has published many books on informal logic, including *The Place of Emotion in Argument* (Pennsylvania State University Press, 1992), *Informal Logic* (Cambridge University Press, 1989) and *Slippery Slope Arguments* (Oxford University Press, 1992).

CHARLES ARTHUR WILLARD received his Ph.D. from the University of Illinois. He is the author of *Argumentation and the Social Grounds of Knowledge* (University of Alabama Press, 1983) and *A Theory of Argumentation* (University of Alabama Press, 1989). He edited (with J. Robert Cox) *Advances in Argumentation Theory and Research* (Southern Illinois University Press, 1982), and is on the editorial boards of *Argumentation, Argumentation and Advocacy,* and *Social Epistemology.* Since 1984 he has been professor and chair of the Department of Communication, University of Louisville.

JOHN WOODS is coauthor with Douglas Walton of *Argument: The Logic of the Fallacies* (McGraw-Hill Ryerson, 1982); *Fallacies: Selected Papers, 1972–1982* (Foris, 1989) and *Critique de l'argumentation* (Éditions Kimé, 1992). Woods is also the author of *The Logic of Fiction* (Reidel, 1974) and the soon to be published *Agenda Relevance.* He is head of the Department of Philosophy at the University of Lethbridge.

Index